THE LORDS OF ROMAGNA

Tombstone of the Beccadelli, by Bitino da Bologna (1341): Church of SS. Nicolò and Domenico, Imola

THE LORDS OF ROMAGNA

Romagnol Society and the Origins of the Signorie

BY

JOHN LARNER

CORNELL UNIVERSITY PRESS
Ithaca, New York

First published in the United States of America 1965
Cornell University Press

PRINTED IN GREAT BRITAIN

FOR

PHYLLIS CARR

dolce guida e cara

ACKNOWLEDGEMENTS

IN the first place I should like to express my gratitude to the late Mr. H. E. ('Harry') Bell, of New College, Oxford, who assisted me at every stage in the development of this book from the time when he first directed my attention to the Romagna. The news of his death in the summer of 1964 has brought sadness to all who enjoyed the warmth of his friendship, the breadth of his humane scholarship, and the stimulus of his teaching.

I am also particularly indebted to two other scholars. Dr. Daniel Waley has read the work in typescript, has suggested many alterations, and has saved me from numerous errors. Dr. Philip J. Jones, in addition to reading the typescript, generously allowed me to consult his thesis 'The Malatesta of Rimini'. I hasten to add, however, that I alone must be held responsible for any defects which appear in the final version of this work.

My researches in Romagna were made possible by a scholarship for three years, tenable in Italy, awarded by the British School at Rome. I would like to record the kindness received in Italy from friends and from the custodians of the archives and libraries which I visited. Here in Scotland I gratefully acknowledge the encouragement given me by Professor Lionel Stones of Glasgow, and Professor Lionel Butler of St. Andrews University. My friend and colleague, Mr. Bruce Webster, helped me in selecting the illustrations, and Glasgow University made a grant towards the typing of my manuscript. My wife, Kirsty, has taken time from her own studies to give assistance in mine. Finally, I must thank Egidia and Phyllis, without whom this work would certainly never have been completed.

J. P. L.

Glasgow University, 1964

CONTENTS

Appendices

LIST OF ILLUSTRATIONS

A PRELIMINARY NOTE ON MONEY AND MEASURES

THE many different terms of money used in Romagna in the period covered by this book are very confusing. The money systems of Florence and Venice, of Bologna, Ravenna, and sometimes of other towns, all flourished within the province. The value of these currencies continually fluctuated in relation to each other, not only in the course of a year, but even from week to week. To add to the difficulty many of the terms describe 'moneys of account' which were not represented by any real coin in circulation. Though, for instance, the pound of Bologna was constantly referred to in documents, there was no coin which actually was this pound. It was merely an accountant's symbol for 240 (real) Bolognesi pennies. (So today, in Britain, we reckon in guineas representing twenty-one real shillings.)

In order to help the reader in this difficult field, the currencies based upon the pound of Bologna (£B.) and of Ravenna (£R.) have been taken as a basis of calculation. In each of these systems the pound (£, *libra*, *lira*) consisted of twenty shillings (s., *solidi*, *soldi*), and 240 pence (d., *denarii*, *denari*). In the text (though not in the footnotes and appendices) an approximate estimate of the value of any sum in the currency of Bologna is placed in brackets after each other term of money. The reader will appreciate, however, that the author of this work lacks the very great technical expertise and knowledge of current market values which were demanded of the medieval money changer, and that therefore these figures are only a very rough guide. The money of Ravenna has not been translated into Bolognesi terms, but here it is easy for the reader to bear in mind that £R.1 was roughly equivalent to 19s. B.

Those already familiar with the medieval English monetary system may be helped by remembering that the pound of Bologna in this period was from ten to thirteen times less valuable than the English pound sterling. At this period the unit of international currency (like the dollar today) was the Florentine gold florin. In 1320 the pound Bolognese, which at that time had a very low exchange rate, was valued at half a florin: that is to say at the equivalent of about 1.765 grammes of fine gold, which in terms of present-day English money might be worth 14s. 3d. But such a comparison is of very little help in understanding its real value which can only be discovered by considering its general purchasing power.

Yet this is not easy to find. Many rents and services were paid, not in money, but in foodstuffs. The price of foodstuffs varied widely according to the year's harvest, to which every aspect of the town's economic life was closely tied. Some indication can be given, however, by noting that famine conditions were considered to exist in Forlì when the price of corn had risen to 12s. 6d. B. a bushel. An acceptable price for salt was 4d. B. a pound. It is difficult to assess land values which varied with the condition of the land. At the end of the fourteenth century outright sale of land could produce £B.28 for two and a half acres of a vineyard, £B.50 for four acres of ploughland, and yet at the same time, as little as £B.6 for one and a half acres of ploughland. A two-storied house, suitable for an aristocrat, with a balcony and tiled roof, a courtyard with a well, a garden, some land, outbuildings, and a granary, could cost £B.600. Other houses at the end of the century might cost £B.16 or £B.24 or £B.75 in the town, £B.30 or £B.60 in a village.

Mills were very expensive; they could be valued at £B.1200. Cattle at the middle of the fourteenth century could cost £R.10 before fattening, but the expense of pasturing was high. An ass with two panniers could cost £R.8; an inn, £B.400; the painting of a lunette with three figures of saints, £B.5; a Tartar slave-girl, £R.49 6s.; a rowing-boat, £B.10; a boat with two sails, £B.250; a book, £B.44; a town clock, £B.100; a funeral, £B.10; a public lavatory, £B.15; the erection of a gallows and execution of a thief, £B.4. A chemist's shop could be leased for £B.50 a year. Clothes could be very expensive. A skirt and long cloak, decorated with pearls, second hand, could fetch £R.22; a French purse of silk and gold, £R.4 8s.; a belt of woven silk and silver, £R.14. But cheaper clothes were available. A short loose cloak, if unlined, could cost £B.1 10s., if lined, £B.2; a lady's mantle, lined, £B.1; a loose jacket, 15s. B., a man's jacket in velvet, £B.1 15s.; a surplice, 12s. B.; a lined hood, 3s. B.; a pair of strong heavy shoes, 3s. B. Dowries, which were essential for marriage, were expensive; £B.1500 for the wife of a signore, and £R.400 and £R.50 for the wives of a doctor and cook respectively. Money itself was dear; the official rate of interest was 30 per cent a year, but many bankers charged a much higher percentage.

The Month of July: Book of Offices of the Blessed Virgin, Forlì

Turning to salaries and wages, it is clear that most services were performed on the basis of an *ad hoc* agreement, or for a commission. Notaries, for instance, charged their clients according to the amount of money recorded in the documents they were asked to draw up. Labourers would only have their wages fixed as the result of laws made by the town's property-holders, and these were often difficult to enforce. None the less some figures can be given. A schoolmaster, appointed by the commune, could be paid £R.25 or £R.50 a year, plus individual payments by parents of the children attending the school. A doctor of medicine could receive £R.300 from the commune, and in addition be allowed to charge any patient who was seriously ill up to £R.3. The clerk of a pawn-bank would be paid £B.30 a year; a mercenary foot-soldier, £B.2 a month. A man who gathered and delivered manure to a field would receive £B.2 for the job.

These fees refer to the period before the mid thirteen-forties. Thenceforth it is certain that all forms of labour costs rose, often steeply. At the end of the century the maximum wages of occasional day-labourers could be fixed at 7s. B. a day from mid-March to mid-April, 5s. B. a day from 1 November to 28 February, and 6s. B. from 1 March to mid-March. Mowers could receive 10s. B. in May, and 7s. B. in August and September. In these three months reapers could receive 7s. B. and threshers 6s. B. a day. Masons and carpenters in the same period could receive 7s. B. a day from mid-March to the end of September, and 6s. B. at other times. Builders' labourers could receive 4s. B. from mid-March to 1 October, and for the rest of the year, 3s. 6d. a day and their food. Smiths could charge 2d. B. for sharpening agricultural instruments. For shoeing war-horses they received 2s. 6d. B. for each shoe; for smaller horses, 2s. B., and for asses, 1s. B. a shoe. A man with his own oxen and cart could receive £B.6 10s. for transporting stones and wood for a month. A priest would probably be grateful for an offertory of 2s. B. for saying a mass.

It will be obvious by now why present-day historians assert that it is impossible to draw up any satisfactory cost of living index for the period. One pointer, however, may be of assistance. In the papal taxation of the clergy of the province in December 1291, those who received annually less than £B.15 were classed with those whose 'revenues are so small or lacking that for the sustenance of their lives they have to beg and seek public alms'. From this it may be concluded that at the turn of the thirteenth and fourteenth centuries, £B.15 was the uncomfortable minimum upon which a single man with no responsibilities could live.

The weights and measures of this period, when each town had its own different standards, are, if anything, even more difficult to understand than its money. The square measure, the *tornatura*, could vary from ·4 to ·8 of an acre ; the dry measure, the *staio*, fluctuated from between five and thirty gallons. Some guidance here is given in Appendix IV, though this can be considered as little more than a contribution towards the fuller understanding of the subject. If the reader is confused he may perhaps console himself with the thought that even the merchants' handbooks in the period were not free from obvious errors on these points.

CHAPTER I

Romagna in the Thirteenth Century

Da quella dolce terra latina; id est de Romandiola quae inter alias provincias Italiae est maxima amoena et omnium bonorum fertilis.

BENVENUTO DA IMOLA[1]

I

ONE of the most moving incidents in the *Divine Comedy* is the meeting of Virgil and Sordello in the sixth canto of the *Purgatorio*. Dante describes how the troubadour, still proud and disdainful in death, stands alone on the eastern side of the Holy Mount. At Virgil's approach the soul stiffens like a crouching lion, and refuses to answer the poet's questions, but, instead, asks him whence he came and who he was. Virgil begins to answer with the word: ' Mantua. . . '. At this, the shade, with sudden joy, leaps to him and they embrace. ' That gentle spirit was thus swift, at the mere mention of his city, to greet there his fellow citizen.'

In this scene Dante has symbolised something which is essentially Italian, and which runs through all Italian history: the passionate local loyalties of the men of the city states. Virgil and Sordello, divided by so many centuries, greet each other as friends, not because they are both poets, but because they are both Mantuans. Yet for Dante the encounter inspires not so much joy as wonder. It contrasts so forcibly with the circumstances of his own day, and moves him to bitter imprecations. ' Ah Italy, hostel of sorrow, ship without pilot in a mighty tempest!' The dead could greet each other in this way, but among the living, citizens fought savagely with their neighbours inside each town, and civil war was universal. What part of Italy now enjoys peace? The Emperor no longer abides by his sacred duty to bring justice to the peninsula, and through his neglect new rulers have arisen. ' For the cities of Italy are full of tyrants, and every peasant becomes a partisan and thinks himself a Marcellus.'

le città d' Italia tutte piene
son di tiranni . . .

In these words Dante described the breakdown of the communes through factions, and the first stages in the slow emergence of the *signorie*, or single-person governments. How was it that this change came about? Why did the old commune fail? Who were the new tyrants, and how did they seize power? Did the feeling between Virgil and Sordello survive the change?

These are some of the questions which the passage provokes, and which this work will seek to answer, in so far as the Romagna is concerned. Romagna itself left an impression upon Dante's poem second only to that of his native Tuscany. The rivers of the province flow through the *Divine Comedy* : the Santerno, the Lamone, the Savio and the Montone echoing from the mountains above San Benedetto as it falls. In its pages the Romagnols live again ; the small town nobles, the brigands of the high Apennine passes, the corrupt *signori*, all gain immortality. And not the corrupt alone, 'for Romagna has its celestial minds, even as its diabolical '.[2] Any full understanding of the great poem of the medieval world requires a knowledge of the history of the Romagna, for to Dante it was this province, before all others, which was the home of the tyrants.

II

The Romagna was a small world of wooded mountain, fertile plain, and bare seashore : 'A little province ', wrote a friar who lived there in the thirteenth century, ' but good, fertile and prosperous.'[3] Its boundaries were the River Sillaro, Cattolica, the watershed of the Etruscan Apennines and the Adriatic coast. Along the line of the Apennine foothills ran the Via Emilia ; on this route stood five of the six principal towns : Rimini, Cesena, Forlì, Faenza, and Imola. To meet the towns upon the road, five rivers flowed from the mountains : the Marecchia, Savio, Montone, Lamone, and Santerno. The whole area was no larger than the combined counties of Norfolk and Suffolk.

In the Romagnol Apennines, low foothills give place by gradual stages to mountains with harsh eocene rocks, standing between 3,000 and 5,000 feet. Erosion of the middle and lower slopes caused villages and roads to avoid the valley bottoms. The villages sit perched on the tops of hills, to which rough tracks lead at an angle of from forty to sixty degrees ; the roads rise abruptly to the protection of mountain spurs. There is a sharp contrast between this lonely, cloud-capped region and the plain, where long, flat, rectangular fields monotonously unfold at right-angles to the road.

In the thirteenth century, a day's ride along the great Roman highway of the Via Emilia carried the traveller from one end of the province to the other. Leaving Bologna he entered the Romagna on crossing the Sillaro, and came in succession to three small towns : Imola, Faenza, and Forlì. Each had been founded by Roman colonists in the second century B.C. and revealed its origins in its layout of straight streets built at right-angles. The first of these was Imola, with a canal running round its walls, and with the cylindrical campanili of the churches, and the towers of the new aristocracy, rising above them.

Imola, alone among the towns of the province, had never been able to extend its control over its own *contado* (or surrounding countryside). Only for a few miles around were the local villages subject to the jurisdiction of the commune. Beyond, to the south-west, where the Santerno valley strikes into the Apennines, the Via Montanara, built by the Bolognesi in the thirteenth century, led through the fiefs of virtually independent nobles : the Alidosi, Pagani, Sassatelli, Ubaldini ; to where, in the fourteenth century, Firenzuola was to be built. To the north of the Via Emilia a canal ran from the town up through marshland to Conselice, a small port on the Po.[4]

Ten miles on from Imola stood the pleasant town of Faenza, at the centre of a road network which made it ' the key to Romagna '.[5] To the south-west the river Lamone flowed down from Marradi, through territories subject to the commune and its noble families : the Fantolini, the Manfredi, the great Conti Guidi, the Accarisi, and the Zambrasi. Here, past Brisighella and Pieve di Tò, with its seventh-century church, lay the ancient road to Florence recorded in the Antonine Itinerary. From Faenza, other roads struck south to Modigliana, and northwards to Ravenna and to Bagnacavallo, which was the seat of the Counts of that name.

Ten miles from Faenza was Forlì, with its huge piazza, on which the diminutive cathedral of San Mercuriale stood incongruously beside a towering Romanesque campanile. From here, following the line of the Montone to the south-west, a road ran deep into the mountains, across the Alpi di San Benedetto into the Casentino. Here again were the fiefs of powerful nobles : the Counts of Castrocaro, the Calboli, the Conti Guidi da Dovadola.

Two miles on, the traveller would cross the Ronco where a road, coming from Arezzo, via Bagno di Romagna and Meldola, met the Via Emilia. Passing on the right,

> il dolce alto ridente
> colle di Bertinoro

and then going through the small Forlimpopoli, he would arrive at Cesena. This town was on a pre-Roman site, built half on the plain, and half stretching up upon a spur of the Apennines. From here roads ran to Cervia, and south through the mountains, past the strongholds of numerous feudal lords ; past Mercato Saraceno and Sarsina (the birthplace of Plautus), to meet the Arezzo road.

Past Savignano and the little ditch of the historic Rubicon, past Sant' Arcangelo, he would cross the Marecchia by the bridge of Tiberius, and enter Rimini, with its small port and narrow streets. The southern gateway of the town was formed by the Arch of Augustus, built in 27 B.C., and standing at the head of the Via Flaminia, the road to Cattolica and the south. What was then, and is still today, little more than a track ran through Montefiore to Urbino.

From Rimini, a road ran northwards along the shore, past Cervia and its salt flats, through the pine forests to Classe, the once thriving port of which nothing now remained but the splendid church of Sant' Apollinare, and the monastery beside it. Two and a half miles on was Ravenna, at one time the capital of the world ; by then a small provincial town with ancient walls ' that seem through age like glass '.[6] By 1371 the coast was three miles away, and was linked to the town by the Padareno and the Padenna, two subsidiaries of the Po ; but the harbour was already beginning to silt up. The monuments of the past still stood : the Mausoleum of Theodoric among the cypress trees ; the Basilica Ursiana with its five naves and gleaming mosaics ; the convent of Santa Maria in Porta :

> casa
> di nostra donna in sul lito Adriano

S. Andrea dei Goti, Santa Croce, S. Apollinare Nuovo and San Vitale, the basilicas of the Greek emperors. There must always have been here an atmosphere of decay, a sense of lost greatness : ' Ravenna erat in florenti statu quae nunc est in languido '. The elegaic note of Benvenuto echoes the tones of Boccaccio : ' come che la sua vecchiezza alquanto la rende deforme, ella fu nella sua giovinezza troppo più florida '.[7] When, in December 1231, the Emperor Frederick II excavated the mausoleum of Galla Placidia, to reveal the sarcophagi of St. Elisha, Theodosius II, and Galla Placidia herself, the men of the town must have received almost with incredulity this testimony to its imperial glories.[8]

Despite its small size, Romagna was a land of strong contrast. The jurisdictions of the towns along the Via Emilia had expanded laterally into the countryside, that is to say, over both plain and mountains. Yet without the resources of Florence at their command, they were seldom able to dominate the central watershed of the Apennines, and in the thirteenth century, this area was given up to small feudal nobles, who supplemented their meagre agricultural revenues by occasional banditry.[9] When at Christmas 1202, Gerald the Welshman passed from Faenza to Bagno di Santa Maria in the Spoleto valley, he remarked on the perils of the journey and the terror inspired in him by the sheer mountains, 'no less for their snow-peaks than for the robbers that dwell there'. He claimed that, when he had descended the pass, the men whom he met were amazed at his good fortune in not being robbed.[10]

It would be misleading, however, to generalise from a foreigner's impressions of a journey made in winter. The physical difficulties presented by the mountains must not be over-emphasised. From the beginning of the thirteenth century communications over the Apennines were quite firmly established. The carbonic acid springs of Bagno di Romagna were already frequented by wealthy invalids of Florence, and by the fifteenth century the baths of the *montagna* were even fashionable.

The routes across the Apennines, and the hundred kilometres between Faenza and Florence, always served without any serious hindrance for the passage of trade and of armed men. This is not to say that their condition was good, or that travel by them was comfortable. Local communes were held responsible for their viability, but repair work was spasmodic. In bad weather it was necessary to transport salt from Ravenna to Bologna by sea to Marcabò, and thence up the Po, rather than by road, 'propter vias malas de Romandiola'.[11] Actually in all weathers transport by water was preferred. At Ravenna in 1357, Jacopo, rector of the church of the hospital of San Salvatore, registered a notarial protocol, saying that he was unable to appear before Cardinal Albornoz at Ancona, as commanded, because 'hindered by the contrary force of wind and sea'.[12] This in itself was clearly considered sufficient excuse. Again, the normal method of travel from Ferrara to Florence via Faenza, was to go first by river to Conselice, and only then to take horse for Faenza.[13]

The Romagna was a land of comparative prosperity. Around 1380 Benvenuto of Imola wrote:

> This land is in the happiest position. At its back it has the Apennines as a shield against the south wind, nature's enemy, while in

front it has free open access to the north wind, propitious to generation. In it are assembled all the things that are sparse in other places : sea, land, mountains, plain, numerous rivers, fountains, hills, woods, healthy air, wine, oil, honey, flesh, fish, rich stocks of corn, numerous inhabitants, great riches, and in a small area, towns, castles, villages, and markets.

This is little more than conventional rhetoric. On other occasions the same author drops into gloomy asides upon the province : ' hardly any part of it flourishes today except Rimini '.[14] The population of the area seems indeed quite high ; it has been estimated at over 150,000 souls in 1371, yet research on this problem still gives ambiguous answers. ' Great riches ' it certainly did not possess. Until the fifteenth century, manufacture was almost exclusively confined to such minor occupations as the shoemaking and smithing necessary to satisfy local needs. Trade was in the hands of ' foreigners ', and the pawnbroker and the pedlar were more in evidence than the banker or merchant. The whole wealth of the province lay in its production of food.

The *montagna* is infertile. It was less so in the middle ages, when deforestation was slight, and the Apennines were covered thickly with oak, beech, and chestnut. But at any time it must have been difficult to wring a living from those eroded slopes. The remoter villages harvested thin crops of spelt, spring-sown wheat, barley, and chestnuts (from which chestnut-bread was made). Vines and olives (today rarely seen in the province) were grown up the steep hillsides. Within the forests, charcoal burners and woodsmen went in fear of bears and wolves, and in summer the herds were led to pasture on such grazing land as the hills provided.[15] A harsh land : only on the foothills did cultivation become easier. Here vineyards and orchards relieved the landscape, and the words of Don Alberti, in the sixteenth century, can have been little exaggerated : ' the Apennine hills appear clothed in vines, figs, olives, and other fruit-bearing trees, as if they were gardens '.[16] Industry was almost non-existent, though a little sulphur was mined in the hollows where chalk was exposed.[17]

The plain, as Columella and Varro observed in classical times, was extremely fertile. In an elaborate simile, Benvenuto compared Tuscany, rich and ornately decorated, with its beautiful women and wise councils, to a living room ; Lombardy, with its great powers and splendid feasting, to a hall ; Apulia, with its fine horses, to a stable. But Romagna, all green fields, was the garden. It was the envied fertility of the province, he claimed, that was the principal cause of all the wars which arose there.[18]

Yet some reservations must be made. Nature had been capricious in her gifts. The apparent placidity of the landscape of the plain was broken at times by earthquakes which struck with frightening force.[19] In other years, amid the summer heat, plagues of locusts descended upon the crops in such strength that they could only be burnt out.[20] Again, the land was badly drained. The rivers of high Romagna flowed along different routes from those of today. The Po ran south of a line followed now by the Reno, and from it branched the Po di Primaro, that led above Conselice, Lugo and Fusignano to enter the sea, twelve miles to the north of Ravenna :

su la marina dove il Po discende
per aver pace coi seguaci sui.

(On the sea shore where the Po descends
to have peace with its tributary streams.)[21]

Two lesser streams linked Ravenna with the river, and intersected and encircled the town. The Santerno, the Senio, the Lamone, and the Montone all flowed from the Apennines into the Po ; only the Savio at Ravenna ran directly into the sea, as all the rivers do today.[22] Around this meeting of the waters a score of place-names such as Bagnacavallo, Bagnara, Laguna, and Bagnorolo, are the sole indications of what was once a wide expanse of land permanently under water. By 1371 both Comacchio and Adria were submerged. All that remained of their inhabitants were a few families living on high ground left as islands. Cardinal Grimoard wrote in this year : ' the territory is low and the waters do not hold the course they should, nor are there any adequate ditches or dykes. . . . Now from day to day villages are submerged, and the land is returning to marsh. In time, little by little, the greater part of this area will be under water.'[23]

Biondo da Forlì, in the fifteenth century, estimated that for fifty miles around the Po there were marsh lands and ' dead waters '.[24] Here the landscape must have been much as Virgil saw it, with the harsh cries of swans echoing through its stagnant waters. This land was incapable of cultivation, yet not entirely unproductive. Fishing and fowling rights there were profitably leased by the great monasteries of Ravenna, and exploited by the Ravennati fishermen.

Yet it was dangerous territory : these lands, and others throughout the plain, were a breeding ground for malaria. Piero da Vigne wrote from Faenza in 1240 : ' You must see that the very frogs here are proud of their marshes' injection of poison into men . . . from this land comes a vapour of corruption that strikes down the gently-nurtured body.'

C' è un breve gre gre di ranelle —

The frogs of Pascoli's Romagna had their predecessors : Martial wrote of them, and in the fifth century Sidonius Apollinarius made play with their croakings, in a letter to a native of Cesena :

> You have shown your own opinion of the attractiveness and amenities of that natal soil of yours by quitting it — yet in your 'happier' existence as an exile in Ravenna, your ears are pierced by the mosquitoes of the Po, and a chattering company of your fellow burghers, the frogs, keeps jumping about on every side of you.[25]

The rains of spring and autumn still transform the summer streams. In previous ages their effect was devastating. Pliny gave an account of the yearly inundations of the Po, and the damage done to adjacent fields 'at the melting of the snows, when the dog star rises'. In the middle ages, all the rivers of Romagna were still liable to ruinous flooding. In October 1384, for instance, the twenty-day rising of the Montone brought disaster. Houses in Forlì were submerged ; its bridge was broken and the Faenza road blocked. The animals died in the fields, and the townspeople, without grain, wandered in misery into the mountains to seek for food. Accounts of similar misfortunes are almost commonplace in the chronicles.[26]

Again, the plain was widely interspersed with forest and pasture lands. In place of today's unchanging expanse of cultivated fields, there still stood much of the ancient Silva Latina, which survives now only in the Pineta, the pine forest of Ravenna.

The principal wealth of the plain lay in cultivation. Flax had been grown here in Roman times (when the linen of Faenza had been held to be the second best in Europe) and it still flourished. Faenza was now celebrated for its broad beans, its principal crop ; while Cesena (which Benvenuto described as 'most fertile') was noted for figs, and Forlì for its aromatic seeds.[27] Vines were tended all over the province, already giving the Muscatello and white Albano wines we know today ; fruit was grown extensively.

But more important were the grain crops : panic or Italian millet, barley, spelt, and wheat. In these the province was extremely rich. The *contado* of Faenza, it was estimated in 1504, produced 130,000 *staia* each year, of which only 60,000 were consumed locally.[28] Ravenna probably produced as much or more.[29] By 1524, Rimini produced 24,000 *staia* of corn, of which

12,000 *staia* were for home consumption and 4,000 kept back for seed.[30] In years when there was general famine in Italy (as in 1329 and 1372) Romagna still exported wheat to Florence.[31] Bologna too, depended upon the province for its corn. When grain lacked there, wrote Cardinal Grimoard, ' remedia sunt de Romandiola '. This does not mean, however, that the province did not have its own famine years, when corn had to be imported from Apulia or the Marche.[32]

One last product must be mentioned : the salt from the flats of Cervia. In this era, when it was often impossible to feed cattle during winter, meat had to be preserved until the spring months. Consequently, salt was almost as important as wheat. Alberti described the shore at Cervia as ' burdened with so many mountains of white salt, that it seemed impossible to see so much together at the same time ', and in the town, he saw in the piazza ' a hill of white salt, gleaming like marble,' a hundred feet round and twenty feet high. The small stretch of seashore outside the town produced enough salt to satisfy the needs of Romagna and all Lombardy, and was an essential part of their economy ; when salt failed to arrive in Bologna, there were riots within a week. In consequence, its control was valuable : ' we have more from little Cervia,' wrote Cardinal Poujet, in the middle of the fourteenth century, ' than from the whole of Romagna '.[33]

III

In considering the government of the towns, and the slow emergence of the *signorie*, it is important to keep in mind the economy of the province. In the bourgeois republics of Tuscany, merchants and bankers succeeded, through their economic power, in bringing the *contado* under the authority of the urban commune. In Tuscany the town had more importance than the countryside. Wealth depended upon trade, industry, and capital, rather than upon agriculture.

A Florentine, speaking to French ambassadors, said that the prosperity of his city came ' not from the riches of the field, but rather from the industry that sent Florentines to do business through the whole Christian world, and to seek their fortunes from merchandise. It is through this that the strength of the state is increased and maintained.'[34] With this economy, Florence, and other towns with a predominantly mercantile structure, came under the dominion of a capitalist class that, in a long struggle extending into the fourteenth century, was able to absorb or displace the feudal nobility of its *contado*. This development created what might be considered as the classic balance of the free commune. In contrast, the communes of Romagna had few citizens, and were primarily agrarian in their economy. For this reason their constitutional development was to be radically different.

The Romagnol town communes of the twelfth century were small and simple in structure. At Faenza, in 1138, the number of citizens was so small that council meetings were held in a church cloister, and the commune was unable to put more than 150 soldiers into the field. The chronicler of the thirteenth century remarks on this with surprise, yet it is unlikely that any of the towns ever exceeded 10,000 souls; the first certain figures we possess, for Rimini in 1511, give the number of inhabitants at 5,000.[35] In these communes there were no great merchants and no bankers, and in the thirteenth century there was little manufacture except for domestic consumption.

Rimini had its port, which served as an *entrepôt* for Dubrovnik, and which carried on a mildly prosperous business in the wines of the hinterland;[36] but it was small, and unsuitable for large craft. 'Here enter small little ships', said the Venetian *portolan* of 1490.[37] Cervia, apart from its production of salt, was little more than a fishing village; Cesenatico, built between 1302 and 1314,[38] never became anything more.

Ravenna was unable to expand because its port and trade had fallen under the control of Venice. By a treaty of 1261 the trade of the commune was severely restricted; an armed Venetian galley was permanently stationed in the port of Santa Maria di Ravenna; and a Venetian consul resided in the town, at the expense of the commune, to ensure that nothing was done against the interests of the Serenissima. Three years later a castle called Marcabò was built on land at the mouth of the Po di Primaro which had been leased to Venice by the Ravenna commune. From this centre, Venice was able to secure monopolistic control of local trade, and rival ships could take nothing from Romagna or the March of Ancona. Marcabò was destroyed in 1308, and Ravenna made spasmodic attempts throughout the century to throw off Venetian domination, but in vain. In 1328, Ravenna agreed to a treaty by which she promised to have no trade with Syria, Barbary, the Byzantine Empire, Apulia, Naples, Sicily, or Alexandria. Anything required from these areas was to be obtained through Venice. Even in famine years, corn could only be imported directly from Apulia if the Doge's licence were obtained.

Officials were appointed to ensure that these terms were obeyed.[39] The ecclesiastical government of the province was powerless to do anything but protest against this, and the Venetian economic hegemony continued. When, in November 1424, Milan wished to provision her troops in Romagna from the grain lands of the Regno, it was only with difficulty that she could persuade the Venetians to allow her ships to unload at Cesenatico, Ravenna, and Primaro, without first passing to Venice.

Venice, in its search for monopoly in the Adriatic, had been the first external power to seek control of Romagnol trade. As early as 1201, in her treaty with the men of the Fourth Crusade, she had prohibited them from buying provisions from Imola and Faenza, ' save by our leave '.[40] Though Ferrara[41] and Bologna also sought the salt and corn of the province, Venice maintained her lead to the second half of the century.[42] After that she was faced with the competition of Florence,[43] which was to prove much more serious.

All the commercial agreements signed by the Romagnol communes, both with these powers and among themselves,[44] were exclusively concerned with salt, wine, and foodstuffs. The wealth of the province was found in the produce of the countryside which Salimbene indicated : ' corn, wine, oil, fish, flesh, salt, figs, eggs, cheese, fruit, and every sort of food '. Yet there was no class of native Romagnol entrepreneurs who profited from the trading of these goods. The communes of the towns insisted upon complete control of all exports, and marketed corn as a communal monopoly. They themselves were the entrepreneurs, and only rarely were the land-owning nobility and ecclesiastics able to market their products directly.

This communal monopolistic control of export was of considerable importance in the political conflicts within the towns. Each land-owning family wanted to negotiate individually when selling produce from its estates, and thus escape communal control. They could only hope to do this as lords of their towns. Once in power, they could sell their corn where they wanted and could ' regrate ' (*i.e.* hold back supplies for higher prices) whenever they wished. The problem of the marketing of food also explains in large part the resistance of the communes to the papacy when the province became a part of the papal states. For under papal rule the export of foodstuffs was only permitted by licence, and with due regard to the needs of the province as a whole. In 1288, for instance, the papal rector of Romagna wrote to Guido di Lamberto da Polenta, *podestà* of Ravenna, to say that

Ravenna, Guido in his own person, and his sons, were to be fined by the provincial government. This was because, between September 1287 and January 1288, they had all exported corn outside the province, '*et in maxima et magna quantitate* . . . so that the said province stands and is placed in danger of famine'.[45] It was to avoid such restrictions that the signori and the communes which they ruled, resisted the papacy so stubbornly. *Campanalismo* : local patriotism, had a strong economic basis.

Up to 1278, Romagna formed a part of the medieval Empire. Yet local autonomy within the wider imperial structure had been secured by the towns during the eleventh and twelfth centuries. This was confirmed, with the imperial right of regalia (which gave them the right to make their own laws and elect their own magistrates), by the Peace of Constance in 1183. At the beginning of the thirteenth century, power within these communes rested in the *concilium comunis* : the Council of the Commune, composed of the more substantial men of the town. Under the presidency of the *podestà*, the council decided policy, and elected from its members the principal officers of the commune. The *podestà* and his vicar (generally foreigners to the town) held office for six-monthly periods, and acted as the chief executive officers of the commune, with full powers of justice. From the Council of the Commune emanated a small executive council called the *consiglio di credenza* (or Small Council), whose members were called *savii* or *sapientes*. This served as a check upon the *podestà*, and, by authorising minor administrative decisions, obviated the necessity of calling the Council of the Commune to settle anything but important matters.

At Faenza in 1103, and at Cesena in 1142, there were conflicts between the town nobility and the people of the commune.[46] Had the communes of this era preserved their simple structure, and had their territorial boundaries remained unchanged, it is possible to imagine circumstances where the *popolo*, through their numerical strength, could have triumphed over the town nobility and secured a democratic government. Indeed, the oligarchic monopoly of office was largely broken down during the thirteenth century. The 'people', organised in the trade-guilds of the 'Arts', were then inserted into the old structure of the commune to form the new constitution of 'the commune and people'. The *podestà*, the Council of the Commune and the *anziani* or representatives of the Arts, now combined to form the *consiglio generale* (or General Council). At the same time a new senior executive office was created, that of the Captain of the People, the representative of the *popolo* and the Arts. He took over many rights (especially those concerning military organisation) from the *podestà*, the representative of the old commune. In this, Romagna followed the example of Bologna. Indeed this widening of the base of the communal organisation was primarily due to the influence of that city, which, in the years after 1248, held political hegemony over Romagna.

This process was uneven, and assumed differing forms in each town. It is poorly documented but the broad outlines are clearly distinguishable. Imola, under Bolognese rule, had Captains of the People in 1255 and 1258 and a General Council in 1263. There was also a Small Council formed by the twelve *anziani* who were the heads of the trade guilds.[47] In Faenza in 1218, the *podestà* formed ' a community of arms ' in an attempt to persuade ' the magnates ' to share office with the people. The attempt failed, but later, in the years of Bolognese domination, popular institutions were imposed upon the commune : Captains of the People, first found in 1256, and officials called *consules mercatorum* (consuls of the Arts) in 1262. There were ' *anziani* of the people ' in 1280, while in 1294 there was a variety of popular institutions : a Council of the People, a General Council, a Council of the *anziani* : and working with these councils, a Small Council of the Twenty-eight *Savii*.[48] By this time the popular elements of the town were fully assimilated within the commune, and the communal seal bore the inscription : ' Sigillum Comunis et Populi Favencie '. Bolognese influence at Bagnacavallo, a small commune twelve miles to the north of Imola, introduced the same elements. Here in 1267 there was a General Council, with *podestà* and five *anziani*.[49]

Rimini alone escaped from the Bolognese domination of Romagna during the middle years of the century, yet here too there was the same development. From 1232, the heads of the Arts were summoned to council, and with them officials representing each of the *contrade* or minor administrative subdivisions of the town. By 1254, the four major administrative divisions, the quarters of the town, elected the ' captains of the societies and Arts ' who had powers to deal with matters of peace and war. From about 1278 these men became known as the ' Four Officials '. Chosen each month in the General Council, they helped the *podestà* to rule the commune. They could propose any measure in the council, while the *podestà* might only offer measures for debate with their consent. They appointed all extraordinary officials, nominated the Small Council, and had considerable control of finance.[50]

At Ravenna, the surviving statutes of the thirteenth century indicate that varying systems were adopted throughout the century, without specifying the periods in which they were operating. There were arrangements for one *podestà*, two *podestà* and a *podestà* and captain of the town. A Small Council was held once a month, and the ' orders and universal societies of Ravenna and its suburbs ' were ruled by a *capitularius* and *maiores* who held posts as *anziani*. Side by side with these measures there were attempts to limit popular control. The *podestà* was supposed to elect, within fifteen days of his entry to office, two men from the ' people ' and two ' knights ' to ' reform ' the General and Small councils. The General Council was not to have more than 200 members, while the Small Council was limited to seventy. A specified object of the reform was to ensure that no-one who was a servant should take part in the councils. A later decree transferred the appointment of the ' reformers ' of the councils to the ' curiales comunis Ravenne,' though who these were is not clear. The *podestà* was also entrusted with the ' reform ' of the Arts.[51]

Our knowledge of Forlì is slight, but by 1292, the town certainly had a communal organisation comparable with others of the province. In that year, the town's General Council met in the Palazzo del Popolo, together with the *podestà*, captain, and *anziani*.[52] In all probability this constitution, too, dated from the middle period of the century, when Bologna ruled the town.

Any effect that this popular legislation might have had, however, was nullified by *comitatinanza* : the expansion of the commune into the *contado*, the attempt to subdue the feudal lords and independent village communes. This took place in the same era. Taking advantage of aristocratic rivalries, now in alliance with one noble house, now with another, utilising imperial support for measures seemingly designed to introduce greater unity, the towns compelled or persuaded the feudality of the *contado* to swear allegiance, and to play their part in intercommunal war and the administration of communal office. In coercing these men into submission, the commune had seemed to triumph. In fact it had sealed its fate. Such was the structure of the new commune that it was inevitably the nobility, whether originating from the town or the *contado*, who would eventually dominate it. These men possessed territorial, military, and social power, and no other class was sufficiently strong to resist their influence.

Sometimes *comitatinanza* was made at the expense of the episcopacies of the province. These acquisitions, though they were often the cause of war with other communes, brought clear gain to the towns; conflicts were generally resolved by some 'compromise,' in which the ecclesiastical authorities complied with a situation they were powerless to change. Less happy were the communes' extensions at the expense of the independent nobility. These attacks on the feudality were accelerated at the beginning of the century. The chronicler, Tolosano, describes one of these incidents in 1208:

> Because Pietro Pagani did not wish to obey Gerardo Rolendini, the *podestà*, and hold to his oath, the men of Faenza rode to Susinana and the parish of Milleo, cutting down vines and ancient trees, burning crops, and carrying out other hostile acts that before they had not attempted, on account of the difficulty of the place and the harshness of the roads.[53]

It would be wrong to take from accounts such as this the impression that the armed strength of the commune was by itself sufficient to assault feudatories and compel them to submission. Considerable forces were required to besiege a castle in the *contado*, and it is doubtful if the citizen militia were able or willing to provide them. The military actions of the commune were mainly confined to hit-and-run raids with destruction of crops.

There were in fact three principal ways by which the feudality was drawn under the jurisdiction of the commune. First, there was imperial pressure. Frederick I, for instance, had granted the *contado* of Rimini to the commune in 1157, and it was at imperial instigation that Imola had destroyed Castel Imola in December 1209.[54] Second, the commune would ally with one feudatory to subjugate another, as did Faenza with the Conti Guidi. Finally — and most frequently — *comitatinanza* was brought about by bribery.

Sometimes, as in Faenza's purchase of Donegallia from Count Alberico in 1215, the commune simply bought the feudality out.[55] More frequently, where the feudal lord actually swore allegiance and citizenship, he did so on advantageous terms. It was often laid down that he did not have to dwell in the town in time of peace, and that in war there was no obligation on him to bring his family to the town. He was exempt from the taxes upon the *contado*. The town promised not to receive any of the lord's men as citizens, and indemnified the nobles for any damage done to their property whilst they were fighting for the commune.[56]

The long-term effect of *comitatinanza*, under these conditions, was to transfer power within the commune from the town notables to the feudal nobility. It ensured that, though minor offices might be held by the 'people', true authority was to rest with the *contado* nobility. The inclusion of the feudality, more than outweighed the self-assertion of the popular orders in the Arts in the era of Bolognese hegemony. In this period the communes had often promulgated decrees derived from Bolognesi precedents against the undue influence of 'magnates'. In the statutes of Faenza, as late as 1410, it was decreed that to remove their 'oppressions, fears, and threats,' no magnate might come to council or enter the Palazzo Comunale.[57] Again, in Imola in 1315, the captain decreed that 'none from the nobles and magnates of the town of Imola shall dare or presume to offend any of the people of the town of Imola under capital pain, according to the statutes'.[58] Conservative legalism ensured that these provisions remained in the statute books, but they were never put into force. Another passage of the statutes of Faenza, already cited, enumerates those families considered by the commune as magnates. Of these, three had long been extinct, and a fourth, the Manfredi, had for forty years held the *signoria* of the town, had the right of authorising or rejecting the publication of the statutes, and, in fact, had ordered their compilation in this particular instance.[59]

The truth was that any magnate, by ascription to the Arts, by becoming a member of a guild, by assuming the rank, if not the status, of a butcher or a smith, a ploughman or a flaxworker, could avoid the legal stigma attached to being a magnate. Indeed, on analysis, the Arts themselves are found to be dominated by the feudal nobility from an early date. In Imola in 1272, the 'society of merchants' for instance, was composed of 'foreigners' — principally Tuscans; of tradesmen — there are two tailors recorded; of notaries; — and of nobles. By 1312, the Arts of Imola were completely dominated by the feudality. The Alidosi are found in that year among the butchers; the Sassatelli among the smiths; and the della Bordella among the society of peasants.[60] Similarly, the da Polenta, in the fourteenth century, headed the names of those belonging to the guild of fishermen in Ravenna.[61] Thus the feudal nobility acted as *anziani*, and by the middle of the thirteenth century had virtually begun to monopolise the podestàship and captaincy.[62] The word 'magnate' no longer meant a member of the aristocracy as such; it had become a generic term of abuse to describe anyone of a different party.

In fact, whereas in Tuscany, *comitatinanza* had brought about the control of the *contado* by the town, in Romagna it had brought about the control of the town by the *contado*. Only when the *signoria* replaced the commune was the balance to be in part restored. For the *signore* could only rise to power in the town by attaining supremacy over his fellow nobility of the *contado*. Once *comitatinanza* had taken place in Romagna, the question was no longer whether communal institutions would ever have any real validity; but only which of the *signori* would attain *signoria*. In his *Discourses on Livy*, Machiavelli, with unerring judgment, was to place his finger on the defect in communal society that led to signorial rule: *gentiluomini*. 'Gentlemen' he defined as those who lived on rents:

> Such are pernicious to every republic in every province. But more pernicious still are those who in addition to this fortune control a castle and have subjects who obey them. The Kingdom of Naples, Rome, Romagna, and Lombardy are full of these two sorts of men. And from this it comes, that in those provinces there has never risen any republic nor any political life, for such generations of men are complete enemies of any civic government. And it would be impossible to produce a republic there in any way. Anyone who wished to re-order these provinces should he be master of them, would have no alternative but to create a kingdom. And for this reason: that when society is so corrupt that law does not suffice to enchain it, a royal hand is needed, that with absolute and excessive power, may check the excessive ambition and corruption of powerful men.[63]

These words might serve as a commentary on the history of the communes of Romagna between *comitatinanza* and *signoria*.

IV

Feudalism in Romagna originated in the era of the Ottonian Emperors of the tenth century; in the eleventh and twelfth centuries the principal tenants-in-chief were the cathedral and other churches of Ravenna. Of the government of 'the Exarchate' of this age, our knowledge is slight and disordered; nor is this the place to attempt any greater illumination. Enough to say that, with the Investiture Contest, the supremacy of the churches was broken. The new communes now claimed the jurisdiction once held by their bishops. In the *contado* a number of feudal lords, the descendants perhaps of Byzantine, Langobard, imperial, or archiepiscopal officials, strove, with equal success, to wrest land from their ecclesiastical overlords. This they did by securing the right to the inheritance and automatic renewal of long-term leases. Thus almost all lay landholding or jurisdiction in Romagna was based upon some past usurpation of ecclesiastical right, either gradual, almost unperceived, and tacitly accepted, or violent, and fruitlessly resisted. The origins of the communes — both urban and rural — might be explained in terms of a landlord-tenant conflict in which the landlord is expropriated. The origins of the territorial power of the Romagnol nobility could be partly explained as the rise of powerful servants, taking over the property of a weak master.

Of the feudatories of Romagna, at the beginning of the thirteenth century, some, as the Traversari and Conti Guidi, were great and powerful in the Italy of their day ; others, such as the Malatesti, were to attain eminence in future centuries. Most were obscure and petty, or even — as with the Tignosi — known to us only through some reference in the *Divine Comedy*. Yet on the relationships of these men ; on their personal hates and enmities, friendships and alliances, the history of Romagna was to rest. From their numbers, five families, who were by no means the most powerful at the beginning of the thirteenth century, were to rise in the fourteenth to seize the *signoria* of the five principal towns of the province. They are the Alidosi of Imola, the Manfredi of Faenza, the Ordelaffi of Forlì, the Malatesti of Rimini, and the da Polenta of Ravenna.

Each in the course of time was to evolve a series of legends concerning its early history. The polite historians of the Alidosi claimed, for example, that the family originated from two captains of Justinian who entered Italy with Belisarius. A similar Byzantine motif adorned the Manfredi legend, in which the father of the family eloped from Constantinople with a daughter of Constantine II. But the family name, ' Manfredi,' suggests rather a Teutonic origin, while the family motto was German : ' Wann Ich Mach '. To satisfy anyone thinking along these lines, another story ascribed the family fortunes to a good-looking barber, resident in Reggio. This man begat four sons upon the daughter of an emperor, in a clandestine love-affair, and had as reward the strange good fortune of ennoblement. The story has every appearance of being believed by the family itself, for they incorporated the *salasso*, or bleeding instruments of the medieval barber, on one of their coats of arms.[64]

The Ordelaffi claimed descent from a German baron called Dell' Affia, who married the daughter of Berengarius, Duke of Friuli. Dell' Affia, the story says, was Berengarius' legate at Forlì, and had his name corrupted by Italian speech to Ordelaf, before being expelled and forced to take refuge in Venice. There, he plotted against the republic, and his son's life was only spared by the magistrates on the condition that he should spell his name backwards. Thus from him was descended the illustrious family of the Venetian Faledro. This story does not lack for a wealth of corroborative detail that may more justly be considered rather the explanation of its origin than the proof of its veracity. Thus Ordelaffo was a not uncommon name in the Italy of this period. It was borne, for instance, by a Trevisan family of the thirteenth century, and a fourteenth-century poet of that town claimed that this was the original stock from which the signorial family had sprung. By chance the Venetian Faledri too, originated from Treviso — and then, of course, Treviso is not far from the Friuli of Berengarius.[65]

An historian of the Malatesti in the fourteenth century traced their descent to Noah, through Croesus, King of Crete, the Tarquins, and a brother of the Emperor Henry III. The fifteenth-century chroniclers, doubtless under the influence of the classical studies of the age, preferred a simple Roman origin : two noble knights of the house of Scipio Africanus, whose manifold merits and virtues had caused them to be envied and thus exiled from Rome to Romagna. The family of the da Polenta alone (perhaps because it was the first to become extinct), had no well-developed fables concerning its origin, apart from the comparatively dreary exercise of deriving its name from the River Polenz, a tributary of the Elbe.[66]

In an age when our vanity prefers to ascribe good fortune to the hard struggle of merit against the disadvantages of birth, the claims of the signorial families to noble origins must appear strange. The true story — the story of little landowners, step by step building up their fortunes, regardless of setbacks, driven onward by greed, lust of dominion, and pride of family, until they had reached a position where they could claim *signoria* — this, one feels, should have interested them far more than the narration of fables. The true story, though less flattering to their pride, would have served at least as a stimulus and guide to future action. But literary convention and courtly manners alike demanded that they should consider themselves, not as local men who had made good, but as imperial stock, who, it must be confessed, had come down in the world considerably. Nor was it this alone that inspired them. With these fables, against the sneers of the bourgeois republics, the *signori* were asserting their legitimacy, a point on which they were justly sensitive : the primacy of their blood in an age in which even the republics had the greatest respect for noble ancestry.

But perhaps after all there is some significance behind these legends. Might they not mirror the descent of officials of the Exarchate, or of Lombard or Imperial nobility? The aunt of the great Maghinardo de' Pagani gloried in the name of 'Galla Placidia', and one remembers the name Teodorico in the Ordelaffi family. Little can be derived from all this: Byzantine and Langobard blood probably ran through the veins of every thirteenth-century Romagnol. In fact any attempt to trace the descent of the signorial families from periods before the eleventh century, or from localities outside Romagna, is doomed to be lost in fruitless speculation.

Returning to reality, the materials for the true story of the origins of the signorial families are too fragmentary and inadequate for any coherent picture to emerge.[67] In the eleventh and early twelfth centuries the families had not generally acquired a family name, though men who may or may not be members of the signorial house, appear with such Christian names as Alidosio or Ordelaffo. Then came the growth of family self-consciousness: the Christian name of one of its members who had gained some local fame was adopted as a cognomen. This seems to have happened to the Malatesti, the Ordelaffi, and the da Polenta in the second half of the twelfth century. The Alidosi, on the other hand, are recorded with a name only at the beginning of the thirteenth century. But even at this stage, family names were extremely flexible. If a striking personality emerged, the house might, in the course of his life, change its cognomen to his Christian name. This is perhaps what happened to the signorial house of Faenza. By the twelfth century they had come to be called the Manfredi. At the beginning of the thirteenth century one of their number, Alberghetto, gained fame as *podestà* of Vicenza against the attacks of Ezzelino da Romano. As a result his kinsmen wavered between calling themselves the Manfredi or the Alberghetti, and the faction dominated by the family in Faenza was called indifferently, the 'pars de Alberghettis' and the 'party of the Manfredi'.[68]

In these circumstances little can be gleaned from the chronicles and documents that have survived. All we can hope for are a few short glimpses of their lives. There is a brief picture, for instance, of the Manfredi playing a part in the communal politics of Faenza in 1103. In that year there was division within the family, the first of many which were to rend it, down to the sixteenth century. Alberico di Guido de' Manfredi, 'and many other nobles', left the town, and allied with Ravenna against its citizens. At the same time, a Guido Manfredi and the Accarisi family (who were to be the great opponents of the Manfredi in the thirteenth century) supported the town against them. Twelve years later, the chronicler tells us, Guido Manfredi was driven out of the town by an alliance of Alberico Manfredi and other nobles. Alberico and his party then occupied the houses of the exiles.[69]

Even brief notices such as these are rare. Generally all that remains are a few ambiguous references. Sometimes men of the families are found in connection with imperial officials ;[70] the Manfredi even entertained the Emperor Frederick I in their house.[71] Sometimes they were associated in some minor way with the greater families of the time : the Conti Guidi and the Ravenna house of the Traversari,[72] or found, like the da Polenta, acting as agents of the Archbishops of Ravenna.[73] All these families at this time were small and insignificant, and their history was inevitably dependent upon their relations with the great feudal houses and the administrators of the Empire and the Ravenna church.

It was presumably through services to these powers that the signorial families came to be landowners within the *contado*. By the first decades of the thirteenth century, it can definitely be said that all were established in the countryside. In 1186, the Malatesti were able to acquire considerable possessions between the Marecchia and Rubicon rivers. By 1197, they had control of Verucchio, from where, perhaps, they had originated. In that year, and again in 1216, the dealings of Giovanni di Malatesta and his nephew, Malatesta dalla Penna, with the commune of Rimini, illustrate well the landed power which the Malatesti had acquired, and the bribes which the towns were forced to make to secure control of the *contado*. The Malatesti promised to dwell in the town six months out of every year in peace time, and continually in time of war ; to hold the enemies of the commune for their enemies, its friends for their friends. By this deed, the Malatesti alone, not the inhabitants under their jurisdiction, enjoyed the rights of citizenship in the town. The two Malatesti were exempt from the payment of *gabelles*, and were assured of compensation for damage done to their property, through war fought by them on behalf of the commune. The following month the commune paid the two men £R.100 that they might buy a house in Rimini, and gave another £R.100 to Giovanni to restore a house with ' a tower ', that he already held there.[74]

At the same time the other families were extending their possessions. The da Polenta may have acquired the village of Polenta itself (which probably took its name from the family and not the other way about) in the middle of the twelfth century. This property, in the mountains near Bertinoro, was held by emphyteutic lease (that is to say a lease for three generations) from the monastery of San Giovanni Evangelista of Ravenna. By 1201, the Ordelaffi were leasing land, in fifty-three different places in the *contado*, from the Abbey of San Mercuriale of Forlì.[75]

The Alidosi had established themselves on the Massa Ambrogio by 1212. On the ridge here to the north of the Santerno, they built their principal castle, and this area came to be known as the Massa Alidosia. In the valley below, there grew up the market-place known as the Mercatale della Massa Alidosia, where stands the present-day village of Castel del Rio. From here, during the thirteenth century, the family was to extend its domain over the neighbouring rural communes of the *montagna* : Castiglione, Visignano, Castelvecchio, Valsalva, Belvedere, and Osta : jurisdictions penetrating the Tuscan Apennines, and bounded on the south-west by the properties of the Pagani. Farther down the valley, within ten miles of Imola, the Alidosi extended their power over Codrignano and Linaro.

With landed power such as this behind them, the lords came to play a larger role in the life of the province during the thirteenth century. An Alidosio degli Alidosi, for example, acted as one of the two consuls of the town of Imola in 1230.[76] In Rimini, Malatesta dalla Penna de' Malatesti (1183–1248) defeated some pirate Slavs from Dubrovnik, served as *podestà* of Pistoia in 1233, and as *podestà* of Rimini in 1239.[77] But isolated instances, such as these, must not be interpreted as indicating that the men of the families yet predominated within their communes. In fact, they were still minor players in a drama whose significance they had not themselves come to realise. Perhaps they had not yet acquired even the ambitions of their descendants. It was only with the growth and intensification of the party struggles that their names were to be heard throughout the Romagna.

CHAPTER II

The Origins of Party Conflict

Dentro a questi termini, idest praedictos confines, *è ripieno di venenosi sterpi,* scilicet tyrannis parvis et magnis vere pestiferis.

BENVENUTO DA IMOLA[1]

I

FROM the end of the tenth century, ' the Exarchate of Ravenna ', which included the whole of Romagna, was within the medieval Empire. At the beginning of the thirteenth century, the papacy attempted to reassert its right to possession of the province, but only with the conflict of Frederick II and Gregory IX, did its claims take on any immediacy. Every town and noble in the province was then faced with the problem of allegiance : to pope or emperor, to Guelf or Ghibelline.

Until 1239, all the communes, with the exception of Faenza, followed the Ghibelline and imperial cause. In that year, however, the powerful Ravennate noble, Paolo Traversari, until then the constant ally of Frederick, declared for the Guelfs, and joined with Bologna to drive the imperial supporters from Ravenna.[2] In August 1240, the Emperor replied by marching north from Ancona. After a six-day siege he re-took Ravenna, and then turned on Faenza, which, despite unexpected resistance, fell on 14 April 1241.[3] For the following seven years Romagna remained Ghibelline, and only with the imperial defeat at Parma, and the triumphant northward advance of the papal legate, the Cardinal Ottaviano degli Ubaldini, did each town of the province come under Guelf control.[4]

The original orientation of Guelf–Ghibelline allegiance in Romagna had been dictated, in part, by the traditional authority conceded to the empire. More important, as a fourteenth-century chronicler explained, it was engendered by hostility to, or suspicion of, Guelf Bologna[5] — it is significant that Faenza alone, the ally of Bologna, had been a member of the anti-imperial Lombard League. In Florence and Bologna, the names of Guelf and Ghibelline were the expressions of relations to empire and papacy, and then again, of class conflict within the cities. In the

Romagnol communes, the alignments of party allegiance were dictated primarily by their fears for their autonomy, and by their relations with other communes.

But there were interior cross-currents of allegiance to complicate these original patterns. The feudatories of the Apennine *montagna* had relations with Florence and Bologna, independent of their relations with the communes of Romagna, and indeed, mutually contradictory on any abstract plane. Giovanni Villani wrote of Maghinardo Pagani of Faenza : ' Ghibelline he was in his nation and in his works, but with the Florentines he was Guelf and enemy of all their enemies, whether they were Guelf or Ghibelline '.

This contrast enraged Dante, who stigmatised him as :

> il leoncel del nido bianco
> Che muta parte dall' estate al verno.
>
> (The lion cub of the white lair [a reference to the Pagani coat of arms : a lion, azure, on a field, argent] who changes party from summer to winter.)[6]

But Bartolo da Sassoferrato, writing in the fourteenth century, would have appreciated very clearly Maghinardo's position. ' As these words are used to-day ', he wrote, ' a man may be a Guelf in one place and a Ghibelline in another, because allegiances of this type refer to a variety of issues.' Indeed he might be Guelf and Ghibelline in the same place — Bartolus cites as example certain citizens of Perugia, ' who wish to be thought of as Ghibellines, because long ago their ancestors had been nobles of the Ghibelline party. But because of the present state of the town, they are Guelfs.'[7]

The second and more important complication was that the Guelf or Ghibelline complexion of each town was bound up and associated with whatever noble faction was dominating the commune. Inevitably, any feudatories who opposed the party in power would assume the other allegiance and, under the specious colour of loyalty to pope or emperor, pursue their own territorial and personal aims within the framework of the commune. In this way, at an early stage of the war between the two great powers, factions of nobles, within each town, struggled to retain or usurp influence under the pretext of papal or imperial allegiance. In Imola were the parties of the Ghibelline Mendoli, and the Guelf Brizzi ; in Faenza, the Guelf Manfredi and Ghibelline Accarisi ; in Ravenna, the Guelf Traversari and the Ghibelline Anastagi ;

in Rimini, the Guelf Gambancerri and the Ghibelline Parcitadi.

It was these parties of nobles, and not any of the communal institutions by which the *homines* of the commune were supposed to declare their will, that now ruled the destinies of the towns. In his *Encyclica Bellica contra Gregorium IX*, Frederick II justly complained, not that Ravenna had withdrawn its allegiance from him, but rather, that Paolo Traversari had led the town into the Guelf alliance. Again, the reason for Frederick's attack on Ravenna two years later was 'that he had heard that Paolo Traversari was dead'.[8] Already it was the nobility and not the *homines* who were the key factor in communal government. Ravenna, indeed was already virtually the *signoria* of the Traversari family.

Neither the defeat and death of Frederick II, nor the triumph of Charles of Anjou, ended artistocratic party conflict. The violence precipitated by the war, the feuds of noble houses that it had engendered or reinforced, the temptations of profitable usurpation in town or *contado*, all served to prolong the struggles. The noble partisans were unmoved by any of the theoretical concepts to be found in the *De Monarchia*; they were engaged, rather, in a struggle for local gain and personal advantage. In Romagna, the words Guelf and Ghibelline were already divorced from their historic meaning; they defined alignments, not of theory, but of interest. With the end of papal–imperial conflict in the province, they were used only as evocations of traditional loyalties, diverted now from their source; as names to justify feudal anarchy.

Names of ill-omen for Romagna. In each town and throughout its *contado*, violence and force prevailed. Within each commune, trivial incidents: some sudden murder, some hasty and mistaken rumour, some true or groundless suspicion, served to bring the factions to conflict. One party would be expelled, would nurse its strength in exile, and, at the opportune moment, return to expel its opponents. Marriage alliances between the nobility of different towns served as links to connect the feuds and factions of neighbouring communes. Strife in one town led inevitably to a chain reaction of similar conflict throughout the whole province. In this way the whole feudality of Romagna were ranged under the banner of opposing allegiance. Marriage alliances with the great feudatories of the Tuscan or Bolognesi Apennines, with noble houses themselves involved in the party struggle of Florence and Bologna, also served to make Romagna sensitive to political mutations in these towns. Insurrection, and the expulsion of parties there, would provoke the same phenomena in Romagna.

This is the age in which the province became, as Dante described it, *mai senza guerra*, never without war.

Thirty years were to pass before the empire was to relinquish its nominal supremacy to the papacy. Yet during this period it was realised that the popes were seeking the cession of the province. Imperial officials, when they appeared, were received with respect, but did not venture on any foolhardy attempt to rule. There was a certain ambiguity as to who, even in theory, held control. The manner of the visit of the apostolic legate and the imperial chancellor to the province, in 1275, almost suggests that there was a theoretical co-dominium.[9] In fact no real central control was exercised by either power. There was a political vacuum in which anarchy flourished.

This vacuum might properly have been filled by the commune of Bologna. Bologna, at the centre of the Via Emilia, was dependent upon Romagna for corn and salt. Geographically, the communications, running from Bologna to each of the towns of the plain, suggest a natural and profitable alliance between the agrarian and rural interests of the province with the commercial concerns of the city. Indeed, in the years after 1248, when she had all the prestige that came from association with Cardinal Ubaldini's levies in the defeat of Frederick, Bologna acquired considerable interests in the province, and appeared to be on the point of absorbing at least the northern segment. The triumph of Guelfism was bound up with the triumph of the Guelf city.[10] It was, therefore, natural that in the third quarter of the century, Bologna's influence should grow. In fact, she appointed the *podestà* at Faenza between 1256 and 1274 ; absorbed completely the town and *contado* of Imola between 1254 and 1278 ; and controlled the podestàship of Forlì until 1272.[11] But Bologna was unable to bring peace between the factions ; her presence, indeed, served only to inflame them. Within her own walls, strife grew between the parties of the Guelf Geremei and the Ghibelline Lambertazzi. The poison of this conflict weakened her power and frustrated her attempts to crush the endemic quarrels of Romagna. The expulsion of the Lambertazzi from Bologna, in 1274, intensified a struggle, the effects of which were to be felt for over thirty years. Nor was this all ; interference in Romagnol factions was to add to party bitterness in Bologna itself.[12] Thus anarchy in Romagna continued unchecked, and its nobility prepared for unceasing strife :

Sforçu monstran grande ;   remore e la paura
Per Romagna se spande,   nulla part' è segura

Chè no porta girlande che fa forteçe e mura
Che desfà.
Chom' è usu de guerra, chosì (or) andarà ;
Tal ne crede aquistar terra, che la perderà ;
Tutta Romagna è en erra batagla pur serà
Secom'eo credo.[13]

(Great stand their forces; rumour and fear spread through Romagna; no one is safe, not he who bears garlands, who makes fortresses and walls, nor he who destroys them. As is the way of war, so now will it go; some think to gain land, yet they will lose it ; all Romagna is in turbulence ; there will be battle, so does it seem to me.)

II

The conflicts in the *contado* were fought out by the comparatively small numbers of troops that the aristocracy could put in the field. But they were violent and destructive. The chronicler Cantinelli gives some vivid pictures of these contests :

In the same year [1276] in the month of May, the honourable Count Urso da Mangona,[14] Captain of the party of the Lambertazzi dwelling at Faenza, together with the Faventines and the Bolognesi and Imolesi exiles, rode towards Imola above the Via Emilia towards Selice, within two miles of the town. There they met some knights who had ridden towards Sant' Agata and had taken great booty. These men were in good spirits as they rode back to Imola, but soon their pleasure was turned to sorrow and grief. For seeing those who had come from Faenza, and wishing to defend themselves, they left their booty immediately — though too late. They were killed or captured there in the meadow called Taviano. There were forty dead and twenty-five who were captured and led back to Faenza, and with them all the booty and cattle and horses that had been abandoned.

Two years later :

The Geremei party which dominated at Bologna led their army above Piancaldoli, intending to capture it. They sent Count Maghinardo da Panico, Ubaldino da Lauglione and the Lord Rainaldo Bornio de' Samaratini with two hundred knights and all available foot-soldiers, above the Via Emilia into the mountains of the *contado* of Bologna, and they camped there on Monday 2nd May. On the Sunday following, Maghinardo da Susinana, with Andrea of the Castellani of Andalò, Lord Brancaleo d' Andalò and Aliotto de' Pipini of Forlì, who was then captain of the Lambertazzi party, with all the soldiers of the party and with a hundred knights of the commune of Forlì, rode to Modigliana, and there captured the Lord Count Tigrino, son of Count Guido of Modigliana, with a great number of foot soldiers who were his *fideles*. Then going on towards Marradi, that Sunday and the night following, they came to San Stefano in Palazzuolo, in the properties of Maghinardo de' Pagani, and there they and their horses rested, though it was raining all the time. Then, on Monday, riding through the mountains, across rocks and woods, they came up to the castle of Piancaldoli, where the army of the Geremei was gathered. When those in the Geremei army realised the size of the army coming in aid of Piancaldoli, they turned their backs immediately and fled, leaving their booty behind. But some of their people gathered in a little fort and called out insults, whereat the knights with the d' Andalò took it by force, killing and wounding many, capturing over two hundred. These they led back to Faenza, with the banner they had abandoned. Through this, those within Castel Piancaldoli received bread, wine, tents, oxen and other spoils from the army, and took them into their camp, together with two mangonels that the Geremei had built there.

A last example shows the effect of the fighting in the towns :

In the same year [1273] the Lord Guido Accarisi and the Lord Maghinardo, son of the Lord Pietro Pagani da Susinana, caused a fort to be built at Gallisterna in hate of the men of Sassadello. Thereupon, Alberghetto de' Manfredi, with all his forces, went in aid of those of Sassadello, to destroy the fort. At this, the friends of the Accarisi went to its defence, complaining bitterly that the Manfredi had broken the peace with the Accarisi. They defended the fort well, but on Wednesday 4th April, when Bonifaccio da Susinana and Paganino, son of the Lord Pietro Pagani, together with some of their friends, came to it to give help, those of Sassadello ran up insulting them. And it befell that Bonifaccio and Paganino were wounded and died of their wounds, and many who were with them were wounded or killed. At this rumours ran through Faenza, and barricades were raised between the divisions of the town, in order that one party should not attack the other. And the men of Faenza carried their goods for safety to the churches, to the houses of the Franciscans and Dominicans, to the Priory of Santa Perpetua and the vaults of the Cathedral of San Pietro.[15]

The complaints of Machiavelli, on the lack of blood and devastation in Italian military practice, would not be true of this period. ' So mortal was that strife ' says the chronicler of the War of Ferrara, ' that whoever was captured by either side, straightaway was he dead.'[16] Nor did the soldiery refrain from inflicting on their fellow-countrymen those savageries which, at a later date, they forbore from pressing upon the foreigner. To destroy the crops and fields of the enemy was as important as to defeat his soldiers in battle. When Guido da Montefeltro led the Forlivesi against Ravenna in 1281 :

They destroyed all the corn, trees, vines and plants, and carried out the maximum devastation right up to the walls of the town itself, both on that day and during the night. On the following Sunday they returned honourably to Forlì during the evening, burning all the houses that they passed on the roads by which they came back. In this attack 10,000 *tornature* of corn land were destroyed and innumerable trees and vines.[17]

Again, when Maghinardo Pagani attacked the Bolognese *contado*, on 9 June 1296, he passed above Castel San Pietro, 'burning the houses in these parts, taking sheep and oxen, men and corn. He did the same about Medicina, so that it was said that on that Wednesday over 2,000 houses were burnt in the *contado* of Bologna.'[18]

The result of such conflicts was general devastation. This is how Salimbene had described the province after 1248:

After this long and heavy war, the peasants could neither sow nor thresh, plough, nor plant the vines nor harvest the grapes, nor dwell in their villages. They worked instead near to the towns, defended by the town militia, who distributed themselves according to the gates of the town. And all day, armed soldiers guarded those who worked in the fields. And it was necessary to do this because of the murderers, thieves and robbers who had multiplied out of all measure. And they took men prisoner to gain their ransoms, and they stole and ate their cattle. And if the prisoners would not pay, they hung them up by the feet or hands and pulled out their teeth, and to force them to pay, put toads in their mouths, and this of all forms of torture was most cruel and detested. And they were crueller than demons. And in those days, seeing a stranger on the road was like seeing the devil, for each thought that the other would seek to capture and imprison him. And the territory was reduced to a desert; there were no farmers there, nor travellers, for in the age of Frederick, especially after he was deposed from the Empire, and Parma had rebelled and struck out against him, the principal roads were deserted, and travellers went by secret paths, and ills multiplied upon the land. And birds and beasts — ravens and wild boars and wolves — were overplentiful. The wolves, not finding their prey in sheep and cattle near the villages now ravaged by fire, came in packs, howling for hunger up to the moat of the towns, and even entered them, tearing to pieces the men who slept under the porticos and on the wains. Sometimes they made a hole through the walls of a house and seized the children in the cradle. None could believe it, unless they had seen, as I saw then, the vile things that were done by men and beasts.[19]

The devastation of war created a vicious circle. The reduction of land values naturally stimulated the appetite of local feudatories to extend their properties. This could be done at the expense of their lay neighbours ; but easier prey were the ecclesiastical proprietors — men who had not been nurtured in those feats of arms which in this age provided the strongest title to possession. A patrimony of declining worth called out for some profitable usurpation to redress the balance. Yet such usurpation could only generate further war, further devastation, and further ambition. The result was a continual pattern of seizure and reprisal, an unchanging atmosphere of violence and rapacity.

As might be expected then, all the evidence for the thirteenth and fourteenth centuries shows a sharp fall in the value of land, continual usurpations, and constant war. Salimbene di Adam wrote that he had lived five years in Imola, five in Faenza, one in Bagnacavallo, and one in Montereggio, and that during all these years ' the malediction of wars occupied, invaded and destroyed all '. In 1224, the canons of San Cassiano of Imola leased all the land they possessed between the River Sillaro and Sellustra, to Catio di Ugolino di Muso and Jacopo Beccario of Bologna, in return for two pieces of wax of one pound each, to be given yearly on the feast of San Cassiano. In addition the lessees were supposed to pay tithes of straw, corn, beans and other fruits of the land. The canons did this, they said, because the territories, ' have no use or value to our canonry, on account of the war, the remoteness of the place, and the presence of powerful neighbours '.[20] In 1228, a canon of Faenza was judging a case in which the sons of Guido da Polenta with other laymen and clerics refused to return certain possessions which by right pertained to the Ravenna church.[21] In 1282, the *cantor* of the Ravenna church and other clerics, with the consent of the archbishop, leased to Lamberto da Polenta properties belonging to the monastery of San Giovanni Battista. The lease was for twenty-nine years at a rent of only one penny a year. As an entry-fine, Lamberto undertook 'the burdens of defending the properties as they are at present, and of recovering those usurped '.[22]

In the *montagna*, local war and violence were even more intense than in the plain. In a lawsuit of 1287, between the two branches of the Onesti family, it was declared that over half of the inheritance of Onesto degli Onesti, in the Savio valley, was sterile and unworked land. In their properties of the *montagna* there had been no sowing or ploughing for five years ; while in the plain, possessions had been leased at half rent.[23] In 1308, again, Don Amatore — one almost writes Don Abbondio, so much does he seem a prototype of Manzoni's character — 'wishing to save his own life, to take counsel of his soul, and to avoid danger ', asked that he might renounce his parish of the Massa Ambrogia, in the Santerno valley, because, he said, the church was placed where there were 'perpetual wars, accompanied by continual homicides and arson'.[24]

If the parish priest had his difficulties, those of the higher clergy were more serious still, and heavier responsibilities brought greater dangers. On 1 September 1266, Guido, Bishop of Sarsina, was murdered by Lord Raniero da Massa Aldrovando de Monte Abeto and his son, and by one Maineto, 'because he did not wish to concede to them the rights of his bishopric'.[25] In 1273, his successor had to face an attack upon Castel Ceule by the commune of Forlì, 'wishing ever to subjugate that territory as their own'.[26] The churches were not only doomed to spoliation by commune and feudatory, even the remoter authorities of the province combined to milch them. In 1253, the monastery of San Giovanni Evangelista declared that, through expropriation by Frederick II during war, its lands returned no revenue. It went on to complain of the alienation of monastic goods by papal legates and nuncios. The same year the Abbey of Santa Maria Rotunda, 'is scarcely able to support three monks', and the Abbey of San Vitale, weighed down by debts after five years' war and alienations by the Emperor, is similarly 'scarcely able to support three monks.'[27]

The fourteenth century heard the same complaints. Ramberto, Count of Giaggiolo murdered Giordano, Archpriest of Castelnuovo, and his brother, in 1336, and seized Valdenuccio.[28] In 1362, San Vitale was still asserting that through wars and other burdens, it was unable to purchase the necessities of life.[29] In the following year, Filippa and Pace, sisters of the priest Basilio, sold their land as incapable of cultivation, explaining that this was due 'to taxes and many other burdens, and considering their poverty, and also the war at present raging in the province of Romagna'.[30] In 1376, the monastery of Sant' Apollinare leased land because, the document declared, its revenues were deficient, and its debts growing, as the result of the long wars of Romagna.[31] Two years later, the monastery of San Pietro in Vincula gave a lease, with the declaration that the monastery was unable to bear any further by itself the direct support of its properties : 'through the lack of labourers and their daily withdrawal from the town and district of Ravenna, and as a result of the numerous taxes and duties, weights and burdens imposed by the town, and through the trials and difficulties from many sources, especially due to the wars, that were in the past, and still are, raging in Romagna . . .'.[32] In 1426, there was a petition of Don Pietro to the Bishop of Imola. He had been, he said, for many years, rector of the church of Sant' Agata. Owing to wars and plagues in the town of Imola, its possessions had not been worked — any that were cultivated gave only half-return. He was therefore unable to live, and asked to be invested with the chapel and altar of Sant' Apollinare, situated in the church of Santa Maria in Regola.[33] Six years before, the clergy of Faenza had declared that it was impossible to pay taxes to the papacy, ' through the incursions of robbers and armed men, who devastate all '.[34] Clerical lands were peculiarly vulnerable, but there can be no doubt that constant war had a deleterious effect upon all landed property. A papal taxation roll of the *contado* of Imola, in 1367, shows six villages exempt from taxation, and fifteen paying only half their tax, because they had been devastated in the war between Bernabò Visconti and Cardinal Albornoz.[35]

On the conflict between feudatory and feudatory in this era, it is hardly necessary to dwell. The struggle between the two branches of the Montefeltri family to control the bishopric of San Leo after 1248 :[36] the war of the Pagani and Sassatelli in 1273, the attack of the lords of Valbona on the Ubertini in 1294 ;[37] such episodes are the everyday staple of Romagnol life, while the party struggles in the towns are essentially reflections of *contado* interests. There is also ample evidence of the usurpations of properties within families ; usurpations to which women were particularly vulnerable. A letter of Alexander IV, for example, shows Guido Riccio, and Guido il Vecchio da Polenta, attempting to defraud their cousin Clara di Geremea da Polenta. The Pope reassures her, that despite the fact that, ' veritate tacita ', her cousins have made no mention of her, she shall none the less have her rights in lands within the Lunigiana.[38] In fact, the absence of primogeniture, and the fractioning and division of family holdings, was to make for the most violent quarrels throughout the whole of the middle ages. This is the origin of the murderous conflicts inside the signorial families in the thirteenth century ; as between Alberico Manfredi and Manfredo Manfredi ; between Guido 'Riccio' and Guido 'il Vecchio' da Polenta ; between Teodorico and Guglielmo Ordelaffi ; and between Malatesta Malatesti of Verucchio and the line of Paolo Malatesti of Giaggolo.

Once embarked upon the road of usurpation it was not easy to turn back. Guido ' Riccio ' da Polenta, for instance, with his sons, had been elected ' perpetual lords and governors ' of Comacchio in 1275.[39] In his later life, perhaps through the influence of his wife, Giulietta, ' a great and noble lady ' and a patron of the

Franciscans,[40] he repented of the means by which he had secured this power. Two fragments of an interrogation from the end of the century show the result. In the first, a witness declared that while crossing over the bridge of the Comacchio canal, he saw the Lord Guido 'Riccio' da Polenta, with many other people, and the notary Succio Uspinelli, gathered under the portico of the family house. He himself thereupon joined the party, to find that Guido, before these witnesses, was declaring himself penitent for the properties and rights he had extorted in Comacchio. He concluded with the words, ' I renounce them and call upon you, Succio, to draw up the instruments '. At this, his son Geremea drew a dagger, and drove it into a pillar of the portico, saying ' Be warned, Succio Uspinelli ; if you write this, the Lord Alberico and my brothers will be ruined and destroyed '. His brothers, Francesco and Alberico, then told the notary that their father was out of his mind (' extra memoriam '). A second witness confirmed the story. Guido had told how his confessor, Brother Guido of the Eremite Friars, had ordered restitution of the usurped lands as his sole penance, adding ' I am guilty, for without right or cause, I possess and have possessed them to the peril of my soul '. According to this witness, Geremea had said, ' Be warned Succio, if you write this, we'll be driven to begging '.[41]

The issue of this case remains unknown, but a similar repentance is found in the will of his cousin, Guido il Vecchio in 1316. Here he asked that there should be restored to each individual or collegiate body, lay, clerical or monastic, all goods that ' through whatever unjust cause, or unlawful acquisition ', or through any other unlawful manner had come to him, or to any of his name. How diligently his executors carried out their duties, can only be a subject for speculation.[42] More specifically, Malatesta da Verucchio and his wife Concordia had been granted permission by Pope Urban IV, in 1263, ' to convert into pious use anything which had come to them through rapine and other illicit means ', which they were unable otherwise to restore.[43] Again, in 1307, Onestina, daughter of Onesto degli Onesti, widow of Giovanni da Fontana, had returned property to the monastery of Santa Maria Rotunda, ' recognising that the seashore, called the Litus Planetoli, found in the district of Ravenna, by the sea, was by her predecessors and herself, unjustly occupied '.[44]

Against this background of aristocratic violence, four principal causes may be given for the continuance of the party struggles ; first, the allegiance of nobles as mercenaries to the arms of pope and emperor ; second, the desire to obtain land in the *contado* by defeating rivals within the town ; third, the wish to control the administration of the town in order to be able to market agrarian produce independently of communal control. Finally there is that greed or lust for power which the age stigmatised as, ' libido voluntatis '.

Beside these realities, the influence of saint or king availed nothing. In 1249, St Peter Martyr appeared before the councils of Rimini, Faenza, and Cervia, to preach peace between the factions. Everywhere he was received with enthusiasm and his pleas accepted unanimously. Everywhere, once he had departed, conflicts rose again.[45] In 1273, the Lord Edward of England and his wife Eleanor were passing through the province, on their way home to be crowned. He, too, attempted, as many had before, to impose peace. But the Geremei were bent upon war, and the prince found his plans defeated by the stubborness of the Romagnols.[46]

III

It would be wearying to narrate the interminable and complicated development of these local conflicts within the six towns, and to catalogue all the attempts of Bologna to bring peace. The events of the years 1249–79 are better summarised briefly as they effect the future signorial families. Amidst the anarchy, certain general patterns can be discerned.

(a) *Imola and the Alidosi*

In Imola there were savage conflicts between the Guelf Brizzi — among whom were the Alidosi family, and the Ghibelline Mendoli.[47] In September 1248, a treaty ranged the town behind the Guelf cause, and laid down that ' the said commune ought to stand to the ordering and disposition of the city of Bologna'. But the settlement brought no stability, and strife broke out anew in 1249, 1250, 1254, and 1263. In 1274, with the expulsion of the Lambertazzi from Bologna, the Imolesi Ghibellines were forced to take refuge, as exiles, in Faenza, where they remained for the following five years.[48]

(b) *Faenza and the Manfredi*

If, in Imola, little is heard of any prominent role being filled by the future signorial family, party conflict in Faenza was dominated, from 1238, by the Manfredi and their Ghibelline rivals, the Accarisi.[49] With the fall of the town to Frederick II in April 1241 the Guelf partly suffered severely.[50] But after the Hohenstaufen defeat at Parma, the parties clashed again. The attempts at pacification by *podestà* — like Ugolino di Fantolino (the hero of *Purgatorio*, Canto XIV) — broke down, and in 1256, Faenza appealed in desperation to Bologna to intervene : 'clearly recognising that if you refuse to do this our town will be destroyed. — Come lords, moved by pity, come without delay!'[51] Bologna's efforts were ineffectual, and in 1274, the Accarisi, in alliance with Guido da Montefeltro of Forlì, seized the town and drove the Manfredi into exile.

(c) *Forlì, Guido da Montefeltro, and the Ordelaffi*

Like Faenza, Forlì in mid-century fell, in part, under Bolognese domination, and received Bolognese *podestà* and captains.[52] This control the town threw off in 1273. It allied with the Lambertazzi (the Ghibelline exiles of Bologna), and opened war on all the Guelf parties of the province. There now emerged the great Ghibelline noble, Guido da Montefeltro, who, as its captain, or with his nominees as captains and *podestà*, controlled Forlì in the years 1274–84.

Moreover, as Captain-General of the Ghibellines, he dominated the whole province in those years. Locally, his party allegiance was dictated by his hostility to the Guelf Malatesti, with whom he had unsuccessfully disputed the inheritance of the Counts of Giaggiolo in 1263.[53] But he was an ambiguous figure. He had acted as deputy-senator of Rome, in 1268, and after the battle of Tagliacozzo, may have betrayed the city to Charles of Anjou. To Dante, he was both the 'nostro nobilissimo Latino' of the Convivio,[54] and the 'scelerum inventor', the Ulysses of Italy, in the *Inferno*, the man who boasts that :

> Gli accorgimenti e le coperte vie,
> io seppi tutte, e sì menai lor arte,
> ch' al fine della terra il suono uscie.
>
> (Wiles and covert ways, I knew them all,
> and so did master them, that their fame sounded
> to the ends of the earth.)[55]

In his role as Ghibelline champion of Forlì, Guido was virtually the first of the new *signori*. Since his power was only temporary, and his control of Forlì owed nothing to his territorial possessions, but rested rather upon his fame as a Ghibelline warrior and statesman, he might be called the first ‘ tyrant ’. As ‘ uom d’ arme ’ he was able to preserve Forlivese unity and independence against Bolognesi and Guelf threats. Nothing is known about the internal organisation of Forlì during this period, but his control must have arisen principally from his personal quality. ‘ He was a noble man, feeling, discreet and affable,’ wrote a Guelf contemporary who knew him there, ‘ liberal, courtly and openhanded, a valiant knight, skilled in arms, and experienced in war’.[56] Qualities of leadership enabled him to sway the General Council of the commune and the noble factions, without requiring any change in the communal organisation to confirm or consolidate his power.

From Forlì Guido extended Ghibelline power throughout the whole province. In April 1274 he attacked Faenza, and imposed his allies, the Accarisi, upon the town. He defeated the Bolognesi in April 1275, and then again in June, in the resounding victory at the bridge of San Procolo (two miles from Faenza). At the end of June Guido took Cervia, and in September, Cesena.[57] Daunted by these successes, the Guelf nobles of the province — among them Malatesta of Rimini and Guido da Polenta of Ravenna — sent to the papal curia, in 1277, to ask that Romagna should be incorporated within the papal states.[58]

Under the leadership of Guido, two houses of Forlì; the future signorial family of the Ordelaffi, and the Orgogliosi, came to prominence as supporters of the Ghibelline regime. But though the town remained Ghibelline until the end of the century, both families were distracted by internal disputes,[59] and were still of minor importance beside Guido and his successor, Maghinardo da Susinana.

(d) *Ravenna, the Traversari, and the da Polenta*

From 1239, when Paolo Traversari changed the traditional Ghibelline allegiance of Ravenna, the conflicts of that town had been fought between two parties, led by the Traversari for the Guelfs, and the Anastagi and the Counts of Bagnacavallo from the Ghibellines. The Anastagi were in decline, however, and were soon to become extinct; for most of the period the party was led by Ruggiero, Count of Bagnacavallo, with others of his house, and the Ghibellines came to be known as ‘ the party of the Counts ’.[60] The monopoly of power held by the Traversari was broken when, in 1240, Ravenna surrendered to Frederick II. At this time Geremea and Lamberto da Polenta of the future signorial family were imprisoned by Frederick II, and Lamberto was executed.[61]

In that same year, Paolo Traversari, 'a most handsome knight, a great baron, extremely rich, and loved by the citizens' died without male heirs. The rival house of Anastagi was similarly to pass away within thirty years.

> La casa Traversara e gli Anastagi

were to be lamented, as part of the past glory of the province, by Guido del Duca in the fourteenth canto of the *Purgatorio.* Paolo's granddaughter, Traversaria, married first, Tommaso da Fogliano of Reggio, and then at his death, Stephen, the exiled son of King Andrew II of Hungary. Both men assumed the title of 'Lord of the house of the Traversari', and attempted to carry on its traditions, but neither produced heirs who survived. After Traversaria's death, one Guglielmo Francesco came to Ravenna and claimed that his wife, Aicha, was a daughter of Paolo Traversari, who had been taken as hostage to Apulia by Frederick II. This claim was accepted by the council of Ravenna, but many believed it to be false, and inevitably the prestige of the family declined.[62] In their place, the branch of the Polenta family under Guido il Vecchio began to assume the leading position in the town. Their cousins, however, the family of Guido 'Riccio' ('the frizzy') di Alberico da Polenta, remained loyal to the Traversari, and opposed the new ambitions of their kinsmen.

Violent party conflicts continued until 1275, when Guido di Lamberto da Polenta, with the aid of the Malatesti, seized the town and drove out the two rival factions of the Counts and the Traversari.[63] It was probably at this time, as a seal to the alliance of the da Polenta and the Malatesti, that Francesca, daughter of Guido da Polenta, married Giovanni Scianciotto, 'the Lame', son of Malatesta da Verucchio. In 1283 or the following year,[64] Giovanni discovered the adultery of Francesca with his brother, Paolo 'il Bello', and killed them both. The first chronicle reference to this is brief and casual: 'Paolo was killed by his brother Giovanni the Lame, *causa luxurie*.'[65] Yet from this incident Dante was to create the story of the fifth canto of the Inferno, the simple yet heartrending words which are spoken in the sudden silence which falls in the second circle:

> Noi leggevamo un giorno per diletto
> di Lancilotto, come amor lo strinse;
> soli eravamo e senza alcun sospetto . . .

'It is possible', wrote Boccaccio of this canto, 'that it happened like that. But I hold it to be a possible fiction rather than based on anything known to the author.'[66] No words could bring out more clearly perhaps the contrast between the quality of truth revealed respectively by history and by art.

(e) *Rimini and the Malatesti*

In Rimini, until 1248, the party struggles had been dominated by the Guelf Gambancerri in conflict with the Ghibelline Parcitadi. From that date, however, the Malatesti rose to prominence among the town's Guelfs. Malatesta da Verucchio, in the first half of the century, had prospered in the Ghibelline allegiance. He had married Concordia di Arrigherio, whose mother had belonged to the Parcitadi family, and had received a substantial dowry from her: 'much money, vast possessions, Giovedia, San Mauro, and an enormous number of other places'. 'From this moment', remarks the chronicler, 'he began to be great and rich and to be named as among the greater men of Rimini.'[67]

The news of the defeat of Frederick II at Parma was to prove the key moment in the rise of the family fortunes. Malatesta, at that time, was on the Via Emilia, leading a party of the town's levies to the aid of the imperial army. A fourteenth-century story says that Malatesta, at this point, intercepted a letter of the commune to the imperial count, recommending that he should be imprisoned, as being of doubtful loyalty, and that it was this which persuaded him to change his allegiance.[68] But even without such provocation, one may picture Malatesta as a man with the intelligence to judge the significance of Parma, the courage to gamble on his judgment, and the lack of scruple to abandon the party under whose auspices he had prospered. Dexterously changing sides, he returned to the town with his forces and re-imposed there the exiled Guelf Gambancerri; 'and from thenceforth he began to have the largest party and followers in Rimini'.[69]

By the end of the century, Malatesta had served as vicar of Charles of Anjou in Tuscany, and it had been forgotten that he had ever been a Ghibelline.[70] In the years that followed, the Omodei and Gambancerri continued the struggle, but in 1268, Malatesta seized the town from a predominantly Ghibelline government and expelled its supporters. Henceforth he was the constant ally of the Guelfs of the province. Conflict with Guido da Montefeltro in 1271 over properties in Giaggiolo, confirmed him in opposition to Romagnol Ghibellinism, and in that year he again expelled the imperialist party from Rimini.[71] In 1275 he was captain of the people at Bologna, and though defeated by Guido in April and June, he still held sway among the Romagnol Guelfs. This predominance was reflected by his standing within the commune of Rimini.[72]

Reviewing the thirty years of 1249–79, it can be seen that the province was in the grip of an anarchy, which neither Bologna nor any other central power was able to check. The rivalry of nobles for power and influence in the *contado* was matched by the attempts of aristocratic factions to gain control of the towns. Here the mark of the party's success was the podestàship. Possession of the office was not in itself of primary importance ; the *podestà* was supposed to be no more than the principal executive official for carrying through the decisions of the General Council. Yet the securing of the podestàship meant that the dominant faction controlled, whether by force or persuasion or a union of both, the *homines* : the men of the communes who voted in the General Council. There was nothing new in this situation, and it is unlikely that there was anything unusual in the conflicts between the nobility to control the *homines*. All that was new was the intensification of these struggles as a result of papal-imperial rivalries, and the lack of any central authority whatsoever with power to restrain them. By 1278, these antagonisms had temporarily brought to the fore in Imola, Rimini, and Ravenna, nobles who professed the Guelf allegiance, and who were allied, albeit by tenuous bonds, to the Guelf governments of Bologna and Florence. Forlì, Faenza, and Cesena, under Guido da Montefeltro, held to the Ghibellines. But exiles from each town — and most prominently the Ghibelline exiles of Bologna, the Lambertazzi — were seeking to overthrow this position ; the situation was fluid, and there was little promise of any stability. Of the future signorial families, two alone, the Malatesti and the da Polenta, had yet attained real authority in the commune. The Manfredi were head of a faction, but were still in exile. The Alidosi and the Ordelaffi were still subordinates in parties led by more powerful men.

CHAPTER III

The Rule of the Church and the Tyrant

> For they did not fight to determine whether one man should rule and be the supreme dictator of the state, but to decide who that one man should be. For not only were their standards, eagles and weapons equally matched; on both sides was the same disloyalty, savagery and ambition. Both wished to oppress the citizens, to put aside the laws, and to hold as just anything which pleased and profited the victors. It was a struggle, not to preserve the republic, but to seize control of it. As the poet said: 'Quis iustius induit arma, scire nefas'.
>
> COLUCCIO SALUTATI[1]

I

THE donations of Pipin and Charlemagne, in the eighth and ninth centuries, had given to the papacy the land known as the Exarchate of Ravenna, and within this territory, specifically Ravenna itself, Rimini, Cesena, Forlimpopoli, Forlì, and the Montefeltro. These grants had been confirmed by many of their successors : by Louis the Pious in 817, by Otto I in 962, by Henry II in 1020, and by Otto IV in 1201. Yet from the tenth century, the province had been administered *de facto* as a part of the Empire. In 1275, Gregory X, fearing perhaps the pretensions of Charles d'Anjou, opened negotiations with Rudolph of Habsburg for the transfer of Romagna and Bologna back to direct papal administration. After long discussions, on the 29 May 1278, the province was formally handed to Nicholas III. On 30 June, Rudolph renounced all oaths of loyalty to the Empire from the men of the province. The individual towns acknowledged their new loyalty, and on 24 September, Bertoldo Orsini, nephew of the Pope, was appointed as rector of the two new papal provinces. The Empire had abandoned a territory that it could not own ; the papacy had accepted a possession that it was to find difficult to hold.[2]

The papacy had already evolved an administrative machine for the rule of its temporal dominions, and the system was to expand until it reached its fullest development with Albornoz. Each province was ruled by a rector, with powers defined by the Bull announcing his appointment. To assist him, he had, if he were a layman, a rector for spiritual matters. Police duties were supervised by a marshal and subordinate constable. The army, formed from feudal levies and communal contingents, was commanded by a Captain-General. Revenues were raised from fines on criminal offences, from the *tallia militum*, from the *focaticum* or hearth tax, from subsidies paid by the clergy, and from various other sources. These revenues were controlled by a treasurer and vice-treasurer. Judicial functions, consisting of the right of judgment in appeal, or between entities possessing rights of justice, were carried out by two judges. On his assumption of office, the rector held a parliament, where delegates of the churches and chapters, the principal nobility, and the representatives of the communes swore obedience. Parliaments would be summoned at intervals throughout his turn of office to discuss business, to learn of papal decisions, and to arrange for the equitable distribution of extraordinary taxation.[3] This machinery has attracted the praise of modern scholars, but in Romagna, at least, three things are obvious : that it was unable to quell party conflict, that it could not prevent anarchy, and that it was violently unpopular.

The aims of the papacy, as shown in the various 'constitutions' of the thirteenth century,[4] might seem innocuous enough. First, they specify the liberty of the Church. The ecclesiastics of the province were to be delivered from all burdens and taxes imposed by the communes, from all illegal distraints, and from all statutes hostile to their interests. Second, they enjoined peace and order ; feudatories were to be reconciled, heretics to be suppressed, reprisals forbidden, theft, murder, and blasphemy punished. No castles were to be built without rectorial permission. Rebels against the Church were not to be received ; resistance to its officials was chastised ; disloyalty was to be punished with death. Third, all judgments in appeal were reserved exclusively to the rector's court. Fourth, in the interests of the province as a whole, it was forbidden to export food without rectorial licence.

Yet these provisions alone gave ample cause for dissatisfaction to the communes. The claim to control foodstuffs struck at their considerable profits from the marketing of corn in time of famine. The claim to jurisdiction in appeal was prejudicial, not only to their revenues from the profits of justice, but to their authority. Even the claim to reconcile the factions was inimical to communal government, for its whole structure was inevitably bound up with the exclusive supremacy of one party.

It is no easy matter to decide how far, in fact, the central power wished to interfere in the communal organisation of the towns. The papacy gave no clear indication of its attitude, and the various rectors adopted differing policies. But, in an ambiguous situation, every definition gave rise to conflict. Bertoldo Orsini appointed his own *podestà* to each town and such a policy struck at the roots of civic independence and freedom of action. Later rectors, faced with opposition, abandoned this as a regular policy, but were to revive it fitfully as opportunity offered. Nor is it easy to state the rights of the communes *vis-à-vis* the papacy. In fact, until the era of Albornoz, despite numerous constitutions published by provincial parliaments, this fatal lack of clear definition of papal and communal rights was to give rise to continual tension. Again, the very novelty of papal claims, in a province which for so long had recognised no authority, except that of a distant emperor, made the work of imposing order more difficult. Every command was met with resistance, every resistance met with harsh papal reaction. What was normal to the papacy was new to the towns. When the papacy claimed jurisdiction in appeal, the town resentfully protested that this was 'against the rights, privileges, and customs of the commune of Ravenna'.[5] So, of course it was, but now there existed a new framework in which rights had to be considered.

Finally, taxation. Taxation under the empire had been light and occasional. With the papacy it became heavy, was increased in the fourteenth century, and was regularly levied. The papal rectors brought with them continual demands for money and military service, and faced with these, the communes may well have considered 'the prophecies of Merlin' to have been in course of fulfilment:

> Romandiola sub iugo teneatur et stola
> Quae in perpensum tallionem reddit immensum.[6]

But it was not just the idea of papal government that was repugnant, it was also the manner of its rule. Perhaps the most fruitful source of dissatisfaction was the frequent venality of many of the papal officials. In 1291, for instance, Alessandro da Romena, marshal to his brother, Ildebrandino, the rector, tried to hang the factor of Agnesina, widow of Taddeo da Montefeltro, because that lady had sold lands, not to him, as he had expected, but to Maghinardo Pagani and the Counts of Cunio. 'Those of Faenza, however, seeing such great iniquity and injustice to be intended, went after them, and by force took Jacopo from them, that he might receive no injury upon his person.'[7]

This is no isolated example. Until the time of Albornoz,

complaints by the papacy itself, against the corruption of rectors and their officials, are a commonplace. They are said to distribute gifts to their own families, to fail to give adequate accounts of their revenues, and to assume the character of tyrants.[8]

Again, the very essence of papal monarchy ensured a permanent weakness in the temporal domain. Men were elected as popes at what is normally considered to be an advanced age. Hence their reigns were short in comparison with hereditary monarchs. Every change of pope involved a change in policy, and a change in administrative personnel, and it was difficult to build up any long-term loyalties to personalities or programmes, doomed to be ephemeral by the very nature of the state. ' Why ', asked Benvenuto, ' is Romagna never without war? ' And the answer comes : ' First, through the avarice of the pastors of the church, who sell now this land, now that, now favour one tyrant, now another, as often as they change their officials.'[9]

' Prima est avaritia pastorum ecclesiae ' : with these words Benvenuto comes back to what lay at the root of the papacy's unpopularity : finance. In effect, the papal relations with the communes moved in a vicious circle. The popes required money, the raising of money excited resistance, the resistance brought forth the need for more and yet more money to crush it : hence further revolt. Added to this were passions of xenophobia. The mercenary troops, who, in this situation, came to the aid of the popes, were generally foreigners : Catalans, Germans, or French, and their presence was already preparing the ground for the violent feelings of Petrarch's *Italia Mia*. The verses of an unknown Italian poet, writing in Provençal about 1282, express much of the sentiment of the province towards the popes and their foreign servants :

'E si eu aghes penduiz aut al ven
Cons de Monfort e tot sos validors
E des autres tanz valria eissamen :
Lo reis Carles, lo filz el neboz amdos
E quem pogues per Romagna estendre,
Viorel Frances ronpre e malmenar,
Seguramen bartejar es encendre!
Es enaissi volgra nostra gens venjar.'[10]

('Would that I might hang the Count of Montfort high in the wind, and with him all his bravos. I would do as much for those others — King Charles, his son and grandson too. And could I pass through Romagna I would like to beat and smash the French to crush them completely to ashes. It is in this way that I would like to avenge our people.')

In this climate, faced with this government, the Romagnols turned to the feudal nobles who were their natural leaders. The long-term effect of the new papal rule was to speed up the process by which single-person government came to each commune. As the threat of papal exactions grew, the men of the communes became more and more anxious that party conflict might cease, so that the town might be united under one family, to resist whatever impositions might be made against it.

The first rector, Bertoldo Orsini, entered the province in 1278, with Catalan and French soldiers, to impose the papal will and to pacify the rival parties. For a while he succeeded in restoring the exiles to their towns, and in securing sworn treaties of peace between the aristocratic factions. In each town, papal rectors and *podestà* were appointed, and Bertoldo himself secured nomination as *podestà* of Bologna. For a time his work was successful. At Imola, the Mendoli returned to the town, 'with joy and triumph'. There was a murder in July, whereat, 'all Imolesi of both parties remained armed by day and night', with the Guelfs gathering at the Porta Alone, and the Ghibellines at the Porta Spavuglia. But Bertoldo arrived from Bologna in time to quell the conflict. The exiled Ghibellines entered Ravenna (September 1278). In Faenza the Manfredi were restored in the February of the following year. In the piazza of San Pietro, fifty members of each party composed their differences, and exchanged the kiss of peace.[11] At Bologna, Bertoldo secured the return of the Lambertazzi, took hostages from both the parties, and strove to secure a lasting peace between them :

'. . . or ascoltati,
Che 'l ue piace per la vostra bontà,
De mantegnire in bona voluntà,
E no guastare la vostra amista,
Che fata aveti :

Si-ue recordo che compromessi siti
Ostaduxi e segurtà dato aucti
De mantenere liança e esser amici
a tute l'ore . . .'[12]

Thus in the rude Bolognese dialect of the vigorous contemporary *servantes*, Bertoldo addressed the two factions.

In vain. By the end of the year irritation against papal interference reached breaking point. On 23 December, Bologna rose. The Lambertazzi were expelled by the Geremei, and fled to Faenza, through the winter snows, by remote paths in the mountains. When the news of the revolt reached Faenza, the papal *podestà* took the precaution of summoning the magnates of both parties and placing them under arrest. But this only served to precipitate conflict. As rumours of the Bolognesi tumults grew, Faenza too, rose in arms. Accarisi supporters seized the Palazzo Comunale and released their leaders ; while friends of the Ghibellines entered the town. The magnates of the Manfredi were forced to withdraw, and when the Lambertazzi arrived from Bologna, they occupied the houses of the exiles.[13] Simultaneously, the Guelfs seized power in Ravenna. In Imola, the Mendoli party, fearing attack by the Geremei, voluntarily abandoned the town and retired to Faenza. When Bertoldo himself sought their readmission, he was refused. As the conflicts flared up in one town after another, Guido da Montefeltro returned to Forlì to head the Romagnol Ghibellines.

From now on Bertoldo's legation consisted of fruitless efforts to re-establish his authority. With the death of his uncle, Nicholas III, ' seeing that the men of Romagna did not wish to obey him on account of the evil he had done ', he departed the province.[14] His brief tenure as legate serves as a symbol of papal rule in the thirteenth century ; to the end, it was effective only spasmodically, and only then when it tempered its practice by alliance with elements in the feudality.

In fact by 1279 party conflict was far too deeply rooted to be destroyed by the benevolent fiat of a papal decree. Romagna was an uneasy amalgam of armed camps of hostile nobles whose interests were irreconcilable. In June 1280, an attempt was again made to secure peace between the parties, and all appointed their procurators. The list of the nobles who take part is impressive.[15] Notable too are the large numbers of their dependants who were involved — 217 people in the *paese* of Bertinoro, 291 in the small town of Forlimpopoli, 240 in the commune of Bagnacavallo. These figures imply that the majority of the adult male population of the province had been drawn, by bonds of dependence or mutual interest, into the conflict of the nobility. Such bonds ensured that anarchy would continue, and that the end would only come by a long and bloody struggle.

Indeed, the attempt to obtain peace was unsuccessful. On Wednesday 13 November, a Guelf force captured Faenza, after Tebaldello de' Zambrasi had betrayed the Porta Imolese to the attackers. Cantinelli waxes eloquent on the damage inflicted by the Guelfs, who, ' like starving dogs ', or ' avid lions bent on prey ' broke into the citizens' houses, looted San Giovanni Evangelista of the Eremite Friars, entered the church of San

Francesco, and killed some children who had been sent there for safety. Afterwards — and it is an interesting commentary on the manner in which the religious orders had become involved in the factions — the two orders of friars were expelled.

Tebaldello Zambrasi's treachery was particularly castigated by the chronicler, who, in a sudden burst of literary fury, placed it as second only to that of Judas Iscariot. It was something never to be forgotten in the province. The man,

> ch' aprì Faenza quando si dormia
> (who unbarred Faenza while it slept)

was placed in the second ring of the ninth circle of the *Inferno*. Writing over seventy years after the event, Benvenuto di Imola was to remark : 'In my part of the world, if we see anyone who has an ill-look about him, we say, — "He looks like the man who betrayed Faenza!"' But what is really surprising in Tebaldello, is not that he opened the gates, but that he was ever in a position to do so. On 29 April 1280, he had married his daughter, Zanbrasina, to Tano di Ugolino di Fantolino, one of the Guelf leaders who entered the town, and his fellow citizens should have realised that his new family interests were hardly likely to be subordinated to abstract ideals of loyalty.[17]

The Guelf seizure of Faenza harmonised well with papal plans of the moment. The new pope, Martin IV, based his policy on alliance with the Angevins. The rector whom he appointed in Romagna in May 1280, Jean d'Eppe, was a Frenchman, and a councillor of Charles d'Anjou. He decided to abandon Orsini's attempts at pacification and support the Guelfs against the Ghibellines. For this it was necessary to subdue Forlì, from whence Guido da Montefeltro still led the Lambertazzi exiles and the Ghibellines of Romagna. At the end of April 1282, with Taddeo da Montefeltro, Guido's cousin, as his Captain-General and a large force of French mercenaries and Italian militia,[18] he marched against the town. But Guido rallied the citizens, fell on the enemy with his troops, and wiped out a large part of their force, making,

> de Franceschi, il sanguinoso mucchio[19]
> the bloodstained pile of the French

recorded by Dante in the twenty-seventh canto of the *Inferno*.

D'Eppe's epitaph was well-deserved :

> En Abrusse et en Romaine
> Pour l'amour Dieu souffrit grand peine.[20]

In the following year, he had as his Captain-General the unsavoury Englishman, Guy, son of the great Simon de Montfort. This was the man whom Dante saw, ' a shade, on one side, alone ', who, to avenge his father, had murdered Henry of Almain in the church of Viterbo.[21] Guy proved unreliable, and made a separate peace with Guido, before deserting the papal cause.[22] None the less, the papal court succeeded in securing the submission of the town, which had been weakened by lack of supplies, in May 1283.[23]

Guido da Montefeltro yielded, was exiled, and left for that career which was to take him to Asti, to Pisa, and finally to the convent of the Franciscans. But the troubles of the papal government had only begun. In 1284, rebellion in the province broke out again, and this time Forlì was joined by Bologna itself. Suppressed, revolt broke out anew in 1287, 1290, and 1292. The rector's complaint of 1291 was to be true for most of the century : ' except for the town of Cesena, almost all the towns of the province of Romagna and the communes of these territories, that is to say, the town of Imola, of Faenza, of Forlì, of Ravenna, of Cervia, of Forlimopoli, and certain other lands of the aforesaid province and the men of the same, persist in rebellion to the rector and to the Holy Roman Church, and will not give obedience to them.'[24]

If the papacy had relied on the loyalty of men calling themselves Guelf, it was soon to realise its error. Frederick II had discovered that ' no pope could be a Ghibelline '; the popes were to learn that no Romagnol could be a Guelf. It was in this confused situation, in which the papacy sought fruitlessly to impose its rule, that Maghinardo de' Pagani came to dominate the towns of Faenza, Forlì, and Imola. At the same time, Guido da Polenta and Malatesta da Verucchio consolidated the powers of their families in Ravenna and Rimini. These three men became the real rulers of Romagna.

II

It would be merely confusing to give a detailed description of the extremely complicated party quarrels in each town, the family links which bound their members, and the fruitless efforts of the papacy to bring peace.[25] In the pages that follow, therefore, only the main outlines will be discussed.

1 The Supremacy of Maghinardo

Maghinardo de' Pagani da Susinana was born about the year 1243. His father had left him as a ward of the commune of Florence ; he was married to Rengarda, of the famous Florentine della Tosa family ; and he fought for the city at Campaldino. It was an alliance to which he was always faithful, and one in which he prospered. In Romagna, his early years were spent in the service of Guido da Montefeltro. Maghinardo acted as *podestà* for him at Faenza, after the Ghibelline victory of 1275, and he fought by his side in the *sanguinoso mucchio*. With Guido's exile, Maghinardo was left as the principal Ghibelline leader in Romagna. After seizing power in Faenza in 1286, he was foremost in the resistance of the whole province to the papal rectors in the 1290s. From 1295 he allied its Ghibelline forces with Azzo d' Este of Ferrara against Bologna. The wider political history of these years, and the spasmodic and ineffectual attempts of the papacy to assert its rule, can be passed over. But Maghinardo's relations with the factions of the three towns in which he dominated, are of interest when considering the development of the future signorial families.

(a) *Maghinardo and the Parties of Faenza*

Though the Manfredi, with the assistance of the Guelfs, regained Faenza in April 1280, their control lasted for only a short time, and together with their opponents they were exiled from the town by the papal government. In exile, a crime within the family set them at enmity with some of their neighbours, and so lowered their prestige that until the end of the century they were unable to regain power. Alberico de' Manfredi (known as Fra Alberico through his membership of the Frati Gaudenti) had for some time nursed hatred against his cousin, Manfredo de' Manfredi ; a hatred caused by a blow in the face, given to him either by Manfredo himself, or by his son Alberghetto. He skilfully disguised the depth of his feelings, and in May 1285 invited Manfredo and Alberghetto to a dinner at the castle of Cesato, five miles from Faenza. At the end of the meal, Fra Alberico pronounced the words, ' Bring the fruit ' (*Venga le frutte*), a prearranged signal for his son, Ugolino Buzzola, and his cousin Francesco di Alberghetto, to lead in seven assassins. These attacked his kinsmen and their friends as they sat at table. Only one escaped. By crawling under the table, he reached Fra Alberico, and clinging to his robe, begged for mercy. Alberico ordered him to be spared that he might carry news of the deed to Faenza.[26]

As a result of the indignation aroused by this crime, the Manfredi had to flee to their castles in the *montagna*. Perhaps through a feeling of moral isolation, they united with their former Ghibelline enemies, and for the next five years were the allies of Maghinardo de' Pagani. This new alliance was of little value to them. Maghinardo seized control of Faenza in 1290, but turned on the Manfredi immediately, and drove them again into exile. They returned briefly to the town in June 1295, at papal instigation, but were driven out again within three months, this time not to return until after Maghinardo's death.[27]

(b) *Maghinardo and the Factions of Forlì*

It was Guido da Montefeltro, above all others, who had sustained the Ghibelline party in Forlì. After he had left the province, it was natural that the two principal Ghibelline families of the town, the Orgogliosi and the Ordelaffi, should look to Maghinardo de' Pagani, his successor, as their patron. During this period, the Ordelaffi family especially was working in close co-operation with Maghinardo.[28] In 1298, it was prominent in driving papal officials from Forlì, and, with its aid, Maghinardo was able to rule the town until, at least, 1301.[29]

(c) *Maghinardo and Imola*

In March 1280, after the Brizzi had sought pardon of the rector for their actions in the Bolognese rising of November 1279, the Mendoli were re-admitted to Imola. The newly restored Ghibellines still sought their revenge, and in October 1280 made a new plot to seize the town. It failed however. Its participants were killed or executed, and this reverse gave the *coup de grâce* to the old Imolese Ghibellines. It did not, however, end the conflict of factions. The Guelf party, which had been dominated by the Brizzi family, was losing its original character. After 1279, it was led by the Nordigli.[30] But now, the Alidosi who had been supporters of the Brizzi, clashed with the new Guelf leadership. Salimbene, writing of these events, says conflict arose ' from a certain emulation and ambition ', emphasising the personal rather than political or ideological origin of the conflict.[31]

Until August 1286, the Nordigli were predominant. But in that month, presumably hoping to rid themselves of papal interference, the family called in Maghinardo to attack the town. When his attempt failed, the Nordigli and their followers were expelled and their houses destroyed.[32] During the next four years, Litto and Alidosio degli Alidosi were able to achieve a temporary supremacy, holding between them the office of 'capitaneus et defensor'.[33]

This supremacy was broken with the general revolt of the province against the papacy, in November 1290, when the Bolognesi arrived to drive out the Alidosi, and place the Nordigli in power.[34] The papal rector of Romagna, Bishop Ildebrandino da Romena, strove to make peace between the parties, and the Alidosi re-entered the town on 8 September 1291. But trouble continued. In the next four years, against the hostility of a town dominated by the Nordigli and the Bolognesi, the Alidosi family leant on the fragile support of the papal government. But this availed them nothing. Imola attacked and burnt Monte Catone and Dozza, held by Litto, dispersed his followers at Corvara, and destroyed the castle of Linaro.[35]

The war between Bologna and Ferrara restored the Alidosi fortunes. In exile they allied with Maghinardo and Azzo VIII d' Este. Alidosio became Captain of Forlì for Maghinardo,[36] and married Cianghella della Tosa. In the fifteenth canto of the *Paradiso*, Cacciaguida told his descendant that light women like her had been unknown in the Florence of his day; but Alidosio was doubtless able to reconcile himself to her faults, by reflecting that, through her, he was allied to a great Florentine family, the kin of Maghinardo's own wife.[37] Indeed, with Maghinardo, his fortunes were momentarily to prosper. With Maghinardo and the Ghibellines of the province, the Alidosi seized Imola in April 1296.[38] The alliance was short-lived. Maghinardo became *podestà* of Imola, and the Alidosi were presumably resentful. In February 1300 — the year in which Dante believed there had been peace in Romagna — the Alidosi were in exile and Maghinardo was attacking their properties in Linaro.[39]

In 1300, Maghinardo was 'Captain of Faenza and Forlì and head of Imola'. His control over the three towns was due primarily to his position as a Ghibelline warrior. Like his predecessor, Guido da Montefeltro, he was accepted for his personal abilities. 'Ille leo Maghinardus' the chronicler of Ferrara calls him. 'Astutissimus et sagacissimus hominum quales aliqui fuerunt in Romandiola', wrote Benvenuto. He came from a family already prominent in Romagnol politics. His father Pietro: 'great, famed, and skilled in war', as Salimbene had written, had allied with the Mendoli of Imola as early as 1263. His family had an ambiguous but, for this period, fortunate tradition of friendship with Florence and hostility to Bologna. Behind him he had the power of his family fiefs in the upper Lamone, Senio, and Santerno valleys. Yet it would be misleading to over-emphasize the territorial basis of his strength. Writing seventy years after his death, Benvenuto claimed that, 'from being a petty *castellan*, he rose, by his virtue and fortune, to be a great lord in Romagna'. This is erroneous, for the Pagani properties were considerable, even before 1263, but Benvenuto's emphasis, one feels, was correct: Maghinardo rose through his personal qualities, 'sua probitate et felicitate'. In these two words of Benvenuto, there are already Machiavelli's desiderata for the new ruler: *virtù*, and *fortuna*.[40]

Within the town, Maghinardo's power rested upon the old communal organisation. Sometimes he held the podestàship or the captaincy of the people himself, sometimes he allowed allies or nominees to hold the office. Nor was his control limited to secular posts. At the death of Bishop Viviano of Faenza, in August 1287, he secured the election of his wife's relative, Lotterio della Tosa, as successor.[41] He can only be seen as a *signore* in the same sense as Guido da Montefeltro. He was a 'tyrant', whose influence was felt rather through his own personality than through any institutional change. Had his male children survived him, it is possible that he would have laid the foundations of a true *signoria*. As it was, he left only the reputation of his greatness, the memory of the 'uomo, maestro delle cose del mondo'.[42] His death was the signal for renewed party struggles.

2 The Da Polenta in Ravenna

In September 1279, the new papal government made peace in Ravenna between three factions; the dominant family of Guido il Vecchio da Polenta and the parties of the Traversari and the Counts, who had been till then in exile.[43] But this harmony was swiftly dissolved and the da Polenta expelled both their rivals. The family of Guido il Vecchio fought for the Guelfs, assisted the Manfredi in 1279, and were with the Guelf force which attacked Faenza in November 1280. In May 1281, they drove off an attack by Guido da Montefeltro and Guglielmo Francesco di Traversari (who was acting as *podestà* of Forlì), and in alliance with the papal count, Jean d'Eppe, destroyed the castle of Traversaria.[44]

The Guelf policy of Guido il Vecchio changed in 1285, when he allied with Maghinardo and Malatesta da Verucchio,[45] as a result of increasing dissatisfaction with papal encroachments. This reached its climax in November 1290, when the rector Colonna arrived with a demand for the surrender of the town to papal authority. Guido was absent at the time, but his sons, Ostasio and Lamberto, replied by seizing and imprisoning the rector and his officials — a deed which sparked off general revolt throughout the whole province.

The part played by Guido il Vecchio in the conflicts of the province was matched by his fame without (in 1290 he served as *podestà* of Florence[46]), and by his monopoly of power in Ravenna. He held the podestàship of Ravenna from 1286 to February 1290, and again in 1292 and 1293. In this position he dealt successfully both with the hostile parties and with the papacy. Indeed, until his death in 1310, his family easily dominated the commune.[47] Cervia too, where Bernardino di Guido held the podestàship in 1283, and again in 1292, came under Polenta control.[48]

3 Malatesta da Verucchio and Rimini

By 1279, Malatesta de' Malatesti da Verucchio had risen to eminence in Romagna, and to pre-eminence in Rimini, as the principal Guelf leader of the province. As with the da Polenta, however, the rule of the Church was to modify and change this natural allegiance.[49] In the parliament of Imola, of November 1286, the Malatesti and the da Polenta alike opposed the rector's attempts to raise troops and money. January and February 1288 saw processes of treason drawn up against both families. Malatesta replied by forming a league with Maghinardo and his Ghibelline allies, against the papal government. In that way Faenza and Rimini were united against the papacy.[50] With this external support, Malatesta, within Rimini, held the office of *podestà* uninterruptedly between 1282 and 1288. At the same time, in the Marche, the influence of the family was growing.[51]

With the appointment of Armanno de' Monaldeschi as rector, negotiations opened for a reconciliation of Rimini and the Church. This proved harmful to the family's interests. At this time the commune was looking for uncompromising leadership against papal authority, and it turned to Malatesta's Ghibelline opponents — the Parcitadi and their supporters. Montagna de' Parcitadi came to power and the Malatesti were expelled. They did not return to the town until January 1290, and even then their position was delicate. They were forced to realise that their interests would be better served — at least temporarily — by pursuing the anti-papal policy of their fellow citizens. In March 1290 Malatesta made peace with the da Polenta, on the issue of Francesca's murder. In November, when the Polenta imprisoned the rector Colonna in Ravenna, the Malatesti allied with them, and seized power in Rimini against the papacy. Malatesta 'received and had lordship of the said town'.[52] Five years later, the old man (he was eighty-three at the time) established definitive control of Rimini. On 13 December 1295 he drove out the Parcitadi and their followers. Ugolino 'Cignatta' de' Parcitadi, Mostaccio, and many others were killed. Two sons of Ugolino escaped, but they were declared rebels, their property confiscated and their homes destroyed. Montagna de' Parcitadi was captured and murdered in prison by Malatestino.[53]

A later chronicler tells how the conflict between the two parties arose from an attempt of two asses to mate in the piazza of Rimini. This created such an uproar among the spectators, that those in the town, unaware of what was going on, believed that the factions had come to blows. Among them was Ludovico da Camminate, who rode through the town calling out the party cry of the Malatesti. Provoked at this, a Parcitadi supporter killed him with a bolt from a crossbow. Three days' street fighting followed, until Malatesta learnt that Guido da Montefeltro was on his way with troops in support of the Ghibellines. At this news, the chronicler says, he went to the leader of the Parcitadi, and appealed for peace, explaining the absurd origin of the struggle, and his complete desire for friendship. This offer was willingly accepted, and the two men kissed each other 'on the mouth'. Thereupon the Parcitadi sent to Guido, telling him not to come further. Shortly afterwards, Malatesta summoned the town militia, left its Guelf element behind, and with the remainder, marched out towards Verucchio. At midnight he abandoned the force in secret, returned to the town, rallied his supporters and drove out the Parcitadi.[54]

The story may not be true in detail — in fact Guido had abandoned Romagna by 1295 — yet in its portrayal of senseless and treacherous conflict, it shows how the past appeared to men a century later, living under established *signoria*.

Henceforth, all power lay with the Malatesti. Probably the right to arm the people had already been transferred from 'the Four' to the Small Council, where the Malatesta party predominated.[55] When, in 1312, Malatesta da Verucchio died, over a hundred years old, his family was firmly established in control of the town.[56]

4 Conflict of Factions in Cesena

Nothing hitherto has been said of Cesena, but this neglect fairly reflects the minor importance of the town in the thirteenth century. In 1237, it is said, the party of the Rigizio was finally defeated by the Articlini.[57] Conflict continued, nevertheless, between the Calisese family, who looked for support to Malatesta of Rimini, and the Ghibelline Articlini, who were dominated by the Counts of Montefeltro, and, between 1297 and 1300, by the Counts of Giaggiolo (a branch of the Malatesti family hostile to Malatesta da Verucchio[58]). At the beginning of the decade, the Malatesti succeeded in gaining temporary control, which they kept for the following five years. But they were driven out in April 1295, and for the five years after that the town was controlled by Count Galasso da Montefeltro.[59] At Galasso's death, new conflicts broke out. But in Cesena no one man had yet risen to dominate the commune as in the other towns of the province. Galasso's brief Ghibelline supremacy was unique, and the Guelf nobility of the town was overshadowed by the fame of the Lord of Rimini. An uneasy balance existed between the parties, and the absence of any outstanding personality precluded any foundation of a *signoria*. As a result — and it is an interesting commentary on the manner in which the *signoria* preserved local autonomy — Cesena, in the fourteenth century, was reduced to dependence upon the governments of its neighbours.

III

The year 1300 is the imagined time-setting of the *Divine Comedy*, the year of which Dante speaks, when, passing through the circle of Evil Councillors, he encounters the shade of the great Guido da Montefeltro, who cries out to him from the flame, questioning him of the land he knew alive. And Dante replies to him telling him of the province both knew so well :

'Se tu pur mo in questo modo cieco
caduto sei di quella dolce terra
Latina, ond' io mia colpa tutta reco,

dimmi se i Romagnoli han pace o guerra :
chi' io fui de' monti là intra Urbino
e il giogo di che' l Tever si dissera.'

Io era in guiso ancora attento e chino,
  quando il mio duca mi tentò di costa,
  dicendo : 'Parla tu, questi è Latino.'

Ed io ch' avea già pronta la risposta,
  senza indugio a parlare incominciai
  'O anima, che se' laggiù nascosta,

Romagna tua non è, e non fu mai,
  senza guerra ne' cor de' suoi tiranni
  ma 'n palese nessuna or vi lasciai.

Ravenna sta, come stata è molti anni :
  l' aquila da Polenta la si cova,
  sì che Cervia ricopre co' suoi vanni.

La terra, che fe' già la lunga prova,
  a de' Franceschi sanguinoso mucchio,
  sotto le branche verdi si ritrova.

Il mastin vecchio e il nuovo da Verucchio,
  che fecer di Montagna il mal governo,
  là dova soglion fan de' denti succhio.

Le città di Lamone e di Santerno
  conduca il leoncel dal nido bianco,
  che muta parte dalla state al verno ;

E quella a cui il Savio bagno il fianco,
  così com' ella sie' tra il piano e il monte,
  tra tirannia si vive e stato franco.'[60]

('If it is just now you have fallen into this blind world from the sweet Latin land from where I bring all my guilt : tell me if the Romagnols have peace or war : for I was of the mountains there between Urbino and the yoke from which the Tiber springs.' I was still watchful and bent downwards, when my leader touched me on the side, saying : 'Speak, this man is Latin.'[61] And I, who had my reply already then, without hesitation began to speak. 'Oh soul, hidden there below, your Romagna is not and never was without war in the hearts of its tyrants, but open war was there none when I left it. Ravenna stands as it has stood for many years : the eagle of Polenta broods over it, so that it covers Cervia with its pinions. The land that stood the long testing and made the blood-stained pile of the French, is found again under the green claws. The old mastiff of Verucchio and the young, who made ill governance of Montagna, there where is their custom, leave the marks of their teeth. The towns of the Lamone and the Santerno, the lioncel from the white lair controls, he who changes party from summer to winter ; and that town whose side the Savio bathes, just as it lies between plain and hill, lives between tyranny and freedom.')

This passage needs little comment. Guido da Polenta, who bore an eagle on his coat of arms, already controlled Ravenna, and his family's power was extending to Cervia. Malatesta da Verucchio, 'the old mastiff', and his son Malatestino, 'the young', who had executed Montagna de' Parcitadi in prison, had control in Rimini. Faenza on the River Lamone, and Imola on the Santerno, were under Maghinardo da Susinana, whose coat of arms was a lion azure on a field argent.[62] Cesena, extending from a high foothill of the Apennines, down into the Via Emilia, so that it lies 'between plain and hill', had not yet fallen under any lordship.

Only in the lines on Forlì,

'la terra che fe' già la lunga prova'

— which refers to Guido's own victory over Jean d'Eppe at the town in 1282 — is there any difficulty : in the third line,

'sotto le branche verdi si ritrova'
('is found again under the green claws')

The Ordelaffi coat of arms contained a green lion, and the words have always been accepted as meaning that the town, in 1300, was under the control of the Ordelaffi family. Yet Cantinelli, a contemporary, states that in that year, the captain of the town was Maghinardo ; nor does it seem likely that while he lived, the Forlivesi family should be able to claim lordship of Forlì, let alone that the town should find itself again (*si ritrova*) under the Ordelaffi. Possibly the explanation lies in an error by Dante himself. Writing in the second decade after 1300, he knew that Scarpetta had assumed, by 1303, such prominence among the Romagnol Ghibellines that he had led the Whites into the Mugello. He therefore believed that three years earlier the Ordelaffi had held the town.[63]

With this reservation, Dante's description of Romagna may serve as a summary of the political condition of the province, to the death of Maghinardo da Susinana in 1302. Romagna was a land of perpetual unrest, and had reduced its papal officials to impotence. Only the so-called tyrants offered some hope of future stability. The unbroken periods of rule of the Malatesti and the da Polenta must have brought relief to the uncommitted citizens of the towns. With the failure of the papacy, men must inevitably have looked to single person government as the answer to perpetual aristocratic anarchy. Nor was this all. These men, warriors who had risen to power by their ruthlessness, their skill in war, their cunning, were precisely the men required by the communes to protect them from the novel impositions of papal government. Their rule, as yet had no formal basis. Their possession of the podestàship was a symbol of power, rather than its institutional expression. Yet in this period, the necessary foundations were laid for the evolution of new constitutional forms in the fourteenth century. Ravenna and Rimini already had a certain stability. But Imola, Faenza, and Forlì were still to be distracted by conflict, for Maghinardo da Susinana, who was in his sixties, had no surviving male heir to his body.

CHAPTER IV

The Honour of the Romagnols

The men of these parts are *passionatissimi* . . . pay heed to every doubt here, lest you find yourself deceived.

CARDINAL ANGLIC GRIMOARD[1]

I

IN August 1302, in his castle of Benchiaro, within the Imolese mountains at the head of the Senio valley, Maghinardo da Susinana lay dying. With him were his daughters, Francesca and Albera, and the Bishop of Faenza and his chaplains, who had come hurrying at the news. In their presence he disposed of his property, and appointed heirs and executors. His horses were assigned, his servants recalled and recommended. His friends were remembered, the men at whose side he had fought in a lifetime of bloodshed: the Accarisi, the Zambrasi, the nobles of Andriano and Mongiardino, the degli Baroni, Ugolino de' Medici, and those of his house, the Gilloti, the Mazi, Ugolino da Petrabuona, the Binielli, the Nordigli, the Tartagni, the Patarini, the Parentini, the Palmiroli, the Scoglantini, the Aghinolfi, the nobles of Fiagnano, of Laderchio, of Toranello, of Aguccano, the Sarucii of Casal Fiumanese, Arpino and the other nobles of Cantagallo, Filippo da Dozza, and all other ' nobiles et populares amicos ' of Imola and Faenza. He urged that there should ever be peace between their houses, and that they should always hold in reverence and friendship the commune of Florence.

Then he arranged for alms to be given to the Friars of Sant' Apollinare, the Friars of San Prospero, the Friars Minor of Faenza, the Friars of San Perpetua, the Sisters of Santa Catalina, the sisters of S. Bernardo, the sisters of Malta, to S. Maria fuori la Porta, to S. Ippolito, to the Hospital of the Sepulchre, money for dowries and orphans, money to the Bishop of Imola, to the Chapter of Imola, the Friars Minor of Faenza. The list continues, while like some litany the words recur throughout the document: ' pro missis cantandis pro remissione meorum peccatorum et salute anime mee '.

He arranged for his burial in the habit of the Camaldolesi, and fixed its expense at £10. Afterwards, there was nothing to do but to lie and think of his life and its meaning, the life of a lord of Romagna, 'mai senza guerra'. The end came on 27 August: he was buried at Santa Maria di Rio Cesare, by the Senio, at that place, it is said, where the sun first strikes on rising. 'Il demonio' was dead.[2]

The death of Maghinardo marks the end of an epoch in Romagnol history, the end of the period when certain nobles from the feudality ruled over the communes by force, without any institutional framework that might legitimise their rule. In the following fifty years this was to change, but before considering the new Romagna, it is tempting to linger on the old. The conventional piety of Maghinardo's will surprises. It is hard to find the personality behind the lay figures of the chronicles, and little impression remains, except of men whose sole reality is found in scenes of violence. There was the Count Ruggiero of Bagnacavallo; 'great he was among the Imperial party of Ravenna, a sagacious man, astute and worldly-wise and skilled in dissimulation, and a cunning wolf.'[3] On his deathbed, he was anxious, above all, that his daughter should marry an imperialist. The friar who was with him exclaimed that this was not the time for these passions, to which he replied, 'Why not? I'm a man, aren't I?' One feels the uselessness of the reply, — 'Yes, but at death, you should pardon all, struggle no longer for anyone, think only of God.' The real essence of the man's mentality is found in those words, — 'I'm a man, aren't I?' I take part in factions, therefore I am.

To such men religion was a feeble restraint, and ecclesiastics themselves seem to have been morally confused, when the interests of the papacy were so often bound up in the party struggles. Fra Salimbene tells how, one day, Guido di Lamberto da Polenta came upon Guido Malabocca, with only a small company in attendance. Malabocca's brother — upon whom Polenta had already taken revenge — had betrayed his father to death, and he debated within himself whether, with his superior forces, he should now kill Malabocca. To the Friar's admiration, however, he decided to be merciful: 'We have done enough. Evil can always be done, but once done, it cannot be called back.' Admirable sentiments, but what is to be made of a Franciscan who praises someone for exacting vengeance on one man instead of on two? — and in such terms too, as to suggest that he was following the golden mean, — 'sufficienter ultus est et noluit excedere modum'.[4]

The morality of the clergy was also conditioned by local

interests. The aristocratic composition of the cathedral chapters naturally involved the episcopacy in the struggles of their towns, and the *signori* strove to obtain an ecclesiastical regimen that would work easily with the temporal government. Maghinardo secured the appointment of his relative, Lotterio della Tosa, to the bishopric of Faenza, and Peppo degli Ordelaffi was elected, if not consecrated, as Bishop of Forlimpopoli.[5] Similarly, Rinaldo da Polenta became Archbishop of Ravenna in 1321. How these elections came about is suggested by a notice of excommunication dated 1308 against Azzo di Ostasio di Guido da Polenta. Guido had entered the monastery of Classe with an armed following, had forced the monks to annul the election of one man as abbot, and had appointed another in his place.

The effect of this subordination of ecclesiastical to lay interest is indicated by a dispute among the canons of Imola in 1299. Five canons, then at Bologna, asked that the election of a new bishop should take place in the diocese of Florence. Imola answered that this was impossible, because Florence was the ally of Bologna, against whom she was fighting, and that any election must be held in Imola itself. The five — all members of aristocratic families — replied that the town of Imola was no safe or suitable place for them to hold an election, 'on account of the wars and discords raging now between the party within the town and the party of the exiles'. They went on to say that they had been exiled by the enemies of the Roman Church, and that there was no security in the letters of safe conduct allowed to them, 'as no tergiversation can do aught to hide'.[6]

The friars, too, were involved in the struggles. Fra Salimbene, who himself breathes the spirit of a Guelf partisan, tells how an aged bishop of Faenza, whose sexual vagaries he carefully chronicled, was murdered by a young Dominican, 'who was of the party of the Lord Alberghetto'. The Dominican obtained command of the Bishop's treasury, and with this, 'violently and simoniacally' secured his own election as successor. He was expelled when the Accarisi seized power in 1282, and died in the bell-tower of the parish church of Bagnacavallo in which he was wont to take refuge, 'on account of the terrors of night'.[7] Doubtless the expulsion of the two orders from Faenza in 1280 was connected with these events.

The wills of the time give an impression of men whose religion was devoid of moral content. Guido di Lamberto da Polenta, for instance, asked to be buried in a coarse hair cloth, and yet stipulated that his clothes as soldier and lord should be borne before his bier. The arms he had taken from the papal rector in 1290 were to be given back, all goods he had usurped from the church were to be restored, and yet he asked that two of his banners and shields should be hung up in S. Maria in Porto. Many gifts were made to churches and the poor, yet pride in the sword still remained.[8] But to turn from this evidence to other sources, to the tortured Christs of Romagnol painting and the contemporary Riminese school is to realise that the interior life is something which does not permit analysis.

The church had done something to stop conflict. The lay order of the 'Cavalieri Gaudenti': the knights of Santa Maria Gloriosa, had been formed in 1261. The first duty of its members was to bring peace between the factions, and their oath of admission to the order required that they should present themselves unarmed, save for a wand, in the middle of any fighting which might break out. The members were supposed to wear neither gold nor silver ornaments, nor armour. Their ornaments, their armour, were to be prudence, nobility, virtue, and honour. The idea was good, its effect valueless. Catalano de' Malavolti and Loderingo d' Andalò, placed in the sixth circle of the Inferno amidst the hypocrites, symbolise their failure.[9] And from the numbers of the *frati gaudenti* came Alberico da Manfredi, 'the worst spirit of Romagna'.

His crime, the treacherous murder of his kinsmen at table; in the year 1285, has already been described. Alberico was still alive in 1300, when the action of the *Divine Comedy* takes place, but his crime roused such detestation in Dante, that the poet evolved the terrible concept of a soul that suffered in hell, while the body lived still on earth. Dante encounters the soul in Tolomea, the third ring of the ninth circle, where the damned spirit appealed to him to free his face from the crust of ice enclosing it:

> 'levatemi dal viso i duri veli,
> sì ch' io sfoghi il dolor che il cor m' impregna,
> un poco, pria che il pianto si raggeli.'

> ('Take from my face the hard veils, that I may vent a little the sorrow that fills my heart, before weeping freezes them again . . .')

Dante asks of him who he is, and the reply comes:

> 'io son frate Alberigo,
> io son quel delle frutte del mal orto,
> che qui riprendo dattero per figo.'

'O', diss' io lui, 'or sei tu ancor morto?'
Ed egli a me : 'Come il mio corpo stea
nel mondo su nulla scienza porto.

Cotal vantaggio ha questa Tolomea,
che spesse volte l' anima ci cade
innanzi ch' Atropòs mossa le dea

E perchè tu più volentier mi rade
le invetriate lagrime dal volto,
sappi che tosto che l'anima trade,

come fec' io, il corpo su l' è tolto
da un demonio, che poscia il governa
mentre cha il tempo suo tutto sia volto.

Ella ruina in sì fatta cisterna . . .'[10]

('I am Fra Alberico, I am he of the fruits of the ill garden who now receives dates for figs'.[11] 'Oh', I said to him, 'then you are already dead?' And he to me : 'I do not know how in the world above my body might be. Tolomea has this privilege that often the soul falls here before Atropos may take the body. And that you more willingly may remove the glazen tears from my face, know that as soon as soul betrays, as did mine, its body is assumed by a devil who rules it until its time has wholly revolved. But the soul hurls down to a cistern such as this. . . .')

He goes on to speak of his companion Branco d' Oria, and then appeals to Dante to free his eyes. But the poet refuses, ' for to him it was courtesy to be rude ' —

'Ma distendi oramai in qua la mano
aprimi gli occhi' : ed io non gliele apersi,
e cortesia fu in lui esser villano.

The canto ends with Dante's lament that a Genoese should be found in company with ' il peggiore spirto di Romagna '. Dante may have seen him often as he bore the burden of his guilt within him through the narrow streets of the little towns. His will, drawn up in Ravenna, shows the customary prudent piety, and the churches of Romagna received £135 from his testamentary alms.[12]

Romagnol treachery is a recurrent theme in the *Inferno*. Tebaldello Zambrasi we have already seen there —

ch' aprì Faenza quando si dormia.

while the ill-faith of the one-eyed Malatestino, son of Malatesta da Verucchio, is denounced through the mouth of Piero da

Medicina, in the twenty-eighth canto. Piero, a member of the family of the Cattanei of Medicina, had himself been condemned to the Inferno, for creating dissensions between rulers, and more particularly between the Malatesti and Da Polenta. On seeing Dante, whom he had known in life, Piero speaks in prophetic words of the treachery that Malatestino was to execute in the year 1306. It was probably in this year, that Malatestino, wishing to crush opposition to his rule in Fano, called its two principal citizens, Guido dal Cassaro and Angiolello da Cagano, to a meeting under safe conduct at Cattolica. On arrival they were seized and drowned :

'Tu, cui colpa non condanna,
e cui io vidi su in terra Latina,
se troppa simiglianza non m' inganna,

rimembriti di Pier da Medicina,
se mai torni a veder lo dolce piano,
che da Vercelli a Marcabò dichina.

E fa saper ai due miglior di Fano,
a messer Guido ed anco ad Angiolello
che, se l' antiveder qui non è vano,

gittati saran fuor di lor vasello,
e mazzarati presso alla Cattolica,
per tradimento d' un tiranno fello.

Tra l' isola di Cipro e di Maiolica
non vide mai sì gran fallo Nettuno,
non da pirati, non da gente Argolica.

Quel traditor, che vede pur con l' uno,
e tien la terra, che tal è qui meco,
vorebbe di veder esser digiuno,

farà venirli a parlamento seco ;
poi farà sì che al vento di Focara
non farà lor mestier voto nè preco.'[13]

('You, whom no guilt condemns, and whom I have seen above on Latin soil, if over-much resemblance does not deceive me, remember Piero da Medicina, should you return ever to see the sweet plain that sweeps from Vercelli to Marcabò. And tell the two worthiest of Fano, Messer Guido and Angiolello, that if foreseeing here is not vain, they shall be cast from their ship, and murdered near

> Cattolica, through treachery of a fell tyrant. Between the isles of Cyprus and Majorca, Neptune saw never so great a crime, not by pirates, not by the Argive race. That traitor who sees with one eye alone and holds that land that he here with me[14] would wish never to have seen, will call them to parliament with him. Then he will deal with them so that they will need to make no vow nor prayer for the wind of Focara.')

In these crimes, as they appear in the *Inferno*, there seems to be something that almost transcends self-interest. They seem inspired by the passions of aristocratic honour rather than by hope of gain, though this is perhaps merely the effect of Dante's art. Dante himself, of course, was bitterly outspoken against the corruption of the Romagnol aristocracy, yet the sharpness of his words springs from a feeling that here was the corruption of the best of all lay societies. For Dante, the ideal society was the peaceful and unfractured world-dominion of the Empire. But in everyday life, what was probably most congenial to him was the society of the old aristocracy of the Florentine *contado*. *Gentilezza*, nobility, this to him was more a matter of blood and birth than it was, either to the troubadours (whose songs on natural gentility have been seen indeed as protests of low-born knights against overweening aristocratic pretensions) or to the bourgeois writers of the *Dolce stil novo*. To Dante, following Frederick II, nobility was certainly *antica possessione d' avere* (ancient wealth) as well as *reggimenti belli* (fine manners).[15]

In Romagna there were still men who possessed both. They were combined, for instance, in Scarpetta Ordelaffi, *gentiluomo giovane e temperato*, and in Guido Novello da Polenta. But it was the men of the past to whom Dante principally looked : to Pietro Traversari, Ranieri da Calboli, and Guido da Prata, and the men of his own day, he thought, were utterly unworthy of their memory. Dante believed, and the belief of course was a delusion, that in Romagna, an aristocratic society had once existed, enshrining love and courtesy, and that, now, degenerate descendants had abandoned the ideals of chivalry, and were utterly corrupt. The sombre oration of Guido del Duca in the fourteenth canto of the *Purgatorio* is one of the greatest expressions of the political *laudator temporis acti*. Guido speaks in prophecy of the cruelties of Fulcieri da Calboli, and then shows Dante, his companion, Fulcieri's grandfather :

> 'Questi è Rinier, quest' è il pregio e l' onore
> della casa da Calboli, ove nullo
> fatto s' è erede poi del suo valore.

Castle of Montebattaglia, Santerno Valley

E non pur lo suo sangue è fatto brullo,
tra il Po e il monte e la marina e il Reno,
del ben richiesto al vero ed al trastullo :

chè dentro a questi termini è ripieno
di venenosi sterpi, sì che tardi
per coltivare omai verrebber meno.

Ov' è il buon Lizio ed Arrigo Mainardi,
Pier Traversaro e Guido di Carpegna?
O Romagnoli tornati in bastardi!

Quando in Bologna un Fabbro si ralligna?
quando in Faenza un Bernardin di Fosco,
verga gentil di picciola gramigna?

Non ti maravigliar, s' io pigano, Tosco,
quando rimembro con Guido da Prata
Ugolin d' Azzo che vivette nosco,

Federico Tignoso e sua brigata,
la casa Traversara e gli Anastagi
(e l' una gente e l' altra è diretata)

le donne e i cavalier, gli affani e gli agi
che ne invogliava amore e cortesia,
là dove i cor son fatti sì malvagi.

O Brettinoro, chè non fuggi via,
poichè gita se n' è la tua famiglia,
e molta gente per non esser ria?

Ben fa Bagnacavallo, che non rifiglia,
e mal fa Castrocaro, e peggio Cunio,
che di figliar tai conti più s' impiglia ;

ben faranno i Pagan, dacchè il demonio
lor sen girà ; ma non però che puro
giammai rimanga d' essi testimonio.

O Ugolin de' Fantolin, sicuro
è il nome tuo, da che più non s' aspetta
chi far lo possa tralignando oscuro.

Ma va via, Tosco, omai, ch' or mi diletta
troppo di pianger più che di parlare,
si m' ha nostra ragion la mente stretta.'[16]

('This is Ranieri, this is the glory and honour of the house of Calboli, where none since has inherited his worth. Nor is his blood alone, between the Po and the mountains and the seashore and the Reno, stripped of the good required of truth and delight ; for inside these boundaries, poisonous roots are flourishing, difficult now to weed out by cultivation. Where is the good Lizio and Arrigo Mainardi, Piero Traversari and Guido di Carpegna? Oh Romagnols turned into bastards! When in Bologna shall take fresh root a Fabbro, when in Faenza a Bernardino di Fosco, that noble shoot of a lowly plant? Marvel not, Tuscan, if I weep, when I recall with Guido da Prato, Ugolin d' Azzo, who lived among us, Federico Tignoso and his company, the house of the Traversari and the Anastagi (and the one race and the other, now without heirs), the ladies and the knights, the trials and the sports which love and courtesy inspired in us, there where hearts have grown so evil. Oh Bertinoro, why do you not flee, since your household and many people have left you that they may avoid guilt? Well does Bagnacavallo, who breeds no more, and ill does Castrocaro, and worse Cunio, that suffers still to breed such Counts. Well shall the Pagani do when their demon goes away, not that pure witness of them shall ever remain. Oh Ugolino de' Fantolino, your name is safe, since now none can be expected, who, degenerating, may blacken it. But go on your way, Tuscan, for now it delights me much more to weep than to talk, so has our speech wrung my mind.')

Of some of these men, Guido da Prata, the Anastagi, and Federico Tignoso, we know virtually nothing. Others are more familiar : the house of Calboli — with Fulcierio and Ranieri, had been engaged often in the factions of Forlì. Pietro Traversari, of course, had ruled Ravenna at the end of the twelfth century, but with his son Paolo (d. 1240) the male line of his house had ceased. Luzio di Valbona — of the Forlivese *contado* — and Guido di Carpegna — of an ancient line of the house of Montefeltro — these were dead ; yet the counts of Castrocaro and Cunio lived still — and bred! The whole of society was condemned by its ancestors, fortunate were those like Ugolino di Fantolino, whose line had expired, whose children would engender none who could shame their unstained memory.

In part, the tone of Romagnol society can be seen as characteristic of aristocratic societies in their heroic phase, where personal and family honour are the guiding principles of existence. When Luzio da Valbona, 'il buon Lizio', learnt of the death of an unworthy son in battle, he received the announcement without any emotion, commenting merely: 'This isn't news. He was always dead. Tell me some news, has he been buried?'[17] But aristocratic honour was often only a mask for primitive savagery. The story of the Ravaldini lords of Monte Castello in February 1338 is suggestive. Guido, Ravaldino, Zello, Dino, and his son Francesco dined in their castle with the bishop of Sarsina. After the bishop had withdrawn, the family fell to quarrelling at table. Swords were drawn, and the five men managed to kill each other, leaving no survivor.[18] The violence of these men was not something confined to one class, but ran through the whole of society. When his *fideles* murdered Corrado di Petra Rubea in 1298, they slew with him his natural brother, his sister, and his little boy. Then they kept his wife a prisoner, prepared to kill her too, if it were found she was pregnant, 'that the seed from that man might not remain'.[19] Other brief notices in the chronicles suggest that agrarian war, with all its savageries, was quite common in the *montagna*.

II

Such crimes, however, seem almost insignificant when compared with the treacheries and murders within the signorial families in the fourteenth century. No family was exempt. The bald narration of these events, though tedious, gives something of the essential character of aristocratic morality in the age in which the *signorie* were being formed. In the pages that follow I shall therefore briefly outline the principal conflicts within each family. In following the course of these crimes, the reader may be assisted through the unfamiliar, yet often similar, names, by reference to the genealogical tables on pages 240-4.

(a) *Within the Manfredi Family*

When, in 1327, Francesco Manfredi surrendered the lordship of Faenza to Cardinal Poujet, his son, Alberghettino, contemptuous of this abdication, allied with his cousin Cecchino, and seized back the town in his father's absence. Fearing Cecchino as a possible rival, he sent him to treat with the Polenta, and in his absence, expelled his family and supporters. The Cardinal's army, and the persuasions of his father, forced him to surrender in May 1328. He entered the service of the Cardinal, but within a year, he was plotting to betray Bologna to the Emperor Lewis. 'Thus', observed Villani heavily, 'he showed that he had no wish to set aside, in deed or reputation, the precedent set by his uncle, Fra Alberico.' He was discovered and beheaded in the piazza of Bologna in August 1329.[20] In the middle of the century again, there were to be violent conflicts between the cousins, Giovanni di Ricciardo and Giovanni di Alberghetto Manfredi; the line of Giovanni di Alberghetto supporting the Church, while their cousins resisted Cardinal Albornoz.

(b) *The da Polenta*

In Ravenna, the treacheries among the da Polenta family assume at times the scale and improbability of Victorian melodrama. In 1322, the Lord Guido Novello da Polenta left Ravenna to assume the office of Captain of the people at Bologna, and gave the town into the charge of his brother, Archdeacon Rainaldo, the Archbishop-elect. On 20 September 1322, his cousin, Ostasio, who then ruled Cervia, with a few accomplices, murdered Rainaldo in his bedchamber, and seized the town. The following June, with aid from Bologna, and forces from Forlì, Guido Novello sought to regain control. On the 17 July, before dawn, he entered the town. But with daybreak the alarm was raised. His partisans — if there were any — failed to come to his support and he was forced to flee. Like his famous protégé, Guido Novello was to end his days in exile. He died in 1330, and it was the line of Ostasio di Bernardino that continued to rule.[21]

At his death, in November 1346, Ostasio's sons carried on the family tradition. In his will their father had left Ravenna to the eldest brother, Bernardino, and Cervia to Pandolfo. The third brother, Lamberto, received nothing. Pandolfo and Lamberto were dissatisfied with this settlement, and plotted against it. In April 1347, Pandolfo, at Cervia, sent a message to say that Lamberto had been thrown from a horse, and was at the point of death; that if Bernardino wished to see his brother alive, he should come immediately. The ruse was successful. Bernardino visited his brother (who lay moaning convincingly in his chamber) and was immediately arrested and imprisoned when he left the room. Pandolfo then hastily donned mourning, and went to Ravenna with a confidential servant of Bernardino. When they were challenged at the gate, the servant called out: 'I am Balzo, come for medicines for Lamberto'. This convinced the guard, who opened the gates to admit the two men. Once inside, Pandolfo told the guard that Bernardino was dead, and that he himself wanted the lordship of the town. Then he ran to the piazza with drawn sword, crying, ' Viva Pandolfo ', and was accepted as lord by the citizens.[22]

Pandolfo had declared to the guard that Bernardino was dead. But he had lied ; in fact he had only imprisoned his brother. The folly of these half-measures was soon to be revealed. Malatesta Malatesti arrived at Ravenna in June, and arranged a settlement. Bernardino was released from prison, the three brothers swore peace, and agreed to share jointly the lordship of Ravenna and Cervia. The sequel was inevitable. On 7 September, Bernardino imprisoned his brothers in Cervia on the pretext that they were plotting against his life. He himself, intimately aware now of the ill-effects of thoughtless clemency, did not fall into his brothers' error. Within a short space of time it was given out that Lamberto and Pandolfo had died in prison, and their obsequies did not prevent Bernardino from attending the festivities in honour of Lewis of Hungary, at Forlì in December.[23]

Henceforth, until the arrival of Albornoz, Bernardino ruled without opposition. Outside the province he attained a certain fame for his affaires — especially in the Jubilee year, 1350, when he established notable precedents for what, later, was to be a favourite preoccupation of his fellow countrymen : the seduction of visitors to Rome. Yet there seems to be little genial in his character. ' He was dissolute and worldly and of unbridled lust ', wrote Villani, ' a cruel and harsh *signore* ', — and thinking of how he had obtained power, it is not difficult to understand why this should be so. His son, Guido, was similarly to be cursed by the family inheritance. In obscure circumstances, through which can be still discerned the customary treachery, he was deprived of his lordship and imprisoned by his natural sons, Bernardino, Obizzo, Ostasio, and Aldrovandino, in 1390.[24]

(c) *The Malatesti*

The same murderous quarrels were to split the Malatesti family. Malatesta da Verucchio had pleaded in his will for perpetual peace between his descendants, but too much was at stake for his words to be taken seriously. Uberto, Count of Giaggiolo, son of Paolo Malatesta, came into conflict with Malatestino dell' Occhio over the possession of Cesena. In 1324, he was treating secretly with his cousin Ramberto, the son of Giancotto Malatesta, on means by which they might deprive Pandolfo of his rule in Rimini. But Uberto was foolish to trust the son of the man who had murdered his own father. On 21 January,

Ramberto invited him to his castle at Ciolaradi, near Roncofreddo, and had him murdered as he dined, by three bastards of the family.[25]

The death of Pandolfo Malatesta in 1326 precipitated further conflict. Both Ferrantino, the son of Malatestino dell' Occhio, and Malatesta, son of Pandolfo, claimed to be his successor as head of the family. A temporary solution was found, by which Ferrantino succeeded him in Rimini, and Malatesta in Pesaro. From this settlement, Ramberto, son of Giancotto, had been excluded, and he showed his resentment, in the now almost traditional manner, by throwing a dinner party. Ferrantino, and his grandson Ferrantino Novello appeared, but Malatesta was detained in the Marche and could not come. His absence saved the others' lives ; for while Malatesta was still alive and capable of vengeance, Ramberto did not dare to carry out his plan. He imprisoned the two Ferrantinos, but allowed Galeotto, the second son of Malatesta, to go completely free. Once again half measures proved impracticable. At his attempt on Rimini, Polentesia, wife of Malatesta Novello (and daughter of Guido Novello da Polenta), rallied support against him. Malatesta returned, and Ramberto, freeing his prisoners, was forced to withdraw to his castles in the *contado*.[26]

The family of Ramberto and that of Malatesta were reconciled by Cardinal Poujet in 1327. But in the following year, the Archpriest Guido, brother to Ramberto, allied with the Ghibelline Parcitadi, and moved to the attack upon the town. This again was unsuccessful, and followed by a formal reconciliation. By this time, however, Malatestino had decided that any permanent peace was impossible. He lulled his cousin with fair words, but resolved to be finished with him. In 1330, Ramberto came to his castle at Poggiano, that they might hunt and hawk together. His host was out, and he waited for him by the fire, for it was winter, and evening was drawing in. When Malatestino entered, Ramberto fell on his knees at his feet to ask pardon for his past treacheries. Malatestino's answer was to draw out his dagger and plunge it in his cousin's neck. He died instantly.[27]

The events of September 1333 had restored Ferrantino to Rimini, and Malatesta to Pesaro. But each was still jealous and fearful of the other. On 3 June 1334, Malatesta called his cousins, on various pretexts, to his palace at Rimini, and on their arrival, seized them. Thus he captured Ferrantino, Malatestino Novello and Guido. Ferrantino Novello was not in the town at the time and escaped. Meanwhile Malatesta's ally, Ostasio da Polenta, entered the town, and the people of Rimini rose and acclaimed

Malatesta, and his brother Galeotto, as *signori*, and *defensores*. Bolognesi troops were sent to support the new regime. Thus by 'the third betrayal of the Malatesti', the line of Pandolfo Malatesta was assured of the future control of the towns.[28] Malatesta Novello and Guido were imprisoned in the castle of Fossombrone, and died there, doubtless murdered. The elder Ferrantino was released, and went into exile at Urbino. His grandson, Ferrantino Novello, in company with his brother-in-law, the Count Nolfo da Montefeltro, waged war spasmodically against his successful cousin, by now graced with the sinister cognomen of Guastafamiglia ('Destroy Family'). But Ferrantino Novello died in 1352, and in the following year, his grandfather, the elder Ferrantino, breathed his last at Rimini, to where, in his impotent old age, he had been allowed to return. The work to Guastafamiglia had been completed.

(d) *The Alidosi and Ordelaffi*

In comparison with the exploits of the da Polenta and the Malatesti, the quarrels within the Alidosi and Ordelaffi families were almost trivial. The disputes between the brothers Azzo and Roberto degli Alidosi, and between them and their cousins of the line of Massa degli Alidosi, do not seem to have reached the point of bloodshed, while the only incident in the Ordelaffi family, in the fourteenth century, was the deprivation and imprisonment of Sinibaldo degli Ordelaffi by his nephews, Cecco and Pino, in 1385.[29] However, these incidents add to the general impression of lawlessness.

III

As might be expected, the unceasing treacheries and violence of the Romagnols, in this period, gave them an enduring reputation among the peoples of Italy. A French legate of the fourteenth century did not scruple to compare them to the English: 'so treacherous and extravagant, are they,' he wrote, 'that in feasting and falsehood they are little different from Englishmen. But they are much more cunning, and with no shadow of doubt more intelligent than the English, so that in reputation and performance, they hold the monarchy of perfidy among other Italians.'[30] 'An old proverb', wrote Matteo Villani, 'says that the Romagnol bears his faith in his breast. One should not be surprised that the tyrants of Romagna lack faith, since they are both tyrants and

Romagnols.' Two centuries on, Guicciardini, as papal governor of the province, wrote in similar terms : ' The source and foundation of all good is to have a name and reputation for severity. This is necessary in all governments, especially those of the Church, and notably so in Romagna, where there are so many wounds, and so many old and new injuries, and where men are commonly dishonest, malign and ignorant of honour.'[31] When the Bolognesi chroniclers describe some treachery they often add the words, ' e quel fo alla romagnola '.[32] This reputation lasted into modern times, and extended to their women. John Hobhouse once warned Byron : ' they are very vixens. . . . Go to Romagna indeed! Go to old Nick, you'll never be heard of afterwards, except your ghost should be seen racing with Guido Cavalcanti in the wood.'[33] Even today, the conflicts of Sanfedisti and Carbonari, and of Socialists and Republicans, have carried on the same tradition.

How far can the Romagnol reputation for perfidy be justified? The deed of treachery it might be argued, is noted in the chronicle, precisely because it is out of the ordinary. Again, once the tradition is established it is self-perpetuating : every treacherous Romagnol was marked down instantly as a Romagnol. It might be argued, too, that the general level of morality was low, and that of Romagna no lower than other places, such as fourteenth-century Scotland.

There may be some truth in these arguments, but it would be unwise to press them too far. The Romagna was undoubtedly the scene of the grossest crimes, and it is more profitable to explain than to deny the fact. The primary cause was the absence of any central political control. Dante's call for the revival of the Empire has been dismissed as the obsolete fantasy of a dreamer. Yet the poet's analysis of his time was correct : the insensate factions, the constant war, the miseries which made his Italy,

non donna di provincia, ma bordello!

arose precisely from the lack of any imperial authority, the lack of Machiavelli's ' royal hand that with excessive power, may check the excessive ambition and corruption of powerful men '. When Dante claimed that the moral and intellectual virtues depended upon the Empire, the fourteenth century showed at least, that without the Empire, they did not flourish.

Nor, for the reasons shown, was the Church ever able to take the place of the Empire. Thus crime was unchecked, and this in an age when life itself was cheap. The petty politics of the time were played out against a fearful background of plague. The Black Death was endemic ; it was noted by the chroniclers as present in the province in 1316, 1318, 1319, 1339, and 1340. These attacks had been severe enough (the Cesena annalist, writing of 1319 speaks of a ' stupenda mortalitas '), but they were merely a prologue to the climax of the terrible years 1347 and 1348. Bubonic infection was rife again in 1361 and in 1365. when Villola wrote that few people remained to be affected by it, since so many had died off in previous plagues. Yet plague came again in 1368.

Whether its effect was to drive men to the piety of the flagellants, or to crime, the Black Death introduced a contempt for life itself, and for the more human qualities in life. Art changed its direction abruptly, returning from the new naturalism of Giotto, to the symbolism of the age of Margaritone. Laura died in the plague of 1348, and Petrarch became the representative figure of the best in the new age, where the ideal is withdrawal to the contemplative life. Even the more robust Boccaccio saw life as a bubble :

> As each man may plainly perceive, there is nothing stable in this world, and if anything is greatly subject to change, it is this life of ours. A trifle too much cold or heat within us — leaving aside countless other accidents and possibilities — leads us easily from existence to non-existence. Nor is gentle birth immune, nor riches, nor youth, nor any other worldly dignity.[34]

It was easy to be cruel, because it was difficult to be more cruel than nature, than life itself.

The same could be said of the whole of Western Europe at the time of the Black Death ; but in Romagna there were other factors to stimulate crime. The poverty of little lords in an age of falling land values, and fewer peasants to till the soil, could too easily be contrasted with the comparative economic prosperity of those who, with no prescriptive right, had seized lordship of the towns. Force was the only arbiter between ignominious indigence and *signoria*. Honour, lust of dominion, the *libido voluntatis*, all combined to tempt to crime, and constant war blunted sensibilities.

Within families themselves, there was no tradition of primogeniture, no system of undisputed natural inheritance. Roman law, and Romagnol practice, generally secured inheritance *pro indiviso* : where the lands and rights of the father were held in common by all the sons. No system was more likely to bring about enmity between brothers. This was intensified in the second generation between the cousins who were their heirs. To inherit one-eighth *pro indiviso* of someone's lands, was to inherit a lively suspicion of all those with whom one held the land. Suspicion, supported by self-interest and fear, easily turned to treachery. Treachery brought its own vicious circle of revenge and fear of revenge. In this way the province became a byword for cruelty and the object of scorn to the merchant chroniclers of Florence — worthy men who preferred that crimes should be committed quietly, and according to law, with ledgers and notarial documents : ' in the name of God and of Profit '.

IV

The tragedy of the Romagna, the failure of imperial power, was also the tragedy of Dante ; and it was fitting that the province should be the poet's last refuge. Some time after the death of the Emperor Henry VII, probably in 1317, he returned to Romagna, and was offered asylum by the Lord of Ravenna, Guido Novello da Polenta.[35] What town more suitable for the man who had sought to stylise his life that it might be worthy of his poem? ' A general sepulchre of most saintly men ', wrote Boccaccio, ' walking here, there is no part where one does not tread on ashes most worthy of reverence.'[36] It was resplendent with the same imperial memories that had been the motive force of so much of Dante's work. The mosaics of San Vitale come to life again in the sixth canto of the *Paradiso* :

> Cesare fui, e son Guistiniano

while from here Caesar had moved, and

> Quel che fe' poi ch' egli uscì di Ravenna
> e saltò Rubicon, fu di tal volo
> che no seguiteria lingua nè penna.

One sees the poet against the monuments of the imperial past, and the old women of Ravenna pointing him out as he goes ; ' the man who visits hell and brings back to the living news of the shades that dwell there '.[37] Outside the walls, walking in the pine forest by the sea, he would watch the bending of the trees to the wind, and hear the birds' song in the branches ; the inspiration of the image of the Earthly Paradise :

> tal qual di ramo in ramo si raccoglie
> per la pineta in sul lito di Chiassi,
> quand' Eolo Scirocco fuor discoglie.[38]

For Dante these were five years of peace. The society in which he found himself cannot have been displeasing. His patron Guido

Novello was himself a poet, and a certain freshness breaks occasionally into the conventionality of his verse :

> Era l' aer sereno e lo bel tempo ;
> a cantavan gli augei per la riviera
> et in quel giorno apparve primavera
> quand' io ti vidi in prima . . .

He was a poet too who had learnt from Dante. So much he loves his lady, he says to her,

> 'sì che gia mai da te non fia divisa,'

echoing the most memorable line of the canto that celebrates the fate of his kinswoman, Francesca.[39]

Guido Novello, says Boccaccio, was one, ' trained in liberal studies, who gave great honour to men of worth and especially to those who excelled in knowledge '.[40] His cousin — and supplanter — Ostasio, must have had a similar education. He is known to have ordered a translation of Livy, and it was he, with Pino della Tosa, who persuaded Cardinal Bertrand du Poujet not to burn Dante's body (this despite the fact that his brother-in-law had been placed among the gluttons in the *Purgatorio*.[41]) Giotto was in Ravenna in these years, and Vasari's report that it was Dante who persuaded him to come there, may well be true. Archbishop Rainaldo, a saint, and a scholar of sorts, presided over the diocese, while, amidst the society of notaries, the poet could find at least three enthusiasts for the study of *rettorica volgare* : Menghino Mezzani, Pier Giardini, and Bernardo Cinoccio ; men who were to preserve memories of the poet up to the days when Boccaccio was in Ravenna.

In this society, Dante completed the poem of the medieval world, and at his death Romagna and Ravenna became ' the perpetual guardian of him whose works the whole world holds in admiration '.[42]

> Ravenna fummi albergo nel mio esiglio
> et ella ha il corpo . . .

Meanwhile, however, the world Dante had described was slowly passing away. New and more stable governments were emerging, and the tyrannies were everywhere beginning to give way to the new institutions of the captaincy.

CHAPTER V

Captaincy and Vicariate

What shall we say about the actions of certain popes and emperors that we have witnessed? For they have constituted men, who can clearly be identified as tyrants, and who rule through tyranny, as their vicars. . . . I reply that it is to be presumed that such great lords are not acting without very good reasons. BARTOLO DA SASSOFERRATO[1]

I

SO far, the first stage in the formation of the Romagnol *signorie* has been discussed. It has been seen how *comitatinanza*, the subjection of the *contado* by the town, created a new dominant class, formed from two virtually indistinguishable elements : the old feudal nobility of the countryside, and the town nobility who had secured emphyteutic leases in the *contado*. In the absence of any bourgeoisie strong enough to challenge their predominance, these men became the natural leaders of the communes. Yet, at the same time, divisions grew within their ranks ; each family and party wished to dominate the commune in its own interest. Something has been said about their motives in this ; they include, for instance, the wish to control the marketing of their crops. But it would be a distortion to over-emphasise the element of calculation. Romagna in this era was essentially an ' heroic ' society in which the habit of conscious calculation was much weaker than in the bourgeois republics across the Apennines. The Romagnol crimes which figure in the *Divine Comedy*, the treacheries of Fra Alberico and of Tibaldello Zambrasi, for instance, startle precisely because of their irrationality. A blow in the face leads to a massacre several years later, the jest of some party leaders to the betrayal of a town : *ex minima causa tam odiosam vindictam*.[2] But contemporaries felt this incongruity far less ; action was not primarily dictated by hope of gain, but rather by the concepts of aristocratic honour.

In these concepts, *libido voluntatis* or *libido dominandi* was a primary element. As a result the towns were distracted by constant party struggles. As landowners, the nobles were able to call upon their *fideles* as a military force to sustain them in the *contado*. In addition, their position as creditors among the petty tradesmen and artisans ensured a body of dependants who were involved in their cause in the town. In this way, all were drawn into the conflict of factions. The collapse of imperial power, which had never been strong, the failure of Bologna (1248–78), and then of the papacy, to dominate the province, meant that there was no central authority to bring order in place of anarchy.

By the end of the thirteenth century, leaders of the factions had obtained full control of their towns, and had begun to dominate them through their communal machinery. These men can be called ' tyrants '. In an era without law they had seized power without legal justification. Their rule was rooted in violence : the exile of their opponents, the proscription of any possible rivals, the readiness at any moment to face some new attack from their fellow citizens in exile, or some new treachery from their present friends. The basis of government was force and their own strength. ' We call a man a tyrant ', wrote Bartolo, ' from a Greek word meaning " strong ".'[3]

How was it that certain families came to be leaders of the town factions? It might be assumed, from considering their properties, that it was predominance of landed power in the *contado* that gave pre-eminence within the commune. But, in fact, some of the feudatories of the Tusco-Romagnol Apennines had wider fiefs than the future signorial families. Even if this were not so, it would be misleading to give the one as the cause of the other. In this era, the qualities which brought men to power in the commune were precisely the qualities of a successful landlord. They were the ability to train feudal followers in the field, the strength to resist usurpations of property, and the cunning and ruthlessness necessary to usurp land from others. The essence of a man's power was not his property but his *fortuna* and *virtù* : it was personal qualities which gave leadership to the future signorial families.

In the thirteenth century, landholding gave an initial advantage, however, because it provided *fideles*, who formed the nucleus of a military force. But by the middle of the fourteenth century, when feudal forces, as elsewhere in Europe, were being replaced by mercenary companies, the landless man with ability as a soldier comes into prominence : men like Jacopo Sforza, whose family was to rule the Duchy of Milan ; a man who began life as a small farmer in the Romagnol plain, and who threw up the unrewarding cultivation of the soil for military adventure. Another example is Sir John Hawkwood, who was invested with the lordship of Bagnacavallo, for his military services to the papacy.

In the fourteenth century, men were called 'tyrants' in one of two senses of the word. The first meaning implied a moral judgment; implied all those evils which Aristotle saw in tyranny. But the word was also used as a legal term: to describe a ruler who — even though his rule might be virtuous and for the common good — yet held position without the authority of law, without some grant acknowledging his status by a higher power.[4] At the beginning of the fourteenth century, the lords of Romagna were tyrants in this latter sense: their rule had no constitutional or legal justification.

In the second stage in the formation of the *signorie*, this 'tyranny' passed away. First the commune itself gave a form of legitimacy to the rule of its lords, by appointing them to the office of captain or defender. Then the papacy, bending to political realities in its turn, completed the process by legitimising the captaincies with grants of vicariates. In this way, true *signorie*: legitimate states with single-person governments, were created. It is this dual process, spread out over the first seventy-five years of the fourteenth century which will be discussed in this chapter.

II

The institution of the 'captaincy' came within the first forty years of the fourteenth century, and had as its background the impotence of the Avignon papacy and the inability of its rectors to establish any firm governments within the papal states.

Nowhere more than in Romagna was this failure so evident. At the end of 1305, Clement V's legates reported that 'in this province there was no [papal] count in the time when we were there, but a vicar whom almost none obeyed.'[5] Five years later, in part as a precaution against the Emperor Henry VII, in part as an attempt to quell the province, the pope created King Robert of Naples the rector of Romagna, a position which he was to hold for the following seven years (1310–17). But Robert's rule was not a success. By 1316, few in Romagna obeyed his viceroys, and the papacy itself had grown impatient with its own nominee.[6] John XXII's decree, revoking the grant of Romagna, 'which you have held for some time by licence of the apostolic see, without, as we have heard, exuberance of great profit to yourself',[7] must have come as a relief to all.

If the papacy re-assumed the province, in the confident belief that its own officials would succeed where the Angevins had failed, it was doomed to swift disappointment. The Rector

Aimeric de Chatelus, in a letter of 1320, painted his plight in pitiful terms. There was nothing, he said, which he could do to oppose the treacherous and violent abuses of powerful magnates. If he gave an order the reply came: ' " Certainly, if my lord wishes it " — but it is the tyrant he means when he says " my lord "!' He was faced with refusals to pay taxes, he was hustled out of the Palazzi Comunali almost as soon as he had arrived. The tyrants forbade their subjects to invoke justice from the papal court of the province. The wisdom of Solomon would be hard put to it in dealing with them. Only military power could avail against them; but to secure soldiers, taxes were necessary, and for these the rector had to humiliate himself before the tyrants, and refrain from doing anything to displease them. ' Yet they still loathe me.' Perhaps, he concluded, it would be better to return the province to King Robert.[8]

Aimeric struggled manfully against his difficulties, but peace and papal authority were only to come to Romagna — and then temporarily — with the establishment of Cardinal Bertrand du Poujet at Bologna in 1327. In the seven years that followed Poujet succeeded in driving away, one by one, the tyrants from their towns. By 1334, the communes of Romagna were his, and the papal states appeared to acknowledge his authority. Amidst mounting triumph, John XXII prepared to move to Bologna as the first step for the return to Rome:

'Vedrà Bologna e poi il nobil Roma!'

But the exultant cry of Petrarch was lost among the clamour of arms. The legate had unwisely allied with John, King of Bohemia, who, between 1330 and 1331, had built up a large north Italian domain. The meteoric rise of John's power had excited envy and unrest, his union with the papacy aroused alarm, and the one was associated with the other in its tumultuous fall. In August 1331, a league was formed against king and pope under the leadership of Francesco d' Este. Against this threat, with the doubtful aid of the Romagnol lords, the legate marched out in April 1333 to attack the Este power. But on 14 April he was defeated before Ferrara; and the work of years collapsed overnight.[9]

The fall of Poujet caused a virtual interregnum in Romagna for the following eight years. Benedict XII was averse to the shedding of blood, and his rectors were consequently powerless. Such scruples did not affect the more stolid mind of Clement VI, but with him it was extravagance and avarice which prohibited the raising of forces adequate for restoring the papal power.

Aimeric de Chatelus returned to the province in March 1343, to receive the temporary submission of most of the Romagnol lords. Yet in that very year, so weak did papal power appear, that the tyrant of Florence, the Duke of Athens, confidently, albeit unsuccessfully, suggested to the papacy that the province should be given to him.[10]

At this stage there appeared a new factor inimical to papal control: the resurgence of the Visconti state in Lombardy. Luchino Visconti, the Lord of Milan, made allies in Romagna, and dispatched to their aid the Great Company of Werner of Urslingen, the first of those bands of foreign freebooters — mobile states almost — that devastated Italy in the following years. Visconti power advanced still further with the succession of the capable and ruthless Archbishop, Giovanni Visconti (1349–54). Florence, meanwhile, was growing hostile to papal rule in the Romagna, which she herself now regarded with covetous eyes. Faced with these difficulties, Clement's rector, his nephew Durfort, was powerless to control the province, or to defend the northern boundaries of the papal states. In April 1352, the papacy was forced to grant Bologna in vicariate to Archbishop Giovanni, and to recognise tacitly its own impotence in the Romagna.[11]

It was against this background that the lords of Romagna tightened their grip on the towns. The power of the tyrants grew by two means: first as the leaders of their communes against papal oppression; second, in strange contrast, as allies of the papacy against others in the province. The lords oscillated successfully as circumstances dictated, between these two policies to secure a rule which was to become permanent and legitimate.

In the first case, the lords united their communes against the papacy. The nobility realised that their interests could be better served by allying with the party of their former rivals than by submitting to the dictates of papal *podestà*. Consequently, the rivalry of parties gave way, after 1317, to a union of almost all the feudality in the commune behind its leading family. This new rule of the tyrant was accepted by the feudality, and it undoubtedly coincided with the needs and wishes of the greater part of the other elements in the towns. The belief is sometimes expressed that, from the time of Boniface VIII, there was a new correspondence of interest between commune and papacy: an alliance springing from their mutual hostility to the tyrant. But as has been seen, the Romagnol commune was already identified with the interests of the feudality and the tyrants themselves. To the

A representation of Dante at Forlì

ordinary citizen, the question as to which family and its supporters dominated in the commune must have been as immaterial as the merits of Whig and Tory to the English eighteenth-century voter. In each case support was only dictated by links of dependence, promise of future reward, and family alliance. With the triumph of one family, the wise changed their allegiance. One thing was obvious, however : that the stable rule of one family was infinitely preferable to intermittent anarchy.

This became particularly true when the communes were faced by papal attempts to levy taxation and other services. When, in 1317, Staggi, the official of the papal *camera* arrived at Bagnacavallo, with twelve soldiers, to collect the taxes owing to the rector, he found the Counts of Cunio ringing the bells of the village, to summon their followers and the men of the neighbourhood to resist. He was, he declared, faced with opposition so strong that, 'but for flight', he would have been killed. He and his soldiers were pursued through the countryside for many miles by the counts and their followers, who cried out to the villages through which they passed, to rise up against them as they fled.[12] What the Cunii were doing here for Bagnacavallo each lord was to do for his own town at some time during the half century.

At first sight then, one would expect the papacy to have been irreconcilably hostile to the rule of tyrants within its own domain. But it was rarely in a position to pick and choose either its friends or its enemies. In 1321 a papal process was initiated against the commune of Bagnacavallo, because 'it was placed under the domination and protection of an individual against the form of the constitutions of the said province'. But nine years after this Cardinal Poujet formally assigned Bagnacavallo to the Count Ugolino di Cunio as rector for the Church.[13] Tyranny had begun, in part, as an alliance of magnate and commune against the Church, but was to develop on a different basis. The frequent alliances of the Malatesti and the Alidosi with the papal officials suggests the new pattern of politics that was to come.

Once established, the tyrants were faced with unrest in their communes, and rivalries within their own families. They wanted peace and stability. If the Church were prepared to limit its demands and recognise their power, they were prepared to co-operate. This was the political reality which, by the middle of the century, both parties were slowly coming to recognise.

III

The rule of the signorial families during the first half of the fourteenth century was not continuous ; it was broken, for instance, by Cardinal Poujet, from 1327 to 1334, and again, briefly, in March 1343. Yet in this period as a whole signorial rule became the norm ; the government of the tyrant assumed the force of custom. As a natural consequence it came to be recognised by the statutes of the towns. Each commune introduced similar institutions, which may be described in general as ' captaincies ', and which had the effect of legitimising the tyrant's rule.

(a) *Forlì*

Forlì was probably the first town to appoint its lord to the captaincy. With the death of the great Maghinardo Pagani, violent factions had developed in the town, between the Ordelaffi, Orgogliosi, and Calboli families. In these the Ordelaffi had the advantage, for they were clearly best fitted to assume the mantle of Maghinardo. Scarpetta degli Ordelaffi had married his daughter to Maghinardo's grandson, and had attained such prestige as a Ghibelline warrior that he was appointed captain of the Florentine Whites, in their invasion of the Mugello (Spring 1303).[14] In 1315, after a very complicated succession of conflicts between the rival families, Scarpetta's cousin, Cecco, seized power, and it was probably at this moment that he was given the position of captain for life.[15]

However, one cannot be certain of this, for only a couple of documents of the town remain from these years. The first is a treaty between Venice and Forlì, in 1321, which opens with the words : ' the magnificent and powerful man, Cecco degli Ordelaffi, Captain of the people of Forlì, in his own name, and on behalf of the commune and people of Forlì through the arbitrium and power conceded to him by a decree of the council of the four hundred of the town of Forlì . . . etc.' A document of the following year shows ' the secret council of the 400 good men of the town of Forlì ' gathered in the Palazzo Comunale by the Captain Cecco, the Vicar of the *podestà*, Francesco da Zaboli, and the *anziani*, to nominate a proctor to go to Venice to represent the commune.[16] Little can be deduced from these fragments, but probably the *podestà* and his vicar had already been relegated to purely executive and judicial roles. The personal prestige and landed power of the Ordelaffi, together with their proved willingness to resist papal exactions, presumably gave the family a clear predominance over the councils of the *anziani* and the four hundred.

(b) *Faenza*

In Faenza the successors of Maghinardo were to be Guelfs. Largely with the support of the viceroys of King Robert, the Manfredi triumphed over their rivals within the town, and acquired some sort of captaincy in 1322. At the same time, the family acquired the greater part of the old Fantolini and Pagani properties within the *contado*, and became the largest landowners of Faenza. Here again, however, very few documents indeed have survived, and speculation must take the place of certainty.

In 1311, the *podestà*, captain of the people, *anziani* (presided over by the *Gonfaloniere* of justice), the consuls of the merchants, and the fifty *savii*, all united with the General Council, to impose a tax.[17] The old machinery of the commune was still functioning, and the Manfredi were working within it. In 1313, Francesco, 'il vecchio', Manfredi was appointed captain, and he was re-elected in 1314 and 1315.[18] These appointments were probably for six-monthly periods only, as had been the custom in the latter half of the thirteenth century. The captain, in law at least, was still considered as subordinate to the *podestà* in the hierarchy of the commune.[19] Save for 1318, when Ricciardo, son of Francesco, was captain, it is not known who held the office between 1315 and 1322.[20] But in this latter year, according to Azzurini, 'while Francesco de' Manfredi exercised the office of captaincy in the town of Faenza, by force he made himself to be called Lord of Faenza, and for four years ruled the town as Lord'.[21] Probably this means that Francesco intimidated the General Council into granting him the captaincy for life. The circumstances are completely obscure, though some have connected Francesco's seizure of power with a letter of 12 August of that year, insisting upon the payment of taxes to the papal government.[22] Certainly, from 1322 to 1327 the family dominated the town, and, significantly, a papal letter of June 1325, which complained of non-payment of tax, was addressed, not to the commune, but to Francesco and his sons.

In three generations of the Manfredi family there were only two brief periods in which the family held uncontested rule: 1322–27 and 1350–56. None the less, there was continual Manfredi predominance in the councils of the town, and conflicts between factions ended. Their place was taken by internal struggles within the family: the disputes of Alberghettino with Francesco and Cecchino, of Giovanni di Alberghettino with Giovanni di Ricciardo, and of Giovanni di Ricciardo with his relatives the Rogati. Yet, until 1350, papal authority, however weakly administered, was still a reality. Only from 1350 does it seem that Giovanni di Ricciardo obtained lordship. Before this date, apart from the years of Francesco's life captaincy (1322–7), the Manfredi, when they held office, did so under the aegis of the old communal organisation. Even in 1356 the captaincy was theoretically elective. In that year, 'the *anziani* of the town of Faenza, the sixty councillors, and the twelve *savii* of the said town elected Giovanni di fu Ricciardo as captain, rector, and governor of the said town'.[23]

(c) *Ravenna*

In Ravenna, the character of the captaincy can be more clearly discerned. It was probably established in 1322, with the seizure of power by Ostasio di Bernardino da Polenta. The statutes of 1327 suggest what had taken place five years before. In these decrees, Ostasio was given the podestàship, and a ten-year appointment as captain of the people,[24] which ensured him complete control of the town. The 'capitaneus et defensor' was given 'complete custody of the town and district, and whatever pertains and could pertain to their custody', full authority to punish rebels or enemies of the town, and the power to judge himself those whom he accused of rebellion. Ostasio and his descendants were given the right of appointing *podestà*, of controlling the elections of *savii*, and of choosing the town's ambassadors. The *podestà* was deprived of any independent right of issuing decrees. Ostasio, as captain, was given the responbility of ensuring that all monies due to the commune — *gabelles*, fines, etc. — were paid, and his salary was fixed at £R.1,200 a year. He selected the officers of the town guard, and his decrees in respect of the guard could only be changed by a three-quarters majority of the General Council. Yet no council or *arrengo* (union of all the men of the town) could be held without the consent of Ostasio or his sons. None but Ostasio and his servants could bear arms, while fortified houses and castles were made a monopoly of his family. These castles were to be constructed and maintained at the expense of the commune. The commune promised, in the statutes, to preserve the properties of the family of Ostasio.[25] Although this was merely a ten-year grant in the first instance, it was presumably renewed at will.

The statutes of Cervia, of 1328, show that Ostasio ruled there in a similar way. Here, his assent was necessary for the choice of *podestà*, and though most of the other officials were freely elected, he appointed the chancellor. The *massarius* (or treasurer) was not permitted to make payments without his assent. The General Council of the Two Hundred could be ' reformed ' by him, and he appointed the Council of the Four Good Men. Nothing was to be proposed in council save in the presence of the *podestà* or his vicar, and of the *defensor* or his vicar. The making of statutes was the prerogative of the *defensor*. As in Ravenna, he had full control of gates and fortifications, and authority to proceed against traitors. To Ostasio were given full powers for the collection of taxes, and he alone was permitted to alienate communal property. Any order for expenses was to be as valid as if it had been confirmed by council according to the statutes. No assemblies of the councils were to meet without his consent. Only he and his family and faction might carry arms.[26]

Ostasio's rule over Cervia — which after all was only a village — was perhaps more autocratic than over Ravenna. It is curious to note how the Ravennati statutes, despite the control granted to the family, admit the possibility that the General Council might actually override the captain's decisions — as in the case of the town guard.

In another document of the time, the council's formal assent and authority is given considerable prominence. This is the commercial treaty of July 1328, in which the Doge of Venice was allowed to appoint a consul, and other unspecified officials to the town. Here, ' the magnificent and powerful knight, the Lord Ostasio da Polenta, *podestà* and captain of the said town of Ravenna,' appointed a representative to swear agreement to the treaty, ' in the full, general and greater council of the town and commune of Ravenna, gathered in the palace of the said commune by the sound of the bell and the voice of the herald in the accustomed manner,' and ' with the expressed consent and authority of the said council '.[27] But no undue significance should be given to this. Even in the *signorie* of the fifteenth century, such consent by the General Council was always regarded as necessary for the full authentication of the more solemn enactments of the *signore*.

(d) *Rimini*

The captaincy of the Malatesti was established after the seizure of Rimini by Malatesta Guastafamiglia and Galeotto, in

1334, — an event, it has already been seen, involving a popular uprising, whether staged or spontaneous, against the line of Ferrantino.

Malatesta da Verruchio's supremacy in Rimini had been determined by personal factors : his own prestige, the military power he was able to maintain, and his position among the aristocracy of Rimini. Indication of this leadership was given by his monopoly of the office of *podestà*. The reorganisation of the commune in 1295 had not basically altered its constitution. Malatestino and Pandolfo continued in the same traditions ; though they predominated, the communal organisation was fundamentally unchanged. In 1320, the General Council still met, with the ' Four Officials ' under the presidency of the *podestà*.

Yet the family was continuously strengthening the reality of its power. At the initiative of his father, Ferrantino Malatesta had been given the office of ' conservator civitatis et comitatus Arimini ', and with it the presidency of the Small Council. There was already a statute decreeing that anyone found guilty of treachery to the Malatesti should be summarily tried and executed.[28] This *de facto* supremacy was given legal form in 1334. In a General Council of November of that year, it was agreed that Malatesta, Galeotto, and their descendants should be freed from all statutes and ordinances of the commune, and should be able to act against them. The brothers were also empowered to convene the Small Council at their will. Deliberations in the Small Council, even if contrary to previous statutes, were to be binding, and for their acceptance, the consent of the Four Officials, or of any other conciliar body, was unnecessary. The only check placed on the council was that its decisions might not derogate from ' the free and perpetual lordship granted to the magnificent knight the lord Malatesta '. The collection of statutes, compiled at the same time, gave the *dominium* (*signoria* or lordship) and *defensoria* for life to Malatesta. Another statute referred to the *ballia* and *arbitrium* conferred on him, and granted unrestricted control of the revenues, and jurisdiction over the commune.[29]

The following year, in April 1335, the General Council accepted unanimously a resolution, by which the Malatesti were given the right to elect to the podestàship.[30] Henceforth, instead of holding this office directly, Malatesta appointed a nominee, and occupied a position in the commune distinguished by the title of *defensor*. In this he was but imitating what had already been done by the other Romagnol lords. The *podestà* became a judicial and executive office, under the direct control of the captain and *defensor*.

(e) *Imola*

In Imola, the traditions of Maghinardo Pagani were carried on by the Ghibelline 'Society of San Donato', in opposition to the Guelf 'Society of San Martino',[31] but from 1315 the Ghibellines were always in opposition. The new Guelf government found its leader, not in any of the native aristocracy, discredited perhaps as a result of their twenty-year exile, but in Ricciardo, of the Manfredi family of Faenza, who held the office of captain until 1327.[32] The character of Ricciardo's government was aristocratic, though working through the old popular forms. This can be seen from a reformation immediately preceding Ricciardo's first three-year appointment as captain, wherein 'propter novitates', new officials called *sapientes de ballia* were appointed in the 'council of the officers (*ministerialium*) of the societies of the Arts of the people'. These *savii* include such *contado* nobility as Lippo and Massa Alidosi, Zanne de' Nordigli, and Pietro de' Bolgarelli.[33] Similarly, in the following year, Lippo and Zanne acted as *anziani*.[34]

Ricciardo lost the captaincy in September 1327,[35] and until 1334 the town was under the Church. But with the fall of Poujet's power, the Alidosi family drove out the Ghibelline Nordigli and seized the town.[36] The circumstances are obscure, but for the following ninety years the Alidosi were to be the lords of Imola.

The coming to power of the Alidosi was the occasion for promulgating new statutes, in which Lippo was declared to be the captain-elect of the commune of Imola. The captain was to hold his office for five years, and to be 'syndicated' — *i.e.* to answer for all his acts during that period — in the same way as any other official. In all business of the commune, he was to work with the *podestà*, the *anziani*, and the *savii*, and not to act without their consent. He swore in the hands of the *podestà* to exercise his office according to the statutes. He was to guard the district by day and night, and to supervise the town-gates, fortifications, and the locks of the canals. He punished lax officials. He saw that there was a good market, abundance of food, and that no corn was exported without the consent of the *anziani* and *savii*. Where statutory power was lacking, he could punish ill-doers on his own initiative. He could draw up levies of horse and foot, and authorise their payment. He had control of *gabelles* and taxes, and was responsible for recovering the goods of the commune. For all this he was granted a salary of £R.800 every six months, and a *familia* or household, consisting of a judge, who was to act as his vicar, a knight (presumably acting as constable), two notaries, six personal servants, including a cook and a messenger, four armed men as a bodyguard, and six horses.[37]

The powers allotted to the captain here seem considerably narrower than those in other towns. His duties and rights were strictly defined and delineated, and placed him, theoretically at least, in strict subordination to the commune. Imola was unusual too, in that its ruling family emerged suddenly and unexpectedly to power. In the other towns, the future signorial family had clearly predominated from the time of Maghinardo's death. The Alidosi indeed had acquired the captaincy of Imola in the early twelve-nineties. But though Lippo had married a kinsman of Maghinardo, and though his father had acquired a certain esteem as Captain of the People in Florence,[38] the family had played a secondary role in the government of the town. The only explanation, apart from chance, for their abrupt seizure of power in 1334 lies, perhaps, in their territorial position within the *contado*.

In the years which followed, Lippo and his son Roberto, were devoted adherents of papal policy. A letter of Benedict XII to the rector of Romagna, Rambaldo, Bishop of Imola, in 1341, observed that since Lippo was ' the least offensive ' of the tyrants, he was to be excluded from the general process that was being drawn up against them. He was to be persuaded to go to the papal court, where efforts would be made to win him over completely to the support of the Church.[39] It was shortly afterwards that the papacy created a decisive precedent in Romagnol politics by granting a vicariate to the Alidosi as lords of the town.[40] The Church was able to do this without serious risk, for Imola had no direct control over its surrounding countryside, and was dependent for its supply of corn upon the good will of the papal officials who directly controlled the *contado*.[41] Externally the Alidosi were subject to control, but in the internal affairs of Imola, whatever the commune had decreed in its statutes, they were now full *signori* by papal appointment.

Thus the Alidosi were the first of the lords of Romagna to attain full *signoria* : that is to say, *de iure* lordship in which there was no stigma of tyranny *ex defectu tituli*. The powers given to captains in other towns made them the legal governors, as far as the communes themselves were concerned. But fifteen years before the other lords of the province, the Alidosi were confirmed in their rights by an authority superior to the commune, by the papacy itself.

IV

So far, it has been shown how, in default of strong papal government, the lords of Romagna had succeeded by 1350 in securing from their own communes some form of recognition of their right to rule. In the following twenty-five years this grant by the communes was in its turn to be legitimised and reinforced by the papacy itself. The ruling families were to attain full *signoria*: that is, full recognition of their status and legitimacy by their appointment as papal vicars. Indeed, it has been seen that the Alidosi had already achieved this. The other ruling houses must have regarded their success as a precedent, as a recognition that with a discriminating policy they too could obtain from the papacy a virtual abdication of power in their favour.

So indeed it was to be, and, paradoxically, the vicariates were granted in the era when the Church was making its greatest efforts to reassert its temporal power. This was the age of the legations of Cardinal Albornoz (30 June 1353–September 1357, 18 September 1358–26 November 1363), and of the three wars of the Visconti against the Church and its allies (1362–4, 1367–9, 1372–5). The final concessions were brought about by the War of the Eight Saints (July 1375–July 1378).

It was the realism of Cardinal Gil Albornoz, to whom Clement VI had entrusted the task of reconquering the papal states, which brought about the decisive change. Despite his early successes in the Campagna and Umbria, his position by 1354 was still precarious. The power of Bernabò Visconti and his allies presented a formidable challenge. Little reliance was to be placed in the calculated surrender of the communes of the Marche. In Romagna he was faced with the unwavering hostility of Francesco Ordelaffi. Externally his position was weak. Both Florence and Naples were pressing on him the claims of the Romagnol lords to clemency.[42] He needed more troops and secure allies if he were to advance further north through the papal states. He himself, as can be seen in the statutes which he was to issue for Forlì, had no love of communal liberty. In these circumstances he decided upon compromise and conciliation; the Malatesti first, and then the da Polenta, were created papal vicars.[43]

The Manfredi and the Ordelaffi, who had proved more recalcitrant, were temporarily driven into exile, and the legations of Albornoz established a limited papal supremacy within the province. When the legate, Cardinal Anglic Grimoard, wrote his description of Romagna in 1371, the Malatesti ruled Rimini, the da Polenta, Ravenna and Cervia, and the Alidosi, the town of Imola, all as papal vicars. The *contado* of Imola, Faenza, Forlì, Cesena, the vicariates of Montefeltro, Bobbio, Sant' Arcangelo, Val di Bagno and of Galeata, were all under the direct rule of the Church.

This equilibrium was destroyed by the War of the Eight Saints : the conflict between the papacy and Florence (under its war committee of eight magistrates) which filled the years 1375–8. Throughout the fourteenth century Florence had looked with thinly disguised hostility at each attempt of the papacy to secure its own domains. It had been antagonistic to Cardinal Poujet, and cool to Albornoz. In July 1375 it showed its hand, allied with the Visconti, and amidst the hypocritical clamour of its humanists, praising the benefits of ' freedom ', restored the Ordelaffi and Manfredi tyrants to power.[44] The war brought little success to the papacy. When Pope Urban VI signed the peace of Tivoli, the Church was financially exhausted, and morally at a disadvantage. In these circumstances the papacy bowed to expediency, and created both the Manfredi and Ordelaffi, vicars of their towns. The precise date of Astorgio Manfredi's vicariate is unknown, but in February 1379 Sinibaldo Ordelaffi was created vicar of Forlì, its *contado* and district, Forlimpopuli, Sarsina, and Oriolo.[45] The last of the Romagnol tyrants had attained *signoria*.

The grants of vicariates by the papacy gave to the *signori* the *merum et mixtum imperium et gladii potestatem* : full civil and criminal jurisdiction, the right to impose taxes, and to act as full lords of their communes — all things which, *de facto*, they already held. All that the vicariate gave to the *signori* which they did not already possess was a new legal sanction to rule. Theoretically, indeed, the vicariates limited their power. The lords were forced to acknowledge that the grants of lordship to their towns were invalid, and that the source of all privilege in the papal states was the papal government. Although almost always renewed without question the vicariates were granted for limited periods, generally of ten or twelve years. Only the Malatesti succeeded, by the end of the fourteenth century, in securing a grant for two generations. Jurisdiction in appeal, and for such crimes as heresy and treachery to the pope, were reserved for the papal government. It was always stipulated that the lords should rule according to the statutes of their towns, and that taxation should not be oppressive. Further, the vicars had to agree to the payment of papal taxation and to act as papal tax collectors in their communes.[46]

The reality of their limitations was determined solely by the relative strength of *signore* and papacy. It may be that when the vicariates were originally granted, the vicar was considered as the papal agent that his name implied. The grants were perhaps thought of as revocable, and precarious in practice as well as in theory. But the papacy had barely recovered from the War of the Eight Saints before it was plunged into the profound crisis of the Schism (1379–1415). In those years the renewal of the grants of vicariate became customary and the duties of the vicar largely formal. When Martin V came to the reform of the papal states, at the beginning of the fifteenth century, he was unable to make any permanent change in the government of Romagna, and the papal control of the province remained ineffectual until the advent of Cesare Borgia and Julius II.

V

During these years much of the history of the *signori* was concerned with attempts to seize villages in the *contado* from each other or from the papacy. These little places might seem of small importance, yet the captains struggled fiercely to secure them, for in an age of famine there was an imperative necessity to control as large an area of cultivated land as possible. At the same time, amid the new expansionist policies of Milan and Florence, the Romagnol towns participated to a much greater extent than before in the affairs of Italy as a whole. Something has been said already of the conflicts within the signorial families, and in a following chapter the character of their rule will be discussed. But it would be tedious to follow the careers of each lord through these vicissitudes. Instead, in order to give something of the flavour and character of the age, this chapter will end with a brief outline of the fortunes of the Ordelaffi in the era of Albornoz.

Forlì had fallen to the legate Poujet in 1332, but the triumph of the Church was to be short-lived. Henceforth the name of Francesco Ordelaffi, the nephew of Cecco, was to stand out in Italy for bold and unpunished violation of the rights of the papal states. Francesco, brave, resourceful, vigorous, stubborn in will, was one 'who did not wish to live at discretion of priests'. 'A faithless Patarine dog', 'a mortal enemy of clergy',[47] like others of his contemporaries, he had probably absorbed something of the spirit of the Fraticelli, with their anti-clericalism and hostility to papal corruption.[48]

He was the nephew of Fulcieri da Calboli, whose savagery

had been castigated by Dante in the fourteenth canto of the *Purgatorio* ; and cruelty was part of his inheritance. It was exaggerated perhaps by his enemies ; it is improbable that he actually killed his son and daughter with his own hands because they advised him to yield to the Church.[49] That he gave ' the honour of martyrdom ' to seven monks and seven secular clergy, suggests rather impartiality in the chronicler than in the tyrant. But cruelty there undoubtedly was. The mercenary soldiers of his enemies would have their hands struck off, and be left to wander to Avignon to beg for alms.[50] The severed head of a citizen who opposed him would hang for several days by the clock tower of Cesena ; a priest would be castrated.[51] It was a cruelty of policy, aggravated, or mitigated, by the grim vein of humour, which runs through all the stories told of him. When he captured those who fought for the Church as ' crusaders ' against him, he would say to them, with mock seriousness : ' You bear the cross — but it is of cloth and will perish — now shall you put on a cross that is imperishable '. Then he would brand the soles of their feet with a cross. Alternatively, he would explain to them that, as crusaders, they were now in a state of grace, and that it was in their own best interests that he was dispatching them immediately to death and the rewards of heaven. When the bells rang for the excommunication, he ordered other bells to be rung, and himself ' excommunicated ' the Pope and cardinals, burning their effigies in the piazza. ' So we are excommunicated ; still our food and drink tastes as fine and will do us just as much good.'

Are all these stories of the anonymous chronicler true? Perhaps not ; but they illustrate the spiritual climate in which the papacy of Avignon was to count the cost of its involvement in the world. And they throw into relief another of his comments upon Francesco : ' he was completely devoted to the Forlivesi and they loved him greatly. He assumed the disguise of pious charity, gave dowries for orphan girls, obtained places for others, and provided for the poor among his friends.' The chronicler of Cesena too, in a sudden unexpected phrase, speaks of him ' moved by his wonted pity ', paying ransoms for those held as prisoners by a German mercenary company.[52] Matteo Villani again speaks of the Forlivesi being ' completely crazy about him ' (*pazzi di lui disperatamente*), and of his skill in leadership in persuading his troops to serve him for little reward. ' And with this he made himself so much loved by them that for no suspicion did he require any guard.' These paradoxical judgments upon Francesco express something of the ambiguity of the rule of the Romagnol tyrants.

Villani wrote of him : ' with a mass of violent threats, he urged the citizens to be his faithful and loyal friends'.[53] In that sentence lies the essence of tyrannical rule. ' Freedom ', to the citizens of the towns, meant two things ; first, freedom from the Church, from the outsiders ; second, freedom from the noble families who alone could free them from the Church. These were mutually incompatible desires. Thus even when their choice had been made, the citizens' friendship, however real, could only be preserved by threats — which were real too.

Early humanism and tyranny have often been unwarrantably linked together. Yet Francesco, like some others among the Romagnol lords, was a patron of letters in a modest way. His secretary, Cecco da Mileto, was a correspondent and friend of Petrarch and Boccaccio. Boccaccio himself was in Forlì during Francesco's rule, and may have accompanied him as secretary and chronicler in the expedition of Lewis of Hungary upon Naples. Another of Petrarch's acquaintances, Antonio Beccari of Ferrara, a poet of sorts, was also found at his court.[54]

If Francesco degli Ordelaffi was the epitome of the Romagnol tyrant of the fourteenth century, his wife, Cia, of the noble house of the Ubaldini, was his equal in fame. ' That great-souled woman, who despite misfortune and intolerable stress, never so long as she was free, changed her countenance or failed in counsel or courage ', excited the admiration of Italy for her courage and her loyalty to her husband. ' I believe ', wrote Villani, telling of her exploits, ' that should this have happened in the time of the Romans, their great writers would not have failed to honour her with bright fame, as they honoured those other women worthy of singular praise for their constancy.'[55] Cia Ordelaffi is representative of the warlike character of Romagnol women throughout history. She looks forward to Caterina Sforza who was to resist the Borgia in the sixteenth century. She recalls Aldruada Frangipani, the Countess of Bertinoro in the twelfth century in whom was found that same combination of physical beauty and warlike courage. ' In worth and beauty ', wrote a contemporary of Aldruada, ' she shone among other ladies, as when dawn approaches, the star of morning burns above the others ', and she came, ' like some new Judith ', to the relief of Ancona.[56] These characters live again in the verse of Pascoli, whose work best reflects the Romagnol spirit, they are ' womanly ', but they are as remote from femininity as from the ladies of the court of Louis XIV.

Francesco had been captured at the battle of Ferrara, in April

1333. He was released, but was resentful of Cardinal Bertrand's refusal to assist him in paying his ransom. He must have seen that the defeat had undermined papal rule in the province. On 12 September he entered Forlì at night, hidden in a hay-wain. He roused his followers, 'and on hearing of his arrival, they were most joyful, for it appeared to them ill to stand under the lordship of Cahorsins and the men of Languedoc. And instantly they caused the people to take up arms, and ran to the piazza, shouting, "Long live Francesco, and death to the Legate and the men of Languedoc".' At this the Legate and his officials fled to Faenza.[57]

The next day, Francesco seized Forlimpopoli and called a General Council of the two towns and their *contadi*. When convened, five knights, suspected of hostility to the family, were seized. One was murdered instantly, and his body thrown from the window of the Palazzo Comunale into the piazza below. The others were killed later, in prison. On the 22nd, Cesena revolted from the Church. Francesco moved swiftly, and secured his appointment there as Captain, together with Ramberto Malatesta, Count of Giaggiolo, as *podestà*. A counter-attack of the Bishop Francesco of Sarsina, and Count Guido of Bagno was driven off.[58]

These successes were followed, in the next two years, by consolidation of his power and further expansion throughout the *contado*. Francesco drove Ramberto Malatesta from the podestàship in Cesena, and thereafter ruled as its sole Lord. He secured peace from his uncle Fulcieri da Calboli (26 December 1334), by yielding Castrocaro to him, but sought to redress the balance by usurpations of ecclesiastical property within the *contado* in the following year. In March 1335, Monte Abete (in the diocese of Forlimpopuli) was snatched from the Archbishop of Ravenna, and Linaro (near Cesena) from the bishop of Sarsina. Monte Cavallo, subject to the bishop of Sarsina, was occupied on May 18, and then Bagnoli, held by Sarsina for the Archbishop of Ravenna. On the 23rd he attacked Meldola, held for the Pope by Paoluccio da Calboli.[59] Only here was his expansion halted. Meldola fell, but Benedict XII sent the treasurer of Romagna to Florence, to secure aid from that commune. The counter-attack came in September, and seemed at one moment on the verge of failure through lack of money to pay soldiers taken into service by the Church. On the 22nd, the treasurer of Romagna was writing to his opposite number in the Patrimony, in tones of desperation, 'Dear Lord and friend, I am in such bewilderment and need that I am unable to write patiently to you : for I fear that through lack of money, the Roman Church will lose its honour in this siege of

Meldola '.[60] With the aid of the Florentines, the Church recovered this particular village, but there the momentum of its attack expired, not to be revived. The Archbishop of Ravenna, in the following year, encountered no less humiliation in his attempt to recover Oriolo, taken from him in 1335. Sinibaldo and Francesco seized his person, stripped him to his shirt, tied him backwards upon an ass, and led him in triumph to Forlì.[61]

In the years that followed, nothing is known of Francesco's internal rule over his territories but externally he showed all his customary vigour. He allied, in 1342, with Luchino Visconti and the Gonzaga, against Florence and Arezzo, and conducted the dreaded Company of Werner Urslingen, then in Visconti pay, into the Romagna. With their support he was able to beat off the attack of the Rector on Cesena and Forlì in October of that year.[62] Five years later, when Lewis of Hungary passed through the province, it was Francesco who was his principal host, receiving him with an escort of 200 knights and 500 foot. Francesco with his sons was knighted by the king and followed in his service to Naples; but he was forced to return by an attack upon Forlì by the papal rector. He was temporarily reconciled to the Church, but in February 1350 he gave aid to the rebellion of Giovanni Manfredi, and together with him again called the company of Urslingen into Romagna. Taking advantage of the confusion in the province, he besieged Bertinoro, and, in July 1350, seized the other chief papal centres in the *contado*: Meldola, Castrocaro, and Castelnuovo.[64] Then he mounted an attack against the Conticino Malatesta of Giaggiolo and Count Carlo of Dovadola in a curious alliance with the Abbot of Galeata, from whom Malatesta held properties for which he refused service. In these actions, Francesco, with his son, Ludovico, took Fontanafredda and Cusercoli.[65] At the end of this campaign, he assisted the Visconti attack on Imola in 1351.

The advent of Cardinal Albornoz, who renewed his excommunication, found Francesco undismayed. He believed 'that the skies had rather thunder to affright than lightning to strike'[66] and he proved the soul of the resistance to the papal army. He tried to unite the lords of the Marche and Romagna against the papal threat, and visited the Emperor Charles IV at Florence, in an attempt to persuade him to favour their cause. However, Albornoz' grants of vicariate to the Malatesti and da Polenta, the Emperor's caution before the papacy, and the weak support given by Faenza to the Manfredi, left Francesco isolated. None the less he determined to resist even the army of Albornoz.

Francesco, it was said, had called the Council of Sapientes at the coming of the Cardinal. They told him that the affection and loyalty which the people of Forlì felt for him was unchanged. But the Church was strong, and they were alone: they advised him to seek for terms. Francesco's answer was uncompromising: 'Now I want you to listen to my plan. I do not intend to make any agreement with the Church unless Forlì and the other places I now hold are to stay in my hands, and these I propose to hold and defend to the death: first Cesena and its *contado*, then Forlimpopoli, and if these are lost, the walls of Forlì, and if the walls are lost, its streets and squares, and then this palace of mine, and finally the last tower upon it, before a single one of them shall be given up with my consent.'[67] This determination was not mere foolhardiness; in Forlì at least, Francesco had the support of the citizens, and externally he possessed the alliance of the Visconti, and of the Great Company who were dependent upon Visconti gold. Even Florence was seeking to mediate on his behalf.[68]

Cesena, however, was not enthusiastic for the cause of the Ordelaffi. Francesco's wife, Cia degli Ubaldini, mounted on horseback, and clothed in armour, defended the town, 'with more than a man's courage and energy', but the townspeople themselves were hostile, and rose against her. She retreated into the citadel of the upper part of the town, seized and executed the two ringleaders of the opposition, and vented her rage by burning the campanile of the Cathedral and the houses standing around. Exposed to the attack of eight mangonels, she still held out. To the plea of her father, Giovanni da Susinana degli Ubaldini, that she could surrender now with honour; she replied with scorn: 'My father, when you gave me to my lord, you told me to obey him before all else. I have done this till now, and I mean to do so till I die. He entrusted this town to me, ordering me not to surrender it for any reason except in his presence, or by his secret command. As long as I obey his commands, I care nothing for death, or anything else.' Cia was faithful to her words, and only yielded at the insistence of her followers, after the castle had been undermined by the besiegers, and was about to collapse. Cesena was completely in the hands of Albornoz by the end of June 1357. Cia was imprisoned in Ancona, but the resistance of her husband continued.[69]

In September, Albornoz, who championed a strong anti-Visconti policy against the Papal Curia, who sought to appease their ambitions, was relieved of his post, and replaced by Andrion de la Roche, Abbot of Cluny. The appointment was unfortunate.

Androin was incompetent; the Visconti seemed irreconcilable, and Francesco Ordelaffi continued to resist successfully.

As the months went on, he began to doubt the ability of his townspeople to continue independent resistance, and, with secret Visconti connivance, he called in the mercenary migrant army of the Great Company. The licence of these troops alienated the Forlivesi, and revealed, as Villani with his customary smugness observed: 'the error of a mistaken and servile people who through gross stupidity wasted an unreasoning affection upon their lords and tyrants.'[70] In was in this situation that Albornoz was re-appointed to the legation, in September 1358, and began to wear down the town by constant attacks.

As a result, Francesco was finally forced to surrender, 3 July 1359. In the following week he made public confession of his sins, implored mercy, and was sent on an expiatory pilgrimage to the churches of Faenza. The legate absolved him, and seems to have planned to invest him with the vicariate of Forlimpopoli and Castrocaro.[71] But the old enemy of the Church was not so easily tamed or satisfied. By the end of the year he had deserted to the Visconti, and was established as their captain at Lugo, where he served with distinction in the Milanese cause. With the end of the Visconti–Papal war, he remained in the service of Bernabò, and acted as his lieutenant at Cremona in January 1368. He died in exile at Chiozza in 1374.[72]

Within twelve years his family had won back control of Forlì. Cardinal Grimoard had warned his successor as rector, that

> This town like others is divided between Guelfs and Ghibellines. The Ghibellines are powerful among the great of the town, and have an inner eye open to the Lord Francesco. I know very well that these Ghibellines want him to recover the lordship, for they have been ill-treated in their goods and persons. They may seem to be quite content with the Church now, but none the less the town is not wholly to be trusted . . . there is innate hostility between parties. It should be ruled with the utmost caution and care, and with a strong force of soldiers. . . . This town is suspect for all time through its predilections which I have mentioned. . . . There is so much diversity and astuteness in Francesco degli Ordelaffi and his followers, that it is impossible to be overcautious.[73]

These forebodings proved all too well founded. In the War of the Eight Saints Forlì rose spontaneously against the Church in December 1375. The Guelfs of the town sought a free commune, and the Ghibellines, under Giuliano Numai, a doctor of medicine from an old Forlivese family,[74] declared for the rule of

Sinibaldo, the son of Francesco. As a result, two deputations went from the town to Florence to seek alliance. The city replied courteously to both. To the Guelfs, the 'Eight', on 6 January 1376, explained that nothing was dearer to their hearts than freedom, and freedom for all peoples. They had, it was true, sent Sinibaldo degli Ordelaffi to Forlì, but only in the hope of pleasing them, and as a result of a deputation claiming to be acting on behalf of the town's General Council. Two days later, however, the news came that Sinibaldo, with his nephews Cecco and Pino, had seized power. In their letter to the family, congratulating them on this achievement, the 'Eight' made no further impolitic references to freedom. They wrote instead that they had learnt with the greatest pleasure that the people had recognised the Ordelaffi as lords. They exhorted them to forget old injuries, their exile and the confiscation of their property, and to reflect, rather, with compassion, on the injustice and expense to which their fellow citizens had been recently exposed.[75]

Unfortunately, Sinibaldo had already gone against the spirit of this admirable, if somewhat academic advice. 110 houses of Guelf families had been sacked and destroyed; and their owners killed or exiled.[76] By these means, the Ordelaffi firmly re-established their power in the town, and in February 1379 the papacy, helpless, was forced to concede them the vicariate of Forlì, Forlimpopoli, and Sarsina.[77] Two years later, the bodies of Francesco and his wife Cia were brought back to Forlì and buried, 'in la spoltura digl' altri Ordelaffi, ai fra' menori, dove senpre in quella era la uxada; la quale è sotta una antiga capela de Santo Andrea, antigamente degl' Ordelaffi'.[78]

VI

In this chapter, the final stage in the creation of the Romagnol *signorie* has been indicated: the course of political events, in which the *signori* obtained, first, the captaincies, and then the grants of vicariate, over their communes. But, as had already been suggested, the structure of government in Romagna was intimately bound up with, and shaped by society. Land tenure, credit facilities, economic strength and weakness, played as large a part in the triumph of the new rule, as did the strength or weakness of the papacy. In the following pages, then, we must consider the life of the town and countryside of this era, the permanent elements behind the political struggles.

CHAPTER VI

The Countryside

> Looking at all ways of making money, I hold that there is nothing superior to agriculture, nothing, as Cicero observes, more abundant, sweeter, or worthier of a free man. It is in the cultivation of the farm that one finds most easily the peaceful life.
>
> PIERO DE' CRESCENZII[1]

I

FOR the age in which he lived, the words of the Bolognese agriculturalist quoted above ring ironically upon the ear. How, asked Crescenzii, should one choose and furnish a farm? His answer was, ' If you should find yourself in a dangerous neighbourhood, subject to the control of powerful enemies, it is safer to abandon such a place rather than insanely and recklessly to put yourself in a position, where, unless by some chance a Lord with great wealth should be persuaded to build a castle, you will have to prepare yourself for death.' Were there no protection from a Lord and were there robbers and bandits, and you still decided to stay, Crescenzii gives advice on how to fortify the place, with streams, ditches, dykes, hedges, palisades, and a watchtower, ' where the head of the household and his servants may take refuge with their property when there is need '. Try too, he advised, to find some place where they do not often change their lord.[2] It is needless to remark that Romagna was just such an area as Crescenzii had advised his reader to quit.

Yet it is this rural life that was the main preoccupation of the inhabitants of Romagna. The real interest of its chroniclers lay, not in the signorial courts, but first, in the description of supernatural wonders and astrological predictions, and then, second only to these, in the state of the weather, and the harvest. The March snow that destroyed the vines, foot-and-mouth disease, plagues of locusts ; it is with these matters that their annals acquire an immediacy and actuality, often lacking elsewhere.

It was a simple story. In winter, when the snow reached from the high Apennine peaks to the Adriatic shore, the peasants dug the drainage ditches of the woods and fields, stripped the trees for firewood, removed the lichens from the olives, trimmed the vines, and repaired their carts. With the thaw in February, they manured and ploughed their fields. Then spring came, and with it the pruning and planting of the vines, the planting of trees, the sowing of the March grain, the flax, beans, millet, and hemp, and the digging of the kitchen gardens. In May and June they ploughed again, planted hawthorn hedges, clipped the sheep, mowed the meadows, hoed and reaped the corn, and formed the stooks in the fields. Then in high summer, under a heat relieved only by sudden thunderstorms, they cut the flax, brought the grain to the granary, hoed the vines, and cut the hemp. Lupins were sown that they might be ploughed into the field as fertiliser. With autumn, there was ploughing again, and the digging out of the corn roots before ploughing, there was the threshing of the corn ears on the granary-floor, and the grape harvest. In October and November the fruit trees were stripped, the olives gathered, the honey taken from the hives. Then the cycle recommenced. Placucci, at the beginning of the nineteenth century, described it month by month, in his treatise on the life of the Romagnol peasant, and his description differs only in details from that of Piero Crescenzii, who was judge in Imola at the end of the thirteenth century. Indeed it differed little from the agricultural practice of Roman times. ' Our contadini,' wrote Placucci, and the words are not mere rhetoric, ' instructed by their elders, know the practical execution of what Virgil with sublime mastery taught in his Georgics.'[3]

The workers of the land in the province can be divided into four principal classes. First were the *fideles* of the mountains, holding land from aristocratic or feudal authorities. These will be discussed when considering the feudal estates. Second were those fortunate enough to have secured their land at long lease.

In this class of lease, annual rents were generally low, and profit to the lessor was mainly derived from the re-entry fine, paid at the renewal of the lease on its expiry after twenty-nine, forty-eight, sixty, or sixty-eight years. In 1301, the monastery of San Severo, for instance, renewed for sixty years a lease of one *tornatura*, one *pertica*, four feet and six inches of land for an entry fine of eight shillings and a rent of a penny a year. Again, the same monastery leased one *tornatura* for sixty years, for an entry fine of fifteen shillings and an annual rent of one ounce of wax. Sometimes the leases were given in return for a food rent. Thus the monastery of San Severo leased land for a third of a *staio* of grain rent, and an entry fine of eight shillings.[4] These leases were renewable, and could be freely alienated ; with time they came to be virtual freeholds. For this reason, when ecclesiastical authorities granted leases in the thirteenth and fourteenth centuries, they always explained why they were doing so, and stressed that no other course was open to them. Often they obtained the permission of the bishop to alienate their lands in this way.

The third type of peasant was the man holding land on share-cropping tenure. In this system, the peasant held his land in return for the annual presentation of part of his crops to the landlord. The share of the produce of the land to be given to the landlord varied from place to place. A Bolognese decree of 1376 ordained that it should not be greater than 75 per cent. Statutory enactments of the Romagnol communes laid down that a peasant, holding land under this tenure, had to give ' half, or more, or less, according to the contract '. Normally, the return of crops due to the landlord was a half, and in this case, was known as *mezzadria*. In these contracts the proprietor gave the peasant a piece of land, and half the seed necessary for its sowing. In return, he received half the produce of the land. If the proprietor also gave a house with the land, then the lessee himself had normally to deliver the lord's portion of the crops to wherever it was required of him. All the statutes of the Romagnol communes guaranteed these contracts, and offered support to the landlord in securing their performance. Workers of the land, it was decreed, were not to thresh or reap corn, collect the grape harvest, nor even glean from the stubble without the permission of the proprietor. They were forbidden to sow without previously ploughing the land four times,[5] and each time they ploughed and manured the land they were supposed to inform the lord, so that he could inspect the fields, and see if the work had been satisfactorily performed. If they failed to inform the proprietor before ploughing, they could be forced to plough again, whether the ploughing had been satisfactory or not. Threshing had to be carried out in the proprietor's granary, in the presence of his agent. The peasants were bound to maintain the ditches of their fields, and, if the lord required it, had to plant two trees a year for every *tornatura* of land they held from him. All these decrees were aimed at ensuring the efficient working of the land, that the proprietor might receive a sufficient return upon his investment. If peasants worked the land badly, failed to manure it, or worked it otherwise than was decreed in the statutes, they had to give the lord the equivalent value of what the land would have produced, had it been worked well.

Contracts of *mezzadria* were sometimes drawn up for a fixed period, sometimes indefinitely. In the case of indefinite tenure for an unspecified time, the peasant was bound to give notice of his intention to quit, at least a month before the grain harvest. Otherwise he assumed the liability of working the land, under the same tenure, for the following year. Were he to quit his farm, having assumed this obligation, he was liable to the payment of damages. If holding under a fixed tenure, he was required to vacate his land, without opposition, at the end of his lease.

To argue on the merits of *mezzadria* is to enter contemporary Italian politics. One or two observations may be made, however, about its operation within the era of the communes. The supervision of the proprietor made for more efficient farming. Again, the proprietor filled an important function in the provision of seed. To sow half a *tornatura* required up to a *staio* of corn.[6] On the other hand, peasants naturally would have preferred a lease in return for a fixed rent, without the burdensome control of the landlord and the heavy due on the land. But the property-owners of the town communes in the fourteenth century sought to convert all land to *mezzadria*. In Bologna, it was decreed, in 1376, that there were to be no further leases at fixed rents, because the attempts of peasants to change from sharecropping ' might bring no small damage to proprietors '. In Romagna, Ravenna had gone further, and by 1360 seems to have decreed that all lessees of immobile goods were to return them to their owners.[7] As a result, probably most of the land, in the plain at least, was farmed at *mezzadria* by the end of the fourteenth century. But many pockets of lease-holding at fixed rent must have survived. As late as 1536, the statutes of Forlimpopoli made provision for proprietors who wished to change their land from fixed rent to *mezzadria*.[8]

The last class of agricultural worker, and the most unfortunate, was the day labourer. The statutes of Faenza show these men waiting to be hired each morning, in the piazza of San Pietro (as they still do today) and tell us the maximum wages they were to be paid. Labourers were to receive seven shillings from mid-March to mid-April, five shillings from 1 November to 28 February, and six shillings from 1 March to mid-March. They were instructed to go straight to work and not to return until the hour of the closing of the town gates. Mowers were to be paid ten shillings, and their expenses, for each day they worked in May, and seven shillings in August and September. Reapers of corn were to be paid seven shillings, and threshers six shillings a day, and their expenses. These prices were laid down, ostensibly ' to stop immoderate disputes over payment.' These wages were high, but work was purely seasonal. In the communal era there were insufficient day labourers in peak periods of the year, and wide-scale unemployment for the remainder of the time. This phenomenon has lasted into modern times ; today Romagna has still the highest level of agrarian 'under-employment' in Italy.[9]

II

In the Romagnol countryside it is possible to distinguish three basic units in this period ; first the feudal villages ; then the independent larger *castelli* ; and finally, the small rural communes formed from the countless hamlets of the province.

(a) *The Feudal Estates*

The feudal estates were those owned directly by ecclesiastical or lay proprietors. Obviously these lords differed much in importance. Some, like the houses of the Conti Guidi, the da Dovadula, da Bagno, the Ubertini and the Ubaldini were connected primarily with Tuscany, and after the thirteenth century played no important role in Romagnol life. Had they, like Maghinardo Pagani, resisted the temptation to dabble in the political life of Florence, they might well, with their wealth and possessions, have lorded it in Romagna as he did, and as much lesser families were going to do. But the lure of the city on the Arno, the prizes which were offered there, caused them to abandon a serious possibility of power, for a vain hope of dominion in a wider field.

Together with these, there were a whole series of obscure and petty nobles. Cardinal Anglic's description of the province in 1371 records scores of small feudatories holding single castles. There were Lollio and Cione, for example, who held Certalto with its *palatium forte* and its thirty-five hearths, near Macerata, between the Conca and Foglia valleys, or Dondaccio della Fontana, holding Petragudola (' with a very strong rocca, 35 hearths ') from the Count of Montefeltro, above the Marecchia on the Rimini–San Sepolchro road on which he exacted toll.[10]

Life in remote places like these, by

the forked rocks of Penna and Billi, on Carpegna
with the road leading under the cliff,
in the wind-shelter into Tuscany,
And the north road ; towards the Marecchia
the mud-stretch full of cobbles . . .[11]

seems bounded by the line of the mountains all around. Here was a society not unlike that of the eighteenth-century Friuli, portrayed in Nievo's *Confessioni di un Italiano*, with an illiterate lord, and a quasi-literate chaplain, with mud choking the courtyard of the castle, the dogs lying across the rushes in the hall, and a sullen, subject village commune. The household of a great lord would be more elaborate, but the basic pattern was the same. The will of Maghinardo Pagani, gives some information. He left money to his notary ' Mazzolo, my old and most faithful servant ' who had acted as his chancellor, and would have kept his seal.[12] He freed his cook, Rainuccio, and the cook's relatives, from all obligations as *fideles* and asked his daughter Francesca to look after them. Money was left to thirteen other personal servants, including three squires, a muleteer, and a groom. All were asked to stay with his daughters. Finally, instructions were given that his three horses, Fanestro, Caprana, and Palfredo, were to be sold.

The concern of the lord for his *fideles* shown in Maghinardo's will was not universal. The murder of the family of Corrado di Petra Rubea by his serfs has already been noted. Other brief references in the chronicles suggest that in Romagna, as elsewhere, agrarian war was the inevitable concomitant of feudalism. In April 1316, for instance, ' certain rustics ' attacked and killed a party of aristocrats near Poggio de la Lastra. In 1348, the vassals of Count Galeotto de' Conti Guidi rose up against him, ' in that for a long time he had treated them ill, and also for his dissolute life '.[13]

None the less, the impression remains that violence in the province was still principally played out within families. The affair of the Count of Giaggiolo, in May 1360, is typical. He had fought with Albornoz, and was then over sixty years old. Yet his sons were fearful of the influence of his concubine Rosina. So they imprisoned him, seized his property for themselves, threw Rosina into the River Cusercoli, with a stone around her neck, and drove her bastards from the castle.[14]

In fact, their behaviour caused an outcry, yet such passages induce doubt that there ever existed that feudal paradise painted by Dante, with :

> le donne e i cavalieri, gli affani e gli agi
> che ne invogliava amore e cortesia.

Something of a chivalric spirit there was. It showed itself, chiefly, at the solemn feasts of the nobility, such as that given by the

Count of Montefeltro in honour of the knighting of one of his sons, when St. Francis came to the castle, and preached there, 'so that all stood with their eyes and ears fixed on him, listening as though an angel of God were speaking.'[15] In June 1324 at the feast for the knighting of the Malatesti and other nobles, at Rimini, 'there was great triumph, for honour of which came there Florentines, Perugians, Senesi, Bolognesi, and all the nobles and powers of Tuscany, the Marche, Romagna, and nearly all Lombardy'. The Provençal Rector, Aimeric de Chatelus, who was present, cannot have felt himself so very far removed from the traditions of his own land.[16] But these moments cannot have been common.

Some of the landed power of the Lords of Romagna had arisen through direct imperial enfeoffment. In 1220, for instance, Frederick II invested Uberto, Count of Castelnuovo, with the castle of the same name; while in confirming the rights of the Ravenna church in the same year, he specifically excluded those enfeoffments made within Romagna by the empire.[17] Again, a Bull of Innocent IV to his nephew, Tommaso da Fogliano, told him that William, King of the Romans, had enfeoffed him and his successors of lands in Cervia and Bertinoro, 'iure feudi, seu in feudum sicut domini feudatorii'.[18] Most of the lands of the Conti Guidi and the Counts of Montefeltro were held, at least theoretically, from the Empire, and when, during the fourteenth century, emperors appeared in Italy, the counts would go to them for confirmation of their holdings.[19] After 1279, the papacy took over this imperial right. Benedict XII, for example, wrote in 1336 to the rector of Romagna, ordering him to invest Albertaccio di Bindato Ricasoli with Premilcuore and Montevecchio Rocche. Eugenius IV, in 1441, asked the Bishop of Bertinoro if it would be expedient to enfeoff Antonio Assassini with Montigliano, previously possessed by 'certain nobles of the Malatesti'.[20] Right up to the Napoleonic abolition of feudalism in 1797, and especially from the sixteenth century, these papal enfeoffments were to be of great importance in establishing the proprietary map of the province. Even in the middle ages they had considerable effect.

Sometimes the abbeys and episcopacies gave land in the same way. In 1248, Archbishop Teodorico of Ravenna enfeoffed land in the Imolese and near Argenta to Pietro Forza: 'iuravit fidelitatem dando eidem de dicto feudo cum uno baculo investitionem cum introitu et exitu suo'. The fief was given, 'per feudum et iure feudi ad usum Regni et hoc sub sacramento fidelitatis'.[21] But the most characteristic form of feudal lease was that known as emphyteutic : the long lease, generally for three lives. This had become automatically renewable and hereditary. From the tenth and eleventh centuries such contracts covered the whole of Romagna, and their effect was to remove control over the land, from the great churches of Ravenna, to the feudatories and communes. These emphyteutic leases, generally at nominal rents, alienated to the lessees all but the vaguest proprietary rights, and imposed none of the obligations of military service exacted in other feudal societies.

With the grant of these lands went the grant of the men who dwelt upon them ; at the ceremony of investiture in which the notary would give the new lord corporeal possession, the vassals were called to the castle to take oaths of fidelity.[22]

It is useful to give some examples. In the fourteenth century the Calisese family of Cesena paid an annual rent of one Ravennate shilling to the monastery of San Lorenzo in Ceserea, for ' the *castello* of Monte Crepato and its whole court *cum zuppa et monte* '.[23] In the fifteenth century Simone and Filippo, of the same family, were paying four pounds of wax annually to the monastery of Classe, for Castel Pergola, with its court and lands, and Castel Quarada.[24] In 1351, the Bishop of Sarsina leased emphyteutically the considerable lands, that had once belonged to the Onesti family in Sarsina, to Malatestino di fu Manfredo di Valbona, for an entry fine of £B.25, and an annual payment of one ounce of new wax and six Ravennati pennies.[25] Again, in 1416, Bishop Zanfilippo of Sarsina leased to Carlo di Lappi of Cesena the *castello* of Linaro, ' with its men and serfs, rights and dignities ', for an entry fine of fifty gold ducats, and an annual pension of two knives in a sheath, to the value of 2s. 6d.[26] Even when the male line of a family of lessees had expired, as had happened to the Onesti, it was almost impossible for the ecclesiastical landlord to take over his proprietary rights. When they attempted to do so, their failure only emphasised their impotence.

In the thirteenth century almost all forms of ascription to the glebe were abolished. It was difficult to administer on any servile basis estates which were scattered piecemeal throughout the province, and there was already a shortage of agricultural labour. The towns were not only willing but eager to accept as a citizen any peasant who came to them, provided only that he was not a serf from their own *contado*. In 1271 two men promised at Ravenna to be ' peasants and continual dwellers in the district of Ravenna '. In return, they with their heirs, were promised exemption from all financial and other burdens for a hundred years. They swore that they were not 'vassals or serfs of anyone from Ravenna or its district'. The document recording this transaction preserves a discreet silence on whether they were the serfs of anyone else.[27] In Rimini a marble stone was placed in the *loggia* of the Palazzo Comunale, inscribed with the declaration that all serfs who lived in the town for a year and a day were to be free. The serfs of Riminesi alone were excepted.[28]

In this manner, even on monastic estates, pure serfdom withered away.

The process was uneven. Sometimes the freedom of the former serf was not absolute. Cash rents were imposed upon him; he was given a personality in law; and yet certain *angaria* or days of free work for the landlord remained. When the canons of Faenza liberated a serf in 1220, the land he had worked was leased to him for sixty years. The conditions imposed were a payment of £R.12 as entry fine, and a yearly rent of three shillings; in addition he gave 'a work and a half' with his oxen each year and 'a work and a half' without oxen. Finally, he gave the Chapter six *mezzeni* of grain every first day of August, and four *corbe* of wine at the time of harvest.[29] Gradually, however, such agreements were superseded by twenty-nine, forty-eight or sixty year leases, or by contracts of *mezzadria*. Occasionally men still promised themselves as serfs, but the general tendency was towards enfranchisement.[30] The mid-thirteenth-century statutes of Ravenna reveal a system of ascription to the glebe still in existence; rustics who fled their farms were to be returned; and only after a full five years of successful undiscovered flight to a town, could a serf be considered as a free man; should a serf die without sons, his lord took half his inheritance. But in the statutes of 1327, these provisions were no longer found; serfdom had given way to new forms of lease.

Pure serfdom, then, was dying; yet a form of vassalage continued to flourish in the province, especially in the *montagna*. This was the service given by *fideles*, men not bound to the soil, but generally holding their lands on emphyteutic leases, in return for certain military and other obligations. By the *Paradisum* of 1256, Bologna annulled the service of *fideles*, alongside all other servile tenures. But the frequent repetition of decrees, throughout the fourteenth century, abolishing contractual renewals of serfdom, suggest that, even here, military feudalism continued to have a vigorous life.[31] In Romagna, the statutes of Forlì of 1359, and of Faenza of 1410, prohibited anyone from swearing fidelity as a vassal, or receiving such homage in future.[32] But they did not specifically annul existing contracts, and it is improbable that they had ever any real validity. In 1352, 1372, and 1374, men were swearing 'fidelitatem, servitutem et vassalaticum' to the da Polenta.[33] As late as 1411, the Bishop of Sarsina received a promise of fidelity, incorporating the feudal obligations, while in the eighteenth century, the chancellery of the bishopric contained formulas, still in use, for the investment of fiefs, and the swearing of fidelity by vassals.[34]

The general characteristics of this form of tenure may be illustrated by a document of 1331, in which one Cecharello Nardi promised, on his behalf and on behalf of his male legitimate heirs, to be faithful and obedient to Lippo degli Alidosi, his sons, heirs, and successors. 'In name of fief, lease, or servitude'[35] he agreed to pay each year on the feast of St. Mary in the month of August three-quarters of a *staio* of corn to Lippo or his factor.[36] He further promised to do guard and *castellan* duties, whenever his lord wished, and to form part of his lord's fighting force at his own expense, as often as he should be called upon to do so.[37] Finally, he swore to answer all the obligations imposed upon him by his lord's powers of jurisdiction.[38] These threefold obligations — of food-rent, military service, and judicial service — it is explained, arose from the fact that Cecherello had formerly owed all these 'real and personal services' to Cando de' Malavolti of Bologna, 'both through purchase and age old custom', and that Malavolti's rights had been granted to Lippo Alidosi through purchase.

This is not the invariable form of such contracts. In 1399 a man swore vassalage only 'for the next ten years'.[39] But most contracts probably embodied the three principal obligations, and were binding upon all male legitimate heirs of the man who swore vassalage.

The vassals of each village subject to a lord were organised, or organised themselves, into a rural commune, in the same way as the other villages of the province. When a village had two lords, it formed two communes, co-existing territorially over the same area. In 1428, for instance, Florence noted that the commune of Tredozio, in the Romagnol Apennines, which had belonged to Malatesta de' Conti Guidi da Dovadula, was composed of eighteen houses and families, and that these were intermingled with the houses and families of the commune of Montesecco, subject to Florence, despite the fact that 'many men of the two communes are of the same people and parish'.[40]

Apart from such executive tasks as the equitable allocation of taxation imposed from above, or the appointment of rural police, these communes had little power of independent action, and were firmly subject to their lords. The grant by Archbishop Teodorico of Ravenna, in 1238, permitting the men of Tuderano to have consuls and a commune, explicitly forbade them to interfere in any way with the marketing of corn and wine outside the village. It allowed the *homines* to appoint *saltuarii* (agrarian police) to arrange for the imposition of taxes, and such other trivialities as the punishment of theft to the value of ten Ravennati shillings. On the estates of the Archbishop of Ravenna in 1298, six men called the ' defenders ' of the commune of Oriolo, ' under the vault of the house of Donato of Oriolo, where he gives judgment ', asked the *gastald* or factor of the archbishop for confirmation of the statutes they had drawn up for the village, ' for it was not convenient that the commune and men of Oriolo should be without statutes '. In reply the *gastald* had to refer them to the ' chamberlain and other greater officials ' of the episcopate. In another instance, in 1376, the archbishop actually imposed statutes on the rural commune of Monte Colombo. Among other provisions — the prohibition of swearing, of carrying arms etc. — these established a council of sixteen men from the village. The consuls of the commune were to be responsible for its debts.[41]

Of course, the communes could revolt against their lords. In 1299, the bishop of Faenza excommunicated the men of Oriolo for rebelling against the archbishop. He named twenty-one men, who ' with the whole of the said *castello* and its subject villages, hostilely, under arms, with their flag, to the sound of the bell ', had attacked both him and Archbishop Obizzo of Ravenna. With almost masochistic emphasis, he dilated on how the two of them had had to seek shelter in a house, how the house had been set on fire, how tiles and stones had been thrown down upon them, and bricks hurled through the windows, while, the whole time, the cry of ' Let them die!' had risen against them and their servants.[42] Yet it must have been easier to revolt against an ecclesiastical than against a lay landlord ; and in neither case would revolt have any permanent effect.

Within each family, the feudal properties were subject to intensive subdivision by inheritance. It has been noticed, previously, that there was no rule of primogeniture, such as was characteristic of later northern feudal law. Almost all properties were held *pro indiviso* between heirs. As an example, the inventory of properties held by Ottaviano degli Ubaldini, in 1371, might be cited ; properties principally inherited from the Pagani. These consisted of :

The whole of Castel Visano, with its court and district (the court being the area of the countryside subject to the village) ;
7/12ths of the Village of Salecchia — with territory, court, and district ; 'quas septem partes habet et tenet pro indiviso partim et partim pro indiviso ab heredibus et cum heredibus' of Ugolino Tano and Maffei Oddi degli Ubaldini ;
The village of Piedemonte, with its court and district ; a fulling mill with its two beams, on the river Senno at the place called La Prisaglia ;
¼ part *pro indiviso* of the *pedagium* (exaction of tolls upon the road) of Palazzuolo, taken at the place called Villiano ;
½ *pro indiviso* of all *pedagia* exacted in the court of Castel Pagano ;
Goods and properties pertaining to him in Borgo Palazzuolo ;
¼ part *pro indiviso* of the villages and courts of Castel Ozzole ;
A house in Castel Pagano, and an orchard around it.

Ottaviano's rights in these places were summarised as ; 'omagium fidelitatem, afictum [lease], censuum [the levying of dues], pedagium, toloneum [toll], dirictus [supervision?] aqueductum [water rights] et patronatum [ecclesiastical patronage] et cum mero et mixto imperio et omni etiam gladii potestate [full judicial and political control]'.[43]

To give another example ; in May 1349, Imeldina de' Medici, widow of Guido da Salutare, recognised Niccolo di Burniolo di Campalmonte, husband of her sister Agnesina, as her heir to

⅓ part of Castel Montefiore — held *pro indiviso* by the Medici with the nobles of Campalmonte and the nobles of Mongiardino ;
Lands in Cavina, Campalmonte and Pagano — held *pro indiviso* with the nobles of Campalmonte, Montefiore and Battaglia ;
⅓ part of rights in Montebattaglia — held *pro indiviso* with nobles of Campalamonte, Montefiore and Battaglia ;
⅓ part of *fideles* of Campalmonte.[44]

The holding of properties *pro indiviso* obviously implied considerable difficulties for their owners ; difficulties, it has been seen, which were often resolved by bloodshed. In happier circumstances, they gave rise to complex settlements between the part owners. In 1369, for example, following disputes within the Alidosi family, Galeotto Malatesta acted as arbiter in an equal division of their properties. The division took place between that half of the family that held *signoria* : that is to say, the sons of Roberto : Azzo and Beltrando, for the one part, and the sons of Roberto's brother, Massa, for the other. First the fortifications of the family were divided. One side of the family received the Rocca of Castel del Rio, the Torre del Ponte della Massa, and the Torre Antica di Linaro. The other was given the Rocca of Monte della Fine, and Castiglione. Lots were to be cast to decide which group of property each side should hold. With Castiglione were included all the *fideles* and jurisdictions of Squaranibolo. Except in the *curia* of Visignano, and at Castelvecchio, no new fortresses might be constructed. In fact, in the drawing of lots, the Beltrando branch must have obtained Castiglione and its linked properties, and the Massa branch, Castel del Rio, for these they were noted as holding in 1371.

The 'jurisdictio, merum et mistum imperium' of all the territories described above were to be held in common, as were all the revenues from them, except, as has been noted, in Castiglione and its court, in which the 'iurisdicio imperii' and revenues were to belong exclusively to the lord who obtained it by lot. Similarly, the revenues of the *dazii* and *gabelles* were to be in common.

There followed, then, the division of the 'fideles seu vassales' with their farms, in the various properties of the Alidosi. The names of the heads of each family, together with their brothers, sons, and grandsons were given, and divided between the two branches of the Alidosi. The result of this division may be summarised thus:

	To the sons of Roberto	To the sons of Massa
From Osta	36	21
Massa Alidosia	72	80
Visignano	23	46
Nuncio	7	7
Valsalva	3	4
Belvedere	20	22
	(161)	(180)

Following this an unspecified number of all the *fideles* of Carburacia, with all the farms and leases of that place were given to the sons of Roberto. Similarly, in Budrignano and Barisano, all rights were given to the sons of Massa and Giacomo.

There followed further divisions. In the Mercatale of the Massa Alidosia, the sons of Roberto received seven houses, a cottage, and a chestnut orchard. Then there was a further division of farms and inhabitants, in Massa and Osta, presumably of men holding land, not as *fideles*, but by other tenure.

In the administration of the Alidosi estates, the revenues, as distinct from the military service of the vassals, were to be held in common (apart, of course, from the properties in the Mercatale and in the court of Castiglione.) Two vicariates were created by Galeotto, one for the Massa Alidosia, and the *montagna*, the other for Linaro. Each branch of the family appointed a vicar to one of the vicariates in alternate years ; thus the Massa branch in the first year would appoint to Linaro, while the Roberto branch would appoint to Massa Alidosia. Each vicar would swear allegiance in the hands of all members of the Alidosi family.[45]

In the plain, the properties of the aristocracy were run as demesne farms, rather like the *cascina* (or fortified fortress farm) of today. It was this form of farming which Crescenzii had in mind in his treatise on agriculture. Typical was the dowry assigned to Parisina Malatesta in 1419. It consisted of two principal blocks ; first Torre di Gualdo, and then Poggio Berni. Torre di Gualdo, a village in the parish of San Pietro in Campito, on the main road just outside Rimini, consisted of 111 *tornature* of ploughland, three *tornature* of meadow, where wild boar had been kept, and eleven *tornature* of woods. There was a central compound, fortified by a ditch with two houses inside. Outside was a large farm building, divided into seven parts, where the farm labourers lived, and a threshing floor. Beside it were six other houses. On the road itself stood the *hospitium*, probably the residence of the lord, which had a garden, a well, an oven for baking, and stabling for between thirty-five and forty horses. At Poggio Berni, there was a fortified house, with thirty-five *tornature* of vineland, and forty *tornature* of olives. The lord of this farm had full civil jurisdiction over the inhabitants, and could fine or beat those accused of criminal offences. More severe punishments would have to be referred to Rimini.[46]

The estates in the fourteenth century were administered by the private vicar, or *gastald*, of the *signore*, with the title of ' officialis et custos generalis ' or ' factor et Gastaldus et negotiorum gestor '.[47]

These *gastalds* did not administer purely feudal revenues. The noble families also leased land to tenants on non-feudal terms, in return for money rents or rents at *mezzadria*. They rented houses in the towns, owned inns, salt flats, mills, and fulling mills, and exacted rights from the patronage of churches. Yet it would be a mistake to think that economic rather than military power was at the base of their prosperity. Gian Galeazzo Manfredi recognised this when he preceded his statutes for the Val di Lamone with the words from the 121st Psalm : ' levavi oculos meos ad montes unde

Montefiore Conca

veniet auxilium mihi,'[48] — it was the feudal properties which were of prime importance. The feudal properties of the *montagna* were economically poor but they were invaluable politically for the *fideles* owing military service who dwelt upon them. The 404 men that the Onesti owned in the Savio valley in 1292, the 113 *fideles* of Bandino and Guido di Battifolle and the Counts of Modigliana, at Marradi in 1313, even the twenty-five soldiers of Sandro da Campalmonte in 1367,[49] these were the measure of a man's power.

The castles held by the nobles were of considerably less importance. In his description of the province in 1371, Cardinal Anglic Grimoard noted over a hundred *cassara*, *rocche*, *turres*, or *palatia*; but they varied very much in strength. Uguccione da Montebello held Montebello, 'on a very high rock on an impregnable mountain, where there is rocca'. Count Enrico da Corniolo held 'a strong rocca and tower above the high and impregnable mountain' by which he could control the Galeata–Tuscany road. The Abbot of Verghetto held 'a tower, very strong and very apt for war, which dominates the surrounding district'. At Castiglioncho, the Manfredi held a castle with an inner wall, an outer wall, a keep with portcullis, and inaccessible rocks to the south-west.[50] But these owners and their like were the fortunate ones. The impregnability of their castles was almost entirely the work of nature rather than of man.

Probably many of them were merely wooden buildings. But in this period, it is remarkable how easily the strongest fortress crumbled before an attack. The assault on Calboli in 1278 was typical:

> In the said year, Wednesday 6 April, the great man, the Lord Count Guido da Montefeltro, captain of the people and commune of Forlì, made a general attack upon the castle of Calboli, in which castle were enclosed the Lord Ranieri da Calboli and his brother the Lord Guido, and the Lords of Perticeto, and certain others who did not wish to obey the commune of Forlì. They had in that castle over seven hundred experienced men for its defence. The commune of Bologna had given £B.12,000 to the Lord Ranieri that he might be well equipped and might have great store of corn, to defend it for ten months or more. But the commune of Forlì caused seven mangonels to be built there which by day and night, continually, shot into the castle, breaking down and destroying walls and killing its men, so that those within were unable to resist, and came to treat with the commune of Forlì. And leaving the castle, safe in their persons and their goods, which they were allowed to take away, they went off. On Wednesday 1 June, the commune of Forlì ordered the undermining and burning of the castle.[51]

Such notices are very common in the chronicles.

Throughout the era of the struggle for *signoria*, the aristocracy of the *contado* continued to dominate the life of the province. In the fourteenth century they became of lesser importance, as the *condotta*, the hired mercenary soldier, replaced the old feudal *cavalcata*. Yet Romagna's nucleus of *fideles* was to make the province still the principal centre for the recruitment of soldiers, and their military traditions were carried on in the companies of such Romagnols as Alberico da Barbiano and Iacopo Sforza.

After the establishment of the *signoria*, the nobles remained, as adherents of the new powers dominating within the province.[52] But during the fifteenth century many of the families of Dante's era were dying out. By 1500, the male line of the da Polenta, the Nordigli, of the da Dovadula, da Romena, da Modigliana, of the Counts of Giaggiolo, of the Zambrasi, and many others, had all failed, 'Where are Facci, Sigismondi, the Berengarii, the Orgogliosi, the Calboli?', lamented Cobelli, '*tutti alla Morte!*' 'Where are Lettiosi, Ruggiero de Numai, and Pier Maldenti?'[53]

'Mais où est le preux Charlemaigne!'

Cobelli was lamenting the passing of the old and the coming of the new, as Dante had done almost two centuries before.

(b) *The Castelli*

In administrative documents of the age, some of the villages of the *contado* were referred to as *castre*, others as *ville*. There was no invariable distinction between them, but the larger and more important units were almost always called *castra*, and it is these which will be discussed in the following pages. Unfortunately, little documentary evidence of their life remains from the thirteenth and fourteenth centuries, and it is occasionally necessary to draw on later material to give any impression of them. However, this in no way distorts the general picture.

Montefiore Conca, on a hill between the rivers Foglia and Conca, might be taken as typical of the *castelli*. It lies midway on the thirty miles of old road (which today would be considered as a mere track) running between Rimini and Urbino. It was on a principal route to Rome, and was the village at which Rinaldo, in *Orlando furioso*, did not stop:

A Rimino passò la notte ancora
Ne in Monte Fiore aspetta il mattutino
Ma quasi a par col sol Sol giunge in Urbino.

This is its only certain claim to fame. Looking north-east from here, the traveller can see the coastal plain and the towns of Rimini, Riccione, and Cattolica, and beyond, the mountains of Dalmatia across the sea. At all other points of the compass, hills rise up, and to the west, the great mountains of the Apennine range. The *castello* itself was bisected by the Rimini–Urbino road, which struck south over a stone bridge across the Conca. It was encircled by a continuous wall with towers, around which stood the wood of the commune. At each end, the road was guarded by gates, the Porta Romana and the Porta San Martino.[54] In the centre was the piazza, with an inn, the Locanda della Corona,[55] and the Palazzo Comunale.[56] Outside the walls, to the west, the *borgo* or suburb extended. The whole village was dominated from above by a stone castle, with massive *donjon* and outer wall, which could only be entered by the drawbridge to the north.

In a document of 1227, the 'Priors' of Montefiore had promised their landlords, the cathedral canons of Rimini, not to quarrel with the Church, and to submit their statutes for approval. It was probably for this type of negotiation that the commune had originally been formed. The Priors still went in procession each year, on the feast of Corpus Christi, to the parish church of S. Paolo to present twenty candles as recognition of the canons' proprietary rights, and the church itself was in the gift of the canons until the sixteenth century. By 1223, the *castello* was subject to the commune of Rimini, and incorporated within the *balia* of Montescudolo. In the fourteenth century the Malatesti appointed officials, with the title of Captain, to guard it. Consequently its power of independent action was always severely limited.

The *castello* itself had its own little *contado*, extending about four miles north-south, and eight miles east-west, with subject villages, in the same way as the towns of the plain. Its jurisdiction was bounded by the river Conca to the north, and by the frontiers of two other *castelli*, San Clemente and Saludeccio, to the west. The stream called the Ventenna (then flowing along a different route) marked the boundary with Saludeccio, and, further south, divided the jurisdictions of Montefiore from the communes of Mondaino, Cereta, and Tavoletta. To the east, the rule of Montefiore was bounded by the *contado* of Castelnuovo, and to the north-east by that of Gemmano. Most of the subject hamlets, Levora, S. Godenza, S. Felice, Serbadone, Liceto, S. Giovanni in Insula, have today disappeared or changed their names.

The boundaries of the commune corresponded roughly with

the parish of Montefiore, based upon the mother church of S. Paolo, whose incumbent was called the Archpriest, and was normally a canon of Rimini. There was at least one other church in Montefiore itself (called La Majestade del Piano della Porta,) and over ten others scattered through the *contado*. By 1370, the lay 'Society of the Blessed Virgin of Mercy' ran a hospital in the suburb, with a church attached, presided over by a chaplain elected by the confraternity. Within the *contado*, a mile from the village, there was an oratory of the third order of penance and at Monte Faggeto, a Franciscan friary.

By the fifteenth century, the *castello* had its own statutes and seal.[57] It appointed a *podestà*; and two syndicators, chosen by lot 'from the wisest and more prudent men', to supervise him. To assist him, the *podestà* had a knight, called the *Socio* or companion, and two 'chancellors' who acted as judges; one for civil, the other for criminal offences.[58] The chancellor for civil crime had to be a 'foreigner', while his colleague was chosen by lot from names inscribed in the *castello's* list of notaries and doctors of law. Three *plazarii* or messengers served the *podestà*.

Two councils gave the commune a fully representative character. The small *consiglio di credenza* was composed of thirty, and the *consiglio generale* of sixty members (including the thirty of the *credenza*). They were controlled by the five priors, the chief of whom held the seal of the commune and the keys of the gates. Their office lasted two months and was chosen by lot. Nothing was to be proposed in the *credenza*, without the previous approval of the priors. Nothing was discussed in the General Council unless previously approved by a majority of votes in the *credenza*. Without the permission of the priors and *podestà*, no more than five councillors could speak on any motion. Members of both councils were co-opted to bring their numbers to full strength. The *credenza* was not able to spend more than £B.25, nor change any statute without a vote of the General Council.

The General Council had authority to impose taxes and *gabelles*, to name the *podestà*, and to distribute the offices which did not pass by lot. The general councils of the *castelli* acted in all cases where it was necessary for the villages to deal with external authorities. They were the instrument for authorising the submission of the *castello* to the commune of the town or its lord.[59] They discussed disputes with other rural communes and elected procurators or representatives to negotiate with them.[60] They took leases of lands or woods, and discharged their formal obligations to the ecclesiastical proprietors who were technically their landlords.[61] They could also, if necessary, borrow money as a corporate body.[62] At Montefiore, the General Council met at least every fortnight, and more often, if the priors required it. A quorum of two-thirds of its members was necessary.

The *massarius*, or treasurer, was chosen by lot from among the members of the *credenza* and held office for a year. To supervise him there were two *regulatores* or accountants, who were also supposed to see that the boundaries of the commune were preserved. One man looked after the books of the *catasto*, or assessment for land tax, while another preserved the public archives, and registered notarial deeds for the local government. The ' lawyer of the commune and the poor ' was chosen each year by lot. The official of the weights was responsible for the weighing of grain taken to the mill. The council also elected the two *gualdarii* or supervisors from each of the subject villages.

Civil justice was simple. Cases concerned with sums below twenty shillings were dealt with summarily ; with sums between twenty and a hundred shillings within two months ; and over a hundred shillings within four months. Cases between relatives were given to third parties, who acted as compromisers. In each of the various *cappelle*, or administrative divisions within the village, one or two men were appointed to denounce crimes. The *cappelle* too, provided the guards upon the gates. Every two months, two men were appointed to see that there were honest weights and measures in the shops and that the price of food was reasonable. Other officials acted as *saltuarii*, or agrarian police, to prevent damage to crops from wandering beasts. Four of the councillors were appointed as ' Friendly Pacifiers ' of any dispute.

Naturally enough, the statutes seek to defend the local interests of the *castello* against outsiders. It was forbidden to mortgage any goods within the commune to a ' foreigner '. Every outsider had to give security to pay any taxes due and to satisfy creditors. No non-citizen might act as notary within the jurisdiction of the *castello*. Anyone wishing to become ' a citizen ' had first to be approved by a two-thirds majority of the General Council. For three generations, the new citizen would be unable to be a member of the *credenza* or to hold the office of prior. None the less, to encourage settlement, a new emigrant was freed from all the financial and personal burdens of the commune except in time of war. The coldness of this *campanalismo* was matched by a warmth of neighbourliness among the villagers themselves. It was even decreed in the statutes that one person from each family of the *cappella* of a dead man should, under pain of a ten pound fine for non-compliance, attend his funeral (though excessive mourning was forbidden).

The majority of the inhabitants of the *castello* were peasants working land outside its walls. With these there was a small *petite bourgeoisie* composed of notaries, tailors, shoemakers, and shopkeepers. The swift mountain streams were suitable for fulling mills, and many of the *castelli*, like Montefiore, had their weavers and other wool and cloth workers.[63] By the fifteenth century at latest, they had resident families of Jews ; (those from Montefiore are supposed to be the ancestors of the famous London banking family[64]). The *castello* itself, with its market every Thursday, acted as an economic focus for the *ville* of the neighbourhood.[65]

When the Venetian ambassadors visited Montefiore in 1503, their first impression was quite favourable. They estimated that there were about 1,000 inhabitants in the *castello* itself, and another 3,000 in the area around.[66] They were greeted by thirty children, crying out ' Marco, Marco ! ', 400 men carrying arms, and a schoolmaster, who delivered himself of an oration in praise of Venice. ' Li è gente assa' civile ', was the conclusion. But they soon recognised the real poverty of the place. The revenues, in so far as they were recorded, were modest enough ; £60 from fines on damage to agrarian property, £70 from the tax on meat, and £70 from the inn. The *podestà* was paid £12 a month ; and a census of £200 had been paid to the overlord — at that time the pope. ' The inhabitants of this place are most poor, some of them are literate ; the *contadini* are better off.' The General Council was largely composed of peasants. ' The district is abundant in wine and oil and in every other thing except corn, for which there is little land. The *castello* in that year lacked 100 *somme* (equivalent to 160 Venetian *staia*) of grain to feed its population. There were sixty pairs of oxen in the territory, of which thirty-five worked in the lands of Montefiore, and the others in its *contado*.

(c) *The smaller Villages and Hamlets*

In the same way as the *castelli* and the towns of the province, the small villages were organised into communes, called *ville*, or, as in the *contadi* of Ravenna and Faenza, *scole*. These units consisted of all the men of the hamlet who had *locum et focum* ; that is to say, the *homines* : the male heads of all families possessing property sufficient to be valued for taxation. These might be as few as five in number ; even so they would form their own commune. Under the presidency of their *massarius* or head, elected from among their numbers every six months, these rural councils fulfilled the same functions within their own sphere as the larger communes.

The rural commune itself was the legal entity which formally submitted the village to the lordship of the dominant town, and the town kept a tight hold upon its actions. Most of their functions were duties rather than rights. The *massarius* was compelled to keep an ' esteem ', or assessment for the land tax, by which the impositions of the town upon the village might be equitably distributed.[67] He was held responsible for the performance of *corvées*, and for ensuring that the roads of the district were properly maintained. He would report crime to the town, and deliver criminals to its justice. In all, he was the agent, doubtless unwilling, of the central government. Despite the stereotyped formulas of the notaries who recorded their meetings, the councils of the communes, over which the *massarius* presided, were extremely informal. The bell of the church was rung, someone shouted out a reminder, and then the *homines* gathered together in any convenient place in the village. In 1292, Orsara met in the square, Fiagnano in the church of San Giovanni ; Casalfiumanese at the crossroads ; Toranello in the cemetery of the church of San Stefano ; Linaro in the church of San Pietro.[68]

To a certain extent the village communes also dealt with local business of their own. In 1311, the men of Codronco gathered with their *massarius*, ' and the flag of the commune ', to do honour to their bishop. 120 years later, by which time the commune was free of episcopal lordship, the commune was leasing Codroncho for sixty-nine years from the bishop.[69] The commune of Campuino, a village in the *contado* of Imola, near to Orsara, south of the Via Emilia, similarly negotiated with the monastery of Santa Maria in Regola, the payment of its yearly rent of fourpence.[70] The communes also purchased land jointly, bought houses in the town, and leased communal property in return for rent.[71] Again, in time of need they would negotiate loans from Jewish money-lenders.

One of the most important administrative duties of the rural communes was to appoint *saltuarii* or agrarian police. Significantly, for it illustrates their semi-rural character, the towns too, elected these officials. The statutes of Ravenna of 1327 ordained that the men of each village *scola* should elect two *saltuarii*, and that the officials of the town should elect two for each gate of Ravenna, to exercise their office for a year, over all land within five miles of the town.[72] The first responsibility of the *saltuarii* was the preservation of the roads, canals, and ditches of the commune in the countryside. They reported all damage to the officials of the town. They were supposed to preserve bridges, to keep streams free from stones that the waters might flow freely, and preserve the boundary stones of the *scole*. All work of this type, up to a value of £B.5 in the *contado* of Faenza, was done by the *scola* itself. If the cost were greater than £B.5 the work was undertaken by the town commune. Sometimes the work of the *saltuarii* was in part taken over by two *aquaroli* ; these were similarly elected by the *scole* and supervised rivers and dykes.

Another duty of the *saltuarii* was the care of the crops. They prevented damage by stray beasts and reported such damage to the town officials. Those responsible were cited to judgment in the town, to pay fines for the damage according to a fixed scale. The *saltuarii* were also supposed to prevent anyone taking wood belonging to another, to see that dogs wore collars, that ditches were not widened without the consent of the neighbouring proprietor, and that wine was not made before the date laid down for *vindemia*. The office was imposed rather than sought. If damage was done, and those responsible were not reported, half the cost of the offence was borne by the *saltuarii* and the other half by the *scola* itself. Security had to be given before the *saltuarii* assumed their offices ; in the *contado* of Faenza, this was £B.25.

The quality of life in the small hamlets of the province may easily be imagined. The village would consist almost entirely of peasants (as late as 1928, no-one in Casalfiumanese earned his living solely by exercising a trade.[73]) The answers to the Napoleonic inquest on Romagnol folklore show a life basically unchanged for five centuries. ' The inhabitants of this countryside ', wrote the archpriest of Villafranca, ' are wretched but ambitious. They are malicious and obstinate to excess in their thought ; the effect of their complete lack of education and their total ignorance. They are most attached to the religion of their fathers.'[74] Their beliefs were not free from the old pagan ceremonies of centuries before. There were the superstitions of May ; the refusal of the peasants to marry in that month, and the May songs under the window of the loved one. There were the superstitions of March too. On 1 March, the peasant went to the roof of his house, took down his trousers and exposed his buttocks to the sun, saying : ' Sol d'Merz cusum e cul, e nom cusr etar ' (' March sun, barn ma doup, but dinna barn me '). In the fourteenth century, Galeotto Malatesti had legislated against the custom of lighting fires to March, which, as he pointed out, was ' a custom of the heathen ', but the practice still lingers in the province today. Fires were lit at midnight on the last days of February and the first three days of March; and the peasants, taking brands from them, would wander through the fields. A full harvest depended on their doing this. The words of their song at this time go back perhaps centuries beyond the age of the Communes:

Lemna, lemna d' Merz
Una spiga faza un berch.

(Licht to March, licht to March,
The twig by strivin'
Kyths a branch.[75])

All the songs of the Romagnol peasant 'turn on love-making and are almost all without sentiment or rhyme, for they compose them themselves'. Romantic love here was an enemy, for marriage was considered as an instrument of family aggrandisement. The *Commedia nuova* of Pietro Francesco, a poem attributed to the end of the fifteenth century, reveals this attitude well. It was written in Tuscan, but the peasant who is its protagonist speaks in Romagnol. The poem tells how he manages to capture and bind Love:

el traditore
che tradisse tutta la gente.

Apollo, Venus, Mercury, Juno, and Mars, all ask with threats or promises that he should release his prisoner; but only one thing will satisfy Love's captor:

'An dighe a cusì ie o cantarin
a dighe bisogna quatrin quatrin
e no bese.'

('I dinna say aye to that, singer lad, I say it's bawbees, bawbees, and nae' kisses, I'm wanting.')

He asks for a thousand florins gold. Venus offers half cash-down, and the rest later, but the peasant insists on full immediate payment, and she has to give way. Before he lets Love go, he makes a pact with him:

'chum prometta d' in sinpazza
me più con sa vilen.'

('to promise me he'll nae taegle ony mair wi' peasants.'[76])

The peasants had few amusements. There was the *trébb* or social meeting of neighbours for singing and dancing, and there were the rough and childish games, in which they imitated and mocked, in little playlets, those who fringed their lives: the notary, hawker, and so on. But life in the hamlets was hard. In the thirteenth century wooden hovels were giving way to stone houses with small windows and doors, yet it is doubtful how much protection they gave from the weather. A nineteenth-century landlord observed that the tenants never shut a door when they entered his house, for the consciousness of draughts was denied to those who always lived among them.[77] Farm buildings were almost always wooden with thatched roofs. The stock of the farms was poor, and agricultural instruments rudimentary.[78] There were few carts in the mountains, while those in the plain, with their front wheels higher and bigger than those at the back, excited the derision of Leonardo da Vinci. Such an arrangement was only, he implied, to be expected in a province which was the 'source of every stupidity'.[79]

Relations with the landlords were marked by the clash of bourgeois and peasant cunning; the townsmen of Forlì and Faenza grew hot about 'the many frauds and malices of rustics', and Crescenzii warned against 'the importunate voracity of workers', who 'fear nothing so much as the presence and caution of their lord'.[80] On the other hand, they were free from the nagging bitterness of later class feelings; it was good-humouredly accepted that both sides would seek to break their obligations. Benvenuto tells a story about a peasant who came to deliver a load of stones to Guido da Montefeltro in Forlì and was invited by him to stay and eat at his house. The peasant, however, insisted upon going straight back, saying that it was going to rain, and that he wanted to be home before the storm burst. Guido replied that his astrologer, the famous Guido Bonatti (of *Inferno*, XX, 118), had told him that it would be a fine day. The peasant answered that this was all very well, but that he himself was certain that it would rain by the twitching of his ass's ears. Despite the pleas of Guido and the astrologer he made off, amidst the jeers of the bystanders at his ignorance, but sure enough, a sudden storm did break soon afterwards. The interest of the story is the relaxed and independent way in which the peasant and Guido are made to speak to each other.[81]

Much has already been said of war and violence throughout the province. The peasants were particularly vulnerable to this; but, especially in the mountains, they helped to augment it by wars between rural communes, and blood feuds between families. In April 1334, while there was war in the upper Savio valley between some rural communes, the men of Colonata marched out to Borgo

San Damiani and burnt the village and its church, ' on account of the death of someone from Colonata '.[82] In May 1383, a deed was drawn up in Castel del Rio, by which representatives were appointed by the *homines* to make peace with Codronco, ' concerning each and every injury, word, beating, insult, and violence of every sort done by either party '.[83] As the more efficient Florentine administration expanded over the Apennines, evidence grows on the mass of violence within the countryside, with written complaints from the city to the lords of Romagna, and vice versa. Cattle raiding was common ; and criminals, such as the counterfeiter, Domenico Stangelino of Fornione, would cross and recross the borders of Tuscany and Romagna, when the officials of either place came to seek them.[84] The activities of professional criminals were supplemented by those of the amateurs. Florence complained to Imola that thirty men of the *contado* had attacked Giovanni da Mato, ' to take from him by force two girls that he had in his house. They broke in, entering violently, wounded the said Giovanni, and would have snatched away the said girls if at the sound many persons had not approached.' Imola replied that Salvestro di Benedetto of Gamberaldo had been attacked by Gentile da San Enontimo and his sons at Gattara ; and so on.[85]

III

It is not easy to interpret the economic life of the countryside in this era. Not until the fifteenth century has any village left continuous evidence of its life in the notarial protocols. The proportion of lease-hold to tenure by *mezzadria* is uncertain ; though *mezzadria* seems to have gained ground in the fourteenth century.[86] Even on so fundamental a question as population, the evidence, examined in Appendix II, is obscure.

Much of the land had not yet been made suitable for agriculture, and was put to other uses. The monasteries of Ravenna, especially, gave leases of fishing and hunting rights in the large areas of marshland which they held about the Po basin. The abbot of Santa Maria Rotunda in 1330, leased the Isola di Palazzolo in Planetolo to Coccho Glauzano, butcher of Ravenna, in return for an annual payment of £R.80, the head of any animal captured there, and the presentation at Christmas of a hundred large eels, and at the due season, of 500 pine cones.[87] These rights were largely exploited by the ancient Ravennate guild of fishermen.

Sheep and cattle raising were much more common than they

are today. In summer sheep grazed upon the Apennine slopes. The Tuscan Camaldolesi pastured their beasts here, and 800 sheep fed upon the properties of the Bishop of Faenza at Accerata and Marradi.[88] In the plain, Cardinal Anglic estimated that around Ravenna alone there were 1,500 pairs of cows and oxen, and a communal revenue of over £R.4,000 from the pasturage of beasts.[89] Extensive woods and pastures were held by all the communes, and each *cappella* of the towns normally had its own pasture where beasts could be reared free of charge. The right of exacting money for use of the woods, both for pasture and fuel, was generally farmed with the other *gabelles* of the town,[90] and encroachments were severely punished.[91] In the woods of Ravenna, some shelters had been built by the end of the fifteenth century, so that the cattle might feed all the year through, but even then, as in the rest of Italy, the majority of the beasts had to be taken home or slaughtered with the onset of winter.[92]

The difficulties of the small landowner in securing satisfactory grazing for his beasts were reflected in numerous contracts of *soccidia* and *colatico*. The contract of *soccidia* can be illustrated by an example of 1357. In October of that year, Piero Menghi of Gamberlaria received 'in soccedam et ad meliorandum', three cows valued at £R.32, from Iacopo Barenci. Pietro agreed to give pasture to the cows until such time as they were sufficiently fattened for market. Iacopo agreed that when the sale had taken place, he would give Pietro half its proceeds after the sum of £R.32 had been deducted from the purchase sum.[93] In contracts of *colatico*, oxen were leased for ploughing in return for money or a produce payment.[94] Contracts were drawn up, too, for the provision of manure.[95]

To what extent waste land was brought under cultivation is an important question, but one which it is difficult to answer. Throughout the period water was being harnessed, both for irrigation and for the mills; new locks and dykes were constructed and the old repaired.[96] Such schemes were sometimes the cause of war between communes, as between Faenza and Forlì in 1217, and in war the enemy always sought to destroy the town's barriers against the waters.[97] Side by side with the work of the communes, private individuals were constantly banding together to drain their properties.[98] With the character of the evidence it is difficult to say whether there was any diminution in activity between the middle of the thirteenth and fifteenth centuries. Certainly, with the fall in land values, and the incidence of plague, is it probable that there would be.

The same might be said of schemes for land reclamation. Here there are only two pieces of evidence. The first dates from 1251. In that year, Lombard exiles, fleeing from the tyranny of Ezzelino da Romano, were offered refuge by the commune of Imola, and given a lease of land at Massa San Paolo, by the side of the Po. The eighty-seven families concerned agreed to live together there, within an enclosed hedge, fortified by dykes and ditches. Each family was given sixty *tornature* of land, and was supposed to bring one *tornatura* of wooded land to cultivation each year. They were allowed to use the wood of Bagnarolo in the same way as Imolesi citizens, and were assigned a hundred *tornature* of the wood of Massa for building houses, and for making repairs to their stockade. They agreed to build a road from Prato Selice at Imola to the Massa, and were allowed to draw water from the river Santerno for milling or other uses. They were to hold a cattle market twice a year. In return they were each individually to pay £B.5, and collectively to present a silk flag to the commune of Imola, at the renewal of their lease every twenty-nine years.

The emigrants were given the right to elect a *massarius*, consuls, the rector of their church and other officials, though these were to be confirmed by Imola. In the following year other families joined, and by 1257 there were a hundred houses in the village and its district. In 1277, it changed its name to Massa Lombarda, by which it is still known today. Imola itself had leased the land on which it had been built from the abbey of Santa Maria in Cosmedin.[99]

Only in the middle of the fifteenth century is any comparable evidence to be found. In 1448, the commune of Imola, under Taddeo Manfredi, leased sixty *tornature* of waste, scrub, and woodland in Cantalupo to one Gabriele de' Menti, for twenty-nine years. Menti, in return, paid nothing; the only condition of the lease was that the land be made fertile.[100] In the protocols of the notary Guasconi, there are twenty-two similar contracts made, between February 1459 and January 1461, by which the commune leased a complex of 4,904 *tornature* of waste land.[101] The leases themselves explain the motive of the *signore*:

> In the territory and land of Imola in the farm of Barignano . . . there are many possessions and lands, once in past times cultivated and ploughed; which possessions in the said farm of Barignano are now shrub, gravel, wood, and pond, useless, uncultivated and unfruitful. It has long been so, through lack of men and people, and on account of the troubles of war and floods. Wherefore our

> magnificent Lord Taddeo etc. desires the same places to be brought to fertility and, for the honour and state of his dominion, to be dwelt in as once they were.[102]

The lessees received plots of wasteland (varying in size from fifty to a hundred *tornature*) for twenty-nine years without any immediate payments. Thus, for example, the rent of the 1,000 *tornature* leased to Antonio Forlani was fixed at a hawk each month of May. However, at each renewal of the lease, Forlani was to pay twelve shillings for each pound at which the land was valued for taxation purposes. The lessee and inhabitants of the area had to swear each year that they would remain under the jurisdiction of the *podestà* of Imola, and that they would not become followers of any other lord of Romagna. Forlani, like the other lessees, was allowed to bring into Imola, free of tax, the produce of the lands he had leased under this contract.[103] These leases were given at very advantageous terms, and, of course, they were initiated by the *signore*. None the less, the fact that land was again being brought to cultivation suggests a revival of agriculture during the fifteenth century.[104]

CHAPTER VII

The Town

It seemed the greatest and proudest thing I had ever seen.

COBELLI, on the Forlì of his youth

I

THOUGH the wealth of Romagna lay in the countryside, the loyalties of the Romagnols, as of all Latins in Southern Europe, was to the town. Civil society, urban life, to the Italian, as to the Greek of the fifth century, was the highest expression of civilisation. The naive delight of the Romagnol town dweller of today in his birthplace echoes the emotions of the native chroniclers of the fourteenth and fifteenth centuries. *Campanalismo*, local patriotism, was much more than an economic force ; it was the deep emotional expression of something rooted in the Italian soul.

None of the towns can be taken as typical. Rimini was a small port ; Ravenna, even at that date, a museum ; Cesena, pre-Roman ; Imola, Faenza, and Forlì all had distinctive characteristics. But for our purposes Imola might be taken as an example. As seen in the map drawn by Leonardo da Vinci, its Roman origins stand out clearly. The Via Emilia itself, in passing through the town, has lost its straightness and taken two wide curves between the walls, but almost all the other principal streets are broad, straight, and set at right-angles to each other. There were two centres to the town, corresponding to its lay and ecclesiastical government. The first, the ecclesiastical, was on the slight eminence where stood the Cathedral of San Cassiano, built between 1187 and 1271, and named from the town's early bishop and martyr. A piazza stood before it, and the episcopal palace opposite. Looking from here, the spires and towers of over a score of religious institutions would greet the eye : the cylindrical tower of the ancient Benedictine Abbey of S. Maria in Regola, S. Niccolo of the Dominicans, S. Francesco of the Friars Minor, S. Eustacio of the Camaldolesi, S. Annunziata, S. Michele, S. Paolo e Donato, S. Giovanni Battista, S. Spirito, the convents of the Franciscan, Dominican, and Augustinian nuns, the chapels of the hospitals and lay societies, and many other buildings which attested to the faith of the citizens. The new Gothic would stand out with startling modernity against the older Romanesque and Ravennate architecture.

The second focus of town life was the piazza, where stood the Palazzo Comunale, by the church of San Lorenzo, from where the great bell of the commune rang through the town and out into the countryside beyond.[1] Around the town extended the walls, with four principal gates, and the dyke of the commune. In the south-west corner stood a castle with moat and drawbridge. Outside the gates a few straggling houses formed suburbs. For administrative purposes the town and suburbs were divided into four quarters. These were each again subdivided into three *cappelle*, all with boundaries on the Via Emilia. The whole town, with inns, markets, churches, shops, and houses, was still largely interspersed with fields, gardens, and orchards. (Today in the southern part of Cesena, by the castle, where squalid two-storied houses stand isolated among vineyards, the semi-rural character of the old Romagnol town can still be recaptured.) Perhaps about 5,000 people lived there.

The houses of the citizens were in no way impressive. The nobles — the Alidosi, the Cunii, the Sassatelli — lived in semi-fortresses, with gardens and high towers, which stood out above the rest of the town. None of these buildings has survived in its original form. Some of the houses of the *bourgeoisie* — modest, two-storied dwellings with tiled roofs — can still be seen. The so-called Casa di Isotta at Rimini with its balcony, and the so-called Casa di Benvenuto in Imola, with fragments of fresco on its walls, are pleasant enough. Other houses which have survived to the present era, such as the Case Polentane in Ravenna are not very attractive. The labourers of the town lived in *casupole*: cottages or hovels. Many of these buildings were of wood, and the towns were in constant danger of disastrous fires.[2] The most wretched made their homes under the eaves of the churches or the porticos[3] of the great. Most of the buildings of the town were rented on lease from the nobility. Some contracts of the Manfredi, from the thirteen-seventies, illustrate the way in which a landlord might build up his urban estates. Contracts were made for twenty-nine year leases of building land in the *cappella* of S. Maria in Brolio in Faenza. It was specified that if, at the end of the lease, the landlords wished to take over the property, then they and the lessees should appoint valuers for the valuation of any building erected upon the land. These would be bought by the ground landlords at the price fixed by the valuers. If the lease

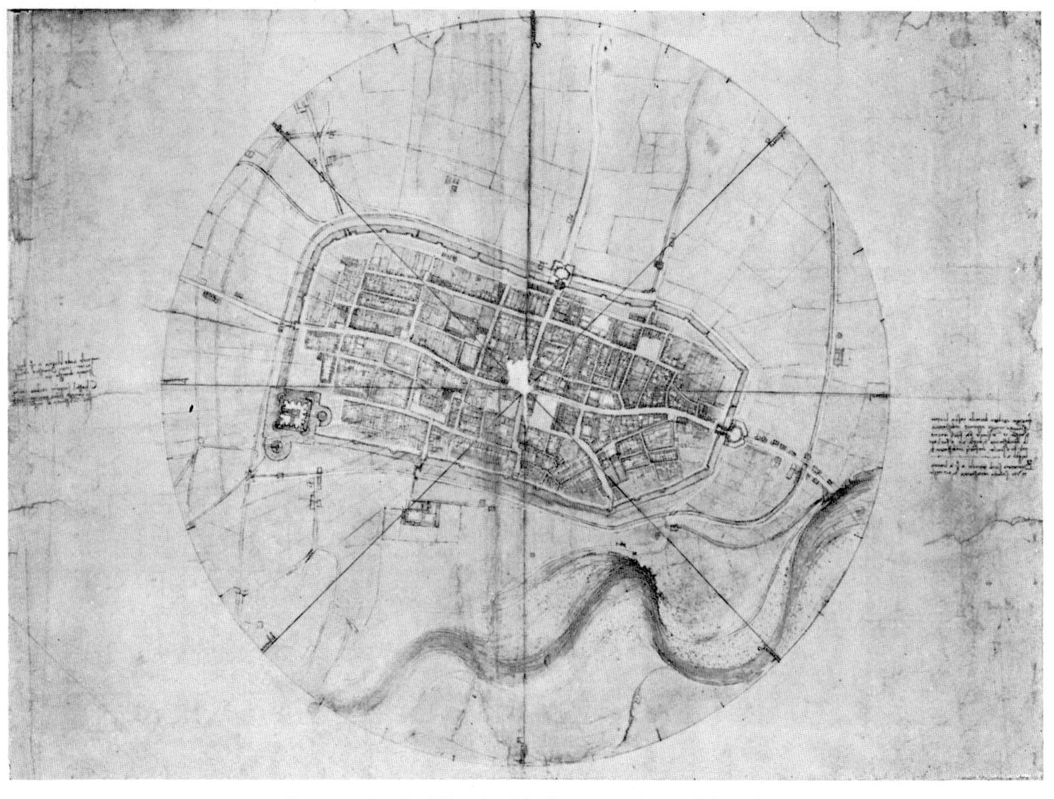

Leonardo da Vinci: Bird's-eye view of Imola

were renewed, the re-entry fine was fixed at twelve shillings.[4]

Life here was insanitary. The piazza comunale was cleaned at public expense, but the rest of the town was left to those who lived there. Technically, a citizen was held responsible for the condition of the street before his house, but, in the fifteenth century at least, the roads in Rimini were so choked with mud that they could only be crossed by stepping-stones.[5] In 1433, Ambrogio Traversari wrote to Cosimo de' Medici to say that the streets of Ravenna were so filled with mud that it was impossible for him to go about on foot.[6] The town statutes forbade anyone to throw house refuse into the streets, and specifically inveighed against emptying chamber pots; but these were probably counsels of perfection. There were some privately owned public lavatories,[7] but the sewers were often open.[8] There were prohibitions against any citizen keeping more than one goat, but again, this was probably disregarded and the pungent smell of animal would be everywhere.[9] In all, the air of the town would be fetid and disease-ridden.

II

The economy of the towns was wholly bound up with agriculture. They were *terre*; market centres for their *contadi*. Many of their inhabitants were peasants or day labourers, who went out each morning beyond the walls to their work, and returned at night. Economic life in the town centred on the markets in fish, corn, and meat.

The sale of food was very closely controlled by the commune, and private enterprise in its marketing was virtually prohibited. All the statutes insisted that corn and other food from the villages in the *contado* should be sold exclusively in the town.[10] The nobility were subject to the same regulations. When Pietro di Guglielmo Traversari refused, in 1303, to bring corn from his estates at Traversaria to Ravenna, the men of the town rode out to his castle, destroyed it, and sent him into exile.[11] Corn could only be exported with the licence of the commune.[12] This normally meant that the dominant family, or group of families, among the landowners, would secure a monopoly of all the surplus corn and sell it, in the name of the commune, on their own behalf. Here was the economic basis of the conflicts of parties.

Even inside the commune, the practice of 'regrating' was common. Landowners would store their corn in warehouses in the town, and create an artificial shortage by refusing to sell until the price had been inflated by the consequent demand. In 1287, for instance, Bishop Viviano of Faenza held 2,000 *corbe* of old corn in his granaries, 'which he refused to sell until it reached the price of £B.1 the *corbe*'.[13] When in 1380, a corn ring at Rimini drove up prices to £6 and £7 the *staio*, Galeotto Malatesta allowed this, the chronicler says, 'to satisfy the greater citizens' until March, when he acted so that the price fell to £3 the *staio*.[14] In the fifteenth century the signorial manipulation of the corn market was to become one of the most important factors in the instability of the *signorie*.[15]

Apart from this marketing of corn by the noble families, there was very little scope for the native entrepreneur. Florentine and Venetian merchants dominated everywhere, and firmly controlled the trade of the ports. There were some small native merchants, but they operated on a very limited scale indeed.[16] At the beginning of the thirteenth century it was difficult even to cash bills of exchange in the towns, as Gerald the Welshman discovered.[17]

In each town there was a small professional element, composed of notaries, doctors, and schoolteachers. Doctors of medicine were comparatively rare (though there were no less than nine in Imola in 1288),[18] and were well paid. In 1314, for instance, Dr. Alberto di Galvano of Bologna promised Lamberto da Polenta, the *podestà* of Ravenna, that he would visit all the sick of the town in the coming year. His salary was fixed at £R.300, and in addition he was permitted to charge any patient who was seriously ill up to £R.3.[19] Medical practice at the time was a curious combination of empirical knowledge and esoteric astrological lore.[20] It was supplemented by the work of the barbers, who in this age performed certain surgical functions such as bleeding.

Schoolteachers did not enjoy the prestige and high salary of doctors, but they lived comfortably. In the early thirteenth century education was principally in the hands of the episcopal schools, such as that of Faenza, where Canon Tolosano, the chronicler, probably taught, and from which a textbook on the *ars dictandi*, or writing of Latin letters, has survived. In the following hundred years the lay school established by the commune became general in Romagna, as in all the small towns of Northern Italy. Above all, these schools taught Latin, but at Rimini a second master was appointed for instruction in law, doubtless for those who wished to become notaries. Normally the master was paid a fixed sum by the commune: £R.25 at Ravenna in 1304, £R.50 at Rimini in 1334, which was supplemented by individual payments by the parents of children attending his school.[21] The masters appointed by the communes were rarley natives of the towns in which they taught, and seem to have lead migrant lives, travelling from town to town each year. Corso di Santo Fiore, *doctor grammaticus*, for instance, had by 1294 taught at Bologna, Forlì, Cesena, and San Gimignano. The statutes of Faenza actually insisted that no master should remain at his post for more than two years.[22] In addition to publicly-established schools, there were a fairly considerable number of private schools, run by local teachers.

Trade was confined to what might be expected in a market town. The tradesmen of the province can be divided into five principal categories.

The first comprised those concerned with food. There were the bakers, fishmongers, and butchers. The butchers were gathered in the Piazza de' Bovi, each with their work benches. Together they formed the *beccaria*, which, in Imola at least, seems to have been run upon a joint stock basis by members of the town nobility.[23] The *pescheria*, or fish market, operated in a similar way.[24] Although most of the fish of northern Romagna came from the marshes and *valli* of Ravenna, the ships and seamen noted in some contracts of the fourteenth century were probably principally concerned with the fishing trade.[25]

The second group of trades concerned the artisan. There were builders,[26] carpenters,[27] brickmakers, smiths, and potters.[28] At the end of the fifteenth century, Faenza became famous for its *maiolica* and gave to the world the name *faience*, but in the thirteenth and fourteenth centuries the secrets of glazing with stanniferous enamels had not yet been discovered.

Those concerned with clothing form another group. There are provisions on wool and cloth working in the statutes of all the towns ; some contracts have survived, and at the end of the thirteenth century *romagnuolo*, the coarse cloth of the province, was exported to Tuscany.[29] But the industry was small and had little importance. Between 1416 and 1476, only seventy-six men were engaged in the Arte della Lana of Faenza.[30] Again, there were leather-workers, shoemakers, skin-dressers, flax workers, furriers, and tailors ; but all with a similarly limited scope.

Mention should also be made of the gold-workers,[31] chemists or apothecaries,[32] paper-workers,[33] and money-changers. Often they were foreigners to the town in which they worked. Finally, there were the normal lowly occupations to be expected in any town, the rag-and-bone merchants, the *brentatores* or wine and water-carriers (who acted as firemen when necessary), muleteers, and innkeepers.

All the principal trades of the town had their Arts or guilds. In Faenza, there was the Art of Notaries and Judges, the Art of Merchants (composed of money-changers, drapers, chemists, and gold and silver workers), the Art of the Skin-dealers and Barbers, the Art of the wood-workers and carpenters, and the Art of the Bakers.[34] In 1272, Imola had nine guilds :

1	Judges, notaries, and doctors	(231 members)
2	Butchers	(236 ,,)
3	Peasants	(177 ,,)
4	Shoemakers	(251 ,,)
5	Masons and carpenters	(161 ,,)
6	Hemp dressers	(119 ,,)
7	Merchants	(731 ,,)
8	Skinworkers	(182 ,,)
9	Smiths and artisans	(95 ,,)[35]

At this time very few members of a guild in fact exercised the trade from which the Art took its name. In Romagna, the guilds had been introduced during the period of Bolognese hegemony in the middle of the thirteenth century, as political rather than economic institutions. In the political struggles at Bologna, the bourgeoisie, organised in their trade associations, had triumphed over the feudal nobility of the *contado*. In Romagna the Arts were never powerful enough to come into conflict with the nobility, but the same legal ideas were applied. No-one who was not enrolled in an Art could properly be called a citizen. Thus the fact that there were 236 men enrolled in the Art of the Butchers in Imola did not mean that there were 236 butchers. All it meant was that the guild gave full rights as citizens to 236 people by enrolling them as members.

It has already been seen that the Arts were dominated by the nobility. Therefore, to equate full citizenship with membership of a guild was a legal fiction which in no way corresponded with political reality, and as a result, in the fourteenth century the guilds came to have a more purely economic role. By the fifteenth century, the Art of Lana Gentile in Faenza was emphasising, ' che niuno ne debbia esse matriculado sel non exercita larte dela lana '.[36] Custom gave the guilds a voice in the election of some town officials, but their principal task was to lay down rules for work and prices, and to act as a social focus for men exercising a trade.

The guild statutes show the Arts, then, arranging for joint attendance at Mass every month (the members being forbidden to leave before permission had been given),[37] prohibiting work on feast days,[38] fixing minimum prices,[39] and appointing *satari* to supervise the quality of work done. They arranged for masses to be said for the deceased members of the guild, and for visiting any sick brethren. Membership was open to those who could prove themselves as 'good and sufficient tradesmen', or, as in the Casa Matha, the ancient Ravennate guild of fishermen, to those whose fathers had been in the guild.[40] The Scola Pescatorum or Casa Matha, acted as a joint marketing body, almost as a limited company, leasing marsh land of Ravenna from the monasteries and churches, and assigning the land taken to its members.

III

How were the trades of the town financed? All taking of interest on loans was considered as usury, and as such, corrupt and unnatural. 'To lend a hundred florins', wrote Sacchetti, 'and to receive back a hundred and ten, is no sustenance of nature, but its consumption, and for that it is unlawful.'[41] This sentiment was faithfully reflected in all the statutes of the towns. The decrees of Imola of 1334, for instance, declared that all instruments drawn up in favour of anyone whom public fame denounced as a usurer, should be deemed fictitious. The instrument of any such person would only be considered as valid if he produced witnesses to swear that it was not a usurious transaction. The statutes of Faenza decreed that a debtor might avoid full payment of his debt by securing witnesses to swear that his creditor was a 'manifest usurer'. In these circumstances, the witnesses told the court how much interest the usurer normally exacted, and this amount, calculated on the capital sum, was cancelled from the debt. Again, 'because the whirlpool of usury, condemned in the pages of the Old and New Testaments is much to be detested . . .' any contract by a Jew or other usurer was held invalid after six years. No-one who was, or was thought to be, a usurer, might be a member of the Art of Merchants, and no member of the Art of Judges and Advocates might act on behalf of any usurer.[42] Such or similar decrees are reproduced in all the statutory compilations of the towns of Romagna.

This attitude to money-lending has long been recognised as a painful and ambiguous element in the commercial practice of the banking centres of Italy. What has been ignored is that even in predominantly agrarian communities, this morality was at variance with the whole practice of society. The small, internal, domestic loan lay behind almost every aspect of social life. Most trades were initiated and sustained through the borrowing of money at interest. Dowries were raised, taxes paid, land and food bought, as a result of usurious transactions. Of necessity, side by side with the formal condemnation of usury in the statutes, there appeared all the practical legal mechanism for the protection of credit. There was the three-day notice of liability for debt before prosecution, the ten-day warning before distraint of security, the imprisonment and public stripping (' to the shirt ') of the failed debtor, and the outlawry of the absconder.[43] The *signore* himself, eager to establish secure credit, wrote to rulers of neighbouring states that they might apprehend debtors who had fled their obligations.[44]

The credit needs of the province were satisfied in part by Jewish bankers. By 1369, the Jews of Rimini were already prominent in establishing loan banks in other centres of Italy. Forlì was a centre of Hebraic studies from the thirteenth century. At Ravenna Frederick II in 1226 had intervened to save a Jew from unjust exactions, and the Jewish community here had probably been established since the Dark Ages. Cesena and Imola too had their families. In the countryside, the Jews held banks at Castelbolognese, Montefiore, Tossignano, Castrocaro, Meldola, Bertinoro, Cervia, and Lugo. Lugo, indeed, grew during the fifteenth century to be an important centre of Hebrew culture.[45]

The *signori* of the towns licensed the Jewish bankers directly, and acknowledged the need for their activity. In 1458, for instance, Taddeo Manfredi conceded to Iacopo Alvincini and Solomon Vitali of Vicenza the right to operate a bank in the town of Imola. He did this, ' considering it to be useful and extremely valuable that Jews should rest and remain in the town of Imola for the purposes of holding a public bank of usury and lending money *ad usurias* to the commune, citizens and subjects of the said town '. Citizens who gave pledges equal in value to their loan were charged interest of six Bolognesi pennies in the pound each month. Those who borrowed under a publicly written instrument (' sub instrumentis et publicis scripturis ') or on faith, could be charged up to eightpence in the pound per month. In the first instance (loan under pledge), the concessionaires were bound to lend money. There was no obligation upon them, however, to lend money without pledge. The grant was made for ten years in return for an annual payment of £B.300.[46]

A similar concession, in 1420, allowed Daniel of Forlì to expand his business to Castrocaro, in the Tusco–Romagnol Apennines. The interest rates were calculated on the same scale, and for exercising his trade in the *castello*, the concessionnaire paid forty florins a year. He paid no other taxes or *gabelles*, and the captain of the Florentine Romagna was obliged to assist him, on petition, with the exaction of debts.[47] Again, in 1490, the Madonna Caterina Sforza, with the Council of Forlì, asked Guglielmo d' Aia to establish a bank in the town. As his first condition of acceptance, d' Aia asked that the community should stand complete security for any goods he might lose in the event of war, revolution, or civil disturbance. Caterina, realising, ' what great damage there had been from not having a Jew ', agreed to this, and authorised d' Aia to lend in the town at an interest rate of sixpence in the pound per month. In the previous two years, following the sack of the banks after the assassination of Girolamo Riario, the citizens had had to go to other places to take out loans, and had had to pay interest of eightpence in the pound.[48]

The tone of these transactions is clearly at variance with the contemporary ethical concept of usury. The high rates of interest are significant too.[49] These bankers were allowed to take a yearly interest of 30 per cent against full security, and of 40 per cent against a public instrument. When money was lent under security, the transaction was rarely recorded in a notarial deed. The banker's own records, and his possession of the borrower's pledge, gave sufficient validity to the transaction. When money was lent without full security, a notarial deed was necessary to protect the contract. In fact, loans without full security were normally only made to corporate bodies, such as rural communes. It was extremely rare for private individuals to be able to borrow on faith or public instrument. The private individual would almost always have to give security in kind. He would pay the lower rate of interest, a public notarial document would be unnecessary, and the sole record of the transaction would be preserved in the banker's own accounts.

Anything of value could be accepted as a pledge or security. In 1428, Simone di Aquila, captain at arms of the temporary papal government of Imola and Forlì, ordered Daniel, son of Isaiah, to consign some armour to the treasurer of Imola. This included five cuirasses, two arm-pieces, a pair of gloves and a helmet adorned with silver and crest. This armour, which was papal property, had been pledged as security against a private loan by one Antonello di Sicilia, armigero. The treasurer was instructed to pay off his debt.[50] Again, a dispute in law, between Andrea Androzolo and a Jewish banker of Cervia called Alivicio, shows Andrea to have pledged some silk cloth. Alivicio also held a roll of linen of eighty *bracchia*, which, Andrea claimed, had been given to the banker in exchange for the original pledge of silk. This was denied by the creditor, who asserted that both the items were originally pledged against the debt. As with most civil cases, the settlement was put to the arbitration of two men, in this case one Christian and one Jew.[51] The securities demanded exceeded considerably the value of the loan made.

As a general rule, then, licensed usury exacted pledges giving the fullest security, and charged yearly interest of 30 per cent. Only Ravenna was able to secure more advantageous credit terms. When in 1441 the town threw off the rule of the da Polenta and submitted itself to the Venetians, one of the articles in which it bound itself to Venice spoke expressly of licensed usury. The town asked that the new government should allow Ravenna to have Jews who would lend money at a rate of five pence in the pound per month for citizens, and at sixpence for non-citizens. The previous interest rate had been eightpence in the pound.[52] Domination by a larger commercial centre brought easier credit terms. But even the 25 per cent interest paid at Ravenna is a high rate. It is explained in part by the taxation exacted both by the governments of the town, and by the papacy, taxation described in 1469 as oppressive.[53] Again, the initial capital necessary for the establishment of a bank was high,[54] there were bad debts, and legal and other expenses. But ultimately the principal explanation must be the strength of unsatisfied demand for credit facilities. Non-professional usurers exacted even higher interest than that taken by the licensed bankers.

Though unable to be full citizens of the towns in which they lived, the Jews followed a life of comparative, if not undisturbed, security. In law they had the same rights as Christians. They took oath in court upon the Talmud, and by the Mosaic law (' manibus tactis scripturis ebrayeis per legem Moyseis et per deum omnipotentem').[55] They could bring civil cases against Christians. Disputes between themselves were also brought before the judges of the towns.[56] With the *signori*, the Jews had generally amicable relations, though they were kept under surveillance to ensure that their contracts were being fulfilled. In 1456, for instance, Taddeo Manfredi, writing from Tossignano, instructed his vicar in Imola to impound the books of the bankers, and the pledges they had taken. When the citizens came to reclaim their pledges, they were to be asked what interest they had been charged.[57]

Until the middle of the fifteenth century there were few signs of religious fanaticism. One of Sacchetti's stories, set in Cervia, illustrates a popular contempt for the Jews, and occasionally they were subject to such indignities as that of 1379 in Forlì, when they were forced to listen to the preachings of Giovanni, 'from being a Jew, newly converted to Christianity', in the church of San Mercuriale.[58] But they had their synagogues, and until the advent of Saint Bernardino, were allowed to live as neighbours with the Christians of the Papal States.

The Jews were not the sole professional money-lenders of the provinces. The *campsores*, or money-changers, essential in an economy of many different coinages, and the goldsmiths, carried on that usury to which their other activities gave scope. Moreover, Tuscan financiers were found with banks in the province, at Imola, Faenza, and Rimini.[59] Yet, reading the notarial protocols, it is tempting to see the professional usurers as being merely supplementary to the amateur. The credit transactions of the aristocracy of the towns dominated economic life, and ensured them a body of dependents as loyal as their *fideles* in the *contado*.

There were two principal methods by which trades were financed. In the first of these, the form of the notarial deed recording the transaction is extremely simple. A admits to having received from B a certain sum of money on loan in order to work on some specific craft. The sums involved might range from £B.12 to 300 florins, though the average investment was between £B.25 and £B.50. The term of the loan was not generally registered, but often a later entry in the margin recorded repayment. These entries show that money was borrowed for periods varying from a month to eleven years. Though there was no mention of interest, it is certain that interest was paid. Gratuitous loans, on the rare occasions they occurred, were heavily emphasised with the explicit statement that they were given, 'ex puro amore et gratia speciale'.[60] Probably, as in Florence, the interest was comprised in the capital sum recorded in the deed.

The second, and most common, contract was akin in spirit to the agrarian tenure of *mezzadria*. A craftsman who wished to set up in business would take a loan from a member of the town nobility. Until he was repaid, the creditor received half the profits, and met half the losses of the trade he had financed. In 1387, for instance, Guido da Zarli lent one Oddo £B.40 for a year that he might work at shoe-making 'ad medietatem lucri et dampni'.[61] In other contracts, where the term of the loan was not stated, the profit and loss division continued until the money was repaid. Even when a time limit was given to a deed, it was possible to extend its term with little formality.

Contracts of this type were made by all the more prosperous men of the towns. Among the signorial families, for instance, Roberto Alidosi in 1360, lent 30 ducats gold to three men to work at cloth-making.[62] In 1383, his son Beltrando made a loan of 12 ducats gold to three men, to work at pot-making.[63] The other aristocracy frequently invested their money in the same way. Members of the house of the Counts of Sassatelli gave sums of between £B.25 and £B.100 to men working as cotton merchants, timber contractors, wool and cloth-workers, and chemists.[64] The family of the Cantagalli, Counts of Paventa, lent money to the goldsmiths and shoe-makers.[65] The professional classes followed their example. A physician's wife lent money to a chemist; a notary lent to a cotton worker, a sword-maker, a potter, or a glass-worker. A schoolmaster lent to a furrier.[66] The extent to which a non-professional money-lender, without really extensive means, might take part in such transactions, is shown by the registrations that have survived, between 1422 and 1429, of one Bartolomeo, an apparently successful painter. During the seven years, he was involved in credit transactions with tradesmen to a value of at least £B.403.[67]

Land was perhaps ultimately a more profitable form of investment than this type of loan. But land was not a short term, nor was it a passive investment. The supervision of the share-croppers who farmed the landlord's property at *mezzadria* required considerable agrarian knowledge. This explains the large number of trade loans made by widows. The average woman was not likely to have specialised knowledge of agricultural practice, and would prefer to invest her money in trade. Capital would come from her dowry, which, by normal practice in Romagna, returned to the wife on the death of her husband.

Other circumstances in which money might be invested in trade are revealed by a law-suit held before the vice-*podestà* of Imola in 1423. This case turned upon the validity of some sections of the will of Baldassare, Count of Bordella. The will had endowed his daughter Lucrezia with £B.1,200, on condition that she did not marry before her sixteenth birthday. On his wife, Francesca, had been imposed the duty of placing the money with some honest merchants. From it, from time to time, she was to spend what was necessary for her daughter's maintenance. Of this sum, she had spent £B.300 at her death. The remaining £B.900 came into the hands of the executors of the count's will, who re-deposited the money with tradesmen. In fact, Lucrezia married before her sixteenth birthday, and in this suit, her husband asked that he might receive his wife's dowry despite her father's will.[68] In the handling of this dowry it is possible to see the value of being able to make short-term trade investments, when part of the capital sum might have to be utilised, at short notice, for some other purpose.

The particular contracts by which trade was financed were only a part of the money-lender's activities in the towns. Not that it is easy to track down and identify their transactions in the notarial protocols. In his textbook for notaries, Rolandino Passagieri had inveighed bitterly against the large number of fictitious deeds, by which the nakedness of usury was clothed in respectability. Would you, he asked, for a few pennies, make out such a deed to the grave peril of your soul?[69] The answer was, of course, that many would only too willingly. Every act of *de ulterius non petendo* that does not specifically state the cause of payment made, may hide a usurious transaction. Every act by which money was placed *in depositum* is almost certain to hide usury.[70] The recipient of money in deposit swore under pain of judgment to preserve the money he had taken against any fortuitous chance : fire, shipwreck, ruin, rapine, theft, violence, and every other eventuality arising from divine or human agency, and to return it at a certain date.[71]

Land contracts of the beginning of the thirteenth century recognise clearly the possibilities of disguised usurious transactions. Such contracts were normally accompanied by the promise of the forfeiture of money if its conditions were not fulfilled. Thus, when in 1223, Cacciaguerra of Monte Petra sold lands for £R.2,201, he promised to observe the contract, ' under pain of double the said price '. The aim of the usurious contract was to set impossible conditions for its performance, so that the money pledged in this way returned to the man who had lent it, with, of course, substantial interest. The notary who drew up the contract for Cacciaguerra realised this, and explicitly stated, ' quod dicta pena non fuerit promissa in fraude usurarum '.[72]

Another method of drawing usurious contracts may be illustrated from the fifteenth century. In 1458, Pietro dell' Antonio paid a yearly rent of £B.40 for an inn called L' Albergo del Cavelletto to its landlady, Nina, widow of the knight Nanne da Vigiano. The document recording the payment includes the information that Pietro had sold the inn to Nina, previously, for £B.400, on the understanding that he had pledged himself to buy it back for the same sum. Here is an example of a disguised loan at 10 per cent interest, under the most favourable security. In fact, three years later, the security had fallen to the creditor, for she sold the inn again for £B.400.[73]

In most cases the skill of the notary triumphed, and the extent to which private persons were engaged in money-lending can only be discerned through documents primarily concerned with other matters. In 1465, for instance, Taddeo Manfredi rewarded his follower de Zuccaro, with property confiscated to the camera of Imola from one accused of treason. De Zuccaro, however, being the debtor of Giovanni Pirotti of Casola, and having pledged land to him for a debt, renounced what Taddeo had given him in exchange for £B.280.[74] Probably, as with loans made by Florentine capitalists in Tuscany, money was lent with the primary hope of obtaining the land pledged as security should the debtor be unable to meet his obligations.[75]

The extent to which men, who were primarily landowners, might lend and borrow money is revealed by an inquisition *post mortem* ordered by Ludovico Alidosi in 1419, to settle the estate of Rainuccio di Gasperino da Pediano. The four commissioners, in their report, found that da Pediano had credits from Ludovico himself for £B.544 5 6, from Count Ludovico di Zagonara for £B.75 10, and from Count Roberto of Fusignano for £B.81 2 0. Pediano's social position may be assumed from the knowledge that his daughter was married to Count Orsatto di Cantagallo.[76]

The ordinary individual of the town, too, lived upon a credit chain made up in no small part by money-lending transactions. The numerous grants of wardship among the notarial protocols give abundant proof of this. These grants, made before one of the town's judges, required a complete inventory of the possessions, credits, and debts of the deceased. The inventory in 1386 of the goods of Nicoluccio Garfagni, a shoe-maker, of Faenza, may be cited as typical. His credits in all amounted to £B.96. Of this money, £B.46 was owing for shoes he had made, and £B.37 from two other shoe-makers. Another £B.3 was for a loan that he had made to one Grundo da Reda, and £B.10 was marked as owing in his books ' a pluribus personis'. His debts amounted to £B.186 2 0. Of this sum, £B.18 16 0 was owed to several people for leather, and £B.10 to three men for cloth. The remainder was composed of two debts, *ex causa mutui*, one for £B.143 6 0, and another of £B.14.[77]

The final evidence for usurious transactions are those deeds in which money-lenders publicly professed their repentance. In 1355, for instance, Pietro, a builder of Bagnacavallo, had a deed drawn up under the portico of his parish church, in which he said that he intended to visit the churches of Rome, and to cross the threshold of the churches of Saint Peter and Paul. Before doing so he promised to restore the money that he had extorted *per usurariam pravitatem*, in all £B.45.[78] Two years later, Biondo Frigerio, ' wishing to save his soul ', confessed that he had lent money for two years in Ravenna, ' though not publicly and openly '. Under the interrogation of the notary, he admitted that he normally lent money under pledge, and only on three occasions under a written deed. He kept no record of his transactions, but when giving loans under public instrument, registered in the deed double the sum actually lent. Asked what interest he took under pledge, he replied 8d. in the pound per month. He was unable to repay the money he had extorted, but promised to restore it should he recover his health, and arrive ' at fatter fortune '.[79]

In the same year, Giovanna, wife of Blasio degli Alberti, in the presence of the Archbishop of Ravenna, restored £R.10 that her husband had taken in usury. She explained that he had gone mad and that in his madness, could talk of nothing but his usury. She was afraid, she said, that he would be denied burial in consecrated ground, and the sacraments of the Church, if the money were not restored.[80] At the end of the century, Daddo di Martino, 'corpore languens', made similar restitution as death approached. He admitted having lent corn and money at an interest of a shilling in the pound each month.[81]

These repentances leave a painful impression. Usury was regarded morally as forbidden, and legally as an evil to be tolerated in the same way as the licensed gaming houses of the town were tolerated. Indeed usury was less tolerated than gambling. The evils attached to gaming, explained Coluccio Salutati, were accidents, but the evil of usury arose from its essence.[82] Yet money-lending, unlike gaming, was essential to social life, a convenience for the middle class, a necessity for the poor. The bank established at Forlì by Caterina Sforza, for example, was established ' for aid and favour of the whole republic and especially of the wretchedly poor '.[83] Only at the end of the fifteenth century, with the establishments of Monti di Pietà under the stimulus of Franciscan preaching, did the ethic begin to come to terms with economic reality.

IV

The centre of Romagnol life was the family, and the *capocchio* or head of the family, was for each class in the community, whether peasant or lord, the most important person in the world. There were two schools of thought on the way in which he should treat his wife and daughters ; the first claimed that women should only be beaten when they acted against his commands ; the second quoted the proverb : ' a good horse and a bad horse both require the spur, a good woman and a bad both need the stick '.[84] Occasionally, the civil authorities would intervene in family life. At Tossignano, for instance, the captain of the village bound Feltrino Contarin, under a pledge of 100 gold ducats, that he would not beat or whip his wife, ' ineptly *et praeter modum correctionis* '.[85] But these attempts at marriage guidance were rare. Men too, were subject to the father of the family, and when they could no longer be beaten, the penalty for disobedience was formal expulsion. A notarial instrument survives, in which the town-crier of Imola agreed with the Mercati family to call, ' in a high and audible voice ', the news that Giulio de' Mercati had committed scandal and excess and violence against his own blood, ' and that the said Giulio had not wished, and does not wish, to live decently according to the wish of his father. And therefore the family of the Mercati do not wish the said Giulio to be of their number, and do not wish to have him as a relative.'[86]

Family life was a very business-like matter, and not surprisingly it frequently intruded into the notarial protocols. Betrothals, giving details of dowries, and the breaking of betrothals too, appeared in them. Marriages were arranged and at an early age. In consequence, there was large scope for divorce, under that provision in canon law which insisted that marriage could only be entered into with the active consent of both parties. In 1362, for example, the vicar of the Ravenna church declared invalid a marriage made between Francesca di Bonfiglio, who was twelve years old, and Nicolo de' Grundi, ' having heard them declare in turn that they had not wished to be married '.[87] If the marriage had been consummated, this was often registered by the notary recording the contract. Again, this might be important when the time came to claim divorce on the grounds of non-consummation.[88] The baptism of children was sometimes recorded by the notaries, and the names of those who had sponsored them. Illustrious people would sometimes cause deeds of procuration to be made out, by which they appointed someone as their representative, to act for them in this *in absentia*.[89] The adultery of wives, normally terminated by murder, occasionally caused scandal among the upper classes, but was comparatively rare. In law it was punishable by death.[90]

The dowry was an essential in marriage, and a prestige symbol among all classes. Beltrando Alidosi sought to limit dowries to the value of £B.100,[91] but in the pressure of social competition, the *signori* themselves were the first to go beyond this. Azzo Alidosi, for instance, received a dowry of 1,000 gold ducats with his wife, Margerita di Guglielmo di Castrocaro.[92] At the same time the cook of the *signore* would expect his wife to be dowered with £R.50 in money and goods.[93] Normally, the dowry returned to the wife on her husband's death. If the wife died without children, half the dowry would return to her relatives.[94] For this reason, a wife could appeal in law if her husband were squandering her dowry.[95]

Girls without dowries generally ended up as servants in the taverns, where they drifted easily into prostitution. Salimbene depicted the agony of mind of a father unable to dower his daughter, and fearing this fate for her; in this case the chronicler himself appealed to the Lord Guido da Polenta, who from charity gave her a suitable dower.[96] Many wills left money for the provision of dowries for poor girls, but private charity was never sufficient. The prostitutes were closely controlled by the communes ; and the commune and papacy exploited them by heavy taxation.[97]

The furniture of the houses of the moderately prosperous was often inventoried in their wills. They include feather beds, the large elegant chests known as *cassoni*, mattresses, sheets, quilts, and cushions. Among the kitchen utensils were copper cooking-pots, frying-pans, wine vessels, churns, and buckets.[98] Dress and personal ornaments were as costly as the purse could afford. The communes occasionally issued sumptuary decrees ; in Imola, it was laid down that none, whether knight or doctor of law or medicine, was to wear gold or silver ornaments.[99] In Ravenna, sumptuary laws were passed in a General Council of 1331. Here it was ordained that no-one was to wear a gold or silver coronet or belt, or anything costing more than £R.10 ; trains were not to be longer than five feet. The measure was only passed with difficulty, after one Guido Ravaldo had demonstrated how pleasing it was to God that the unbridled cupidity of women should be restrained in this way, and had pointed out that every well-constituted state, such as that of the Romans, had passed similar laws.[100] In fact, these statutes were generally ignored. The inventory, for instance, of the goods of the lady Francesca, wife of the notary Giovanni de' Lambardini, included a velvet dress, decorated with thirty-four large and eighty-four small pearl buttons, and seven rings ; one, a small emerald set in gold, one a large sapphire set in gold, one a ruby set in gold, and one wholly of gold. She also had a dress of scarlet cloth, a loose jacket of fine linen, a hood of white cloth with a golden pin to attach it, and a belt of green silk with silver gilt buckles.[101] Such clothing was expensive ; a codicil to the will of Ser Carnevale di Zese of Faenza recorded the clothes he had given to his betrothed, ' to be worn when she married him and on feast days '. They included a tunic of five *bracchia* of cloth, costing £R.1 7 6 a *bracchio*, a skirt and long cloak with worn silver buttons, bought second hand for £R.22, a French purse of silk and gold worth £R.4 8 0, and a belt of woven silk and silver worth £R.14.[102] Fashions in general came from Venice and Florence.[103]

The hired servants of the town nobility were almost completely at the mercy of their masters. In 1320, the Commune of Imola was fined £B.1,300 by the papal authorities, for failing to pursue a case against one of the town notaries. This man, Giovanni de' Baglioli Capucci, with two of his servants, Aurelio and Giacomo, had been accused of holding his servant Lucia as a prisoner, and of amputating her nose and ears because she refused to yield to his desires. The commune had completely neglected the case.[104] By the end of the fourteenth century, Eastern slaves were being bought in the province. In 1376, for instance, the lady Lena, wife of Oddo Oddi, sold a ' slave girl of Tartar race and speech ' who had been given the name of Citta at baptism, to Tommaso da Porcellino for £R.49 6 0.[105] In 1397, the heirs of Masio Florino of Forlì sold Lucia, ' from Russia ', (or ' from Rascia ' [in Serbia]?), to Demoldo da Ravaglia of Ravenna, with the stipulation that, in accordance with Masio's will, she should be released after three years.[106] In 1440, Bartolemeo de' Palazzi sold a slave called Cilta, ' of black skin and colour ', whom he had bought at Venice, to Mercato Mercati, for 100 *corbe* of corn.[107]

Opportunities for private reading in the thirteenth and fourteenth centuries were limited. Ecclesiastical libraries were presumably open to those interested, but the only inventories which have survived, those of the Archbishop of Ravenna, listing about 260 books, show a very conservative selection.[108] The nobility amused themselves with the tales of Lancelot of the Lake — *Galeotto fu il libro* — and kindred matter, but even in the fifteenth century books were very expensive. To a certain extent the signorial courts patronised the new humanism of the fourteenth century, which found some followers in the province. Of these the most notable was Benvenuto da Imola, of whom we shall say something more shortly. Iacopo Allegretti, the son of a judge of

Forlì and himself a doctor, was friendly with the Florentine humanist, Salutati, attained some fame in literary studies, and was patronised by the Ordelaffi and the Malatesti. Galeotto and Pandolfo Malatesti had friendly relations with Petrarch, and Pandolfo himself, a man of culture, protected Francesco da Fiano who was destined to be ' one of the minor stars in the humanistic constellation ' in the age of Salutati.[109]

Again, we have already noted the presence of the poet Antonio da Ferrara, and, at the end of 1347 and the beginning of 1348, of Giovanni Boccaccio at the court of Francesco degli Ordelaffi. Boccaccio had lived some time before that date at Ravenna, under Ostasio da Polenta, a man of liberal education. At Ravenna we find notaries with strong literary interests, and at least one schoolmaster, Donato degli Albanzani, who must have had a first-rate talent for the teaching of the *studia humanitatis*. Among his pupils Giovanni di Conversino (1343–1408) was to occupy chancellary posts in Northern Italy and strongly influence the development of classical studies in Lombardy while Giovanni di Iacopo Malpaghina (*c.* 1346–1417) was to become the *amanuensis* of Petrarch, and then, later, to fill the chair of rhetoric at Florence at an important moment in the development of civic humanism in Tuscany.[110]

Yet literary culture, both Latin and Italian, was inspired from other centres in Italy. Some poets, such as Tommaso da Faenza, and Ugolino Buzzola, had already begun, in the thirteenth century, to write in Tuscan.[111] Those who cultivated literature in Romagna must have felt themselves to be apostles of Florentine civilisation rather than as embodying any distinctive local school. In other forms of intellectual activity, the houses of the friars provided a focus for local scholars. The Dominican Guido Vernani, a lecturer at Bologna, who probably died in 1348 in the convent of his native Rimini, wrote commentaries on Aristotle's *De Anima*, Rhetoric, and Nicomachean Ethics, and various works in favour of the papal *plenitudo potestatis*, including an interesting attack upon Dante's *De Monarchia*. Also a Dominican was Enrico da Rimini, who lived around 1312, and left various writings : sermons and a treatise on the Four Cardinal Virtues. From the Augustinian Friars, came Fra Gregorio (*c.* 1272–1358) who after teaching theology at Paris, returned to Rimini in 1354.[112]

If theological scholars found a home in the province, men who attained distinction in legal studies, whether in canon or civil law, inevitably migrated to other centres where their talents could be better utilised. Among these were Gozio de' Battagli of Rimini (*c.* 1270–1348), who ended his days as a cardinal, and Raniero Arsendi of Forlì (d. probably in 1348), an eminent contemporary civilian.[113] But in the field of history Romagna produced some interesting chroniclers. In the thirteenth century Canon Tolosano of Faenza told the story of his town to 1236, and Pietro Cantinelli, a notary, gave an often vivid narrative of the wars of Romagna from 1226 to 1306. With these should be mentioned the Franciscan Salimbene, who passed many years in the province. In the fourteenth century we have the Annals of Cesena from an anonymous ecclesiastic, and the *Annali forlivesi* of Pietro Ravennate, most of whose chronicle, though known to seventeenth-century historians, has now been lost.[114] Finally we may mention two chronicles by laymen : the *Marcha* of Marco Battagli (died between 1370 and 1376), and the anonymous *Cronaca malatestiana* of the same period.

All in all, the evidences of literary culture in the province, if we look at any comparable non-Italian area, are quite impressive. Away from the study, there were hunting, chess, and visits to the spas of the Apennine *montagna*. Sometimes the whole signorial court — as that of Giorgio Ordelaffi in 1418 — would go off in festive mood to take the waters ; on other occasions the visits were made strictly for reasons of health. Rengarda Manfredi wrote to Ludovico Gonzago that she had visited the baths of Petriolo, 'which some distinguished doctors believed would be soothing and helpful for a certain pain in my stomach '.[115] For the lower classes there were the taverns, and the licensed gaming houses of the commune. All betting was a communal monopoly, and the statutes generally had provisions against playing at dice in taverns.[116] Every year there was the entertainment of the *palio*, the races run upon the commune's feast day.[117] But to many kinds of temperament the quality of life in the little towns must have been inexpressibly boring, and those who could not distract themselves with the exercises of religion, must have turned eagerly to the excitements of crime. The Florentine poet, Pieraccio Tedaldi, passed a long period in the province in the thirteen-seventies. He had a Romagnal lady, whose memory he was to recall fondly later at Lucca, and from time to time he was able to put a brave face on his exile :

'come Carlo in Francia
o come il conte in Poppi, i' sto in Faenza.'

('As Charles (IV) in France, or as the Count in his castle of Poppi, so am I in Faenza.')

But at other times he breaks forth in lines which will find an echo in the hearts of all strangers who have passed a long time in the province :

> ' Ché i' sono oggimai sazio
> del tanto dimorare qui in Romagna,
> che a considerallo è uno strazio,
> Vorrei partir omai d'esta campagna
> e ritornar nel dilettoso spazio
> de la nobil città gioiosa e magna.'

(' For I am now so weary of staying so long here in Romagna, that to think of it is painful. I wish to leave henceforth this countryside, and return to the delightful terrain of the noble, joyous, and great city.')

Romagna was clearly not considered as an ideal residence by Italians of the time. In his satirical reply to the famous monthly wishes of Folgore da San Gimignano, Cenne de la Chitara (*c.* 1332), in his sonnet on April wished that Folgore's band might undergo various unsavoury experiences, and that then they should ' be revived among the men who lug hoes in the plain of Romagna ' — a fate which he clearly thought was unpleasant.[118] The boredom of provincial existence accounts in no small part for the virulence and persistence of the conflict of factions. It also explains the popularity of the *signoria*, once it had been established. The new form of government at least provided a colourful pageant in the ceremonies which grew up around the personality of the *signore*.

V

In October 1334, a list was drawn up of the ' Equites de Cavalcata ' of Imola.[119] These were the men with horses, who were liable to military service for the commune, and who constituted the aristocracy of the town. On this occasion there were in all fifty-two families. They can be divided into two principal groups. First came the upper class, the men who held emphyteutic leases of substantial properties in the *contado*. Among these were the Alidosi, the Cantagalli and the Nordigli, the families from whom the *signorie* were to be established. The other names among the *equites* ; Carvassali, Binielli, Oraboni, Baioli, Giraldi, Ugodonici, Bolgarelli, Broccardi, are almost entirely those of notarial families. Here was the only substantial group in the town which could have resisted the imposition of single person rule, which might have had an interest in preserving the communal government. Patently it is an element of the greatest importance in the establishment of the *signorie*.

If ever ' the state as a work of art ' existed, the product of calculation, measurement, and ordered reasoning, it was the public notary who made it possible. In the notarial protocols all the life of the town appears, with richness and precision of detail. It was the notary who drew up every administrative act, but his scope was far wider than that. All economic life flowed through the pages of his cartulary, the establishment of trades, the buying of houses, the leasing of land. Social life was here too, the births, baptisms, marriages, and deaths. In all, the notarial protocols provide the most important source for the understanding of Romagna. The artists of the province portray the immutables of life. Giovanni da Rimini's Christ on the Cross speaks of a living faith : the body twisted in agony, the bloody sweat, the crown of thorns, the triumph. Dante tells of romantic love :

> a che e come concedette amore,
> che conosceste i dubbiosi desiri?

— and Francesca replies, telling of the day without suspicion, the eyes meeting, the lips touching, *tutto tremante*. In the protocols religion is absent, romance is absent. All we have are the testaments of men about to die, the squabbles of monks and the ostentatious gifts. Love is not mentioned, but there are the dowries, the marital quarrels, and the divorces. All life, of a certain sort, is here. Who held the land, who held office? Who owed money, how much was taken from the peasants? The notarial contracts provided the answers.

Any act, once registered in the notary's cartulary, had the force of law ; indeed it could create law, and abrogate the *lex* of the communes, nor could anyone question in law the findings of a protocol, or the notary's competence in drawing up a deed. The notary could do his work anywhere ; in the Palazzo Comunale, in church, by the roadside, in a shop. It would be a lengthy process ; the parties coming to agreement, explaining what they wanted, the pen moving slowly on the rough draft, stopping again as a point was discussed and clarified, doodling a face in the margin before carrying on. It is a tradition that lies deep within the Italian consciousness, the origin of the countless hours spent before bureaucrats writing on *carta bollata*. Later the rough draft would be written up in a cartulary, and deposited in the archives of the commune. The statutes of the towns sometimes insisted, 'since many notaries, importunate in taking their fees, are negligent in producing their writings', that this should be done within five days.[120]

The scale of notaries' charges was established according to the sums of money mentioned in the deed; for writing a contract of £B.10, the notary would receive twelve shillings, and for 'authenticating' it by writing it up in the cartulary, another four shillings. The charges rose progressively; for a public instrument dealing with sums of between £60 and £100, he would receive eighteen shillings for rogation, and ten shillings for authentication.[121] Once registered, the notarial documents were open to inspection by all interested parties; sometimes a foreign notary would be appointed by the commune to read and translate the documents to anyone who wished to know their provisions.[122] If the notary died after writing the rough draft, and before formally registering and authenticating his acts, the authority of a General Council was generally necessary to enable another notary to complete his work.

The notary in Romagna was generally taught his craft in some local school, such as that which Benvenuto's father ran in Imola.[123] By origin, the office of notary was closely bound up with Roman law, and with the Roman Empire, and this connection was still jealously maintained; notaries signed themselves 'imperiali auctoritate notarius'. This was not a mere rhetorical flourish; notaries were in fact created from the plenitude of imperial power, by the authority of the Emperor delegated to some Count Palatine, and were entitled to exercise their art 'per totum Romanum imperium'. Deeds recording the creation of a notary echo with the splendid sonority of a greater world; 'the right of the distinguished man Lord Iacopo, Count Palatine of Cerro in the diocese of Zara, and of his sons, and successors throughout the whole world and the Roman Empire, to create notaries and ordinary judges, to legitimise bastards etc. . . . is known to have emanated from the imperial plenitude of power of the most excellent, most serene and most unconquered Emperor Lord Charles IV, through divine clemency, Emperor of the Romans and ever Augustus. . . .' Kneeling before the imperial representative the notary was invested, 'cum penna et calamario'. He exchanged the kiss of peace with him, and swore an oath of fidelity, touching the Gospels.[124] Afterwards he would be received at a dinner of the notaries of the town and would be enrolled in their Art.[125] Though sometimes the sons of artisans (shoe-makers, for instance) became notaries, on the whole the society was closely knit, with sons and grandsons following the father's profession.

The first impression of the notarial mind revealed in the protocols is one of comprehensiveness. The next is of essential sobriety. In so far as a generalisation can be made, this sober, almost austere outlook was characteristic of the notary himself. This notarial mentality is clearly shown in the work of Benvenuto de' Rambaldi of Imola, the son, grandson and brother of a notary, and himself the most famous of Romagnol notaries. Coluccio Salutati, with the wonted humanist phrase, described him as ' quasi divinus vir ', words which suggest, somehow, a dynamic imagination. In fact, what prevails in his work is precision, detail, literalness of mind. He remarks, for instance of

l' amor che a nullo amato amar perdona

that this is untrue, that many people fall in love, and that the loved one doesn't return the same feelings. This is insensitive to Dante's complete meaning, and yet the prosaic quality of Benvenuto's mind is what makes his Commentary on the *Divine Comedy* so valuable. He was not really interested, say, in the significance of Guido da Montefeltro in the universal scheme of things, but he was able to explain a lot about Guido's life in Romagna.

Benvenuto's ability was exceptional and gave him access to the dominant intellectual circles of the time. Boccaccio was his master (the Boccaccio of the *De Genealogia Deorum*, rather than that of the *Decameron*), and Petrarch and Salutati his friends. But other notaries had similar interests. If there was a Renaissance, it was due to the new standards set by the educated laymen, and this meant either merchants or notaries. However, one must not exaggerate the speed with which the new currents of thought passed down to the ordinary reader from the elites. As late as the middle of the fifteenth century the library of the notary Ser Tramaccio de Tramoccio was probably typical. This consisted of :

uno libro codice
uno libro aurore — probably a notarial text-book
uno libro virgillis
uno libro loctis — a study of contracts?
uno libro vocabullarum
uno libro super sexto decretalium
summa odofredi super decretalibus
uno libro troyani — perhaps the *De excidio Troiae* of Dares.

uno libro aurore magistri Rolandini — Passagieri's celebrated notarial textbook.

uno libro summe Egidii de Judicario ordine
uno libro tragedarum Senece
una lectura super aliquibus legibus
uno libro epistollarum Cassiodori
uno libro compendiose — perhaps an encyclopedia, such as that of Isidore of Seville

uno libello feudorum
una alia lectura iuris
liber floris super testamentis
uno libello sancti Tome de aquino de anima
uno libello Stacii
septem libris rogatiorum olim Ser Baptiste Sancte de Melendro comitatus Mutiliane[126]

The last item in the list is interesting. It is almost possible to suspect that the favourite reading of notaries was the notarial protocols. To a modern taste, certainly, these might be much more interesting than most of the books mentioned, and they might be profitable too. Lorenzo Guarini, for instance, noted, 'that in 1469, on the last day of February, as I was looking through the instruments of my father at Bagnacavallo, I found the deed of the building of the church of Bonzolino, constructed by Pirovaldo Guarino'. With it was the award to Guarino of the right of presentation to the church. He showed the instrument he had discovered to the Bishop of Faenza, who immediately invested his family with the *ius patronatus*.

The primary source of notarial wealth was not the drawing up of documents. This was well paid, but it did not make a man rich. The forgery of papal bulls, as carried out by Ser Tommaso da Ripasantra, in Rimini, was much more profitable, but much more dangerous; discovery brought the death sentence.[127] The real value of being a notary was that, in a semi-literate society, it guaranteed an opportunity of being an office holder in the commune, as *massarius*, chancellor, etc., with all the accompanying perquisites. Above all, it gave the training necessary for taking out a farm of the revenues of the commune. In these communal enterprises lay the only scope for business talents. Having made money by office holding and tax-farming, the notary would then invest in land, or in the trading contracts of the town; from this point, marriage into the signorial family, and identification of interests with the *signore*, was but a short step. Such ties gave further scope for making profit through the town government.

What this implied can be seen, for instance, in the history of the Counts della Bordella of Mordano. Their unsavoury name may suggest the origins of their wealth, but later generations courteously hinted that it was in fact derived from a noble of Bordeaux who was a follower of the crusades, and who broke his journey at Mordano at the end of the thirteenth century. The truth is otherwise. An Ugo della Bordella was a knight of the commune in 1235.[128] Henceforth, the family took to the notarial profession, with profitable results. Bartolommeo della Bordella was advocate of the commune in 1334, had taken the farm of the *gabelle* of milling in 1336, and was negotiating the purchase of salt in 1337.[129] With this sort of transaction, by 1360, Zello, Bartolomeo, and Alberico of the family were able to take a perpetual lease of most of the territory of Mordano, from Bishop Carlo Alidosi. The terms were an annual rent of £B.300, and a re-entry fine of £200 every sixty-nine years. Shortly afterwards, Innocent VI raised Mordano to a county, and its possessors to the dignity of counts.[130]

The example of the della Bordella was there for all to see. Notaries had an interest in stable government and stable tax collecting, and, given the circumstances of Romagna, this could come only from single person rule. In each commune, this class of officials clung to power through all the changes in government, as *signore* gave way to *signore*. Some of the names of the *equites de cavalcata* of Imola, in 1334, were still found among the town officials in the era of Napoleonic rule. In Rimini, the Benci, Belmonti, Adimari, Perleoni; in Faenza, the Casali, the Viarana, the Pasi, the Zuccoli, Azzurini, and Paganelli; these provided the cadres of communal officials, and formed the leading families of the citizen aristocracy.

These men had been raised in the great traditions of Bolognese law. Perhaps they saw with reluctance the sweeping away of the old order. To some, as to Benvenuto, the change was unbearable. Benvenuto himself took a prominent part in the insurrection against the Alidosi in 1365 and was one of those chosen by the town to appeal at Avignon against signorial rule. As a result he returned no more to Imola, 'town of noble minds'. Like his master he was to end his days as an exile. The *signoria* remained; and with it remained Benvenuto's contemporaries. Practical, hard-headed men, they stayed to serve the *signore* and themselves. And because of this, the commune did not wholly die. The name, the institutions, the administrative structure, the administrative personnel remained. Something of the spirit remained too : the seeking after legality, the search for justice. It was justice conceived in the terms of the age, but justice none the less.

CHAPTER VIII

The Government of the Communes in the Fourteenth Century

Tyrannus autem est pessimus; hoc autem est ita manifestum quod demonstratione non eget.

BARTOLO DA SASSOFERRATO[1]

I

SO far this work has distinguished three eras in the formation of *signorie* : tyranny — when the lords of Romagna ruled without any legal justification ; captaincy — when their rule was legitimised by decree of their communes ; and finally, *signoria* — where the papacy gave a final legitimisation by its grant of the papal vicariates. But in defining the rule of the *signori* by these legal formulas, one misses the reality behind the government of the towns. For whatever the formal constitution, what was important was who held power within it. In fact, during the whole of the fourteenth century, among all the changes in the legal position, the administration of the communes was essentially the same, and its character was unaltered.

This government has been called a ' dyarchy ' — a word implying a sharing of authority between the commune and the *signore*.[1bis] More justly, it might be seen as the final and natural development of communal rule. It would be wrong to describe the commune of the thirteenth century as ' free ' in contrast to the commune of the fourteenth century. The only change was that the commune was now dominated by one man, instead of by a small feudal oligarchy. In fact, the real change in the character of the communes came in the fifteenth century, when some of the lords acquired, through custom, a sense of prescriptive right, and attracted to themselves the sentiment of their subjects, the feeling that they were the natural princes of the state to whom personally their subjects owed loyalty and allegiance.

Such sentiment did not exist in the fourteenth century (and existed only rarely in the fifteenth). Basically, the *signori* were still communal officers. Having seized power and expelled their opponents, they summoned the usual councils to confer upon themselves the offices of captain or *podestà*, and to decree the formal expulsion of their rivals. When they began to tamper with the constitution and become life-captains, they did so by calling upon the communal councils to enforce the new system. As a result, there was only a gradual and insensible relaxation of the idea that their positions as captains rested upon representation and consent. The representative figure of this age was a man like Francesco il vecchio de' Manfredi, whom Sacchetti, in one of his stories, described as 'a wise and worthy lord without any pomp, who had the habits and semblance and manners of an important citizen rather than of a *signore*'.[2] Popular recognition was, of course, a façade ; the consent of recalcitrant *anziani* could always be secured by threats or violence. But since the era of *comitatinanza* this had always been so.

It was the papal vicariate which did most to change this concept of the *signore* as a communal officer. But a generation had to pass before the idea was generally accepted that a ruler was distinct from his commune. Even in the grants of vicariate, the *signori* were enjoined to rule 'according to the statutes', that is, in other words, 'according to the good old law of the communes'.

Signorial rule in the fourteenth century differed from previous rule, only in that it was more continuous and stable than the rule of the faction-leaders which had preceded it. Inevitably it depended upon the character of the *signore*. It would, for that reason, be pointless to claim that as a system of government it was anything but bad. When Bartolo da Sassoferrato (albeit, merely echoing Aristotle) described it as the worst of all forms of government, he was writing with an intimate knowledge of the Italian political situation of the day. Obviously, though, the characters of the lords themselves differed greatly. Some seem, from what brief notices remain, to have had a certain charm. One thinks of Guido Novello da Polenta, the patron of Dante ; of Scarpetta Ordelaffi, whom a political opponent described as 'a young and temperate gentleman' ;[3] of Cecco degli Ordelaffi, who according to Cobelli 'was for his pleasantry well-loved by the people'. Cobelli was writing over a hundred years later, when the Ordelaffi had passed away, but still in his day, Cecco's memory was recorded in the songs of the people :

> Cecco Hordelaffo
> Ongn' omo m' apella
> Per la piu sauia ceruella
> Che al mondo sia ![4]

In the rule of Francesco II Ordelaffi, it has already been seen how there was a large element of popular support. Generally, however, signorial rule in the fourteenth century was treated by its subjects with wary indifference. Its only real advantages were first, that it was better than what had gone before, and second, that it preserved the local independence of the towns against the papacy. But where the *signore* himself was not a native of the town — as with Francesco Ordelaffi at Cesena — he no longer represented any focus for local patriotism, and his rule was based wholly upon fear. At Cesena, Anglic Grimoard reported in 1371 that Francesco 'ruled it tyrannically for some years by so much violence that, as it seems to me, no roots of his remain there '.[5]

But even in their own towns, the *signori's* rule rested mainly upon force. Ostasio di Bernardino da Polenta clearly ruled by intimidation. In Ravenna, Guido de' Traversari, Araldo Spreti, Giovanni Piccinini, and two Monaldini were murdered at his command; the survivors of their houses were forced to flee, and with them three other families: the Onesti, Bicci, and the Sassi.[6] Ostasio also killed Bannino, a bastard of Guido il vecchio, and his son, in 1325.[7] Ostasio's son, Bernardino, 'a cruel and harsh *signore*,'[8] held power by the same methods. In May 1357 there was rioting in the town against taxation, and two signorial officials were killed. But the mob dispersed at evening without pressing their advantage, and the next day Bernardino was able to regain control. As a result, 120 of the citizens were imprisoned, and many subsequently executed. Again, in Faenza in 1350, the citizens, Villani wrote, 'had no love for the lordship of a new tyrant (Giovanni di Ricciardo Manfredi) who was by the wise reputed to be madly made '.[9]

Perhaps the most revealing insight into signorial government of the time comes from the rule of the Alidosi at Imola. Under Roberto Alidosi (papal-vicar, December 1350–63) the internal government of the town had been comparatively peaceful. His death, however, caused a crisis in the affairs of the family. Azzo and Beltrando, the two eldest boys among his six children, were invested jointly with the vicariate and *signoria*. Almost at once, trouble developed with the other branch of the family, their cousins, the sons of Massa Alidosi. More serious still, each of the two brothers sought to establish supremacy over the other. Two factions grew up round the brothers and soon took up arms. 'One robbed the other,' says the chronicler, 'and the friends of one and the other were robbed.' Finally, in May 1363, amidst serious street-fighting, an attempt was made by one party to burn down the Palazzo Comunale. As a result, the papal government intervened and arrested the brothers. They were restored in June, however, but without the control of the castle or the town guard. They were also warned not to tax the citizens beyond the customary amounts.

The government of the Alidosi remained burdensome and yet weak. ' These Alidosi stand but poorly, and have little command in the land, for they were young when their father died and are ill-united.'[10] In January 1365, Rainaldo de' Bolgarelli, of a landed notarial family eminent in the town,[11] who had been exiled by the Alidosi, but restored by Albornoz, attempted, with certain of his friends, to dispossess them of the government. For a moment the insurgents gained control, and began to burn down the signorial palace ; but Azzo and Beltrando were saved by the arrival of their brother Todeschino, who, entering the town with a troop of foot ' with trumpet and drum ', managed to break the rebels and kill their leader.[12]

Disorders continued, however, and in March the commune itself attempted to remove their *signori* from office. On the twentieth of the month the twelve *anziani* and twelve *sapientes* of the town met in the house of the *podestà*, Eduardo de' Cerchi of Florence. In company with his officials, Cerchi proposed that a delegation should be sent to the pope, to protest against the evils which had arisen : ' through the depraved and impious rule and the evil extortions made by the lords Azzo and Beltrando to the damage of the people and men of the town '. The ambassadors, he proposed, should ask for good and just rectors who would govern according to the statutes, and who would hold office for six months only. Some of the *anziani* and *savii*, whose speeches were briefly recorded, supported the motion. Ser Iacopo Gharamondi complained of the ' rapacious and ravening wolves of magnates ', and declared that the people of Imola had fallen into a wretched and miserable condition as a result of the ill government of the two lords. He was supported by Bombone Bomboni and Giuliano de' Calvi. Calvi complained that from the time of Lippo Alidosi, ' as everyone knows ', the finances of the commune had been pocketed by the tyrants. The opposing speeches were not recorded, but in the ballot, the motion was only passed by twenty-four to twenty-two votes. By the rules of procedure the *familia* or officials of the *podestà* who were foreigners to the town, had two votes each. This meant that a majority among the native *anziani* and *savii* must have been opposed to the proposal.

The following day a General Council was called in the cathedral of Imola. It was presided over by the papal-rector, the *podestà*, and the Lord Azzo. A motion was introduced setting out the various crimes of the Alidosi brothers. They had burnt down the Palazzo Comunale, created divisions among the citizens, caused disturbances, usurped the revenues of the town to their own use, and imposed taxes 'to the damage and prejudice of our Holy Mother the Church'. In all this they had been aided by about twenty 'powerful and noble magnates, the accomplices and followers of the said tyrants', who had shared in their spoils. The citizens, it was said, went in continual fear of chance words thrown out by the tyrants.

As a result of this indictment, it was agreed by 512–332 votes that five procurators (among them was Benvenuto da Imola) should go to Avignon, to lay the case of the commune before the Pope.[13]

The result of the deputation was a letter from Urban V dated 1 November, ordering the two brothers to be deprived of their vicariate and sent to Avignon, to be examined personally by him to see if they were fit to rule. The papal rector, Cardinal Androin de la Roche, was told in the meanwhile, to dispatch a report upon the town and its parties.[14] De la Roche, whose massive incompetence displayed itself in every aspect of his life-long and devoted service to the Church, must have given a favourable answer, for in the following year the brothers were restored to rule, though with a *podestà* appointed by the rector. Their troubles were not yet over, however. They plotted to drive away the papal *podestà*, were imprisoned and deprived of lordship. 'This time', wrote Villola, 'it seems to me must be the last.'[15] But the rector again displayed his clemency or weakness; they were restored in October 1357, and seem to have given no further trouble to the Church. Cardinal Grimoard, in 1371 wrote: 'I have found these brothers to be of great fidelity, and so too were their ancestors. They should be kept in good favour and grace.'[16]

The most satisfactory interpretation of these events is that Azzo and Beltrando were young and inexperienced. They ruled by threats and violence, with the aid of a dominant clique of nobles. But the voting records of 1356 show that the town, whether because its citizens were ruled by fear, bonds of dependence, or the preference for native rulers to papal officials, was only half-hearted in its opposition to their rule. Despite the adverse vote, the power of the Alidosi was firmly rooted in the town. This consideration must have influenced the papacy in its decision to maintain the *signoria*. Unstable as they were, the Alidosi were men whom it was better to retain as allies.

The situation in Imola probably reflects roughly the position in each of the communes. Violence was an essential element in signorial rule, yet it would be wrong to imagine that it was the sole constituent. The government of a single person was really necessary for the continued existence of the communes, for the towns could not have survived indefinitely the aristocratic factions which were the inevitable sequel to *comitatinanza*. The captaincy, at least, offered an escape from the anarchic feuds of Guelf and Ghibelline, even if sometimes it replaced them by quarrels within the signorial family.

Again, it was the *signori* who preserved the finances of the communes. The small towns of the province, with their agrarian economies, had none of the great resources and capital backing of the major Italian states ; their financial administration worked on hand-to-mouth expedients, and was always on the brink of chaos. The *signori* came to power partly as a result of the difficulties of the communes when faced with the ever-increasing demands of papal taxation. Historians, looking at the world-wide interests of the Avignon papacy, which stretched from the Mongol missions in China to the parishes of Iceland ; at all its attempts to secure peace in Europe and the launching of a crusade ; have portrayed the resistance of the papal states as meaningless anarchy. Yet narrowing one's vision, looking at the communes from their own essentially provincial standpoint, the early years of the fourteenth century appear principally as a story of unremitting attempts at fiscal oppression by the papacy, and the resistance that these attempts called into being. In this resistance the *signori* were the champions of their communes.

More than this, as a counter-weight to the natural individualism of the citizens, they ensured that there was any revenue at all. Consider the finances of Imola. On 6 February 1366, Pozzoli, the *massarius* for the following six months, recorded a balance of £B.684 8 2. On the 28 August of the same year he deposited with his successor in office, £B.471.[17] Such was the narrow margin within which the commune had to meet papal taxation and its own domestic expenses. Any sudden new expense in excess of such sums could only be met by loan — and the rate of interest was high. Amidst financial crises one finds the use of short term expedients ; in 1287, for instance, the commune alienated 2,000 *tornature* of land ; in 1310 it borrowed £B.600 — significantly enough from its future *signori*.[18] Measures like these did little to touch the heart of the problem ; the principal difficulty was that the citizens were continually seeking to avoid their financial obligations.

There were, for instance, frivolous claims to exemption from taxation: by the laymen of the Cavalieri Gaudenti in 1287, by physicians in 1289.[19] In addition, there was continual dishonesty among those who were not exempt. In a *collecta* of 1312, imposed for the purchase of corn, over 1,500 failed to pay, and were formally sentenced to pay double the sum originally demanded.[20] But it is hardly likely that the commune should have had greater success in executing the sentence of the fine than in securing the original taxes. The answer to this problem was given in the same year, when it was decreed in the General Council that ' because the nobles were refusing to pay taxes ', the lord captain ' who now is, shall have free control and free power to exact all *collecta* placed in the town for the following fifteen months . . . from whatsoever person of whatever grade '. This was carried by eighty to twenty-six votes.[21] Such a grant of new coercive power to the captain almost suggests that the *signore* is the man who comes to revitalise a lost civic tradition.

Patently one would not pursue this line of thought very far. None the less, the members of the signorial family, accustomed from childhood to the exercise of authority, would probably be more efficient than any amateurs likely to be thrown up by a communal democracy. What notary or carpenter was likely to have the experience of, say, Bernardino di Guido, the brother of Lamberto da Polenta? By birth and marriage he was allied to power; his maternal grandfather was Bernadino of the great Ferrarese family of the Fontana; his grandmother, Samaratina, had been daughter of Alberghetto Manfredi. His wife, Maddalena, was the daughter of Malatesta da Verucchio.

All his life he was involved in politics. He was with Jean d' Eppe in the attack on Forlì in 1282, he was *podestà* of Modena in 1287, and had acquired such honour there that he had been offered the podestàship of Milan. In 1292 he was *podestà* of Cervia and Faenza, in 1297 *podestà* and captain of war at Parma, ' from where he returned with the greatest honour to his own'. In 1301, he was *podestà* again at Milan, in 1305 at Ferrara, in 1306 at Bologna, in 1307 at Cervia. In 1308, he was a leader in the war of Ferrara, in 1311, as a councillor of King Robert, he brought troops to the aid of Florence against Henry VII. Only his death in 1313 prevented him from exercising the podestàship at Florence to which he had been appointed.[22]

An ordinary citizen of the towns might have been a better man, a demagogue like Cola di Rienzo might have been more popular. But it cannot be doubted that such a man as Bernardino was more likely to be an efficient ruler.

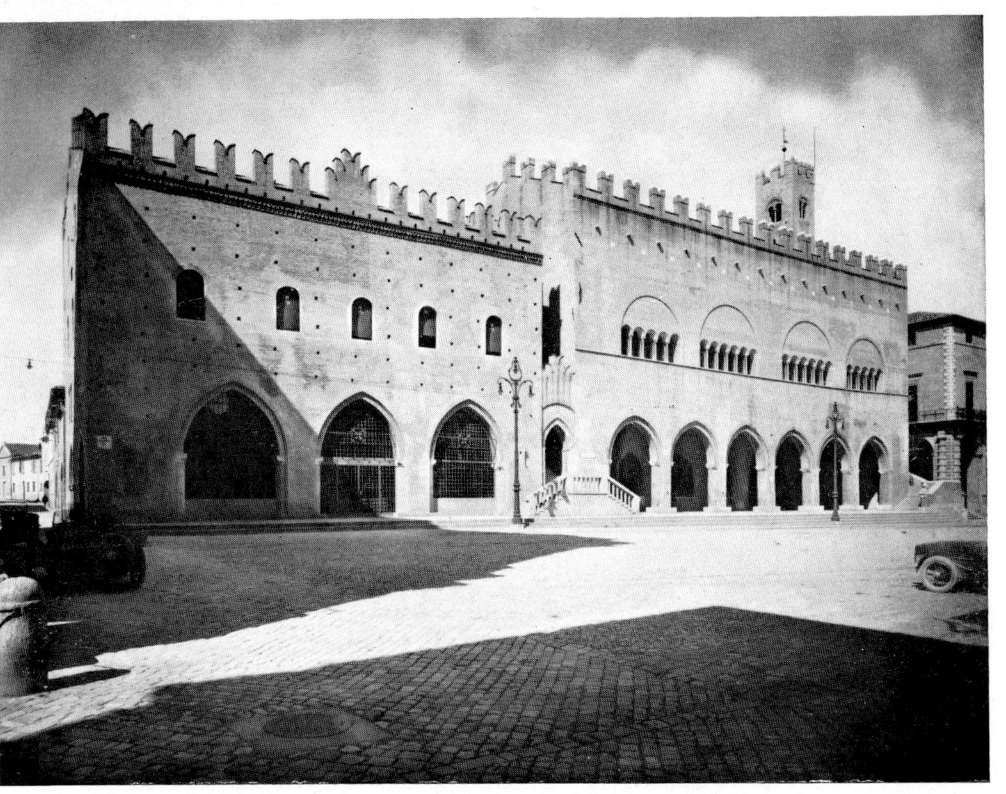

Palazzo del Podestà and Palazzo dell' Arengo Rimini

It is an academic point, for in Romagna there was never any possibility of democratic rule. The only choice presented to the communes was between the government of the *signori* and that of the Church, ' the lordship of the Cahorsins and the men of Languedoc ', as Villani called it. In the event, therefore, the *signori* came not as destroyers but as saviours. For whereas in Florence the rule of a tyrant — of the Duke of Athens for instance — was a sudden usurpation which violently overturned the established order, in Romagna the *signoria* was established slowly and inevitably over a long period of time ; it was the natural fulfilment and development of the commune.

II

The grant to the *signore* of the life-captaincy gave him unfettered control over general policy decisions, and over every aspect of communal administration. Previously his rights and duties had, in theory, been limited, as in the statutes of Imola, but now all was ordered ' at his will '. In making policy decisions he would be influenced, perhaps, by a small circle of intimates, such as those found in attendance with Sinibaldo Ordelaffi — his wife, the Lady Paolo, his nephew Tebaldo, two or three nobles of the *contado*, and Master Meletto di Russi, his doctor and astrologer (the last role an almost indispensable adjunct to the signorial courts of the age).[23] His private secretary might be some minor humanist, such as Cecco da Mileto, who would brave the strictures of his Florentine friends in the hope of finding a genuine patron.

For his administrative work he would keep the ' household ' granted to the captain by the commune. This consisted of a judge, who acted as his vicar, a constable, notaries, messengers, and servants. They lived together with the *signore* in the Palazzo del Popolo, shortly to be renamed ' Palazzo della Signoria '. The *signore* who was efficient in administration would supervise the general running of all aspects of the government, giving special attention to the finances, the defence, and policing of the commune.

His principal executive assistant was the *podestà*, who was always a ' foreigner '. This official, who, in the early thirteenth century, had been the supreme officer of the commune, the executive of the will of the General Council, had by now become the executive of the will of the *signore*. Together with his household, the *podestà* dwelt in the Palazzo Comunale, or Palazzo del Podestà. The size of the household would vary from commune to commune. In Rimini in the fourteenth century it consisted of a knight, three judges (two for civil and one for criminal cases), six servants and a cook (clothed in the same livery), ten policemen (in another livery) and four court-beadles. Sometimes the *podestà* would have the assistance of two knights of justice, who would be citizens of the commune, and who would have jurisdiction over minor cases. Finally he was allotted twelve horses. In Rimini he was paid £900 for a six months' tenure of office. Out of this sum he was expected to keep his household.[24]

The statutes of all the towns — even those of Faenza drawn up after the establishment of the *signoria* — decreed that the *podestà* should be elected by the General Council, and should hold office for not longer than six months, or at most, a year.[25] In fact, here as elsewhere, the will of the *signore* overrode all, and in this period, the podestàship was a signorial appointment. When Franco Sacchetti wanted to extend his holding of the office in Faenza, he simply indited a sonnet of request to the Lord Astorgio Manfredi, and waited for the laboriously constructed confirmation in the same medium :

> Ora tornando a vostra intenzione
> quel che m' addomandaste vi convegno
> comme a rettore e franco campione.
> Sei mesi aggiungo al vostro reggimento
> della podesteria con buon talento.[26]

Now that the podestàship had become merely an executive post, the social standing of those who held it declined. It was no longer an office held by the feudal nobility, as in the thirteenth century. Later, when the Romagnol towns became virtually client states of other powers, the prestige of the office became more important, and the post would be held by some professional diplomat nominated by the dominant city. But in the fourteenth century, the *podestà* was merely a serviceable man of presence, drawn from the middle classes, and trained in civil law. There grew up what was virtually a new class of professional *podestà*.

Of these Franco Sacchetti may be taken as representative. *Podestà* in turn at Empoli, Susinana, Serravalle, Bibbiena, Faenza (in 1396), and San Miniato ; he ended his life in the important office of Captain of the Florentine Romagna. Basically he despised the *signori*, and was ambivalent about his profession. To a fellow Florentine, acting as *podestà* of Bologna, he wrote : ' Can there possibly be a more stunted life than ours . . . one must be quite mad to leave a sweet, temperate life as lord of one's family, to become, not so much a *podestà*, as a servant of ruffians '. He complains of having to punish the crimes of a whole town, of the need to correct the vices of his household, of being subject to the least important person in the signorial court. If there is anything wrong it is always the fault of the *podestà*. 'Yet here I am, white haired, wandering still, forced to go looking for another such post.' 'What is really incredible', he wrote, 'are the people who are actually rich, who are merchants, and want the job. One can understand it once — for the experience, or as a penance — but if they do it for other reasons, they are either avaricious or feeble-minded'. Writing from Faenza, he ends by claiming that his title should be not 'servus servorum dei' like the pope's, but 'servus servorum diaboli'.[27]

This is one mood of Sacchetti, but not the whole man. The intensely human flavour of his writings springs from all the contradictions of human nature in his personality. At one moment he is the brutal realist of the *Novelle*; at other times he reflects in austere terms on human life, and will advise his friends to arm themselves with the philosophy of Seneca and Christ. 'O vanagloria dell' umane posse! Vanitas vanitatum . . .' the least of the hermits of the Camaldolesi leads a nobler life than the greatest lord in the world. Again, in pastoral mood, he walks the mountains and salutes the (extremely artificial) shepherdesses;

> O vaghe montanine pastorelle
> Donde venite sì leggiadre e belle?

At other times this gives way to sonorous and sombre reflections on the state of Italy and of his native Florence: 'quanti omicidii e incendii, e quante morti nominate per iustizia, nella mia città in picciol tempo son occorse!'

The very fullness of Franco's nature must have made him the ideal *podestà*. Socially he was able to deal with the *signori* and to maintain harmonious relations with them during his period of office — and this was perhaps the most important element in his work. When Astorgio Manfredi was presented with some of the rose-apples of Florence, he sent one across to the Palazzo del Podestà, together with an apple of Faenza, to ask his *podestà* which was the better. Sacchetti was at table when they came; he called for a basin to wash his hands, then ate the apples, and, still stitting at table, composed a tactful sonnet declaring that both were best, according to one's taste:

> 'L' una e l' altra è buona tutta e piena
> Secondi gli appetiti e le persone
> che son diverse sotto 'l ciel sereno.'[28]

Such gestures came naturally to him, and eased the whole process of governing. With Sacchetti verse often becomes almost an administrative memorandum. He writes a ballad comparing the Lord Astorgio, with his wife and their son, to the Trinity :

> 'sono tre in un seggio
> e uno in tre perfetti e una essenza'.

He writes verses to each of the *signori* in turn, explaining how their government alone is just and noble. When Ludovico Alidosi replied to a sonnet which praised his father, by explaining that he was very, very busy, and that he wouldn't therefore answer with a sonnet himself, but would send one composed by Venanzio da Camerino, ' which I think should sufficiently satisfy you ',[29] we can imagine a raising of eyebrows at the seriousness with which this sort of thing was now being taken. In writing them, Sacchetti was not (as some historians seem to have thought) on oath.

In general, the *podestà* supervised all the aspects of the administration of the town and *contado*, co-ordinated its various branches, and sought out any irregularities in its operation. He presided over its various representative councils, and was responsible particularly for justice. It was an office of great responsibility and called for gifts of character. The *podestà* had to resist the temptation of the town's women (or like Marco della Torre in Forlì, he might end by being knifed by outraged brothers)[30] and the inevitable opportunities for peculation.[31] At the end of his service, like all the other officials, he was 'syndicated', *i.e.* subjected to a searching scrutiny of his accounts and actions during his period of office. Sometimes towards the end of his tenure, a public announcement would be made by the town-crier, that any wishing to complain of him should present themselves at the Palazzo Comunale for their grievances to be investigated.[32]

The administration over which the *signore* and *podestà* presided ruled over town and *contado*.

III
THE ADMINISTRATION OF THE TOWN

The town administration can be considered under six principal aspects : Justice, Chancellery, Finance, Councils, Local Officials, and Defence.

(a) *Justice*

The dispensing of justice was the most important function of the *podestà*, and occupied most of his time. In the hall of the Palazzo del Podestà in Faenza, for instance, he would sit with his judges at the five benches, each distinguished by a distinctive device : the Bench of the Oxen, for contracts of minors ; the Bench of the Eagle for criminal cases ; the Bench of the Lion for civil cases ; the Bench of the Horse for contracts of women ; and the Bench of the King, for cases dealing with damage to agrarian property.[33] Justice was inevitably based on the teaching of the law schools of Bologna. It was laid down at Faenza that all judges must have studied continuously for five years at Bologna, or some other *studium generale*.[34]

Criminal justice compensated for the ineffectuality of the police by dealing out occasional draconic sentences. Theft was punished by death.[35] Crimes of violence were accepted more philosophically. *Crimes passionnels* were generally pardoned (as in present day Italy). Armed assaults were often punished only by a fine. When in a room in the Palazzo Vecchio of Imola, one Giovanni di San Lorenzo stabbed Corrado of Cesena, ' with a steel dagger in the lower part of his shoulder, so that the blood came, crying out : " Take that, you drunkard " ', the *podestà* merely ordered him to pay a fine of £B.200.[36] This sort of offence indeed, was generally considered to be more a civil cause between the two people concerned. It was probably treated here as a criminal offence because it actually took place in the palace of the *podestà*. Technically the carrying of arms in the town was forbidden, but it was difficult for Romagnol justice to conceive of violence between individuals as being a public matter. As late as 1442, two soldiers were given leave to fight a duel on the piazza of Forlì.[37]

In all criminal cases, torture was used to extract confessions, though under strict rules.[38] Prisons were supervised by a gaoler, who, in Imola, gave security of £B.15 that he would not rob his prisoners, although he was allowed to take their cloak as fee.[39]

In civil justice, for the reasons given, many of the cases dealt with crimes of violence between individuals. The normal procedure here was for the *podestà* to mediate between the two parties, persuade them to exchange the kiss of peace, and to bind them over to good behaviour under pledges of money.[40] In other cases too, the judges aimed at securing amiable composition, rather than making any precise definition of right. When, for instance, in Imola, Pirondino and Francesco quarrelled over a boundary wall, Stefano, a carpenter, and Guglielmo, a mason, were appointed as arbiters to arrange an agreement between them.[41] The judges also appointed arbiters to decide on matters of fact. When

Nino of Carseggio was struck by a stone thrown by one Giovanni, he went to a doctor at Tossignano who claimed to have cured him. But Nino denied that he was now well. In this case, arbiters were appointed to examine the scar, and they reported that Nino was in fact cured.[42]

Despite the practical rough-and-ready manner in which these cases seem to be decided, the procedure was lengthy, with notaries recording all cases ventilated before the judges.[43] For this reason cases concerned with sums below the value of £B.3 were generally dealt with summarily by the *podestà's* officials.[44] Justice as a whole was eminently practical, and in this respect was in clear contrast to the town statutes. Reading through the statutes, one receives an impression of towns so clean and orderly that they would do credit to any modern urban administration. This evidence must always be used with extreme caution ; the statutes had a symbolic rather than a real value. They embodied haphazard attempts to legislate for an ideal city. They were compiled by bringing together various decrees (of different dates) by the General Council. These were sometimes contradictory and often little more than counsels of perfection, which no one took at all seriously. A citizen, for instance, seized with a sudden fit of social consciousness, would propose in the council that everyone should be held responsible for cleaning away each week the mud before his house. The virtue of this proposal could not be gainsaid, and the measure would be carried unanimously. At first the citizens would grudgingly obey the new regulation. Then when winter came, any enthusiasm they may have had for it would die, and the roads would begin to silt up again. But when the judges came to compile the statutes, they would include such an unexceptionable decree as being part of the law and practice of the town, even though the stench of the streets was reaching their nostrils in the council chamber.

The *signore* himself exercised a general control over the operations of justice, without, however, taking part in its routine administration. Cases of treason were dealt with by him,[45] and he could intervene in any matter of interest. Sacchetti tells a story of a peasant of Faenza who was being robbed of his lands by a powerful man in the town, and who, being unable to obtain justice through the wealth and position of his opponent, gave money for all the church bells of the town to be rung, to draw the attention of Francesco de' Manfredi to his plight. Francesco then heard the man's case and secured the return of his land.[46] This is merely a story of course, but it shows that Sacchetti (who should have known) believed in the final jurisdiction of the *signore*, and it suggests that justice was often difficult to come by.

At all times the *signori* could intervene in the operation of justice to pardon offences or to remit sentences. By the end of the fourteenth century, they had acquired, too, a legislative role through their issue of edicts.[47] Sometimes, of course, this signorial influence could be positively malign. In Forlì, in October 1384, goods were stolen from the house of the Numai family and a rumour spread through the town that Sinibaldo degli Ordelaffi had been in league with the thieves and had taken a share of the booty. In September of the following year, there was a theft from the Orselli family. Two of the culprits were caught; one was hanged, the other escaped. But the avarice of Sinibaldo was aroused, through seeing the property of the Orselli which had been stolen and recorded. Accordingly, he instituted a case of false testimony against them. Guido Orselli fled, his brother, Andrea, who remained, was thrust into prison.[48] However, this type of lawlessness was one of the causes of Sinibaldo's deposition in December of the following year.

(b) *Chancellery*

Although there was no particular specialisation of function within the non-judicial parts of the administration, each commune had its chancellor who was responsible for drawing up acts of the commune, and for supervising the preservation of documents. All the principal officers of the commune had their notaries, who were obliged to deposit their completed registers with the chancellor. In Imola the chancellery was a room in the Palazzo Vecchio, but the archives were preserved in a chest in the sacristry of the Franciscan church. There were three keys to the chest, of which one was held by the captain, one by the *anziani*, and one by the sacristan of the Friars.[49] The Franciscans were also the custodians of the archives in Forlì. Here the chest containing the privileges, instruments and rights of the commune had two dissimilar locks; one of whose keys was preserved by the *massarius* of the commune, and the other by the warden of the Friars. It was laid down in the statutes that this box was only to be opened in the General Council and was to be closed before the council separated.[50]

The *signore* himself would have his personal secretary, distinct from the communal administration. By the end of the fourteenth century this was likely to be some minor humanist skilled in the verbal felicities or pomposities of the time.[51]

(c) *Finance*

(i) The chief executive officer of finance in the commune was the *massarius*, or treasurer, or ' magister introitum '. The statutes of Imola and Forlì laid down that he was to be elected by the captain and *anziani*. In Faenza he was supposed to be elected by the *signore's* vicar, together with the twelve *savii*. In effect this probably meant unfettered signorial control, as in Rimini, where all the financial officers of the communes were appointed by the Malatesti. In each case, the *massarius* had to be over twenty-five years of age, and had to give securities (in Imola of £B.3,000 and in Forlì of £B.2,000) that he would perform his office in a proper way. Often he was forbidden to handle the money himself, and his functions were limited to accounting, while the *depositarius* had actual control of the coins.[52] The money itself was held in a normal stout wooden *cassone*. Sacchetti tells a story of how Albornoz called Giovanni di Ricciardo Manfredi to him, at Ancona, to ask for a loan of 10,000 florins. Without hesitation, Giovanni offered him 20,000. Delighted at this, Albornoz sent his treasurer to Bagnacavallo with the lord, to collect the money. When they arrived, however, Giovanni announced that he had just remembered that he had sent the key of the *cassone* to Tuscany, and that he would only receive it back in a week's time. The Cardinal, waiting, 'with open purse', was to be doomed to disappointment, for within the week Giovanni had declared his alliance against him.[53]

The strictest control was exercised over the office of *massarius*. In Imola, in 1334, a conference of *anziani* and the vicar of the captain was necessary for paying out as little as twelve shillings.[54] In Forlì the *massarius* was unable to spend over twenty shillings without the sealed authorisation of the captain. Within a month of the end of his office, he was ' syndicated ' by the ' inquisitores rationum '. He drew up his accounts each month, calculating the totals of revenues and expenses.

(ii) There were three principal sources of communal revenues : the *dazii* or *gabelles* ; revenues from communal properties ; and the *collecta* or graduated tax.

(A) *The* dazii, gabelles, *or internal customs revenues*

The *gabelles* raised in Forlì in the fourteenth century may be taken as characteristic.[55] These consisted of :

1. *Taxes on contracts*. Almost all legal transactions were subject to this tax. On deeds of sale, gift, or exchange, sixpence in each pound of the value of the object bought or sold etc. was

exacted by the commune. 5 per cent was exacted on dowries of women living in Forlì,[56] and 2·5 per cent on dowries of ' foreign ' women marrying Forlivesi citizens. When dowries were restored to wives on the deaths of their husbands, as was the normal practice in Romagna, 5 per cent was taken by the commune. A 1 per cent charge was made upon loans, and another 1 per cent on their restitution, or on the cession of goods to creditors in default of restitution. Divisions of property were subject to 5 per cent tax, and wills to 5 per cent of the property left by the testator. All money and property assigned in civil cases of law was subject to 5 per cent impositions. Leases of houses and lands were subject to a tax of 2·5 per cent on the money paid, each time the lease was made or renewed.

If registered by a notary, the notary was bound to record these transactions in the register of the commune. This not only gave greater validity to the contract, but also served as a check on the payments to be made to the commune. Every year there was a ceremony in which the notaries swore to do this. If the transaction were not made through a notarial document, it had to be reported to the men who had bought the farming of the tax within three days.

2. *Taxes on trade.* Those importing cloth into the town paid a tax of 20 per cent of its value. Valuation was made by the ' esteemer of the *gabelles* ' together with someone from the Art of the town's cloth-workers. On the sale of cloth, both seller and buyer paid sixpence each in the pound. Those importing cloth for their own use and not for re-sale, paid sixpence in the pound. Those exporting cloth paid sixpence for each bale of a weight of 450 pounds.

The import of jewels, silks, and dyes was similarly subject to 5 per cent tax, and their export to 2·5 per cent. The import of ordinary wool was subject to a levy of sixpence in the pound and of *biselli* or heavy wool to elevenpence in the pound. The buying or selling of wool was taxed at threepence in the pound.

Skins and rags were charged a shilling in the pound, sixpence from the buyer and sixpence from the seller. The *rubbia* (whose root was used for a red dye), garlic, and onions, were all taxed at sixpence in the pound on sales. Wines and vinegar, when sold in bulk, were taxed at 2·5 per cent; when sold in small quantities, at 20 per cent. Charges were made on carts and wagons going into the town, a shilling or sixpence according to size.

Animals brought into the town paid 2·5 per cent of their value. A charge of 2·5 per cent was then made on their sale, but there was no charge for taking them again from the town. Butchers who imported beasts from outside the ' district ' of the town paid nothing, though their sales of beef and pork were subject to 20 per cent exactions. For each goat or lamb sold the *gabelles* took four shillings. Except for attendance at the market of Meldola, a licence was necessary for taking beasts out of the town. Finally, fish, fruit, metals, seed, wood, stone, and lime all involved a tax of 5 per cent on sales.

3. *Taxes on corn and milling*. All bringing corn into the town for sale or milling paid 1/2½ on every hundredweight. The same charge was made on flour. For the payment of the milling tax, everyone over the age of four years was inscribed in a ' liber buccharum '. It was assumed that each person here would require to mill, for his own use, six *staia* of grain each year, and was accordingly taxed at a flat rate of twelve shillings a year for milling costs (or two shillings each *staio*). The representatives of the villages of the districts gave a list of all their ' mouths ', each January or February, to the officials of the *gabelles*.

The sale of corn was subject to a tax of a shilling the *staio*, and its export to another shilling. Corn entering the town was taxed at the same rate. This latter exaction was not made on anyone bringing corn into the town from ' an alien territory or district or contado ', nor from Forlimpopoli or its *contado*. Those who stored their corn in the town granaries, paid 2 *staia* of it for every 100 *staia* stored. For the valuation of the weight of corn stored, a charge was made of sixpence for each *staio*.

However, in Forlì, all taxes on corn were relaxed when the price had risen to twenty-five shillings the *staio*.

(B) *Communal Property*

The second source of revenue came from communal properties, the lease of mills and fulling mills, and the lease of rights of pasturage owned by the commune, with rights of taking wood from its forests.[57]

Revenues from communal properties and the *gabelles* were not normally raised directly by the commune. What happened was that the right of exploiting them was sold each year to the highest bidder.[58] Generally each individual *gabelle* was sold separately, but sometimes the wealthier citizens of the town would unite to make a bloc bid for all the *dazii* of the town.[59]

(C) *The* Collecta

The *collecta* was a graduated tax based upon the ' esteem ', a careful assessment of the value of immobile (and sometimes mobile) property. When Rimini drew up a new 'esteem' in 1345, it was decreed that all possessions in the town and *contado* — vineyards, ploughland, orchards, woods, pasturage, meadows, lakes, etc., were to be measured with the stamped measure or *pertica* of the commune. Only the lands of the Malatesti and their '*fideles*' were to be exempt. After measurement, the land was valued and the result entered in the book of 'esteems'. The possessions of churches and religious bodies were also measured, but entered in a separate book. Properties leased from the Church were registered against the names of those who had taken them in lease. It was laid down that all vineyards planted for over three years were to be assessed at £R.2 a *tornatura*; ploughland, orchards and gardens at £R.1, meadow land at fifteen shillings, woods with undergrowth and pasture land at twelve shillings. In the town, each owner-occupied house was assessed at £R.3, and other houses at thirty shillings. If a house were leased, it was the lessee who was subject to the 'esteem'. The property of those who were not subject to the commune of Rimini was registered in two separate books. In the first were entered the valuations on property, whose owners lived in Pesaro, Montefiore, Castelnuovo, and other places subject to the Malatesti. In the second were entered the 'esteems' of those who came from places outside Malatesti jurisdiction; their names being entered under the various districts from which they originated; Montefeltro, Cesena, etc. When land was found to be without an owner, it became the property of the commune. Additions or contractions in the 'esteems' — arising from such things as the conversions of ploughland to vineland, were made every two years.[60]

The 'esteem' was roughly comparable with present day 'rateable value' in English local government. So much money would be exacted upon every pound of 'esteem.' Officials would be elected *ad hoc* by the *podestà* and *anziani* for the collection of the tax.

Before the introduction of the 'esteems', money was probably raised by taxation on cattle; as in Imola in 1301, where, for the purchase of salt, each yoke of oxen was taxed at twenty shillings.[61]

The domestic expenses of the communes were composed of:

(i) The payment of officials; the captain, *podestà*, judges, official notaries, the chancellor, *massarius*, the schoolmaster, trumpeters, etc.

(ii) Customary oblations to religious orders or for town feasts.

(iii) Irregular and miscellaneous payments: for ambassadors, nuncios, spies; for the maintenance of bridges and dykes, and other occasional payments: 'to Guglielmo the painter for painting 25 shields on the 20th of the month'; 'for justice done by hanging on the person of Giovanni Oltremont; and for the gallows constructed at Rio Sanguinario' etc.

(iv) The payment of the guards of the gates, and soldiers hired by the town — the most costly item of all.

(d) *Councils*

Both the decrees creating the life-captaincies, and the grants of vicariate gave the *signori* absolute power within their communes. Yet there was no ideological basis for signorial rule (unless local patriotism were an ideology), and the military supremacy of the ruler would avail little against the opposition of a united town. Accordingly the *signori* had to rule with a certain measure of representation and consent by their subjects.

This was provided — under very strict control — by the General and Small Councils of the communes. In the slow transformation of commune into *signoria*, these councils had always had importance, and their continuing executive functions made them still a significant element in the governments.

The size and composition of the General Council, whose members were drawn from each 'quarter' or administrative division of the town, were controlled by the *signore*. In normal circumstances therefore it would not be likely to propose anything contrary to his interests. Yet in times of crisis, as in Imola in March 1365, the Council could express a clear vote against its rulers.[62] Usually it confirmed the decrees of the *podestà* and elected the minor officials (messengers, agrarian police, trumpeters, etc.) In theory it was still considered as embodying the full will of the commune, and its assent was necessary for treaties with foreign powers.[63]

The General Council met only occasionally, but its interests were represented by a series of Small Councils, which assisted continuously in the work of government. These varied greatly in their composition, from place to place, and from time to time. In Imola in 1334, the Small Council consisted of eight men (two from each quarter) called *anziani*. They held office for a month. At the end of their tenure, each *anziano* proposed four candidates from whom the captain chose the new council. They were supposed to discuss with the captain, 'each and every business or negotiation of the commune', and their deliberations were recorded by a 'notary of the *anziani*'.[64]

Often they combined with the General Council to elect other

committees to deal with such specific matters as supervising the collection of some tax. The councillors of these *ad hoc* committees were generally known as *sapientes* or *savii*. But sometimes there would be other permanent consultative bodies alongside the *anziani*, whose members were also called *sapientes* and whose division of function with the *anziani* it is difficult to define. In 1316 for instance, Sinibaldo Ordelaffi as Defensor of Faenza had around him *anziani*, 'consules mercatorum', and the four, the twenty and the thirty *sapientes*.[65]

The operation of the conciliar system can be illustrated from the records of Ravenna in November 1306. The Lord Lamberto da Polenta, then *podestà*, caused the 'consiglio di credenza' or Small Council to be summoned, 'by the sound of the bell in the usual way' to the *loggia* of the Palazzo Comunale. Here he made a proposal that a new post should be created within the commune, that of a special judge to supervise officials. His speech asked that this 'should have the force of statute and should be written in the book of the statutes of the commune of Ravenna'. Then he suggested 'that counsel should be given to him by the councillors'. The Lord Albertino de' Berordenghi then made a speech in favour of the motion, which was carried unanimously. The Lord Ugolino de' Bozzoli then proposed that the judge, in addition to his other duties, should supervise the officials of the gates and waters. Ser Rodolfino Roglello supported Ugolino, and asked that the judge should be one who had not been born in Romagna or Bologna. However, the Lord Pietro de' Balbi recommended that they should not proceed with these proposals: 'in the meanwhile let my lord *podestà* have twelve *sapientes* with whom he may treat on these matters, and let whatever shall be decided by them be carried to the General Council, and let what pleases the council be put into effect'. The Small Council then formally ratified this decision, 'adding there, what shall be determined and decided by the councils of the town of Ravenna'.

The General Council met the following day. Here the notary, Ser Vitale da Bagnoli, proposed simple acceptance of the *podestà's* proposals, and the 'reformation' was carried with only one contrary vote.[66]

(e) *Local Officials*

Within each *cappella* or *guaita*, that is to say, within each minor administrative division of the town, two officials called *cappellani* or *maiores* were appointed by the *anziani* (as in Imola), or elected by the men of the *cappella* itself (as in Ravenna),[67] to supervise certain aspects of local administration. The *cappellani* were supposed to denounce to the *podestà* all crimes committed within their district, to apprehend criminals, and to assist in the collection of taxes.

The importance of these largely unpaid officials, and of the *cappella* system, seems to have been growing. By 1447, the men of the *cappella* of San Donato in Imola were buying a house for the business of the *cappella*.[68]

(f) *Defence*

The gates of the towns were closed at sunset and guarded night and day by men of the commune. They acted as police to ensure that the customs dues or *dazii* were paid on entry or exit from the town. However they also had military functions when necessary. In Forlì all between the ages of fourteen and seventy could be called upon to serve in the watch as guards. In times of emergency even the judges, advocates, doctors, and masters of grammar, etc., who were normally exempt, could be pressed into service.[69]

In the early part of the fourteenth century, the communal army was formed from the citizenry itself. The statutes of Faenza of 1410, still decreed that no citizen should be elected to any office, ' unless he goes in the host, or in cavalcata '.[70] Again in 1370, the Malatesti were raising troops by taking a man from each household among their citizens.[71] This was perhaps an exceptional measure, but the citizens themselves were still always considered as the principal element in the defence of the town. As late as 1449, for instance, when mercenary forces were the norm in all Italy, the citizens of Faenza were prepared to serve as soldiers in an emergency. In May of that year, when the Imolesi advanced to make a sudden attack upon the town, Astorgio II, called from his bed at the news, ordered the bells to be rung, and beacons to be lit upon the great tower : ' and immediately a great number of the men of Faenza gathered in his aid and defence'.[72]

These communal levies, would, in the fourteenth century, have as their nucleus, the *fideles* of the nobility. The fighting qualities of these troops were beginning to be widely recognised. Romagnol troops were employed by the king of France in his wars in Flanders,[73] and within Italy, Venice especially was already raising large numbers of troops here as *condottieri*.[74]

None the less, for obvious reasons, the *signori* kept a permanent guard of soldiers who were ' foreigners ' to the town, and who sometimes might even be non-Italians. In 1362, Guido da Polenta was employing a German company of horse under one Herman of Bamberg, and in 1367, a company of Hungarian troops under John the Hungarian.[75] So, at the same time, were the Malatesti. According to a story of Giovanni Fiorentino, the leader of the German guard in Rimini was executed for an affaire with Constanza, the niece of Galeotto Malatesti.[76] The castles of the *contado*, too, were naturally enough manned by men in the direct pay of the *signori*.[77]

IV

THE ADMINISTRATION OF THE *CONTADO*

The administration of the *contado* was a problem which was only partially solved by the end of the fourteenth century. The *signori* of the towns were the dominant lay landowners in the *contado*, and their castles and feudal forces provided a nucleus for its control. Yet the other large landowners, even when they were the allies of the *signore*, tended often to form demesnes within the *contado* which were independent of the will of the central authority. Within the *contado* of Imola for instance, the Cantagalli of Paventa, the Sassatelli of Sassadello, and the Bordella of Mordano all managed to raise their lands to the status of independent counties. There were, it will be seen, special circumstances in the Imolese *contado* which assisted this development, but probably communal control was weak wherever the feudal nobility held extensive properties. In the high, deep-wooded mass of the Tusco-Romagnol Apennines, among remote and sometimes inaccessible villages, the principal land-owners were a law unto themselves. The descendants of the Conti Guidi ; the Counts of Modigliana, the Counts of Romena and Dovadola, stayed as exempt from *comitatinanza* as they had during the era of the commune. In fact large parts of Romagna remained independent of the town, and, with the absorption of their lords in Tuscan politics, passed eventually under the dominion of Florence.

Accordingly, any description of the legal boundaries of the *contadi* is misleading. The towns ruled where they could, but their jurisdiction was always fragmented by pockets controlled by feudal landowners. Again, the town's power over the subject villages was effective only in proportion to their proximity. In the district near to the town the administration would conform to what was decreed in the statutes. In the mountains, the grip of the commune would slacken.

The constant wars in the province gave villages on the periphery of the *contado* the chance to change, or to threaten to change, their allegiance to some other commune. In these circumstances, the towns were forced to modify that absolute authority over the *contado* which they claimed in their statutes, and to come to terms with their villages. In September 1408, for instance, when the Lord Ludovico Alidosi, on return from a hunting expedition, was dining under the portico of a house in Castel Guelfo, he was approached by representatives of its rural commune, and informed that no adequate agreement had been made between the village and his *signoria*. The men suggested therefore that the following terms should be drawn up : (i) that they should be free from any burdens or taxes on property and persons ; (ii) that the salary of Ludovico's vicar in the village should be paid by the *signore* himself ; (iii) that the only duties required of them should be the maintenance of roads and bridges ; (iv) that they should be provided with salt at a fixed charge of four Bolognesi pennies a pound ; (v) that they should be charged no *gabelle* for grinding corn within the commune, and that if they wanted to grind corn at Imola they should only be charged a shilling a sack. Castel Guelfo had rebelled from Bologna and had only recently joined the Imolese *contado*. It could easily (and later in fact did) return to its old allegiance. Consequently ' still at table ', with, we are told, ' joyful and willing spirit ', Ludovico agreed to all their terms.[78]

Such contracts are no exception. In 1382, when Codronco changed its allegiance to Beltrando Alidosi, the commune was allowed to keep its castle under its own control. It promised merely to fly the flag of Beltrando ; to hold his friends for friends, enemies for enemies ; to make war upon any persons when called to do so by the *signore* and his sons ; not to make peace without his permission, and to defend, conserve, and augment his state. In return, the *signore* promised to defend them in their liberty and property and to pay off the debt which the commune owed to the Bishop of Imola. He also engaged to secure peace between Codronco and the men of Castel del Rio, and all the other villages dependent upon him.[79] Similar contracts were made by the lords of the *contado* with the *signori*. In 1411, for example, the Lords of Baffadi, Cristoforo, and Sino asked from Ludovico Alidosi a provision of £B.8 a month, for guarding Baffadi for him ; an assurance that their rule would not be disturbed by Lambertino di Gaggio (a noble of the Imolese *contado*) ; and finally the grant of all jurisdiction.[80] Apart from reducing their monthly provision to £B.5, Ludovico agreed. These contracts are similar to the treaties by which the *signorie* of Romagna themselves came to be bound as

A peasant's house in the *montagna*

Scenery in the Savio Valley: Le Scalecce

adherents to Florence and Venice. Indeed, in the case of Codronco, the commune actually asked ' in adherentiam venire '.

It can be seen that the bald submission of the communes of the *contado* of Imola in 1292 (where its men had simply and unconditionally sworn that ' they are and wish to be under the yoke of Imola ')[81] came to be modified considerably in practice. None the less, communes still often submitted to the towns unconditionally ; sometimes the sheer need for protection forced the commune to complete dependence. When Laderchio changed its allegiance from Imola to Faenza in 1376, and submitted to Astorgio I Manfredi in the piazza of Bagnacavallo, the document declared that the village did this : ' Considering the immense dangers and perils arising from the wars that have sprung up in the vicinity ; wishing to live safely and securely ; and to adhere to a lord and protector who may have power and authority to defend the abovementioned men and others of the said commune and to protect their goods '. They promised military service and all other burdens, and in return received only Astorgio's assurance of protection.[82]

Where it could, the town exercised the fullest rights over its subject villages. The *ville* nearest to the town came under the direct control of the *podestà*. The *massarius* of the little communes had to denounce all crimes to the town, to assist in the collection and imposition of taxation, and to assist generally in the administration of the dominant commune. Further from the town, control was exercised by placing a signorial vicar in the principal *castelli* of the *contado*. The *castelli* themselves, as has already been seen in Montefiore, had their own little *contadi*, with villages subject to them.

These systems varied considerably from *contado* to *contado*. Below is a brief summary of what is known of the administration of the *contado* in each commune.

(a) *Rimini*

At the beginning of the thirteenth century, the *contado* of Rimini was divided into three areas : the *balia* of Scorticata, comprising the villages in the valleys of the Marecchia and Rubicon ; the *balia* of Longiano, comprising the villages to the north of the Rubicon valley ; and the *balia* of Montescudolo, which included the villages to the South of Rimini, around the valleys of the Foglia and the Conca rivers.[83] With the extension of the *contado* later, this simple system was abandoned, and the Malatesti ruled by appointing officials with the title of captain or vicar to the principal *castelli*. These exercised the same overriding powers in the rural communes, which the *signori* themselves, whom they represented, enjoyed in the town. But here too, a measure of counsel and consent was preserved. At Savignano, for instance, a General Council exercised its functions, as the statutes of 1378 explicitly stated, on the basis of the canon law maxim: 'quod omnes tangit, ab omnibus debet approbari'. From the General Council, a Small Council of ten men was chosen by lot to exercise conciliar functions for six months. Councillors appointed the officers of the commune: the *massarius* (or treasurer) the four *gualdari* or agrarian police, the two messengers, and the men who corrected the 'esteem'. The vicar himself exercised civil and criminal justice. He swore allegiance only to the *signore*, by whom he was 'syndicated'. His salary was paid by the men of the *castello*.[84]

Similar systems are found in the statutes of Montefiore, Scorticata (1462), of Bertinoro (1431), of Longiano (1448), of Verucchio (of the fifteenth century), Santarcangelo, and Sogliano (1400).[85] Though these statutes were drawn up in the fifteenth century, they reflect and often incorporate the system of earlier years.

(b) *Cesena*

On the administration of the *contado* of Cesena, no information is available. In 1378, the town was given in vicariate to Galeotto Malatesti, and became a dependency of the Riminese family.[86] Its *podestà* was appointed by the Malatesti, and presumably the Riminese system of local captains and vicars was employed in its *contado*.

(c) *Forlì*

In the *contado* of Forlì, the same system of signorial vicars was employed. The men of Castrocaro, as early as 1304, met in General Council, in their 'house of the commune'.[87] Oriolo, when it formed part of the Forlivese *contado*, was ruled by a vicar of the Ordelaffi, who raised the taxes upon it in co-operation with its *massarius* and General Council.[88] The larger Forlimpopoli had both a vicar and a vicar's lieutenant.[89]

Several of the *castelli* had their own statutes.[90] According to one source, the *contado* seems to have been governed, in the fifteenth century, by six men called procurators of the *contado*.[91]

(d) *Ravenna*

The *contado* of Ravenna consisted entirely of the rich, flat lands of the plain. Thus, geographically, it was the easiest to control. It seems to have been administered directly from the town by the *podestà*, working in conjunction with an official called the constable of the *contado*.[92] The *signore* himself is found, sometimes at Ravenna,[93] sometimes at a village in the *contado*,[94] making peace between the local families. Apart from Comacchio (which did not long remain within the *contado*)[95] the *ville* seem to have sworn unconditional obedience to the town.[96]

(e) *Faenza*

More clearly than elsewhere, the administration of the *contado* of Faenza can be divided into two parts, rule over the *montagna*, or Val di Lamone, and rule over the plain.

(i) *The Val di Lamone*. In the early part of the fourteenth century, the area between the Pieve di Tò and Marradi was ruled by a captain who was appointed anew every six months, and who dwelt at Castel Pellegrino near Gattara. The area between Pieve di Tò and Faenza was ruled by a second captain who resided at the town. By 1376, this area had been divided out between the jurisdiction of four *castelli* : Rontana, Brisighella, Calamello, and Fernaccione, to each of which the neighbouring villages were subject.[97]

This system was changed again during the Great Schism. In 1412, Gian Galeazzo Manfredi succeeded in obtaining the consent of Pope Gregory XII to the complete separation of the Val di Lamone from Faenza.[98] By this, two *signorie* were created out of one. The Manfredi henceforth ruled Faenza as papal vicars, but held the Val di Lamone independently with the title of Counts. From this date the county of the Val di Lamone was ruled by a viscount, who was appointed by the Manfredi every six months, and whose rule corresponded to that of other signorial vicars in the *contado*. The viscount, with his household (consisting of a notary, six servants and three horses), resided at Brisighella. He had all the powers of justice of the town *podestà*. He was the only official appointed by the court. All others, the *massarius*, who supervised finance ; the four *plazarii*, or messengers ; the syndics (who ‘ syndicated ’ the viscount, his household, and all other officers) were elected by the men of the valley in the General Council. The General Council, meeting in the church of Santa

Maria di Brisighella, or in the house of the commune, was composed of forty men elected by each of the *scole* of the Val di Lamone, with each man holding his office for a year from the first of October. The *scole* that elected the council were composed of not less than twenty-five *fumantes*. A commune with fewer *fumantes* united with its neighbour to form a quorum. Larger *scole* were able to elect two members to the council. Election was free, although the viscount, with the consent of the two priors, had the right of reforming and correcting the council each month. The priors were chosen by lot from among the elected members of the council, and assisted the viscount in conducting the discussions.[99]

Later, there were twelve ' governors ' of the valley, presumably appointed from the members of the General Council. The county of the Val di Lamone was now entirely separated from the vicariate of Faenza. Yet in matters concerning the signorial family of the Manfredi — *e.g.* for such matters as the establishment of a regency for young Astorgio III — the men of Faenza and of the Val di Lamone, would come together in a united General Council.[100]

(ii) *The Plain of Faenza*. In the plain, the *contado* was ruled, by the fifteenth century, through four vicars established at Russi, Solarolo, Granarolo, and Orioli. Probably the system was already established by the fourteenth century.[101]

(f) *Imola*

In the age of the communes, Imola was able to extend its authority only over the twenty or so villages in its *districtus* or immediate vicinity. This weakness was due to the continual conflicts of the town with its episcopacy and with the lay counts of earlier centuries ; to its struggle with the neighbouring communes of San Cassiano and Castel Imola (destroyed only in 1174 and 1221 respectively), and to the long sustained hostility of Faenza and Bologna.[102] In the middle of the thirteenth century, the Bolognese administration of Imola succeeded in subduing that part of the *contado* which was not already subject to feudal nobles, and it remained under Bolognese rule until 1278, when Romagna was ceded to the Church.

With papal government in the province, the *contado* was given to Imola. The vigorous *podestà*, Bernardino di Cunio, secured the submission of all the communes of the *contado* in 1292. However, in the same year, Imola revolted from the Church, and its *contado* was, as a punishment, awarded by the papal rector to Bologna. By 1298 the grant to Bologna had been revoked, but the *contado*, as distinct from the *districtus* had not been returned to Imola. Instead, it was made into a separate state ruled *immediate* by the papal government.[103]

The papal administration at the beginning of the century did not have any conspicuous success. In June 1305, an agreement was drawn up between the Count of Romagna and the commune of Imola, in an attempt to remedy the lawlessness of the *contado*. The document declared that the *contado* of Imola, ' which belongs to the Roman Church, has now for a long time been split between rival lords. . . . The communes respect lords and tyrants who have violently seized power, and maintain themselves by threats and terror. They do not obey Holy Mother Church, its officials or the Lord Count of Romagna, nor do they pay the taxes to the treasury of the Church as they ought.' It goes on to complain of the ' violences, pressures, extortions, illicit acts and homicides in that contado '. These evils are so unchecked that *fumantes* are daily emigrating, while those remaining, ' ad maximam paupertatem et ad nihil sunt redacti '. To deal with this situation, the commune of the *contado* was now placed jointly in the hands of the Count of Romagna and the commune of the town of Imola. The town assumed the title of ' protector et defensor ' of the *contado*. To the town was given the right of electing and nominating the ' rector or Podestà ', and of nominating officials for the next two years. Of the revenue raised from the *contado*, two-thirds was to go to the Church, and the remaining one-third to the commune of the town. At the same time the Count promised to nominate someone to deliver the *contado* from the hands of the tyrants. The town, for its own part, promised to pay the ' fodrum regale sive fumanterium debitum ' for the next two years.[104]

This was merely a temporary agreement. But five years later, the Papal Count is found acknowledging the receipts of money from the commune of the town, in the presence of the *podestà* of the *contado* of Imola.[105] The town may perhaps still have had some controlling interest in the payment of the revenues of the *contado*. Certainly *contado* and commune worked together in close alliance at times. An apparently innocuous document of May 1315, shows Monalduccio da Nocera, vicar of the Roman Church in the *contado* of Imola, appealing to the *podestà* of the town of Imola, Francesco de' Medici, and its captain, Geraldo Savignano to come to Pediano in defence of the Roman Church, with forty or fifty good soldiers. On the same day, ' before the gate of Pediano ', in the presence of Bitnoi de' Sassadelli, Gambio Banderini and Oderico de' Nordigli, the *podestà* of the town ordered the destruction of Pediano and the devastation of its adjacent district. There follows a papal document opening with the ominous words, ' hec est inquisitio ', a process of inquisition against the *podestà*, captain, *anziani*, council, and commune of the town and against Monalduccio, the *massarius*, and officials of the commune of the *contado* (and among them it specifically mentions Lippo and Litto Alidosi). This declared that Monalduccio, having falsely called himself vicar of the *contado*, had accepted a large sum of money from the commune of the town that an illicit attack might be made upon Toranello and Pediano. Monalduccio's arrest was ordered, the commune of the town was fined 10,000 marks of silver, and Lippo and Litto the sum of £B1,000.[106]

The town commune certainly retained a moral interest in the *contado*. The *podestà* of the *contado* had his seat in Imola, and dispensed justice in the town.[107] With the Alidosi assumption of the *signoria*, this authority was extended through the family lands in the *contado*. In his description of the Romagna in 1371, Cardinal Anglic remarked that though the Alidosi had no *de iure* rights in the government of the *contado*, they yet had considerable authority through their possessions.[108]

None the less, for seventy years, the *contado* of Imola was an administration distinct from the government of any town. The *podestà* and treasurer were appointed (and paid) by the papal government, and occasionally by the Pope himself.[109] The statutes of the commune of 1347 were drawn up by notaries, acting from the authority and commission conceded to them by the ' general parliament of the commune of the *contado* of Imola '. According to their decrees, administration was decentralised into four legations; Dozza, Tossignano, and Montemauro in the *montagna*, and Mordano in the plain. For the election of the Small Council voting was by legations, with three votes to Mordano and Dozza, and two for Monte Mauro and Tossignano. For the election of the ' parliamentum generale ', voting was by the rural communes that went up to form the legations, with one vote for each commune with five *fumantes* or less, two for those with from five to ten *fumantes*, three for those with from ten to fifteen, four from those with over fifteen, and five for Tossignano. Magnates, with their servants and descendants, were excluded from the deliberations of the communes, and the *populus* had rights against the magnates similar in kind to those found in the Bolognesi statutes.[110]

The unity and independence of the commune was broken,

however, during the war of the Eight Saints. In the general attack upon the papacy, the neighbouring communes seized what they could of the *contado*. Some communes submitted to Bologna.[111] Of these, Casalfiumanese, Corvara, and Fiagnano, with their dependencies, remained with that city, and were formed in the following century into the *podesteria* of Casalfiumanese.[112] The other communes were given by the Bolognesi to Beltrando Alidosi in 1386, and united into the vicariate of Fontanalice.[113] A second group of communes fell under the control of the Manfredi of Faenza in 1377. During the Schism, these villages were granted by John XXIII to his supporters, the Alidosi, and by Gregory XII, to the Manfredi.[114]

The pope of Pisa, John XXIII, was still attempting to rule part of the *contado* in 1407,[115] but after that date, all the rival papacies seem to have resigned themselves to its loss.

In the disintegration of the commune of the *contado*, the town of Imola emerged with the greater part of its territories. It ruled them, during the fifteenth century, through three captains or vicars, one at Tossignano, one at Fontanalice, and one at Castel del Rio.[116] But there were still General Councils of the whole *contado* subject to the town, and the statutes of 1347 still had authority in the villages subject to Imola.[117]

These *castelli* which were ruled by the signorial vicars had much the same organisation as that of Montefiore which has already been described. The vicar or captain worked with, and largely directed, the administration of the three *castelli*, which included the lesser neighbouring rural communes. Tossignano, for instance, had a General Council of *arrengo*, 'convoked, congregated and united in the larger hall of the house of the commune by sound of the bell and voice of the herald, as is the custom', and an inner council of twelve men. Its officers included a *massarius*, a vice-*massarius*, a notary, a *sindicus* supervising finances, a procurator who dealt with relations with other communes, and a herald. The vicar or captain, by whose mandate the councils met, was appointed by the *signore* from the more prosperous numbers of the notarial or judicial class of the town commune. Within the rural commune and its subordinate dependencies, he had the same function as the *podestà* in the town.

The *massarius*, elected by the General Council of the commune, swore loyalty in the hands of the vicar, and promised to exercise his office with diligence and honesty; to denounce all malefactors, and to stand to syndication at the end of his period of office. Working with the Small Council, he was responsible for the distribution of taxation imposed by the town, both in the *castello* itself, and between the *castello* and its own subject villages. It was he who appointed men to correct the ' esteem ' upon which taxation was based. With the council he had the right of imposing *gabelles* or tolls, in order to raise money by indirect taxation. On questions concerning the tolls of the vicariates and the dominant communes, the *massarius* at times negotiated directly with the *anziani* and General Council of the town.[118]

From this review, it becomes clear that, with individual variations, the normal method of administering the *contado* was through placing captains, directly subject to the *signore*, over the more important *castelli*.

From the time that the papal vicariates were granted to the captains of the town, the rural communes swore allegiance, not to the town commune, but directly to the *signore*. In strict legal terms, the establishment of the *signoria* separated the town and *contado*, for the government of the *contado* now belonged only to the person of the ruler. Again it has already been shown that the establishment of the *signorie* was a part of that process by which *comitatinanza* was reversed, a part of that process by which the *contado* conquered the town. Accordingly it would be idle to attempt to interpret *contado*-town relations in Romagna in Caggese's classic formula of urban bourgeoisie oppressing *contado*-landowners and peasants. Indeed, even for Tuscany this interpretation is being abandoned.[119] The truth is that town and *contado* reacted naturally upon each other ; power in the one was bound up inevitably with ownership of property in the other. Much of the land in the villages was owned by the notarial and official class dominant in the town, and was worked at short lease or at *mezzadria* by a tenant peasantry.[120] The town dwellers, therefore, would hardly look kindly upon any policy of taxation directed against land as such.

However, having said this, it must be added that the rich, the powerful, and the cunning will always, in the course of nature, seek to exploit the poor and the weak. Inevitably there was landlord-tenant conflict, and inevitably the landlords who drew up the communes' statutes looked to their own interests. Again the *signori*, in the villages they ruled, exploited their subjects just as they did in the towns. *Corvées* could be oppressive. In 1380, the men of Cerasoli were forced to build a castle there. Six years later they petitioned their *signore*, complaining that ' your Official of Roads and Bridges is forcing us to repair a stretch of road from Covignano, which was never before done by us . . . *la qual cosa*

Segnore nostro, ce pare recevare ingiustia'.[121] Taxation, too, was burdensome. The men of Dozza, for instance, complained that when they had been ruled by Lodovico Alidosi, they had been forced to pay more than £B.300 a year to him.[122] The smaller communes must have often found it difficult to pay. In 1453, the rural commune of Mezzocolle, ' gathered, convoked, and united in the public highway, at the place called La Botte, in the accustomed manner, and according to their ancient custom in General Council, and at the request of Domenico Coletto, *massarius* of the commune ', named one of their men as their procurator to negotiate a loan from Daniel di Isaiah of Tossignano. This was to pay the tax demanded by Taddeo de' Manfredi for the expenses involved in the renewal of his vicariate. Twelve years later, the same commune took out a loan of £B.25 at 40 per cent interest from a Jewish banker, Giacomo, in order to pay a subsidy of £B.20 towards the castle which Taddeo was building in Bagnara, the sum of forty shillings towards the bridge being built across the Po, and a florin and four shillings to the officials who had come to the village to register their corn.[123] Even if the commune did not complain at the taxation, its members may have reflected bitterly that the interest they were paying on the loan was going to a money-lender who was licensed (for a considerable sum) by the *signore* himself.

In return, the peasants of the *contado* received little from their government. When selling their produce in the town markets they were exploited by the monopolists of the commune. In the countryside itself, violence and continual feuds were only partially suppressed by the wavering control of the *signore*. It would be unwise to see the administration of the *contadi* in idyllic terms.

CHAPTER IX

Religious Life

> Before all and above all, I advise that the King of Kings and Lord of Lords, who has all power in heaven and earth, should be venerated and honoured.
>
> CARLO MALATESTI TO GIOVANNI MARIA VISCONTI[1]

THE creation of the *signorie* within the Romagna was obviously a defeat for the papacy in the political field. Yet in the same period, the Church won notable victories in terms of its religious doctrines and organisation. Widespread heresy was subdued; the anti-clerical struggles of the communes were resolved; and the grants of vicariate ended by compromise a situation where political hostility to the papal curia could lead to a rejection of its ecclesiastical teaching. As a result, the fourteenth century saw a new and closer linking of all society with the institutions of religion, and the firm establishment of religious orthodoxy.

I

The most important achievement of the Church was the eradication of heresy. There were Manichean sectaries at Ravenna as early as the sixth century,[2] and by the end of the twelfth century heretical thought was probably diffused fairly widely through the towns of the province, as it was through all of central and northern Italy.[3] Rimini, by its links with Lombard and Tuscan heretics, and perhaps, too, by its contacts across the Adriatic with the Slav world of the Bogomils, was an important centre for Catharism. In 1184 the commune had a *podestà* who had refused to swear to the statute expelling heretics, and as a result they were present there in large numbers.[4] In 1204, Innocent III was renewing the complaints of Lucius III on this score.[5] The first major attack upon the Cathars of Rimini was at the instigation of Frederick II in 1226, when the *podestà*, Inghiramo da Macerata, burnt several of their followers. In the following year Honorius III complained to the commune that certain citizens were seeking to avenge Inghiramo's execution of ' their daughters, sisters, and relations ', and he threatened excommunication against those planning such wickedness.[6] In fact the town had the reputation of being a centre of heresy as late as 1275.[7]

In Italy there were two principal schools of Catharist thought: that of Desenzano, and that of Concerezzo, preaching an absolute and modified dualism respectively. If the contemporary document from the Biblioteca Malatestiana of Cesena reflects local opinion, both sects were represented in the province. The Cathars, the description says, hold that there are two omnipotent powers: God, who created all celestial things together with the good angels, and the Prince of Shadows, who has formed the visible world. Some believe, however, that God created the *Urstoff*: the four elements, and that he alone is the true creator *ex nihilo*: Satan has merely used these elements to form men and the material world. On the disputes concerning this point the author refuses to go into detail: 'because relating to this there are told, at will, as many different fables as there are heretics'. The ideal of the Catharists is sexual abstinence. Cain is said to have been born from the adultery of the Serpent with Eve, who then instructed Adam in the knowledge of sexual intercourse: the first fruit of the tree of good and evil. The Cathars argued to the diabolical formation of matter from the sinfulness of man, and such illogicality in creation as the existence of serpents and reptiles 'which serve no purpose'. All the prophets of the Old Testament, apart from Isaiah, were false and damned, though God had sometimes spoken through them despite themselves. Some believed that souls are procreated by souls, as bodies by bodies. Others — though these doctrines are only taught in private — hold that God created all souls, which transmigrate, from the beginning. Christ, John the Evangelist, and the Virgin Mary, were neither human nor divine, but good angels sent by God. Christ had only a phantasmagorical body, and has not, therefore, suffered in the passion.[8]

It is clear that Catharism is more a different religion than a Christian heresy. Much more orthodox — perhaps only heterodox as the result of being persecuted — were the 'Poor men of Lyons' or Waldensians, whose presence at Faenza in 1206, called forth the complaints of Innocent III. Nothing could better exemplify the iron determination of this Pope when faced with heresy than the grim letter with which he instructs the abbot and monks of S. Ippolito in Faenza, under pain of interdict, to cast out from their cemetery the body of one Otto, a heretic, who has been buried there.[9] Yet it is difficult to distinguish sharply between the Waldensians (whom Innocent identifies with the Patarines) and the Humiliati, also found in Faenza, who, after being condemned as heretical in 1174, attained later a precarious orthodoxy. ' Patarine ' was used not only in its technical sense, as describing those who denied the validity of sacraments administered by priests of evil life, but also as a generic term for all those who by their emphasis upon apostolic poverty and purity in the church bordered upon the heretical.

In an age when St. Francis and the Poverelli coexisted with the canon lawyers who proclaimed that ' the earth is the Lord's and the fullness thereof ', the boundaries between heresy and orthodoxy were extremely difficult to determine. In Emilia the local sect of the Apostles is a case in point. The Franciscan, Salimbene, indignantly describes how, at some time in the 1260s, the Apostles had a child preacher who drew such huge crowds to the Basilica Ursiana of Ravenna, that they overflowed on to the steps. He devotes many pages of his chronicle to attacking them, yet the vehemence of his argument — he calls them ' ribalds and pigs and fools and ignoble ' — sprang perhaps from the closeness of the sect to some aspects of the doctrines, or at least, the ethos of his own order.[10] The Apostles, who were condemned as heretical in 1286, emphasised literal adherence to the words of Christ, apostolic poverty, and the life of the primitive church. Their leader, Gherardo Segarelli, was burnt at Parma in 1300, though in his life he had received considerable episcopal encouragement. Later, with the preaching of the heroic Fra Dolcino, the sect moved northward and away from Emilia, to the Veneto, Lombardy, and Piedmont.[11]

A similar ambiguity enveloped the heresy of the Flagellants. Many of the friars in fact seem to have been involved in the origins of this movement which sprang up with sudden force in the year 1260. Bands of men, walking in pairs, naked to the waist, and bearing candles in their hands, passed through the towns of Italy, beating themselves with knotted thongs, singing canticles of praise to the Virgin, and calling to God with wild cries, and with tears streaming from their eyes, for peace and mercy. Following this practice whole towns would march out to their neighbours, as did Imola to Bologna in 1260. But the hysteria engendered by this devotion, with its mingling of the music of the *laude* and the screams of the self-chosen victims, proved too much for both ecclesiastical and lay authorities, who by 1269 had combined to proscribe its performance in public.[12] None the less, flagellation in private, as we shall see, continued to play an important part in popular piety.

In Romagna, as elsewhere in Italy, the source of heresy often lay in this lack of clear definition at the boundaries of orthodoxy and heterodoxy. But always present too, was discontent among lay tenants of ecclesiastical proprietors, the doubts of imperial partisans seeking some firmer rationale for their resistance to the temporal papal party, and the greed of those who wished to appropriate ecclesiastical ' liberties ' and avoid the bitterly disputed payment of tithes. However, the course of the thirteenth century amply demonstrated that the orthodox and Guelf could as easily usurp ecclesiastical rights and lands as those who claimed some higher doctrinal justification for their deeds. Moreover, by the end of the century the communes and the ecclesiastical powers had reached a working compromise on their respective rights and jurisdictions. Consequently the task of those seeking to establish orthodoxy was not too difficult.

The spearhead of the orthodox reaction was formed by the new orders of friars : the Franciscans and Dominicans, who were eagerly welcomed in Romagna, and whose work was generally attended by success. The celebrated Dominican, St. Peter Martyr, passed many years at Cesena (where his finger was later to be revered as a treasured relic), and preached at Ravenna, where, according to his biographers, his sanctity was revealed by various heavenly signs. In popular tradition, his murderer, Carino, is said to have fled from justice through the Romagna, to have fallen ill at Forlì, and to have been admitted to the Dominican hospital. Here, having confessed his crime to none other than the saint's brother, he assumed the Dominican habit, died in an odour of sanctity, and attained beatification.[13]

Still more surprising stories are woven around St. Anthony of Padua, who was provincial minister of the Franciscans for Emilia from 1226 to 1230. After a truly Franciscan preaching to ' my brothers the fish ' at Rimini, ' whereat all the fish raised their heads from the water as if praising God ', he succeeded in converting many of the town's Cathars. In another miracle at Rimini he caused a horse which had been without food for three days to kneel down and adore the blessed sacrament before eating the oats which had been placed before it.[14]

For those unconvinced by such wonders other persuasions were employed, and here too the friars exercised their talents. In 1237 Gregory IX gave to the Dominicans the control of the new Inquisition in Lombardy and Romagna. By 1259 the inquisitors' work had expanded to such an extent that Innocent IV created new administrative arrangements by which the Dominicans became responsible for Lombardy and northern Emilia, and the Franciscans for the Trevisan March, the Marche, and Romagna.

In Romagna the Franciscans had two seats : at Faenza and Rimini. and the size of their organisation may be judged from the fact that by 1302, Fra Guido da Tisii, the Inquisitor of Rimini, had no less than thirty-one officials as his assistants. It was for a successor of his that, between 1320 and 1330, Zanchino Ugolini drew up a treatise on inquisitorial procedure which has merited the description of being ' one of the clearest and best manuals of practice that we possess '.[15]

It is doubtful whether after the closing years of the thirteenth century the inquisitors had much work upon their hands. The only case heard before the Romagnol inquisition of which evidence has so far been brought to light is a prosecution of 1332, and here the ' heresy ' of which the accused is found guilty is merely that of usury.[16] In the fourteenth century heterodoxy largely died out within the province. In neighbouring Bologna there were numerous heretics at the beginning of the fourteenth century, and the condemnation in 1323 of the Spiritual Franciscans and Fraticelli, who asserted the absolute poverty of Christ, revealed widespread unorthodoxy in Umbria, the heartland of Franciscan mysticism, and in the Marche.[17] Michele, the Minster General of the Franciscans who headed the movement of the Spirituals, came from Cesena, and it is possible that his example may have moved others in the province. We have already seen that Francesco degli Ordelaffi was branded as ' a false Patarine dog ' by his enemies. But most probably this is merely an example of the way in which the Papacy indiscriminately condemned as heretical those who resisted its temporal power.[18] Certainly in the grants of vicariate there was an implicit alliance against heresy which meant that by the end of the century the province was unshakeably orthodox. When the inquisitor, Lorenzo da Rimini, appointed Beltrando Alidosi as his vicar for the suppression of heresy in March 1371, he was merely giving a more formal recognition to a position all the *signori* already held.[19]

II

As representative of ecclesiastical organisation in the province, we may take the diocese of Faenza. Here the surviving records of December 1291 for the payment of the papal tax of the Tenth give a fairly complete picture of the local composition and economic strength of church life.[20] The Bishop of Faenza probably had a revenue of about £B.1,000 a year. He was dependent upon the Archbishop of Ravenna, where his election was confirmed, where he was consecrated and given formal possession of his see.[21] To assist him, his chapter had ten canons, whose individual revenues from their canonries ranged from £B.10–£B.80 a year. Attached to the cathedral of S. Pietro were three chaplains of altars whose revenues ranged from £B.31–£B.20 a year, and one other with insufficient income to be taxed.

Four monasteries were found in the *contado*, and many more near or in the town. The Camaldoli had three houses, the Fonte Avellana (a branch of the Camaldoli) one, and the Vallambrosi one. These were taxed upon revenues ranging from £B.160–£B.32 a year. In addition, there were houses of Augustinian, Dominican, and Franciscan friars, and a branch of the Canons Regular of the Congregation of S. Marco at Mantua — this last the wealthiest of the orders, with a taxable revenue of £B.350. For women there was a Camaldoli and a Cistercian convent, and convents of Franciscan and Dominican nuns. There were houses of the two military orders : that of St. John of Jerusalem (with an annual revenue of £B.190), of the Temple (taxed on £B.35 — paid under protest), and finally the hospices and hospitals of Madonna Bianca, of S. Lazzaro di Messina and S. Giuliano (for lepers), of SS. Giacomo and Cristoforo (of the Templars), of S. Sepulcro (of the knights of Jerusalem), of Santo Spirito, and of S. Egidio of Roncoduce.

Within the town, there were thirty rectors of churches whose incomes ranged from £B.80–£B.15 a year, and ten whose incomes were below seven gold florins, or whose ' revenues are so small or lacking that for the sustenance of their lives they have to beg and seek public alms '. Within the *contado* there were 154 churches, organised in twenty rural parishes, the larger of which were generally under the control of an Archpriest, or, more rarely, of a Prior or Canon. Of the rectors of these churches, sixty-two were, similarly, too poor to be taxed.

From the whole document one obtains a powerful impression of the strength of orthodox religious life in a typical Romagnol diocese. Of course, changes in its character were taking place. The crusading idea had fallen. In 1189, Bishop Giovanni of Faenza had led 200 men on the third crusade, most of whom had died during its course.[22] But with the thirteenth century the old dream of participation in ' the world's debate ' was fading, and the military orders : the Templars with three houses, at Rimini, Budrio (in the Riminese *contado*), and Forlì, and the Hospitallers, with a *commenderia* at Faenza,[23] exercised little influence in the province. In Clement V's attack upon the Templars two knights were interrogated at Cesena, and seven at Ravenna, all of whom denied the charges against them, and whose fate is unknown.[24] But even before this scandal the Cavalieri Gaudenti[25] provided a more attractive home for those nobles seeking some ecclesiastical organisation, and the Gaudenti themselves disappear in the fourteenth century. This coolness before the crusading ideal is reflected in the few donations which were made in wills of the period to this end. Giovanni Balbi of Ravenna left, in 1287, £R.270 to ' one who will go overseas in aid of the holy land ',[26] but his example was not followed. Perhaps some Romagnols joined the crusaders who set out from the Romagna and the Marche on the Smyrna expedition in 1344. But the event gained only the briefest and gloomiest mention in the chronicles : ' many went who did not return '.[27] The expeditions of the fourteenth century were thought of by the clergy as matters involving burdensome taxation, while local ' crusades ', like that declared against Francesco Ordelaffi, aroused no enthusiasm. Pilgrimages, on the other hand, were popular. Many wills left money for good works, should a projected pilgrimage prove impossible. Azzo Alidosi, for instance, asked that a chapel should be built in the church of the Franciscans, to the value of 130 ducats, if he were unable to visit the church of S. Maria of Fano, or St. Peter's at Rome.[28] At various times, Galeotto, Malatesta Ungaro, and Pandolfo di Galeotto, went on pilgrimage to the Holy Land. Malatesta Ungaro even visited St. Patrick's Well in Ireland, in the hope, it is said, of communing with the shade of his mistress who had been murdered by her husband.[29]

Rarely were the monasteries mentioned in wills ; in Romagna, as elsewhere, monasticism appears as a declining way of life. Yet another priory of Camaldolesi monks was founded in 1329 by the hermit, Simone de' Pianelli,[30] but this is an isolated incident. There were only five monks in the Cistercian abbey of S. Severo in 1345, and none in 1408.[31] In S. Maria Rotunda ' through the malice of the times ' there was no monk or lay brother at all by 1327. By 1388, Classe had no monks ' on account of the wars in Romagna '.[32] Convents too suffered. There were perhaps among the ladies of Romagna those who emulated the Blessed Margarita of Faenza (d. 1330), follower of S. Umiltà of the Vallambrosians, but if so they did not succeed, like her, in reaching the pages of the *Acta Sanctorum*.[33] The Blessed Chiara of Rimini (fl.1300), whose heroic mortifications, visions, prophecies, miraculous cures, persecutions by devils, and strange paroxysms (cured only through the taking of the Eucharist), were dishumed by the learned Garampi, seems to have belonged to no order.[34] If Giovanni Fiorentino's *Pecorone* has any authority, the religious houses for women in the province can hardly have enjoyed an admirable reputation in the second half of the fourteenth century. Fiorentino's novels have a frame story in which a nun and her lover meet together in the parlour of a convent of Forlì to sing, dance, and tell stories.[35]

If monasticism was declining, the friars, on the other hand, were extremely popular. Three men of Faenza: the Blessed Rainaldo (d. 1222), the Blessed Rodolfo (d. 1228), and the Blessed Giuliano (d. 1241), had all been associated with St. Dominic himself, and with the early growth of the Dominican movement. By 1303, there were convents for men in each of the six principal towns, while Imola and Forlì both had two houses each for the female branch of the order.[36] The Franciscans were equally popular. St. Francis himself had passed through the province, and a popular story tells of his encounter there with the formidable Bishop Mainario Aldighieri of Imola. Convents of the First Franciscan Order are found in Faenza in 1224, in Forlì and Ravenna after 1249, in Cesena in 1250, in Imola shortly after 1250, and in Rimini by 1258. By their side grew up the second Franciscan order of the Sisters of St. Mary the Virgin or 'Poor Clares', and the third order of laymen: the Frati della Penitenza, or Franciscan tertiaries.[37] Many of the citizens in their wills asked to be buried in the Franciscan habits. Along with the principal orders too, the Augustine, Servite, and Carmelite friars all flourished. Unfortunately, by the middle of the fourteenth century quarrels had begun between the various orders which were to be extinguished only a hundred years later.

Of the character of the secular clergy it is difficult to speak. It is noticeable how in the taxation record of 1291, a high proportion of them, almost 35 per cent of the parish clergy of the diocese of Faenza, are recorded as either earning less than seven gold florins a year, or as being dependent on alms. Within the town of Faenza, there had been some re-ordering of the parish system to meet the contemporary needs. The many *cappelle* or parishes of the town had been grouped by 1155 into four principal 'congregations' taking the name of the four larger churches in the quarters of the town, each presided over by a *primicerius*. By 1253, these were united in a College of Urban Parishes, which gave a general organisation to parish life in the town.[38] In the *contado*, parish organisation was less well developed, and presumably there was little economic rationalisation.

In both town and *contado* the election of the parish priests often lay with the parishioners, and the rural communes in particular played a large part in the management of the parish. In 1400, for instance, the *homines* of the parish of Sant' Agnese di Goggianello, vacant through the death of the rector, gathered in the church. Sixteen of them came from Flubano, and eight from Goggianello itself, and these, ' together considering that by right the election belonged to the parishioners ' unanimously elected Don Giovanni di Guido, from the *contado* of Bologna, to the office. He was present at the meeting, accepted, and was later presented to the bishop, who confirmed his appointment.[39] Sometimes the right of presentation was said to belong to the *homines* comprised in the parishioners of the church,[40] at others to the local commune.[41] In fact, the boundaries of the commune and the parish would generally be the same. In addition to electing the priest, the communes would gather money for the business of the church. In the village of Tossignano in 1442 the council even decreed the sale of some of the goods of the convent of the Friars Minor to restore the fabric of the church.[42] Sometimes this control had curious results. When the *homines* of Campuino were having a chapel painted in their church, some of the men wished to entrust the work to Giovanni de' Calegarii, others to Galeotto de' Calvi. As a compromise both men were engaged ; with the stipulation that neither should work in the chapel without the presence or consent of the other. They promised this under a penalty of a fine of 25 gold ducats for non-compliance.[43] Again, as in the *castelli*, the little village communes made formal oblations to their churches. Each year, at high mass on the feast of the Resurrection the commune and *universitas* of Corvara presented a wax candle to the archpriest of the church of Santa Maria.[44]

It is obviously difficult to say whether this rudimentary form of congregationalism secured a worthy clergy. Reference has already been made to the attempts of Don Amatore to ' save his life ' in 1308.[45] Other incidents stand out. In 1358, for instance, Abbot Iacomo of San Vitale, with the chapter of the monastery, deprived Don Francesco Masio of his rectory of the church of San Lorenzo da Scornio, for open concubinage ' by day and night.' He kept his mistress, Gasdia, in the church ' and not content with that, many other unsavoury women, whom he took to taverns, drinking with laymen and playing at dice '.[46] In November 1456, the archpriest Valeriano Zanelli of Santa Maria di Tossignano, a celebrated copyist of the age, ' being afraid of the plague raging at the present time in Tossignano ', stated that he did not wish to remain there. ' Desiring however to provide diligently to the care and needs of his parishioners', he named as his substitutes, Fra Bartolomeo and Fra Battista, both of the order of Servi of Forlì. His parishioners do not seem to have been unduly disturbed by his desertion, for five years later he was back and receiving £B.50 for a new missal he had completed for the lay society of Santa Maria of Tossignano.[47] Again, in 1461, the men of the parish of S. Martino in Gesso gathered above the market of Sassoleone, recognising that Don Giovanni dalla Marca had departed *insalutato hospite*, elected another rector in his place.[48] But such incidents found their way into the notarial protocols, presumably because they were exceptional.

Certainly the system closely identified laymen with the fortunes of their own parish, and many of their wills asked for the decoration of their churches. In 1373, Giacomo Mercati left £B.5 for the painting of a *lunette* containing the figures of the Blessed Virgin, St. John the Baptist, and St. Catherine.[49] In 1387, Margarita di Giovanni asked her heirs to see that someone was commissioned to paint the Virgin with Child, St. Elizabeth, St. Margaret, and St. Anthony. In 1422, the Lady Francesca di Giovanni Mini asked for two figures of St. Anthony to be made: in 1446, Bernardo Donato asked his heirs to place 'a wooden crucifixion with the *testator* on his knees before it with hands raised', in the church of San Pietro of Laguna.[50] Until the middle of the fifteenth century, it was the will of the town aristocrat, and not the *signore*, which gave the greatest patronage to the artist.

Outside the old parish organisation too, the layman came to play a large role in church life through the lay fraternities, noticeably in the Franciscan and Dominican third orders. Indeed the Bull of Honorius III of 16 December 1221, in defence of the Frati di Penitenza of Faenza, is probably the first reference to the Franciscan Tertiaries. Certainly, they are definitely recorded in the town in 1236,[51] and they attained an enormous vogue through the inspiration of Fra Novellone, a local flagellant. When lying on his deathbed in July 1280:

> the whole clergy of the town of Faenza, with the people and a vast horde of men and women, bore Fra Novellone with the greatest joy and honour to the cathedral of S. Pietro, where all living in Faenza, men and women, citizens and foreigners came. And whoever could get something of his clothes rejoiced greatly, since they held him for a saint . . . for his good and chaste and harsh life, and the great penance which he performed in his life. For by day and night he would whip his flesh and give himself to great fasts and prayers and penance . . . going eleven times in his life to the threshold of the

blessed James the Apostle (at Compostella), and five of those times, with bare feet, whipping himself continually, and tearing his flesh.[52]

It was doubtless his inspiration which caused so many of the lay societies of Faenza which sprang up from the mid-fourteenth century to place an emphasis upon flagellation. We hear then of the ' White Beaters ' and the ' Black Beaters ', distinguished according to the colour of their hoods. As typical could be taken the Society of S. Maria de la Misericordia of Faenza whose members were granted an indulgence in 1362, on those occasions when they ' show reverence to the Virgin with lauds and canticles at certain times . . . when they go to bury the bodies of the dead and gather to flog themselves and sing lauds '.[53] Among the lauds sung on such occasions which have been preserved, is one in fact entitled ' Lauda beati Noveloni de Favencia '.[54]

These forms of devotion may appear repulsive, but the *disciplina* had long played a part in orthodox penitential dogma, and the terror engendered by the Black Death of 1348 gave a powerful impulse to the more emotional and hysterical expressions of religion. In all the towns the lay societies were to have a strong hold through the later middle ages. There were nine in Imola by the middle of the fifteenth century. Here, for instance, the will of Lando Galassi of Mezzocolle, after leaving money for the repair of the new *campanile* of San Cassiano, gave £B.10 to each of the following societies : that of Maria Beata, meeting in the church of the Carmelite friars, of Corpus Christi, meeting in San Cassiano, of the Blessed Mary, meeting in San Francesco, of San Pietro, meeting in San Pietro in Laguna, of San Sebastiano, meeting in San Lorenzo, of Santa Maria in Valverde, and of San Giovanni, meeting in San Domenico, and of San Bernardo.[55]

The societies had social as well as devotional functions. The society of the Blessed Virgin Mary, for instance, ran the hospital of Saint Mary the Devout, and was responsible for the upkeep of the bridge over the Santerno.[56] Many of the hospitals of the province in which the sick and indigent were cared for had grown up through the piety of these lay societies.[57] Most of the wills of the townspeople of Imola, at the end of the fourteenth century, left five shillings towards the upkeep of the bridge, and many left money to the various hospitals.[58]

III

Once the vicariates had been granted, the closer integration of lay and ecclesastical society was accompanied by a close union of papal and signorial governments. Hitherto the communes had devoted much energy to attacks upon ecclesiastical properties, especially upon the lands of the Archbishop of Ravenna,[59] but with the establishment of legal *signorie* such incidents almost cease. In part, of course, this was because the towns had already obtained most of what they wanted from the churches. But the laws of the communes give numerous testimonies of their loyalty to orthodox religious ideals. The statutes of Faenza, for instance, required an oath from the *podestà* that he would aid the inquisitor, and would execute heretics.[60] Further, they forbade buying or selling in churches, and prohibited work or trade on Sundays and on the great feasts of Christmas, the Epiphany, Easter, Whitsun, the Assumption, and All Saints (though here numerous exceptions on the grounds of necessity diminished the force of the law).[61] The altar of St. Martin in the cathedral of Faenza was maintained at the expense of the commune, and its chaplain, elected by the *anziani*, received annually twenty-five *corbes* of grain, and twelve *corbes* of pure wine from the communal revenues. Each year on the feast of St. Martin, the *podestà* with the general council, and the representatives of the Arts, went in procession to the altar, where each Art presented a large wax candle, and a banner to the value of £B.10.[62]

Religious life came to be more and more closely bound up with secular government. We have already seen how the church and the friars had become involved in the faction conflicts of the towns, how, for instance, in 1287, Lotterio della Tosa had become Bishop of Faenza 'at the prayers and insistence of Maghinardo da Susinana'.[63] This involvement was to grow with the fourteenth century, and the coming of the *signoria*. From the time of the Liber Censuum the Bishop of Rimini was supposed to be appointed by the Papal See.[64] Bishoprics of the other towns seem to have been reserved to the papacy after 1319, as forming part of the papal states, though it is uncertain if bishops were always in fact papally provided.[65] None the less the personnel of the ecclesiastical hierarchy still reflected to a large extent the social pattern of lay society.

In Imola, for instance, Carlo, brother of Azzo and Roberto Alidosi, was bishop from 1342 to 1354, and was succeeded by Lito, son of Roberto, who held the office until appointed Papal Treasurer in 1380. Guglielmo Alidosi, after being Bishop of Cervia, was translated to Imola in 1382, though his career was cut short by plague in the following year. From 1402 to 1412, Ermanno dei Brancaleoni, a kinsman of Ludovico Alidosi, held the same office. Another member of the family, Alidosio Alidosi, after being

Archpriest of Mezzocolle, was raised to the see of Rimini in 1332.[66] The town aristocracy, of course, dominated the cathedral chapters.[67] The influence of lay society, as a result, was all pervasive. In March 1372, Beltrando Alidosi, as we have already noted, was appointed vicar of the Franciscan inquisitor-general, with the right of seizing heretics within the boundaries of the commune. At the same time, Zollo, rector of the church of Sant' Ambrogio della Massa, acted as *gastald* of the family for their properties in the *montagna*. Again, among the chapter of the Dominican convent of Santa Maria della Carità were the daughters of all the more prominent Imolesi families : Penna de' Caravassalli, Isabella da Tossignano, Agnesina de' Tartagni, Lambertina de' Bolgarelli, Maddalena Broccardi, Margerita della Bordella, Caterina de' Palmiroli, and so on. That the prioress of these ladies in 1334 and 1351 should have been Mattea Alidosi can be explained, according to taste, either by picturing a society keenly attuned to the values outside the cloister, or alternatively by imagining that Mattea had been borne to her office by those same inherited qualities of leadership which had carried her family to *signoria*.[68]

The Alidosi certainly played a greater part in ecclesiastical government than the other *signori* of the province in the fourteenth century. Perhaps they had acquired a reputation, whether true or false, for greater piety, and it was for this that the family was the first in the province to be invested with the papal vicariate. However this may be, the advantages to the papacy of the overlapping of lay and spiritual government are obvious. It was an advantage in that it called a halt to communal-episcopal conflict, which in Imola especially, had been very bitter in the twelfth and thirteenth centuries ; it gave the civil government a vested interest in orthodoxy ; and it ensured an alliance of the two authorities against the usurpations of *contado* nobility. The Pope could confidently write to Bishop Carlo Alidosi in 1346, telling him to guard the properties of the church with the delegated powers of excommunication, and ' invoking, if need be, the aid of the secular arm '. In fact, with the assistance of his uncles, the bishop did restore many properties to the bishopric.[69] It was a disadvantage, on the other hand, in that the signorial bishopric involved the Church very closely with signorial interests. The interests of the bishop's family, it may be suspected, often triumphed over those of the Church. Bishop Carlo leased emphyteutically considerable properties to Roberto Alidosi, and to the della Bordella family which was his ally, and such leases were virtual alienations of episcopal rights.[70] It is not perhaps mere chance that the first complaints to the Pope concerning Alidosi usurpations of ecclesiastical properties should come in the rule of Bishop Marino (1380–82), who had no apparent connection with the family. Again, the usurious transaction of Azzo and Roberto Alidosi which took place in the episcopal palace has already been noted.[71]

On balance the advantages for the Church predominated. Throughout the period of the Great Schism, and then through the Conciliar Movement and the fifteenth century right into the Reformation era, Romagna was to remain staidly orthodox. Whatever it lost in temporal power during the century and a half of signorial rule, the Church, by its compromises with the lay power, preserved and strengthened those beliefs which lay at the centre of its organisation. The advice of Carlo Malatesti, champion of Gregory XII, to Giovanni Maria Visconti, that 'above all, the Signore of Signori should be venerated and honoured' was in large measure a fruit of the papacy's flexibility and willingness, ultimately, to reject ideal in favour of possible solutions.

CONCLUSION

FOR too long the slow transition from commune to *signoria* has been popularly portrayed as a process in which a free and democratic society, represented, as in Carducci's poetry, by virtuous men of heroic stature, was replaced by an evil form of government whose representative was the *signore*, symbol of wickedness, albeit of cultivated wickedness. Such a change could only satisfactorily be explained in moral terms, and historians of the nineteenth century, in considering the phenomenon, drew heavily upon concepts of moral decline. A proud and independent spirit was said to have given way to an enervating acquiescence in tyranny, in which the citizens lost the habit of managing their own affairs.

It is scarcely necessary to say how unsatisfactory is this type of argument. The truth is that there was no antithesis, moral or otherwise, between communal and signorial government. In Romagna, at least, the *signoria* was merely the sophistication of a primitive form of government. Here the commune had hardly been a unity at all, but rather a vague link of a few conflicting interests. The *signoria* emerged with the expansion and development of the original commune, an expansion which incorporated within the primitive political structure the *contado* nobility and the lower orders represented by the guilds. We see here the same process which was repeated in all Western society at the same period : the birth of the state. The *signoria* came as a result of the development of administration, of an increasing centralisation, of a new professionalism in government.

Of course, this government was not democratic. But then neither was the commune from which it had emerged. (Neither were the bourgeois oligarchies of Florence and Venice.) And it is difficult, in fact, — given the weakness of Empire and Papacy, to see what other form of rule could have evolved in the province during the thirteenth and fourteenth centuries. To recognise its virtues — and this without in any way minimising its obvious faults — the *signoria* should be seen, not against some ideal standard erected by modern (or fourth century B.C.) political thinkers, but within the context of its own troubled times. Essentially it was a compromise of conflicting political interests : interests represented by rival nobles, the citizens, and the Church.

This is not to idealise the signorial form of government : ' the worst of all', according to the contemporary Bartolo. But the towns of Romagna had no possibility of producing any other form, for the *signoria* was intimately linked with their society. In considering the government of the communes in the thirteenth and fourteenth centuries, and the life of town and country, one sees how little social change the creation of the *signorie* actually made. The transfer of authority from the factions of nobles who formed the 'free' commune, to one noble family, brought about no alteration in the quality of life. Here too, the establishment of the *signoria* did not introduce a new form of society; it was merely the natural and final development of the old. In Romagna the *signoria* came not to destroy, but to fulfil the original aims of communal government, and it did so by establishing a dyarchy with the commune. For the commune in its origins was not, as the nineteenth-century liberal believed, an attempt to secure democratic freedom. It was a revolutionary conspiracy to destroy the local authority of remote powers claiming a universal dominion; and like all revolutions the communal movement tended to end in single person government. 'Libertas' in that era should not be interpreted as 'democratic liberty', but as *campanalismo*. It was this *campanalismo*, or local loyalty, which was the keystone of the commune, and which was similarly to be the formative influence in the *signorie* of Romagna.

The conclusions reached in the previous pages on the transition from commune to *signoria* in Romagna, can, I believe, in their general outlines, be taken as applicable to all those other towns of Italy — especially in the Marche and in Umbria — which had a similar agrarian economy. In each, aristocratic rivalry, stimulated by the Guelf-Ghibelline conflicts of the thirteenth century, undermined the precarious stability of the communes, and in each the *signori* came to power in the fourteenth century, both as a check to and as a result of this anarchy. Once in control, the *signori* were able to bring about a new balance, which enabled the individual towns to preserve their independence during the following century.

In so far as Romagna is concerned, the *signorie* which were established in the fourteenth century had a precarious and uneven development. The Alidosi *signoria* ended as early as 1424, and Imola in the fifteenth century wavered between the government of the Church, of a branch of the Manfredi family, and of the Riarii. The papal nepotism of Sixtus IV gave Forlì too, to the Riarii family, after the fall of the Ordelaffi in 1480. The da Polenta yielded the lordship of Ravenna to the Venetians in 1441. Only the rule of the Manfredi and the Malatesti lasted into the sixteenth century, and both were cut short by the campaigns of Cesare Borgia in 1500 and 1501. With these men passed the local independence of their states, which the communes had first established.

A final question : did these rulers cull from the experiences of the thirteenth and fourteenth centuries any ideal of government, any higher concept of their role in political life than that of holding on to the power they had attained? It would be easy to be cynical about this. Yet all power structures find eventually their own rationale and moral ideology. The bourgeois oligarchy of Florence — brutal enough if seen from any vantage point other than that of the capitalist apologist — produced the civic humanism of Bruni and his friends. So too, I believe, did the *signori* of Romagna attain in the fourteenth century to some abstract ideal of their role in society.

In part this ideal was created by the concepts of *courtoisie* and *gentilesse* taken from the Arthurian Romances, whose popularity in this period is attested by the names : Galeotto, Lancilotto, Ginevra, and so on, found within the signorial families. In part too, it was formed by the Church whose allies now the *signori* had become and whose concepts of the just ruler were not entirely absent from its grants of vicariate. Again, it was doubtless shaped by the literary moralism of the time, by such men as Petrarch, whose counsel to Francesco da Carrara, Lord of Padua, must have been repeated in his friendly contacts with the Malatesti family. Petrarch urged that a Prince must love his subjects : 'You must not be the lord of your people, but the father of your country, and love them as your children, yes, even as yourself. You should inspire them with love, not quell them with fear, for from fear comes hate.' Like Machiavelli, he asserts that the best defence of the *signore* is not a bodyguard, but the goodwill of his subjects. The prince too, must be just, giving to each his own, and inclining to mercy in judgment. He should promote public works, provide against famine, and explain to his subjects the need for taxation when it is raised. He should exercise control over his officials, and himself be humble, generous, and modest.[1]

All this might seem vague enough. Yet the influence of Petrarch can be clearly seen in the advice given by Carlo Malatesti to Giovanni Maria Visconti, advice which offers a fairly precise indication of how the *signori* regarded themselves in relation to their states. It was written down 'at the ducal camp near Cassano when I mounted my horse to go to my own parts : 27 August 1408, the eighteenth hour'. In the first place, as we have already seen,

Carlo advised that the King of Kings and Lord of Lords should be worshipped and honoured. He counselled Visconti to love his subjects as a return for their love to him, and urged him to be diligent in his rule. He should give no unnecessary gifts. He should avoid war ' as far as he can ', and shun cruelty. He should promise nothing without consideration, but he should keep his promises inviolably. He should not allow dissension in his family, and should punish anyone who tries to bring discord between him and his brother.

He should elect a council which is loyal to him, and allow no others to interfere in the state. ' Lest error arise ', decisions on supplications and letters should be approved by the council before being promulgated. None of the *signore's* servants should be allowed to issue edicts at variance with the statutes of the city : ' for from experience I have observed that love, hate, and gain, very often divert servants and council from the truth. And if he fails to do this, it is certain that he will destroy his state, and in a short time too.' His councillors must not interfere in the administration of justice, save to ensure that it is administered. Offices should not be sold : ' for it is certain that no-one buys his office without hope of profit, and he will not be able to get this without oppressing his subjects '. The holding of office by vicars should not be allowed and office holders should be syndicated at the term of their office according to the statutes. ' As far as he can ', he should have impartial officials. If they are found guilty of offences in their office they should be punished with death, despite pleas for mercy.

Anyone found guilty of interfering with the just apportioning of taxation, ' whether through love or hate ', should be punished most severely, as should tax-defaulters. Taxation should be imposed quickly, and collected diligently. Courtiers should not be allowed to petition for direct or indirect remissions ; if this isn't done : ' it will be easier for an ass to fly than for him to keep his state '. The citizens should not be taxed unreasonably, and should be able to see in what way their money is spent. Taxes should be imposed equitably so that the rich pay more than the poor. Those with power in the state should not be exempt.

Mercenary soldiers should be paid promptly and inspected regularly. He should not proceed against anyone accused of treason without first taking counsel. Rebels should not be put down by pleas or bribes, but punished as an example. Those wishing to return to their loyalty should be received, on their giving securities for future good behaviour. Finally, private citizens should be forbidden to construct fortresses, and all fortresses should be destroyed save those absolutely necessary to the state.[2]

All this advice could be considered as rather the maxims of prudent self-interest than as the expression of an ideal of government (though Carlo's life suggests that he was sensitive to the claims of a higher moral purpose). In such small states as those of the Romagna, rulers could hardly be isolated from their subjects, and the threat of assassination urged discretion in the exercise of autocratic rule. In fact, political murders of *signori* were not uncommon in the fifteenth century, and the threat of assassination was a real spur — though not always effective — to making an attempt at just government.

Of course, the *signore's* position within the state, as an autocrat menaced by the continual threat of assassination, did not, in weaker spirits, make for psychological health and facility of touch in government. Yet once the *signoria* was established its internal rule presented few problems for there was no real class or social struggle in the province. The *signore* had to keep on good terms with his own family, and with the Church. He had to avoid perpetrating any obvious injustice, and he had to preserve the supply of corn. His principal weakness arose from the poor financial position of the communes. If he could obtain a *condotta* as the client of some more powerful state, his financial problem was solved. But such links drew him into a dangerous dependence upon the larger powers of Italy, who in the fifteenth century were to make Romagna the battleground of their conflicting ambitions.

It was through these powers, in fact, that each of the *signori* was eventually to be swept away. Yet while they survived, the Lords of Romagna were able to give to their fellow-citizens the one thing which they desired above all others : local independence. They gave to their subjects a pride and a sense of belonging, almost impossible for us to imagine in a world of giant states — the pride which comes from being a citizen in a community small enough to allow the individual to identify himself intimately with its interests.

APPENDICES

APPENDIX I

The Boundaries of Romagna

THE Italian state of today has no administrative subdivision known as Romagna, and accounts of the boundaries of the province are confused and contradictory. The name itself arose in the era of Byzantine domination. The Lombards called the whole of the Roman-Byzantine territory, ' Romania '.[1] Gradually the word came to be used in a more restricted sense, though there was little agreement as to where exactly Romagna was.

(a) *The Northern Boundary*

In 1396, a legal process was held, to define the northward extent of the province ; even at this date, witnesses gave varying interpretations : that the Romagna began at the Po ; at the Garisenda and Asinelli towers in Bologna ; at the Sillaro, etc.[2] This uncertainty continued throughout the fifteenth and sixteenth centuries. To Biondo da Forlì, the province consisted of the area between the rivers Foglia and Santerno ; Emilia proper lay north of the Santerno.[3] To Pius II, however, Romagna was the whole of Emilia.[4] In this he was followed in the sixteenth century by Don Alberti, who attempted to reconcile the two traditions by distinguishing between Romagna, and Romagna Transpadana.[5] When d' Azeglio, in 1859, led the insurgent nationalists of Bologna, Ferrara, Ravenna, and Forlì, he claimed to speak for ' i popoli delle Romagne ', and the province he formed was called ' le Romagne '.[6]

Following d' Azeglio, some modern scholars have claimed that the term Romagna should imply the territory formerly included in all Emilia to the River Panaro. Among those who maintain this, Rimini, which strictly formed part of the Pentapolis, is none the less incorporated within the province. Certainly, as they point out, there is no geographical or economic unity, in the land south of the Bolognese *contado*, to distinguish it from the rest of Emilia.[7] Others appeal to the authority of Dante, who in *Purgatorio*, XIV, 92, appears to define the Romagna as the land : ' tra il Po e il monte e la marina e il Reno '.[8]

During the thirteenth century the statutes of Ravenna ordained that their *podestà* should be chosen from those, ' qui non sint de romagna, set bononia sit excepta . . . non . . . de romagna, praeter quam de bononia '.[9] Here, Bologna was clearly considered part of the province. Yet Salimbene, in the same era, described it as the land, ' inter marchiam Anconitanam et Bononiam civitatem '.[10]

When, in 1278, Bologna and Romagna were incorporated within the papal states, the administrative documents of the curia distinguished the two, and were to continue to do so throughout the fourteenth century. ' Guilelmus dei gratia Episcopus Muritiatensis provinciarum Marchie Anconitane ac Romaniole, Civitatis quoque Bononie et Comitatus Brictonorii Rector ' — such is the typical form, even though the rector of Romagna almost invariably acted as the rector of Bologna too.[11] Again, Cardinal Anglic, in his celebrated *Descriptiones*, separated the two quite distinctly. If the authority of Dante is to be given weight, as a contrast to *Purgatorio*, XIV, 92, already cited, one can refer to *Inferno*, XXVII, where Dante, asked to describe the condition of the Romagnols, makes no mention of Bologna.

One might make a tentative attempt to reconcile the two passages in the *Divine Comedy* by claiming that, although at line 99, he pauses to condemn the ' Romagnoli tornati in bastardi ', yet the poet in *Purgatorio*, XIV is not attempting to describe Romagna, but rather the whole area where the Calboli were famed. In *Inferno*, XXVII, on the other hand, Guido da Montefeltro has asked for specific information of the Romagnols, and here, one could say, Dante has restricted himself to information on the Romagna. In support of this thesis it could be pointed out that in the *De Vulgari Eloquentia*, Dante distinguished in chapter XIV, *De idiomata Romandiolorum*, the dialect of the Romagnols from that of the Bolognesi. I do not know how much weight this argument carries[12] ; it may be that to praise the poet for ' quella mirabile coscienza storica e geografica ', as Casini does, precisely in that passage where he asserts that Dante in *Purgatorio*, XIV is describing Romagna, is to lay a mistaken emphasis upon his genius.

Dante's remarks upon Romagnol dialect are difficult to interpret correctly.[13] He emphasises its softness, yet to the ear of the foreigner it appears harsh in comparison with Tuscan. Again, it seems difficult to equate dialect with provincial identity, when the speech of Imola is as different from Riminese as Bolognese.[14] The cephalic index, which Comelli uses to show a distinction of race between those north and south of the Sillaro, seems, to the layman in such matters, highly suspect. None the less, I follow Comelli in his general conclusions ; for the purpose of this study the northern demarcation of the Romagna will be fixed at the River Sillaro, which forms the boundary between Bologna and Imola. Such in fact is the general consensus of opinion today.[15] It may be justified by the administrative distinction drawn by the papal curia in the fourteenth century, and still more by the fact that today, the peasants of Castel San Pietro will assert that the men south of the Sillaro are Romagnols, but that they themselves are not.

(b) *The County of Bertinoro*

Although set firmly within the boundaries of Romagna, and subject to the same jurisdiction as other places in the province, Bertinoro was always distinguished from the rest of Romagna in papal documents. The explanation of this is that the county had fallen to the papacy by inheritance in 1178, a century before the rest of the province.[16]

(c) *San Marino*

Though undoubtedly a part of the Romagna, San Marino in the middle ages led a life remote from the rest of the province, and Dante fails to mention it. In consequence I omit any consideration of it.

(d) *The Montefeltro*

Tonini declared that the Montefeltro was not in Romagna[17] and in present-day Italy it is incorporated within the boundaries of the Marche.[18] However, Guido da Montefeltro, in *Inferno*, XXVII, obviously believed himself to be a Romagnol ; Anglic includes it within his *Descriptio*, and Franciosi has assembled sufficient evidence to justify its being considered a part of the province.[19]

(e) *The Massa Trabaria*

Like Bertinoro, the Massa Trabaria which consisted of the upper valleys of the Marecchia, Foglia, and Metauro, and included Sant' Agata Feltria, Penna, and Valbona, had been subject to the Roman see before 1278. In 1288, Nicholas IV drew the boundaries between Romagna and the Massa. These fluctuated throughout the fourteenth century; in Grimoard's description, villages designated earlier to the Massa, were incorporated within the Montefeltro. None the less the greater part of the Massa was always administered separately from Romagna, and the area as a whole, must be considered to lie outside the province.[20] Today it forms part of the Marche.

APPENDIX II

Fumanteria and the Population of Romagna in 1371

I

THE *DESCRIPTIO ROMANDIOLE*

In 1371 Cardinal Anglic Grimoard, papal legate of Romagna and Bologna, compiled for his successor three documents, giving guidance on the government of the provinces which he ruled. The first was a description in general terms of the political problems of the territories.[1] The other two consisted of detailed statistical information concerning, first, Bologna and its *contado*,[2] and second, the various parts of Romagna.[3] These last two documents gave an account of the castles, routes, papal garrisons and officials, the town governments, and papal and communal revenue. Finally they gave the number of *focularia*, or ' hearths ', in each town and village.

The document dealing with Romagna did not include information on the upper Marecchia, or part of the Savio valleys, for these were ascripted at that time to the administration of the Massa Trabaria ; nor did it take into account the inhabitants of the upper Santerno and Savio valleys, who then obeyed Florence and the Tusco-Romagnol house of the Ubaldini. But otherwise it gave statistics of all the Romagna within its traditional boundaries. In this it has been regarded as the most important source for estimates of the population of the province in the fourteenth century and as a primary document towards the understanding of the historical demography of the papal states.

II

THE CONCLUSIONS OF BELOCH AND GAMBI

The *Descriptio provinciae Romandiolae* assessed the total number of *focularia* or *fumantes* of the province as 34,644. Du Cange defined FOCUS and FUMANS as meaning *domus*, *familia*, commenting ' in Italia censentur per focos, maxime in pagis et vicis '. The tax itself was called FUMANS, FOAGIUM, or FUMANTERIA. In Romagna only the last form is found, sometimes spelt *fumantaria*. FOCULARE and FUMANTE were the names of those liable to this tax. Thus Beloch, in his examination of the *Descriptio*, correctly associated *fumantes* with the *fumanteria*, and confidently assumed that the word meant ' all fathers of families '. Taking then an estimate of five souls to each family, he claimed that the population of Romagna in 1371 equalled the total number of *fumantes* multiplied by five.[4]

This conclusion did not meet with the entire approval of Gambi. In a very much more detailed examination[5] he noticed that Anglic had cited three villages twice in the same document. Accordingly he cancelled these from Anglic's total of *fumantes*. He also removed from the total the *fumantes* of certain villages beyond the Po, that he believed should not be considered as part of the province. Thus he was left with 33,494 *fumantes*. Otherwise Gambi followed the broad outlines of Beloch's calculations. *Focularia* implied families. Working by analogy, from modern statistics of Romagnol families he assumed that there was a mean average over the whole province of 4·5 souls to a family.[6] He multiplied 33,494 by 4·5, and to the total thus attained, added the 1,474 soldiers mentioned by Anglic as garrisoned in the province. This brought the population of Romagna to 152,197 souls.[7] This figure, Gambi pointed out, did not include those dwelling in monastic houses. For some reason — probably, he explained, because Anglic's authority was not spiritual but political — the cardinal had not given any indication of the numbers of the religious in the province.

III

The first reason for considering these conclusions invalid lies in the character of the *Descriptio* itself. In the first place it does not, as Beloch and Gambi assumed, describe in its entirety Romagna in the year 1371. Second, its internal accuracy is suspect.

(a) *The composition of the* Descriptio

Though compiled in the year 1371, the *Descriptio* was based upon documents of the administrative subdivisions of Romagna of different periods. Much of the information supplied was in fact already outdated. What at first appears to be a Domesday Book of 1371, a survey based upon enquiry at town and village level, turns out on more careful examination to be no more than a rather careless miscellany of chancellory information of different years.

This becomes apparent if the *fumanteria* and *fumantes* of the *Descriptio* are placed side by side. Here are some of the figures :

	fumanteria (in £B)			*fumantes*
Imola (*town and district*)	2,074	13	8	1,624
Imola (*contado*)	312	2	7	2,881
Faenza (and *contado*)	453	16	2	4,189
Forlì	3,077	4	4	3,482
Cesena	365	14	2	3,375
Ravenna	350	4	10	3,233
Rimini	593	6	8	5,505
Vicariate of Sant' Arcangelo	96	19	0	893
Vicariate of Montefeltro	204	12	0	1,889

Now there is no reason why in 1371 Imola and Forlì should have been subjected to eight or ten times heavier taxation, proportional to their *fumantes*, than the other towns or vicariates. Imola was ruled by a papal vicar, but then so were Ravenna and Rimini. Forlì was *immediate subjecte*, but then so were the *contado* of Imola, Cesena, and Faenza. And in all the *fumanteria* is said to be raised, ' ad rationem 26 den. pro quolibet fumante '.

The explanation must be that the papal clerk, compiling the *Descriptio*, drew for his account of *fumanteria* in Forlì and Imola upon outdated documents which dealt with years when the tax was heavier. Although the traditional annual tax was twenty-six pennies on each *fumante*,[8] yet it could greatly exceed this figure, In the *contado* of Imola, between 1361 and 1367, for instance, it stood at £2 17 6½ each year.[9] It is probably from this time that the 1371 figures for the town of Imola and Forlì were taken.

But if this error arose in *fumanteria*, it is not improbable that similar errors are concealed in the numbers of *fumantes*. Indeed, there is very good evidence that this is so. Gambi himself pointed out that the village of Linaro is assessed, at one point in the document, as having 20 *fumantes*, and at another at 22 ; that, similarly, Pietro ad Uso is assessed at 12, and then 9 ; Marradi as having 60, and then 42 *fumantes*.[10] Yet he failed to grasp the significance of these errors, which reflect clearly the manner in which the *Descriptio* must have been compiled. Pietro ad Uso had at one time been incorporated within the Montefeltro. There the papal assessors had agreed on a valuation of 9 *fumantes*. Some administrative reorganisation, perhaps, had caused it to pass to the *contado* of Rimini, where a different assessor had valued it at 12 *fumantes*. The papal clerk, in drawing up the *Descriptio*, used both accounts in his compilation, and failed to notice that he had duplicated his entry, through the transfer of the village to a new administration.

(b) *The internal accuracy of the* Descriptio

The lack of precision in the statistics of the *Descriptio* should also be emphasised.[11] This rather obvious point offsets the reliance placed by previous students on these figures. Anglic himself said that the figures were ‘ salvo iure calculi ’, and the precise claim of the *Descriptio* that there were 34,644 *focularia* is somewhat muted in Anglic’s letter of advice to his successor : ‘ possunt esse in tota Romandiola, in quibuscumque terris que tenentur ab ecclesia mediate vel immediate 34,000 fumantium non ascendunt ad 35,000 ’.

IV

Despite the fact that the *fumantes* in the *Descriptio* do not refer wholly to 1371, it might yet be assumed that they are roughly valid for a period — say five years — preceding it. However, the second principal reason for rejecting the findings of Beloch and Gambi is that there is not, as they assumed, and as all have assumed who have examined the document since the time of Fantuzzi, any direct relation in Romagna between *fumantes* and families.

In support of this conclusion three arguments may be advanced :

(i) Comparison of *fumantes* recorded in the thirteenth century with those of 1371 fails to show the effects of the Black Death.

(ii) Comparison with other earlier lists of *fumantes* reveals difficulties which suggests the improbability of these units representing families.

(iii) The number of families recorded in the village of Massa Alidosia in 1369 shows no relation to the number of *fumantes* at which it was assessed in 1371.

Each of these points must be examined in turn.

(i) Fumantes *and the Black Death.* The central feature of population change in fourteenth-century Romagna is the succession of bubonic plague infections. Up to 1371 plague struck the province in 1316,[12] 1319,[13] and 1340.[14] These epidemics reached their climax in 1347 and 1348. In May 1348 : ‘ cominzoe in Arimino una grandissima mortalità e poi per lo contado e durò infina adì primo de dicembre. E morì di tre persone le doe.’[15] Most of the chroniclers dwell upon it in similar terms as a disaster.[16] Further outbreaks followed in 1361 — falling severely on Rimini, Cesena, Forlì, and Faenza, though not in Imola[17] — and in 1365. Of this last plague the Bolognese chronicler records: 'che quasi pocha zente gli romaxe, imperzochè per le altre morìe ch' erano stade, tanti glen morì, che mo pochi ne romaxe '[18] — words implying desolation. Plague is recorded again in 1368.[19] It is obvious, then, that the effect of plague in the province was catastrophic ; more so perhaps even than in Florence.[20]

Yet Beloch himself noticed that, in 1288, the town of Imola had been assessed by the provincial curia as having 2,000 *focularia*. This figure, he thought, must have included both the town and its *districtus*. Imola had appealed against this judgment and had secured the reduction of its *fumantes* to 1500. Yet the number of *fumantes* for town and *districtus* in 1371, after the year of the Black Death, was larger than in 1288.[21] Either then, he thought the town had deceived the papal administration, or, despite all probability, the population of Imola had actually increased during the century. He reached this conclusion, undisturbed either by the roundness of the figures involved in 1288 — remarkable if in fact *fumantes* are coterminous numerically with families — or by the apparent arbitrary nature of the two assessments.

In addition to this, a document of 1312 gave the names of 2,378 families living in the town of Imola alone. Thus, assuming that *focularia* means families, if the town had 1,500 families in 1288, the population in twenty-four years had risen by 875 families — 50 per cent.[22]

(ii) *A comparison of some lists of* fumantes. Two other documents referring to the *fumantes* of the *contado* of Imola raise doubts. The first is that drawn up in 1265, by the commune of Bologna, which at that time administered it.[23] The second is a survey of the *contado* by the papal governors in 1367, recording the *fumantes* between the years 1361–7.[24] The first document enumerated only the villages subject to the immediate jurisdiction of Bologna. The document of 1367 recorded only the villages within the commune of the *contado* of Imola. Consequently neither are fully complete. Below, however, are appended the figures of all the *fumantes* of the *montagna* mentioned in both documents, and in the 1371 over *Descriptio* :

	1265	*1367*	*1371*
Dozza	129	46	170
Mezzocolle	59	$12\frac{1}{2}$	33
Casalfiumanese	42	$18\frac{1}{4}$	32
Fiagano	46	20	32

	1265	*1367*	*1371*
Corvara	45	38¼	126
Sassoleone	50	12	31
Cantagallo	21	4	32
Orsara	14	5½	37
Gaggio	6	4	
Fornione	7	2	18
Fontanalice	26	12½	84
Tossignano	114	78½	350
Toranello	14	9	70
Sassoretroso	10	2	23
Mongiardino	6	7	36
Monteoliveto	22	8	22
Porogno	6	1	9
Baffadi	20	7	46
Montemauro	28	10	47
Gallisterna	43	12	43
Pediano	24	5½	42
Mazzolano	23	13	53
Goggianello	7	2½	16
Serra	80	17¾	43
	842	348¼	1,395

In these lists lists one might see the effects of the 1348–9 epidemics. But even accepting that the document of 1367 was utilising administrative records of, say, 1350, it is difficult to assume that by 1371 (twenty years after at most), the number of families should have increased by 600 per cent, as they must have done if *fumantes* in fact equal families. Again, the estimates of *fumantes* in fractions in the document of 1367 suggests the improbability of their representing families ; one can think of half or three-quarters of a unit in taxation, but it is difficult in this context, to think of half a family. However small, a family living in a village is one family.

(iii) *A Document of 1369*. In one village it is possible to check directly the relation between families and *fumantes*. In 1369 two branches of the Alidosi induced Galeotto Malatesta to arrange for the equitable division of their patrimonial properties. In the document recording his decision,[25] Galeotto divided out, not only the land, but also the *fideles* belonging to the family, naming them individually. Forty-two male *fideles* were recorded by Galeotto at Belvedere (which in the *Descriptio* had twenty *fumantes*) and fifty-seven at Osta (which together with Carseggio had thirty *fumantes* in 1371). So far, by accepting an equal ratio of men to women, by assuming (unwarrantably) that these villages were composed entirely of *fideles* and were completely deprived of freeholders, and by accepting that 4·5 is an approximate multiplier to convert 'families' to 'souls', one might agree that in the *Descriptio*, *fumantes* might be justly related to population. But the same document goes on to show that in the Massa Alidosia, the family of Roberto Alidosi had thirty-nine *fideles* with their thirty-six sons, six brothers and five grandchildren. In addition to this there were also men who were not *fideles*, jurisdiction over whose farms was shared out. For the Massa Alidosia then, there were 152 male *fideles* (say 304 souls) and an unspecified number of non-*fideles*. The *fideles* alone came from seventy-one families. Two years later the *Descriptio* recorded the Massa Alidosia as having only twenty-five *fumantes*, and in these two years there is no surviving record of plague in Romagna.

V

These three points, considered together, seem to show conclusively the error of equating the *fumantes* of 1371 with families. What then are *fumantes*?

(a) Fumantes *as Fiscal Units*

In early documents of papal rule, *fumanteria* had been associated with the 'fodrum regale', raised in the province by the old imperial administration.[26] This tax had been graded according to the substance of each man in the province. Those who held one yoke of oxen paid twelve pennies; those with two yokes paid twenty-six pennies; those with three, two shillings, and so on. The man with one ox only paid sixpence, 'pro se et familia sua'. He who worked with his hands paid fourpence, 'similiter pro se et familia sua'.[27] The papacy replaced this with a system less cumbersome, though not more equitable, that had been in use in part of its territories since at least 1092.[28] The origins of this tax were explained by a papal document of the middle of the fourteenth century: 'Focularia, quae habuerunt originaria quod quaelibet domus in qua fiebat focus seu ignis, solvebat Camere S.E. XXVI den., et sequendo numerum focularioriorum quae tunc erat, Communia infrascripta solvunt annis singulis incommutabiliter summas infrascriptas. . . .'[29]

The use of the historic tense here is important. Taxation was raised on the number of *focularia*, 'que tunc erat'. In fact, in the patrimony in Tuscia, Calisse believed that there existed two methods of paying *fumanteria*. The first, the more ancient one, was where a fixed sum, once proportional to population, but later unchanged from year to year, was annually exacted.[30] By the fifteenth century as Bauer claimed,[31] the tax bore no relation to the real number of hearths, though it had once done so. Beloch himself, referring to the figures for the district of Rome in 1422, declared that here *focularia* represented conventional taxation units, unrelated to families.[32]

This is true, too, of Romagna. The *fumanteria* was a tax laid collectively upon each village and town. Each commune was responsible for a payment of twenty-six pennies for each of the *focularia* for which it was assessed. But such *focularia* or *fumantes* were fiscal units, calculated without immediate reference to population. To say that a town had 1,000 *fumantes* did not mean, either that it had 1,000 hearths or that it had 1,000 families ; it meant only that it was liable to payments of twenty-six pennies multiplied by 1,000. Assessment of the number of *fumantes* in each town was arbitrary, and depended not upon the number of families, nor upon the number of souls, but upon a rough calculation of its ability to pay.

Some evidence of this may be cited from the Florentine Romagna. At the village of Bocconi in November 1393, the General Council, at which there were present sixty-three men, representing over two-thirds of the male population, sent to Florence to seek exemption from taxation. Florence replied later : ' these men are poor and live in a sterile place ' ; in future they need only pay the expenses of the captain of the Florentine Romagna when he passed through the village, ' and for any other tax to which they are subject in that province, they shall pay only at the rate of thirty *fumantes*, nor to more *fumantes* shall they be constrained by the captain '.[33] This seems to give unambiguous support to our conclusion. Such a conclusion harmonises, in fact, with the investigations of Sorbelli, who, reviewing population over the whole of the Emilian *montagna*, without reference to the *Descriptio*, asserted that *fumantes* correspond to economic potentialities rather than to souls, and claimed that increase or diminution of families only rarely influenced the number of *fumantes*.[34]

Thus, when Anglic drew up his laborious lists of *fumantes*, he was not attempting to satisfy an academic and disinterested curiosity, he was preparing what was primarily a taxation guide ; he was making a fiscal rather than a demographic survey. One might notice here the misleading emphasis in Gambi's aside on the population of the monasteries. Anglic failed to include these in his account of the province, not through lack of authority, but because religious houses made private tax agreements with the papacy, and were excluded from lay burdens such as the hearth-tax.

(b) Fumantes *as People*

So far, *fumantes* have been defined as fiscal units which were based originally upon population, but which by 1371 were no longer related to population. Confusingly enough, however, the word was also used in the same period to designate people subject to the tax of *fumanteria*. This does not affect the arguments already advanced.

The raising of the hearth tax caused the papal government to assess each rural and town commune at a number of *fumantes*. At the same time, the authorities of the larger towns described as *fumantes*, those of their men having ' locum et focum ' (that is to say, having full civic rights, and being liable to full military and financial burdens). Thus the word was used in two senses. But the assumption that in either sense, *fumantes* can be used to mean ' families ', at least as far as Bologna is concerned, is denied by Anglic himself :

> Item est sciendum, quod in comitatu, in castris et in villis sunt duo genera hominum quo ad contributiones impositionum fiendarum, aliqui vocantur fumantes et terrigene, alii cives malenutriti. Isti ultimi in certis factionibus et expensis contribuunt in civitate, et ecciam in castris in comitatu : alii terregene solum contribuunt in castro et nichil in civitate, prout ista in statutis Comunis Bononiensis particulariter distingunter.[35]

Palmieri defined the *malenutriti* as all poor manual labourers, and those exempt from public burdens. He went on to cite a decree of Bologna, of September 1385, which ordered all the names of *malenutriti* from certain rural communes to be enrolled. The replies convinced him that the *malenutriti* were comparatively rare. Many villages reported none, or only a few ; only one had as many as ten.[36] None the less, even granting a close relation between *fumantes* and families, these *malenutriti* would increase the difficulty of arriving at any final estimate of population.

In fact, the *malenutriti* were probably only one class of many who had been exempt when the hearth tax was originally drawn up. Thus in 1263, when the tax seems still to have been paid on the focus, the men of Aquapendente promised to collect : ' XXVI den. per focularem, exceptis a militibus et a nobilibus hominibus, et a iudicibus, sacerdotibus, notariis, mediciis, iaculatoribus, orfanis, et viduis sine regimine, et ab hominibus qui non sunt consueti dare seu solvere'.[37]

(c) *Another Error in Calculation by* Fumantes

The figures given by the *Descriptio* of the hearth tax of Forlì caused Santini to come to grief in his estimate of Forlivese population in the fourteenth century. Santini noted that a tax on each *fumans* of twenty-six pennies a year yielded £3,077 4 4. This implied that there were 28,405 *fumantes*. Yet the town and *contado* of Forlì had been allotted only 3,482 *focularia*. Santini therefore concluded that *fumantes* meant every member of a family comprised in *focularia*. He divided the 3,482 *focularia* into the 28,405 *fumantes*, to come to the conclusion that the mean average of a family in Romagna was roughly eight souls. Comparison with the *fumanteria* and *focularia* of Rimini would have convinced him of his, or rather, of Anglic's error.[38] The terms *fumantes* and *focularia* are, in fact, used interchangeably throughout the document.

VI

ALTERNATIVE METHODS OF COMPUTING POPULATION

It has been seen that, in Romagna at least, *fumantes* cannot be equated with families. This is an unwelcome conclusion, for it reveals a void where previously there appeared to be reliable evidence. It might be well to indicate briefly two other sources, which could be examined in order to obtain a closer insight into Italian population in the fourteenth century.

(a) *The 'Liber Buccharum'*

In most Italian towns in this era, there was a tax upon the milling of grain, called the ' Datium macine et bucchorum cum menementis et membris suis '. The regulations for the taxes of Forlì, laid down by Cardinal Albornoz in 1364,[39] show how this was raised. The theory behind it was that, when a man went to mill grain for his family, he should be taxed at a rate of two shillings for every *staio* of grain. But in order to prevent evasion of the tax by the use of domestic hand mills, the money was, in fact, raised in a different way. Everyone in the commune, over the age of four, was enrolled in a ' liber buccharum '. It was then assumed that all enrolled in this way needed six *staia* of grain to be milled each year for their personal use. Accordingly, all those enrolled were subject to a capitation tax of twelve shillings a year.

Obviously, the ' liber buccharum ' is valuable demographic evidence. Unfortunately, in Romagna, the earliest to survive seems to be that of Rimini in 1511, when a number of 5,000 mouths was registered.[40]

A warning must be entered here, however. All calculations must be based upon the ' liber buccharum ' itself, and not upon the yield of the *datium macine*. For often the tax was not raised by the commune itself, but sold at auction to some tax farmer. Consequently, to discover population statistics, one cannot simply divide the yield of the *datium macine*, as recorded in the books of the commune, by the tax raised upon each individual. Failing to realise this, Santini was again trapped into error. In Forlì, in 1371, the *datium macine* raised £B.8,500. Santini divided this sum by twelve shillings to arrive at the conclusion that there were 14,175 mouths. But there were 3,482 *focularia*, which he believed represented families. He thus drew near to the conclusion that there was a mean average of five souls to each family. However, as has been seen, he had already decided by his confusion of *fumantes* with *focularia*, that the mean average was eight souls to a family. Consequently he rejected his own conclusions on the *datium macine* for ' molteplici ragioni ' (unspecified).

(b) *The Books of ' Esteem '*

The ' esteems ' of the town and *contado*, upon which the raising of the *collecta* was based, seem, in default of the 'liber buccharum', the best source for estimating population. Certainly it is one which has been very little used. Sometimes (although not always) such ' esteems ' included regulations for the registering of those who were not actually liable for taxation. It is much to be hoped that local scholars will begin the critical examination of these valuable records.

VII

Here, for the present, the subject must be left. Although in the course of this Appendix some criticism has been made of the work of previous scholars, it must be emphasised that none the less their work as a whole has the highest value, and that in this field the possibilities of error are immense. Similarly, it should be remarked that Anglic's *Descriptio* is still an extremely important source, if read critically, for the understanding of Romagnol society.

APPENDIX III

Some Notes on the Finances of the Communes

I

PAPAL TAXATION

THE three principal sources of revenue, exacted by the papal government in Romagna, were the *fumanteria* or hearth tax, the *tallia* or *tallage*, and the *salaria*, or salt monopoly. To give any precise account of the yields of these taxes would demand researches which are outside the scope of this work. But in order to give a general idea of the burdens placed upon the province, some figures are appended below.

(a) *Fumanteria* probably rested lightly upon the communes at the beginning of the fourteenth century, but with the years of conflict in which the Avignon papacy struggled against its enemies in central Italy, the tax grew to enormous proportions.[1] Here are the figures for the yield of the tax for some communes in 1330, and as they were recorded in 1371 :

	1330 (£R)			1371 (£B)		
Rimini	650	–	–	593	6	8
Vicariate of Sant' Arcangelo		—		96	19	–
Vicariate of Galeata	95	16	8	131	7	8
Ravenna	200	14	–	350	4	10
Villa Fontana	63	–	–	14	5	4
Ganzanigo		—		10	16	4
Bertinoro	63	–	–	36	8	–
Bobbio	30	–	–	92	8	2
Town of Imola	501	–	–	2074	13	8
Contado of Imola		—		312	2	7
The Alidosi		—		12	7	–
The Bishop of Imola	26	–	–	28	2	10
Bagnacavallo	44	–	–	47	19	10
The Cunii of Barbiano		—		56	1	4
Faenza	370	–	–	453	16	2
Meldola	25	–	–	21	11	2
Polenta		—		4	8	10
Val di Mezzo	17	12	–		—	
Montefeltro	33	14	–	204	12	10
Cervia	40	–	–	27	1	–

These figures[2] show that where taxation was not increased, it was, at least, maintained at the same level. Even where it had been maintained at the same level, the *per capita* yield had increased, for the population had been considerably reduced by the Black Death. At the same time, the economy had been weakened by constant war. Moreover, the totals given here for the 1371 tax upon the town of Imola, for example, are misleading. As is shown in Appendix II, these figures record receipts for each year of the period 1361–7. In fact, in the thirteen-sixties, *fumanteria* was probably exacted from the whole province at the rate of £B.2 17 6½ on each *fumante*, whereas in 1371 it was being raised at the rate of only twenty-six pennies per *fumante*.[3]

The figures given for 1330 and 1371 represent the ordinary yield of the tax on *focularia*, paid each year by custom. In addition to this, however, Anglic remarked that he had used this system of taxation to raise an extraordinary levy, for the building of a castle at Faenza, at the rate of one *bolognino* on each *fumante*. He admitted this to be an *ex gratia* impost, that would not serve as a precedent, and recommended his successor not to continue with it when the castle was completed.[4]

(b) If the hearth tax were profitable to the church, *tallia* was even more so. Below are the yields from certain communes and feudatories recorded in 1336–7, 1360, and 1371 :[5]

	1336	1360			1371		
Town of Imola	£700	£3,692	–	–	£3,684	11	–
Contado of Imola		2,040	15	9	1,920	18	9
Villa Fontana		574	–	–	474	5	3
Ganzanigo		574	–	–	474	5	3
The Alidosi		105	–	–	105	6	1
The Bishop of Imola		620	–	–	631	13	–
Bagnacavallo					1,025	10	–
Faenza	1,232	148	11	6	6,439	3	6
Rimini	3,318				14,500	–	–
Ravenna	800				3,900	–	–
Cesena	1,025				5,000	–	–
Forlì	1,644				8,038	15	3
Cervia					1,052	15	–[6]

Until the time of Albornoz, *tallia* had only been raised by the technical consent of the communes and feudatories in the parliaments of the province. But at some date during his office the tax had been stabilised at a fixed sum, payable annually, without parliamentary consent.[7]

(c) The third source of papal revenues in Romagna was the

salaria or marketing of salt from Cervia. All feudatories and communes were forced to purchase salt from the papal *camera*, which shared half its vast profits on the deal with the Lord of Cervia. In 1371, this yielded over £B.23,000 from the six principal communes alone.[8]

(d) The curia also drew money for licences to export corn and salt from the province, giving estimated yields of 600 and 2000 gold florins respectively in 1371 ; while, with some surprise, we notice that, before that date, the Marshal of the Holy Roman Church had sold licences to hold brothels and gaming houses. Anglic himself had abolished this, considering that association with the tax was shameful to the Church.[9] Similarly, he had abolished the tax on *bulletini* (licences to travel, or passports) considering that 'it was shameful for the Church to act like the tyrants'. In addition, however, the Church drew money from fines in the provincial court — estimated at about 2,000 gold florins in 1371 ; and all the normal communal revenues of those lands which it ruled directly, such as Castrocaro, the *contado* of Imola, the Vicariate of Galeata, and, in 1371, Faenza and Forlì. These last revenues, when the various expenses had been deducted, yielded in 1371, roughly £B.140,343.

Romagna was not a rich province. Florence could have paid these sums with equanimity; but here they were ruinous. In difficult years the communes had either to borrow money at high rates of interest, or to revolt. Revolt called forth *condempnationes*, swingeing fines on already harassed communes. Imola, in 1282, paid *tallia* of 805 florins ; and in addition, was ordered to send soldiers to attack rebel Forlì. It sent them, and through the incompetence of the papal officials, they underwent the defeat immortalised by Dante as the 'sanguinoso mucchio'. The commune was then ordered to send troops to the papal *cavalcata* besieging Meldola. It refused, and was fined £B.1,600. The following year it was assessed at a *tallia* of £B.2,205, and to pay it had to take out a loan of £B.2,127 from a Bolognese banker.[10] How to obtain the money to meet taxation such as this? By the export of corn, perhaps? But with papal government such export had been forbidden without licence — and Ravenna is fined 10,000 silver marks, its protector Guido da Polenta 2,000 marks and his sons Lamberto and Ostasio 1,000 marks each.[11] Further demands for *tallia* follow.[12]

The period when King Robert held the rectorate saw the imposition of particularly heavy fines for refusal to meet communal obligations. In 1311, Imola paid 2,000 gold florins on Carraciuolo's condemnation.[13] Again, how was the pressure to be met? Perhaps by the extension of the town's boundaries, at the expense of some neighbouring rural communes? Pediano was chosen as the victim, and in an extremely cunning fashion the commune claimed to be acting under the rector's authority. In vain : the customary document follows — ' Hec sunt condempnationes . . .' and the commune finds itself fined a further 10,000 marks of silver.[14]

It would be hazardous, taking into account the nature of medieval arithmetic, to accept the precision of these sums, yet we need not doubt Anglic's assertion that the province yielded 100,000 florins a year after expenses had been deducted.[15] In return for this, the papacy gave nothing. Yet the papal demands had to be met as a first charge upon the economy, and in addition to domestic taxation. Little wonder then, that tyrants easily called forth the loyalty of their communes against such impositions, or that the papacy should finally ally itself with the *signori* to obtain from the communes what money it could.

The story of Vanne di Staggi has already been noted.[16] It is repeated with variations throughout the century. The curia, explained the choleric Aimeric de Chatelus, secured only half the *tallia* it should, because of the ' deceits and violence of the tyrants and their great insolence '.[17] In 1326, Aimeric wrote to the pope, complaining that Forlì and Rimini failed to send procurators to the parliament of Bertinoro. When Rimini finally dispatched a representative, after a special message had been sent, the town claimed that it had been exempted from the tax by the Empire. Well did the papacy know from where these equivocations issued : John XXII showed this by writing, not to the commune, but directly to Ferrantino and Malatesta dei Malatesti, urging payment.[18] When in 1330, the curia sought to make its compulsory sale of salt to Forlì, Cecco and Sinibaldo degli Ordelaffi replied by seizing it themselves and refusing to pay.[19] Gradually, the papacy found itself in a position where, at war with one tyrant who had proved intractable, it was forced to ally with other tyrants to carry on the fight.

This situation was changed through the realism of Albornoz. He saw that, while the communes were led by the *signori*, the papal revenues would always be in jeopardy. It was hopeless to expect taxation to be raised on the scale previously envisaged. Abandoning illusory hopes, he compounded for the smaller sums of census in return for the grant to the *signori* of the papal vicariates. With the war of the Eight Saints, the vicariate was extended to the Ordelaffi and the Manfredi. In each case *tallia* was no longer held to be payable, and in each case the census was less than what *tallia* had been.[20] This may be confirmed by considering the lists of former *tallia* payments recorded in 1371 and comparing them with the census of the new vicariates :

	Tallia			Census
Imola	£3,684	11	4	1,000 florins gold
Ravenna	3,900	–	–	3,000 ,, ,,
Cervia	1,052	15	–	
Rimini	14,500	–	–	6,000 ,, ,,
Forlì	8,033	15	3	1,000 fl. (1379–83)[21]
Forlimpopoli	1,217	–	–	2,000 fl. (1383–91)
Sarsina				
Faenza	6,439	3	6	1,500 fl. gold[22]

These payments of census remained stable until the Schism, when some changes occurred. In 1418, having lost Sarsina, Giorgio Ordelaffi was paying 1,000 florins for Forlì and Forlimpopoli.[23] From 1410, the census for Faenza, and the *contado* in the plain, was lowered to 1,000 florins[24], and the Val di Lamone (the *contado* within the *montagna*) was turned into an hereditary fief, or county, for the Manfredi family.[25] The payments for Rimini rose to 10,000 florins, were reduced to 8,000 in 1431, and then, with substantial losses of territory, to 1,000 florins in 1463.[26] Imola still paid 1,000 florins in 1399. But when Sixtus IV awarded the town to his nephew Girolamo Riario, it was given for 200 florins. To this was added later Forlì at 1,000 florins gold.

It will be seen that the abandonment of *tallia* for census brought immediate profit to the communes. Moreover, although the grants of vicariate declared, in some instances, the right of the papacy to exact *fumanteria*, the communes were able either to avoid future payments altogether or to pay greatly reduced sums. Gradually the papacy found itself forced to assignments, or to selling the tax to the *signore* himself. Thus, between 1405 and 1409, the *fumanteria* of both Rimini and Sant' Arcangelo was sold to Giovanni and Ramberto Malatesti for 200 florins gold. (The tax in 1371 had been : for Rimini £B.593 6 8, and for Sant' Arcangelo £B.96 19 –.) From 1413 to 1420 it was not paid at all. In Imola, Rimini, and Faenza, assignment of the tax had already begun by the end of Martin V's rule.[27] By the middle of the fifteenth century, the recipients of such assignments could only hope to obtain any money at all by re-sale to the *signore*. Thus in 1451, the Abbot of San Paolo fuori le Mura, of Rome, who had been granted the tax of the town, district, and *contado* of Imola by Nicholas V, in order that the monastery might be rebuilt, re-sold it to Marsibilia

Manfredi for £B.170. The same monastery is found giving absolutions of payments of £B.128 annually, for the period 1455–8.[28] More fortunate still was Forlì. When in 1451 a mandate arrived, asking the *signori* for payment of *fumanteria*, the astonished *anziani* and Council of the Forty dragged forth the ‘ omini antighe ’ from their retirement, to testify that the only papal impost that had ever been known to the town was the ‘ censo uxado per la renovaxone consueta ’.[29]

II

COMMUNAL REVENUES

Below is an attempt to draw up the balance of expense and income in each town, as they were estimated in 1371 by Cardinal Anglic Grimoard.[30]

(a) *Forlì*

First, Anglic recorded receipts of £B.41,605 from the *gabelles*. The various items in this yield were :

Contracts	£B.5,700	Measures	£B.400
Milling	8,500	Skins	375
Wine	5,000	Carpenters	1,000
Gates	3,800	Wool and wool cloth	600
Weighing	2,000	Fish	500
Butchers	5,000	Dyed cloth	1,400
Spices etc.	1,100	Bread	550
Communal property	2,000	The piazza	80
Dyes and flax	800	Lease of mills	450
Wood	900	Prisons	200
Fruit	350	Shops	100

The fines of the *podestà* amounted to £500, those of the captain to £50. The revenues from fines for damage to agrarian property reached £200. No other revenues, such as the *collecta*, are mentioned, though provision for raising it is found in the statutes. The total yield recorded was £B.42,415.

The recorded expenses amounted in all to £B.42,415. They were formed in the following way :

All payments to officials noted here are monthly

Captain and household	120 florins
His 19 knights	161
His 20 footsoldiers	50
Podestà with household	60

All payments to officials noted here are monthly

Officers of the guard	10 florins		
Officers of agrarian damage	10		
Exactor of *Gabelles*	10		
Advocate of the Commune	15		
Syndic	15		
Official of corn-weighing	3		
Trumpeters	8		
Messengers	£B.3	13	8
Bellringers	11	16	3
Massarolus	8	–	–
Master of the Clock	3	10	–
Notary of the *anziani*	3	–	–
Four 'Inquisitores Rationum'	12	–	–
Three notaries of the Guard	9	–	–
Four officials of weights	7	–	–
Messenger of above	3	–	–
Messenger of fines	8	–	–
Messenger of the *anziani*	3	10	–

Thus the annual expenses of these officers amount to *circa* £B.9,287 2 –. However, it is obvious that Anglic had not recorded here all the officials paid by the commune.

There follow expenses for soldiers: three constables of cavalry, with forty-seven soldiers, whose pay came to 415 florins, and four constables of foot-soldiers paid 150 florins a month. The annual expense of these soldiers, then, was about £B.11,356 10 –.

In addition, extraordinary expenses, for ambassadors, spies, repair of fortifications, oblations, etc., were calculated at £B.2,220 annually.

These accounts were drawn up when Forlì was ruled *immediate* by the Church. A similar calculation of the revenues was made between 1405 and 1411, when Forlì was again under the Church. At that time, receipts were calculated at £B.34,700 a year, and expenses at £B.1,954 15 – a month (*i.e.* £B.23,457 a year).[31]

(b) *Faenza*

The yield of the *gabelles* of Faenza, set out in a similar way to those of Forlì, was £B.43,530. Fines of justice raised £B.550; fines for agrarian damage, £B.140; fines of *gabelles*, £B.85. No other revenues were recorded. The total yield was given as £B.44,305.

The recorded expenses amounted to £B.25,249 9 –. These were composed of payments to officers of the town, itemised as in

Forlì, coming to £B.2,261 15 – a year. (This sum omits the expenses of the courts of the papal rector who then resided there.) Then there were four *provisionati* ; three constables of horse, with forty-two soldiers ; six constables of foot, with ninety-eight soldiers and four knights ; whose expenses in that year amounted in all to £B.13,533 7 –. The four captains with thirty-nine soldiers, that manned the four gates of the town, and the three captains with the seven soldiers that manned the gates of the suburb, received annually £B.1,959 15 –. The *castellans* of the castles of the *contado*, together with their troops, received annually £B.4,944 12 –. Extraordinary expenses amounted to £B.2,500.

(c) *Cesena*

The yield of the *gabelles* was £B.23,060. Fines of justice produced 500 golden florins, agrarian fines £B.400. Extraordinary revenues amounted to a further £B.160. The total annual yield was about £B.24,457 10 –.

The expenses of Cesena amounted to £B.4,282 12 9 — in so far as Anglic recorded them. The expenses of town officials amounted to £B.281 14 9. The monthly salary of the *castellan* of the castle of Cesena, with twenty-five soldiers, was 85 florins a month. Extraordinary expenses amounted to 600 florins a year.

All the communes detailed above were ruled directly by the Church in 1371. The following communes were ruled by *signori* as papal vicars, and Anglic mentioned them with the warning : ' fuller information cannot be obtained on them because their lords . . . hold under census '.

(d) *Imola*

The yield of the *gabelles* was £B.17,100. Communal properties brought in £B.1,200 ; milling taxes £B.2,000 ; *barrateria* £B.700 ; licence of usury, £B.100 ; lease of shops, £B.200. The *collecta* (raised every month) secured each year, £B.2,000. Agrarian fines amounted to £B.200, and fines of justice, £B.1,500. (But compare here the very much smaller yield of the other communes — all of whom had larger populations. Anglic's calculations are not based upon accounts of uniform dates, and in other ways are often unreliable.)[32] The total yield entered was £B.24,800.

The recorded expenses amounted to £B.6,290 9 –. The salaries of only three officials are noted, amounting to £B.1,407.

The guards of the gate received £B.504 a year. The *castellan* with fifty soldiers received £B.2,714 8 –. Extraordinary expenses amounted to £B.1675 1 –.

(e) *Ravenna*

Only one official was recorded : the vicar, with his household, receiving £402. Soldiers cost annually £4034 10 –. No other expenses were written down.

The total recorded revenues amounted to £54,200. Of this £40,000 came from the *gabelles*. *Collecta* raised £5,000, and dues on pasturage, £4,000. Fines of justice secured £1,200, and the sale of salt £4,000. In addition, the estimated 1,500 yoke of oxen in the *contado* were taxed at 10 *staia* of spelt and 2 *staia* of wheat each.

(b) *Rimini*

The recorded revenues of Rimini amounted to £B.73,700. These were composed of *gabelles* — £49,700 ; fines — £4,000 ; two *collecta* — £10,000. The salt *gabelle* raised £5,000 and the tax upon the *contado*, £5,000.

The expenses of Rimini, as recorded by Anglic, amounted to £B.13,467 5 –. This sum was made up of salaries of officials — £3,867 ; guards of the gates — £2,512 10 – ; *castellans* of the *contado* and their troops — £5,577 15 – : and *provisionati* — £1,510.

However, as with other communes, the information Anglic gave on the communal revenues was incomplete. Tonini has drawn up a balance of the expenses of the commune, based on the payments noted in the town statutes, to arrive at the conclusion that these amounted, in fact, to about £R.23,000 — a considerable difference.[33]

These assessments probably over-emphasize the stability of the towns' revenues. They do not include, for instance, payments of census to the papacy. The expenses of soldiers, which was the most costly element in the budgets, obviously increased enormously in time of war.[34] The revenues from the communes' administration were incorporated with, and supplemented by, the revenues from the patrimonial estates, and private business transactions of the *signori*. But by the middle of the fifteenth century most of the *signorie* were to be faced with severe financial stresses, from which they were to be only partially freed by the interested charity of external powers.

III

Of the coins minted by the Romagnol *signorie*, only those of Ravenna had any wide circulation outside the place in which they were produced. In 1283, the exchequer of Ravenna was administered jointly by the archbishop and commune.[35]

It has been claimed that Francesco 'il Vecchio' Manfredi created a mint in Faenza, though this seems improbable. But certainly, by 1374, there was a ' magister zecce ' in the town. Surviving examples of Manfredi coins are few, and limited entirely to *quattrini* or farthings, with an average content of 2 oz. of silver to 1 lb. of lead. Although in their surrender to Cesare Borgia in the sixteenth century, the town asked that Manfredi coinage might still run within the commune, there is no mention of Manfredi money in any document of sale and it was presumably coined principally for prestige reasons.[36]

The money of Rimini, which bore the name of the Malatesti upon it, from the time of Carlo Malatesta, had perhaps a similar function.[37]

APPENDIX IV

Some Notes on Money, Weights, and Measures

I

ANY work upon the economic history of Romagna demands a precise knowledge of the present-day equivalents of medieval measures. Unfortunately this is not yet available. The following notes merely attempt to show approximate coefficients, and to indicate some of the difficulties.

(a) *Square Measure*

The basic measure of area in Romagna was the *tornatura*, divided into 100 *pertiche*. The *pertica* consisted of 10 *piedi*; the *piedi* of 12 *oncie*.

The *Enciclopedia Italiana* (XXXIV, p. 49) gives the following metric equivalents, to which I add their approximate English values:

Place	Equivalent of *tornatura* in m.²	Approximate equivalent in acres
Bologna	2088·44	·5
Imola	1933·02	·5
Forlì	2384·4505	·6
Cesena	2899·5272	·7
Rimini	2947·9293	·7
Ravenna	3417·66	·8
Lugo	1681·43	·4
Faenza	2301·8	·6

Tonini (*Le imposte pagate in Rimini nel secolo XIV*, Bologna, 1864) assigned 2,948 m.² to the Rimini *tornature*, and Zoli (*Statuto*, 221 n.131) agreed with the figure given above for Ravenna. Rossini, however (*Statuta Faventiae*, 33 n. 1), estimated the *piede* at 0·38 m.², the *pertica* at 3·8 m.² and the *tornature* at ·33 hektare (presumably a misprint for ·38). Later, however (Tolosano, 112 n. 4), he distinguished the nineteenth-century *pertica* of 3·8 m.² from the ancient *pertica* and *piede* of 4·8 m.² and ·48 m.² respectively. This would have given a *tornatura* of ·48 hektare. Thus the confidence of Zoli (and of all who have written on the subject), that : ' l' attuale corrisponde certamente all' antico ' may well be misplaced.

(b) *Linear Measure*

The *pertica*, composed of 10 *piedi*, was also a linear measure.

The Faenza *pertica*, it has been seen, is variously calculated at 3·8 and 4·8 m. (Tolosano, 112 n. 4).

The Forlì *pertica* has been estimated at ' little less than 5m.' in 1914 (Santini, *I dazii*), though this seems to conflict with Forli's figure for square measure.

Other linear measures are

(1) the *passo* ; which in San Marino fluctuated between 1.28.3 m. and 0·53.7 m. (De Montalbo, A. Astruodo, A. G. di Riella, *Dizionario . . . della Repubblica di San Marino*, Paris, 1898).

(2) the *miglio* ; which according to the *Enciclopedia Italiana* (XXII, 118–19) varied throughout Italy from 1.500 – 4.500 cm.

(3) the *bracchio* ; in Forlì, little more than 60 cm. (Santini, *I dazii*, 10).

We read too of the *canna*, equivalent to the *pertica*, and of the *tavola*, a squared *canna*. In cloth, the unit *cavezza*, was used, consisting of 70 *bracchia*.

(c) *Dry Measure*

The principal dry measures of Romagna were the *staio*, the *corbe*, and the *sacco*.

(i) The *staio* is given the following equivalents in the *Enciclopedia Italiana* :

Place	Equivalent in litres	Equivalent in gallons
Tuscany	24·36	5·31
Forlì	72·16	15·78 (almost two bushels)
Cesena	138·17	30·39

Santini (*I dazii*) estimated the *staio* of Forlì as a measure of 140 *libbre*, which he calculated at *circa* 4·7 kg. (which would be only 9½ gallons). Tonini (*Le imposte*, 34) gives the *staio* of Rimini at 400 *libbre*, which would be about 3½ bushels.

The *libbra*, composed of 12 *uncie*, has again been variously calculated. Santini estimated $\frac{1}{3}$ kg. for Forlì (*i.e.* ·7 of a lb. avoirdupois). The *Enciclopedia Italiana* gives the following figures: for Ravenna, 347·83 g.; for Bologna, 361·85 g. Both, however, used the same *Libbra* mercantile of 361·85 g. I am unable to distinguish between the 'libram grossam et mediam et subtilem' cited by P. Sella, *Glossario latino emiliano*, Rome, 1937, *sub voce 'libbra'*.

The *quateruola* or *quartarolo* is identified by the *Vocabulario degli Accademici della Crusca* as a measure equal to a quarter of the *staio*. I assume, without any certainty, that the *quartarius* and *quartaria* are an equivalent measure.

(ii) The *corbe* of Imola, Faenza, Ravenna, and Bologna, were, according to F. Balducci Pegoletti, *La pratica della mercatura* (ed. A. Evans), Cambridge, Mass., 1936, pp. 199, 151, all equivalent to 3 *staia* of Florence, and to $\frac{3}{5}$ of the *staio* of Venice.

Rossini (*Statuta Faventiae*, 385) asserted that the *corbe* of Faenza equalled 72 litres (almost 16 gallons). Yet Tonini asserted that the *corbe frumentaria* of Bologna weighed 140 lb. (14 gallons).

Pegoletti wrote (p.167) that 100 *salme* of grain of Manfredonia equalled 190 *staia* of Rimini, and 400 of Bologna, and (p.113) that 100 *salme* of grain of Sicily equalled 210 *staia* of Rimini and 445 *corbi* of Bologna. This would imply that 2·104 *staia* of Rimini were equivalent to 1 *corbe* of Bologna. Unfortunately, Pegoletti adds that 1 *salma* of grain of Sicily equalled 1,145 *staia* of Florence, which cannot be reconciled with his assertion that 1 *corbe* of Bologna equalled 3 *staia* of Florence. This contradiction must be placed alongside the doubts concerning the practical value of this compilation expressed by P. Grierson, 'The Coin List of Pegoletti' in *Studi in onore di A. Sapori*, Milan, 1957, p. 482.

The Venetian, Sanudo, has a similar contradiction. Writing of Rimini in 1503 (V, 378), he says: 'Una corba è uno staro venitian.' Yet later (V, 494) he makes 1 *staio* of Rimini the equivalent of $\frac{1}{2}$ *staio* of Venice.

(iii) The *sacco* was identified by Tonini as the equivalent of the *staio*, with a weight of 400 Riminesi *libbre*. Sanudo, in 1503, (V, 495) gave its equivalent as 300 *libbre*.

The *sacco* of Bologna in 1434 was the equivalent of 360 *libbre* (Tonini, *Storia*, V, 143). In Imola in 1462, it equalled 340 *libbre* (Archivio Notarile di Imola, L. Monte, 1 June 1462).

The *bernardo di grano* of Rimini was $\frac{1}{12}$ of a *sacco*. By Montalbo, cit., it was estimated in 1898, as 14·5 lit. (3·17 gallons) — in other words, just under ten times the weight of the *sacco* of Rimini. Yet Montalbo gives the *sacco* of Rimini as 1.47.3 Hl.

II

MONEY VALUES

The two coinages most often found in Romagna are the Bolognese and Ravennate. In each, the standard unit was the pound, composed of twenty shillings, or 240 pennies. The silver *grosso* of Ancona, and the *grosso veneziano*, were equal to twenty-four Bolognesi pennies, and to twenty-three Ravennati pennies (Theiner, 1,588). Thus £R.1 equalled 19s. 2d. Bolognesi. This is in the fourteenth century; though earlier the two coinages may have been of equal value (Tonini, *Storia*, III, 586).

The pound Bolognese fluctuated in value with respect to the gold florin of Florence, from 30s. to 32s. at the beginning of the fourteenth century, to 40s. in 1320, to 39s. in 1338, to 32s. in 1362, to 31s. 8d. in 1381. (Zanetti, 99–100, and see the articles of Savioli in *AMR*, 3, XIII, 1895; 3, XIV, 1896; 3, XVI, 1898; Schäfer, *Die Ausgaben . . . unter Johann XXII*, 79–80; *idem*, *Deutsche Ritter*, 36.) The pound Ravennate seems, throughout the first half of the century, to have been valued at about 40s. to the florin (*Monumenti ravennati*, III, 191), rising to 44s. in 1356 (Theiner, II, 347). The ducat and the Savona florin were roughly equivalent to the Florentine gold florin. On the 1 April 1360, the florin was valued at 33s. 1d., the ducat at 33s. 8d., and the Savona at 31s. 4d. (Theiner, II, 418, who shows fluctuation within the year and the month.)

For Florentine currency see R. de Roover, *The Rise and Decline of the Medici Bank*, Cambridge Mass., 1963, 31–4; for the Venetian, G. Luzzatto, *Storia economica di Venezia dall' XI al XVI secolo*, Venice, 1961, 93. On the relation between the *libra denariorum*, used in the local trade of Romagna, and the *liber* composed of *denari grossi* or 'groats' and used in international commerce, see G. Luzzatto, *An Economic History of Italy*, trans. Philip Jones, London, 1961, 126–9.

APPENDIX V

The Sources of Romagnol History in the Thirteenth and Fourteenth Centuries

I

BIBLIOGRAPHIES

THERE are extensive bibliographies of Romagnol history in: G. Cencetti and G. Fasoli, 'Gli studi storici sulle signorie romagnole', *AME*, IV, 1939, — with notes on archives; G. Bagli, 'Contributo agli studi di bibliografica storica romagnola', *AMR*, 3, XIII, 1895, and 3, XIV, 1896; G. Gasperoni, *Saggio di studi storici sulla Romagna*, Imola, 1902, Pt. 1 (mainly concerned, however, with the sixteenth-century material); E. Calvi, *Tavole storiche dei comuni italiani: part III, Romagna*, Rome, 1907 (though the tables are inaccurate); U. Foschi, 'Bibliografia cervese', *SR*, XI, 1960, 155–77. Particularly valuable is A. Vasina, *Cento anni di studi sulla Romagna 1861–1961: Bibliografia storica*, Faenza, 1962.

II

ARCHIVE MATERIAL

For this period, the archive material is very thin. Few communal or signorial documents survive. The notarial archives of the province usually date from the end of the fourteenth century, and are almost wholly uncatalogued. For the manuscript material in general, see: G. Mazzatinti, *Gli archivi della storia d' Italia*, Rocca San Casciano, 1899–1915, Volumes I and II; F. Bonaini, *Gli archivi delle provincie d' Emilia*, Florence, 1861; G. Mazzatinti (and collaborators), *Inventarii dei manoscritti delle biblioteche d'Italia*, Volume II (Rimini), Volumes IV and V (Biblioteca Classense, Ravenna), Volume VI (Bagnacavallo, Longiano, and Faenza), Volume LX (Modigliana and Forlì), Volume LXXXIV (Lugo).

Very many of the manuscripts of the Biblioteca Gambalunga of Rimini have been published by Tonini, in his history of the town. The notarial archives date from 1342 (see Mazzatinti,

Inventarii, II, 132). In Cesena, the Archivio Comunale (see Mazzatinti, *Archivi*, II) provides little material for this period, and the Biblioteca Malatestiana less. In Forlì, the Ordelaffi archives were taken to Mirandola by the widow of the last *signore*, and have disappeared. None of the early acts of the commune or *signoria* have survived (see Mazzatinti, *Inventarii*, I, and B. Brandi, *L' archivio storico del comune di Forlì*, Rome, 1892). The notarial archive dates from 1374. Lack of time prevented me from examining the manuscripts of Bagnacavallo (see L. Balduzzi, ' Sugli archivi di Bagnacavallo ', *AME*, n.s., VII, 1881).

None of the village notarial archives in the province date from before the fifteenth century. There are no documents from before 1480 in the archive of Cervia (G. Plessi, ' Gli archivi di Cervia ', *SR*, XI, 1960, 115–53), and few from before the fifteenth century in Meldola, Civitella, and Galeata (G. Orlandelli, ' Gli archivi della valle del Bidente ', *SR*, X, 1959, 115–44).

In these circumstances, I have confined my reading to the following archives :

(i) The Biblioteca Comunale di Faenza, which contains a few acts of the period (see G. Ballardini, *Inventario critico e bibliografico dei codici e pergamene dell' archivio del comune di Faenza*, Faenza, 1905 ; and Mazzatinti, *Inventarii*, VI, 242, XXVI, 5) and a notarial archive dating from 1367 (see P. Zama, *Indice e cronologia dei notai del vecchio archivio faentino (1367 – 1880)*, Faenza, 1925. Monsignor Rossini has made a *schedario* of the notarial archive, up to and beyond 1500 (see G. Rossini, ' La sistemazione delle fonti archivistici locali ', *SR*, I, 1950).

(ii) The Archivio di Stato of Ravenna (see Mazzatini, *Archivi*, I, 273–318) contains some documents of the thirteenth and fourteenth centuries. The notarial archives (which are well catalogued) in the Archivio di Stato, contain the *rogiti* of nineteen notaries in the period 1307–1438. I cite these by the Mazzo number, in which they have been bound together.

The Biblioteca Classense (Mazzatinti, *Inventarii*, IV, 144 ; V, 3) contains the *Statuti polentani* of 1327, and the *Storia di Romagna*, by the sixteenth-century Vicenzo Carrari.

(iii) The Biblioteca Comunale of Imola contains (among other archives) :

(a) The Ferri Manuscripts, consisting of twenty volumes of notes (often made from documents now lost) upon the history of the town, compiled by the Abate Ferri in the eighteenth century (see R. Galli, *I manoscritti e gli incunabuli della biblioteca comunale di Imola*, Imola, 1894).

(b) The Carte Galli, a similar, most valuable collection made by the former librarian (see F. Mancini, 'I fondi speciali manoscritti della biblioteca comunale d' Imola', *SR*, IV, 1955.

The Carte Galli have been my principal guide through the archives of Imola.

(c) The archive of the Sassatelli family (see G. Bagli, 'L' archivio Sassatelli in Imola', *AMR*, 3, VI, 1888, 423).

(d) The chapter and communal archives, and a notarial archive (see Mazzatinti, *Archivi*, i). I refer to these notarial archives by citing the name of the notary and the date of the *rogito*.

In the Imolese *contado*, the archives of Tossignano and Conselice were destroyed during the last war, and only Dozza survives. Its earliest documents are of the fifteenth century (see *Comune di Dozza: archivio storico*, Imola, 1913).

Outside the province, the Archivo di Stato of Rome, and the Biblioteca del Senato del Regno contain numerous statutes of the town and rural communes of the province (see Mazzatinti, *Inventarii*, Vol. LXXIII ; *Biblioteca del Senato del Regno* ; *Catalogo della raccolta di statuti*, 1943– ; and L. Fontana, *Bibliografica degli statuti dei comuni dell' Italia superiore*, Turin, 1907, III). The Archivio di Stato of Florence contains little for this period apart from its collection of statutes of rural communes in the Tusco-Romagnol Apennines (see *R.A.S. di Firenze: statuti di comunità e luoghi autonomi e soggetti alla Repubblica*, Florence, 1903). The Archivio di Stato di Bologna contains some materials on the province, but they are not easy to discover. The Archivio di Stato di Modena contains nothing for this period, but I have read briefly in the Biblioteca Estense of Modena.

Many documents from the Vatican Archives have been published in collections as that of the Abbe Theiner. Partly for that reason, and partly because I have sought to see the emergence of the *signorie* in their local context, rather than as an incident in the history of the papal states, I have sought no new material there.

GLOSSARY OF UNFAMILIAR WORDS

(For the terms for weights and measures, see Appendix VI)

ANZIANI: 'Elders'; the councillors, who generally represented the Arts, in the Small Council.

ARRENGO: the union of all the men of a town in council.

ARTS: the guilds of tradespeople or professional men.

BALIA: literally, authority. An administrative division.

CAMPANALISMO: local patriotism — the spirit of 'our campanile's higher than yours'.

CAPPELLA: literally, 'chapel', a minor administrative subdivision of the towns.

CASTELLO: (Latin, *castra*) a large village, generally having smaller villages under its control.

CAVALCATA: the obligation of service on horseback with the militia of the commune.

COLATICO: the lease of oxen for ploughing.

COMITATINANZA: the process by which the commune of the town gained authority over its *contado*.

CONDOTTA: a contract for the hire of troops (cf. *condottiere*, one who raises soldiers).

CONSIGLIO DI CREDENZA: Small Council; see pp. 172–3.

CONSIGLIO GENERALE: General Council, see pp. 172–3.

CONTADO: (Latin, *comitatus*) the countryside which surrounded the town, and which was dependent upon it. Generally it corresponded with the boundaries of the town's bishopric.

CONTRADA: one of the administrative subdivisions of the town.

DAZIO: tolls, internal custom duty.

DISTRICTUS: the area of the *contado* immmediately bordering the town; sometimes used to indicate the area ruled (as distinct from *contado*, the area claimed) by the town.

DON: the Italian title for a priest, our 'father'.

EMPHYTEUSIS: a lease for three generations.

FAMILIA: household.

FIDELES: men holding land by a semi-feudal tenure (see pp. 107–8).

FOCULARIA: literally, 'hearth-holders'. By extension a unit of taxation. See Appendix II.

FUMANTES: used interchangeably with *Focularia*.

GASTALD: factor.

GONFALONIERE: literally, 'flag-bearer'; the head of the *anziani*.

HOMINES: the men of the commune who possessed 'locum et focum' (place and hearth) — that is to say, who had full civic rights, and were liable to all military and financial burdens.

MASSARIUS: in the town, the Treasurer; in the rural communes, the head of the commune.

MEZZADRIA: a tenure of land, a form of share-cropping in which the landlord leased land to the tenant, and gave him half the seed necessary for its cultivation. In return he received half its produce.

MONTAGNA: predominantly mountainous terrain; to be distinguished from *collina* (hill country).

PAESE: a substantial village.

PLAZARII: the messengers of the commune.

PODESTÀ: the principal executive officer of the commune.

RENOVATION: renewal of lease.

ROCCA: castle.

SALTUARII: agrarian police, see pp. 119–20.

SAPIENTES: see, *Savii*.

SAVII: 'the wise'; the councillors in the smaller councils of the commune.

SCOLA: a rural commune.

SIGNORE: (Latin, *dominus*) in general any 'lord', but used in this work to mean specifically 'the lord of a town'.

SIGNORIA: (Latin, *dominium*) lordship, dominion; in this work used particularly to indicate the full legitimate single-person governments established in the fourteenth centuries in contrast to the 'tyrannies' or governments without full *de iure* recognition, which had gone before.

SOCCIDIA: *agistment*; the taking in of beasts to graze in return for payment.

SYNDICATE: to investigate an official's conduct in his office on his relinquishment of it.

VILLA: a small village.

VINDEMIA: the grape harvest.

GENEALOGICAL TABLES OF THE SIGNORIAL FAMILIES IN THE FOURTEENTH CENTURY

The only purpose of these tables is to assist the reader in the understanding of the text. For more comprehensive accounts see: Litta-Passerini, *Celebri famiglie italiane*; Ricci, *L' ultimo rifugio*; and Messeri and Calzi, *Faenza nella storia*.

THE ALIDOSI

1257 Alidosio and Margherito Alidosi
1259 Sons and heirs of Alidosio della Massa

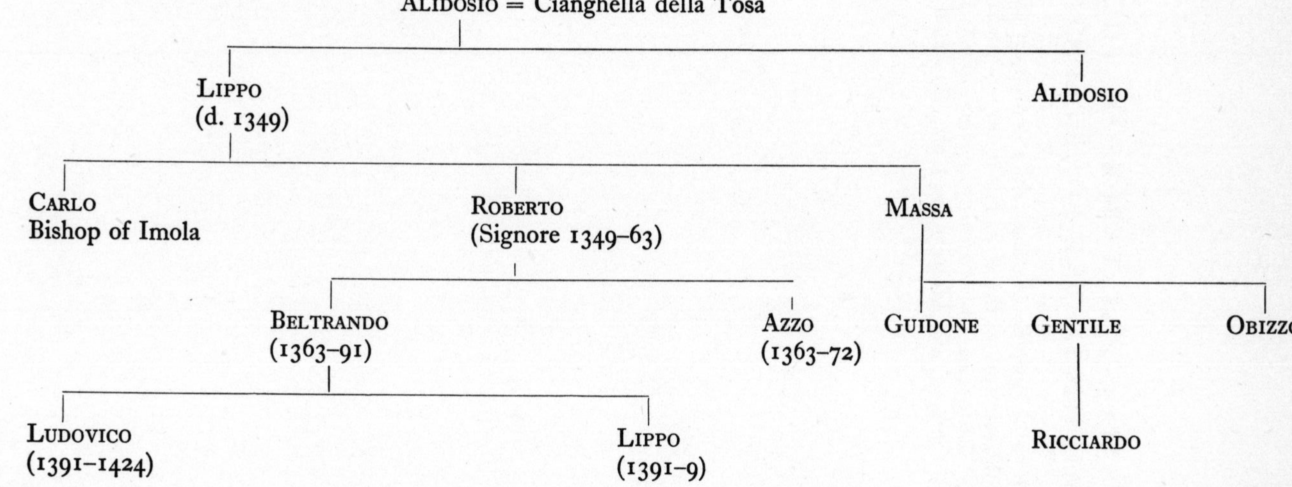

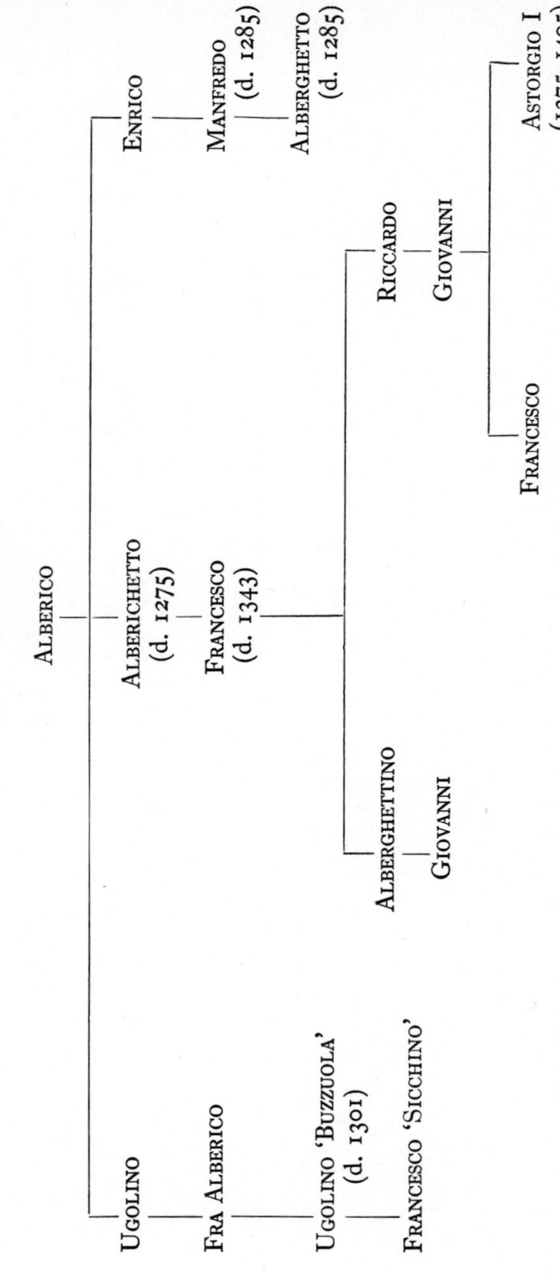
THE MANFREDI
Alberico
Ugolino
Fra Alberico
Ugolino 'Buzzuola'
(d. 1301)
Francesco 'Sicchino'
Alberichetto
(d. 1275)
Francesco
(d. 1343)
Alberghettino
Giovanni
Riccardo
Giovanni
Francesco
Astorgio I
(1375–1405)
Enrico
Manfredo
(d. 1285)
Alberghetto
(d. 1285)

THE DA POLENTA

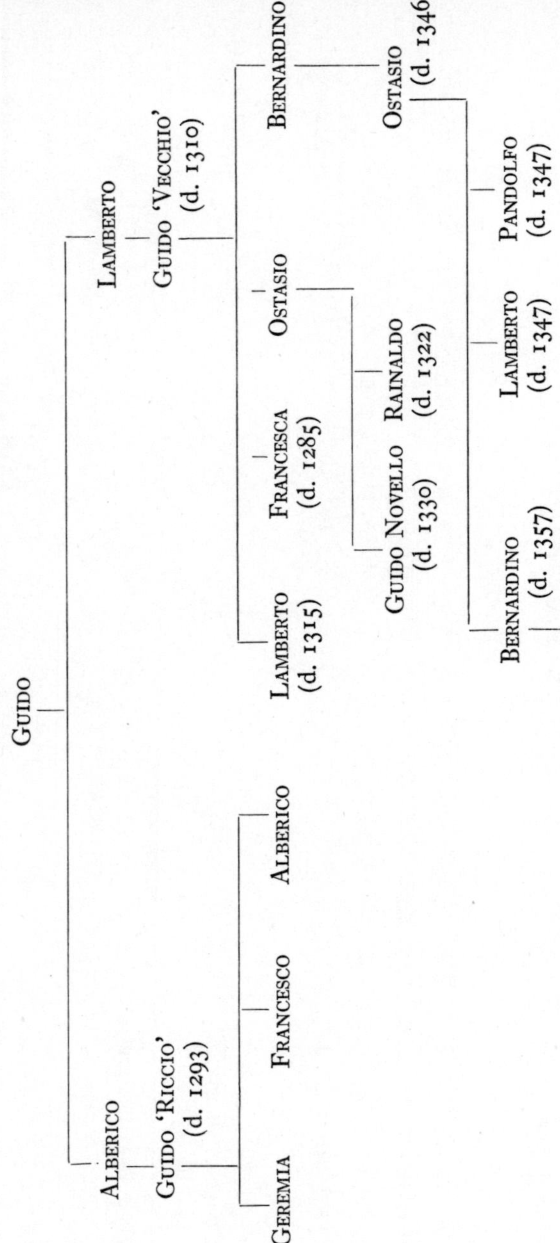

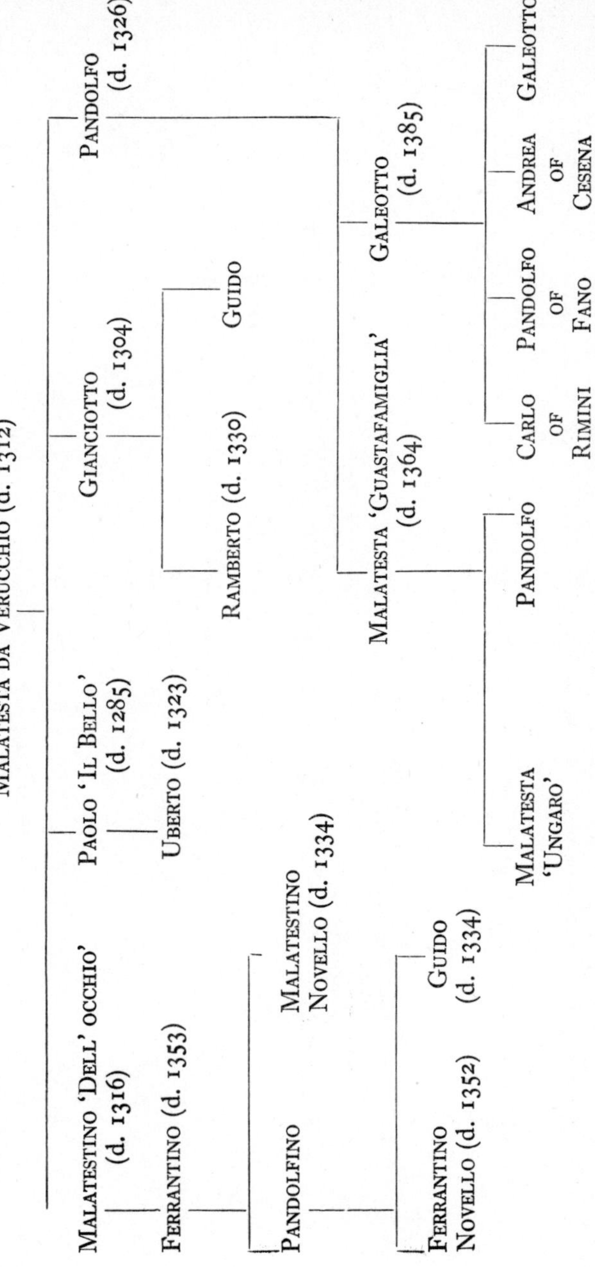
THE MALATESTI
Malatesta Dalla Penna (d. 1248)
Malatesta da Verucchio (d. 1312)
Malatestino 'Dell' occhio' (d. 1316)
Paolo 'Il Bello' (d. 1285)
Gianciotto (d. 1304)
Pandolfo (d. 1326)
Ferrantino (d. 1353)
Uberto (d. 1323)
Ramberto (d. 1330)
Guido
Pandolfino
Malatestino Novello (d. 1334)
Malatesta 'Guastafamiglia' (d. 1364)
Galeotto (d. 1385)
Ferrantino Novello (d. 1352)
Guido (d. 1334)
Malatesta 'Ungaro'
Pandolfo
Carlo of Rimini
Pandolfo of Fano
Andrea of Cesena
Galeotto

THE ORDELAFFI

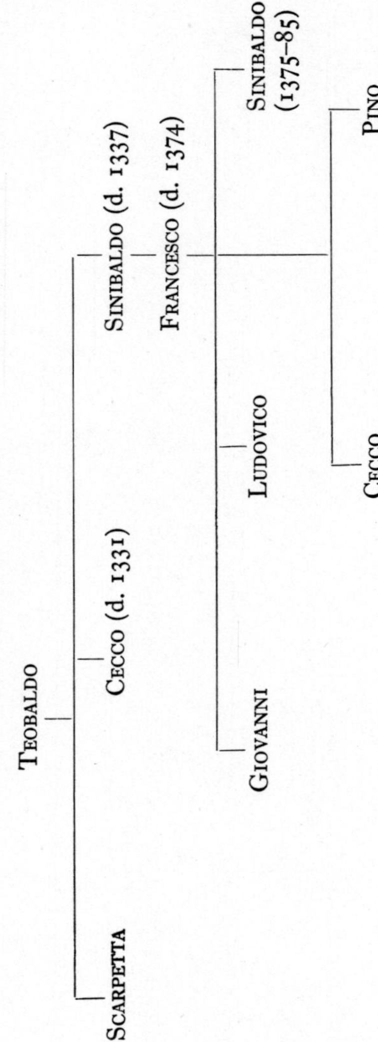

LIST OF ABBREVIATIONS

1. ARCHIVES

AC. Imola	Archivio Comunale di Imola
ACap. Imola	Archivio Capitolare di Imola
AN. Faenza	Archivio Notarile di Faenza
AN. Imola	Archivio Notarile di Imola
AN. Ravenna	Archivio Notarile di Ravenna
AS. Bologna	Archivio di Stato di Bologna
AS. Florence	Archivio di Stato di Firenze
AS. Ravenna	Archivio di Stato di Ravenna
BC. Faenza	Biblioteca Comunale di Faenza
BC. Imola	Biblioteca Comunale di Imola
BC. Ravenna	Biblioteca Classense di Ravenna
BE. Modena	Biblioteca Estense di Modena

2. PERIODICALS

AFH	*Archivium Franciscanum Historicanum*
AME	*Atti e memorie della R. Deputazione di Storia Patria per Emilia*
AMR	*Atti e memorie della Deputazione di Storia Patria per le provincie di Romagna*
ASI	*Archivio Storico Italiano*
ASR	*Archivio della Società Romana di Storia Patria*
BSDI	*Bollettino della Società Dantesca Italiana*
EHR	*English Historical Review*
FR	*Felix Ravenna*
GSLI	*Giornale Storico della Letteratura Italiana*
RGI	*Rivista Geografica Italiana*
RSDI	*Rivista di Storia del Diritto Italiano*
SR	*Studi Romagnoli*

3. ABBREVIATED TITLES OF OTHER WORKS

Fantuzzi	M. Fantuzzi, *Monumenti ravennati de' secoli di mezzo*, Venice, 1801–4
Mittarelli	J. B. Mittarelli, *Ad scriptores rerum italicarum Muratori Accessiones Historicae Faventinae*, Venice, 1771
MGH. SS	*Monumenta Germaniae Historica; Scriptores*
RIS	*Rerum Italicarum Scriptores* (references to the new edition of this work are distinguished by being cited with the name of the editor)
Tarlazzi	A. Tarlazzi, *Appendice ai monumenti ravennati*, Ravenna, 1869–76
Theiner	A. Theiner, *Codex Diplomaticus Dominii Temporalis S. Sedis*, Rome, 1861–2

NOTES

CHAPTER I

1 Benvenuto de' Rambaldi di Imola, *Commentum super Dantis Aldigherii Comoediam*, Florence, 1887, II, 301.

2 *Ibid.*, II, 301.

3 Salimbene di Adam, *Cronica*, ed. O. Holder-Egger, MGH. SS, XXXII, 509.

4 For routes, see the ' Descriptio Romandiole ' written by Cardinal Anglic Grimoard in 1371, in A. Theiner, *Codex Diplomaticus Dominii Temporalis S. Sedis*, Rome, 1861–2 (henceforth cited as Theiner), II, 490–516 ; G. Barbieri, ' Lo sviluppo storico delle vie di communicazione tra Firenze e Bologna ', *RGI*, 1947, 103–16 ; A. Palmieri, ' Le strade medievali fra Bologna e la Toscana ', *AMR*, 4, VIII, 1918, 28 f.

5 M. Sanudo, *I diarii*, Venice, 1879–1902, V, 629.

6 Fazio degli Uberti, *Il dittamondo*, ed. G. Cersi, Bari, 1952, I, 187.

7 Benvenuto, II, 306 ; Giovanni Boccaccio, ' Trattatello in laude di Dante ' in *Le vite di Dante, Petrarca e Boccaccio*, ed. A. Solerti, Milan, 1904, 36.

8 Thomas Tuscius, *Gesta Imperatorum et Pontificum*, ed. E. Ehrenfeuchter, MGH. SS, XXII, 511–12. See, too, *Corpus Chronicorum Bononiensium*, ed. A. Sorbelli, RIS, XVIII, pt. I, II, 114, and H. Rubeus (Rossi), ' Italicarum et Ravennatum Historiarum Libri XI ' in J. G. Graevius, *Thesaurus Antiquitatum et Historiarum Italiae*, Leyden, 1704–25, VII, pt. I, 402.

9 *Corp. Chron. Bon.*, III, 288–9.

10 Giraldus Cambrensis, *Opera*, ed. J. Brewer, Rolls Series, London, 1863, III, 240–1.

11 G. Parks, *The English Traveler to Italy*, Rome, 1954, I, 181, 532 ; Theiner, II, 539.

12 AN. Ravenna, M.5, Tom. Ia, 32r, 24 March 1357.

13 J. Gill, *The Council of Florence*, Cambridge, 1959, 181.

14 Benvenuto, III, 387–8.

15 A. Sorbelli, *Il comune rurale dell'Appenino emiliano nei secoli XIV e XV*, Bologna, 1910, 240–7 ; G. Cortini, *Storia di Imola e della valle di Santerno* (Mss. in Biblioteca dell' Archiginnasio, Bologna), I, 14–17 ; Biondo da Forlì, *Roma ristaurata et Italia illustrata*, Venice, 1543, 139.

16 F. Alberti, *Descrittione di tutta italia*, Venice, 1557, 266.

17 A. Veggioni, ' La fusione dello zolfo dal XV al XVIII secolo nelle miniere di Romagna ', *SR*, VI, 1955, 335. For rights of ' querendi venias solfori ', *Monumenti ravennati de' secoli di mezzo*, ed. M. Fantuzzi, Venice, 1801–4 (henceforth cited as Fantuzzi), III, 262–3.

18 Benvenuto, II, 301–2.

19 Earthquakes are recorded in 1142 ; 1222 (Tolosano, *Chronicon Faventinum*, ed. G. Rossini, RIS, XXVIII, pt. I, 83, 150) ; in May 1277 (*Corp. Chron. Bon.*, II, 199) ; in May 1279 (Salimbene, 500 ; Petrus

Cantinelli, *Chronicon*, ed. F. Torraca, RIS, XXVIII, pt. II, 16); in March 1331 and March 1337 (*Annales Caesenates*, RIS, XV, 1152, 1175); in September 1385 (Giovanni di M. Pedrino Depintore, *Cronica del suo tempo*, ed. G. Borghezio and M. Vattasio, Vatican City, 1929–34, II, 465); in August 1483 (L. Cobelli, *Cronache forlivesi*, Bologna, 1874, 281); and on other occasions.

20 *Corp. Chron. Bon.*, III, 160, 193.

21 *Purgatorio*, XXVIII, 19–21. See A. Zoli, 'Ravenna e il suo territorio nel 1309', *AMR*, 3, XVIII, 1900, 181–200; P. Amaducci, 'Cenni topografici su Ravenna antica', *AMR*, 3, XXV, 1907, 497.

22 See Theiner, II, 490–516 *passim*; *Chartularium Imolense*, ed. S. Gaddoni and G. Zaccherini, Imola, 1910–13, II, 311; Fantuzzi, V, 428.

23 Theiner, II, 514, 529.

24 Biondo, *Roma ristaurata*, 140; *Aeneid*, XI, 456–7; Cantinelli, 90.

25 J. Huillard-Bréholles, *Vie et correspondance de Pierre de la Vigne*, Paris, 1865, 307; Martial, III, 93, 8; Sidonius, *Letters*, tr. W. B. Anderson, Harvard, 1936, I, VIII.

26 Pedrino, II, 453–5. See *e.g.* the flooding of Cesena, September 1299 (*Annal. Caes.*, 1117–18); of Faenza — as far as the episcopal palace — in 1192, and 1228 (Tolosano, 70); of the Po in 1294 (Cantinelli, 76). Giovanni Villani, *Croniche di Giovanni, Matteo e Filippo Villani*, Trieste, 1857, XI, I, notes serious floods in Romagna in 1333.

27 Pliny, *Natural History*, II, 10; Tolosano, 70; Benvenuto, II, 314; Biondo, *Roma ristaurata*, 140.

28 Sanudo, V, 629.

29 Fantuzzi, V, 144–5, 155; export of grain in 1288, *ibid.*, III, 138.

30 L. Tonini, *Le imposte pagate a Rimini nel secolo XIV*, Bologna, 1872, 34; 'Documenti inediti intorno a Sigismondo Malatesta', *La Romagna*, 1910, 367; P. Jones, 'The end of Malatesta rule in Rimini', *Italian Renaissance Studies*, ed. E. Jacob, London, 1960, 238 n.5. See, too, L. Ranke, *The History of the Popes* (English translation), London, 1896, I, 289.

31 G. Villani, X, 121; L. Ciaccio, 'Il Cardinale Legato Beltrando del Poggetto in Bologna', *AMR*, 3, XXV, 1906, 522–3; Theiner, II, 480; L. Mirot, 'La Question des blés dans la rupture entre Florence et le saint-siège', *Mélanges d'Archéologie et d'Histoire*, 1896, 186, 196–7.

32 Theiner, II, 528; G. Ghirardacci, *Della historia di Bologna*, Bologna, 1605, 400; *Ann. Caes.*, 1133–4; Rubeus, 469. In 1368, Romagna was said to yield 60,000 *corbe* of grain to the papacy, J. Glénisson, 'Une Administration médiévale aux prises avec la disette', *Le Moyen Age*, 1951, 304, n.1 *bis*.

33 Alberti, 270–1; Theiner, II, 532; Benvenuto, II, 306.

34 *Négotiations diplomatiques de la France avec la Toscane*, ed. G. Canestrini, Paris, 1859, I, 91.

35 Tolosano, 36. See below, Appendix II.

36 L. Villari, *The Republic of Ragusa*, London, 1904, 118; Theiner, II, 515.

37 L. Tonini, *Il porto di Rimini*, Bologna, 1864; V. Franchini, 'Appunti di diritto marittimo riminese nel secolo XIV', *La Romagna*, 1913, 193–261. For the port in 1402 (in exceptional circumstances);

Commissioni di Rinaldo degli Albizzi, ed. C. Guasti, Florence, 1867, I, 10–19.

38 *Ann. Caes.*, 1122–3, 1134.

39 *Documenti riguardanti antiche relazioni tra Venezia e Ravenna*, ed. P. Pasolini, Imola, 1881, 15–25 ; Salimbene, 481–2 ; 45–55. See, too, A. Torre, ' I patti fra Venezia e Cervia ', *SR*, XI, 1960, 21–61.

40 W. Lenel, *Die Entstehung der Vorherrschaft Venedigs an die Adria*, Strassburg, 1897, 47 n.1 ; see also 65–8 for Marcabò. The first extant Venetian commercial treaty is an agreement of 1099 with Imola, concerned with the export of corn, wine, and meat ; W. Lenel, ' Ein Handelsvertrag Venedigs mit Imola von Jahre 1099 ', *Vierteljahrschrift für Social- und Wirtschaftsgeschichte*, VI, 1908, 203.

41 Theiner, I, 32–4 ; D. Waley, *The Papal State in the Thirteenth Century*, London, 1961, 255.

42 *Acta et Diplomatica e R. Tabulario Veneto*, ed. A.-S. Minotto, Venice, 1873, III, 1, 9–13 ; Fantuzzi, VI, 104.

43 R. Davidsohn, *Forschungen zur älteren Geschichte von Florenz*, Berlin, 1896–1908 ; III, 31, 141, 162, 183 ; IV, 314 ; R. Ciasca, *L' arte dei medici e speziali*, Florence, 1927, 555–8.

44 *Appendice ai monumenti ravennati*, ed. A. Tarlazzi, Ravenna, 1869–76 (henceforth cited as Tarlazzi), I, 261.

45 Fantuzzi, III, 138.

46 Tolosano, 26–7, 32–3.

47 AC. Imola, M.11, 168, 13 August 1255 ; Cortini, *Storia di Imola*, III, 188–9.

48 Tolosano, 133. See Ballardini's introduction to *Statuta Faventiae*, ed. G. Rossini, RIS, XXVIII, pt. V, 1.

49 J. Ficker, *Forschungen zur Reichs- und Rechtsgeschichte Italiens*, Innsbruck, 1868–74, IV, 454–5.

50 L. Tonini, *Storia civile e sacra riminese*, Rimini, 1848–88, III, 193–8.

51 *Statuto del secolo XIII del comune di Ravenna*, ed. A. Zoli and S. Bernicoli, Ravenna, 1904, 15, 22, 28, 108, 151–2, 106, 107, 151–2.

52 Tarlazzi, I, 405–6.

53 Tolosano, 121.

54 Tonini, *Storia*, II, 576–7 (and see too, III, 511–15) ; Ficker, *Forschungen*, IV, 273–4.

55 G. Tonduzzi, *Historie di Faenza*, Faenza, 1675, 241–3.

56 Tonini, *Storia*, II, 603–7 ; III, 408–11, 450–4, 429–35, 495–6, 496–7, 501–2, 506–7.

57 *Statuta Faventiae*, 187, 200, 112.

58 AC. Imola, M.VIII, 6.

59 *Statuta Faventiae*, 131, 148, 171–2.

60 AC. Imola, ' Liber Societatum civitatis Imole, 1272 ', M.III, 94 ; for 1312, *ibid.*, M.VI, 61. The Alidosi, in 1272, were found in the society of the Judges, Doctors, and Notaries, and in the society of Butchers.

61 C. Spreti, *Notizie spettanti all' antichissima scola de' Pescatori in oggi denominata Casa Matha*, Ravenna, 1820.

62 See S. Bernicoli, *Governi di Ravenna e di Romagna*, Ravenna, 1898 ; Cavina's supplement to Tonduzzi ; and Tonini, *Storia*, III, for lists of communal officers.

63 *Discorsi sopra la Prima Deca di Tito Livio*, I, 55.

64 P. Ginanni, *Memorie dell' antica ed illustre famiglia Alidosia*, Rome, 1735, 1–5 ; G. Ballardini, ' Di una impressa dei Manfredi ', *FR*, 1912 ; A. Castiglione, ' Il salasso nell' arma gentilizia dei Manfredi ' in ed. C. Singer and H. Sigerist, *Essays in the History of Medicine presented to Professor K. Sudhoff*, London, 1925, 159–82 ; Giovanni de Mussi, *Chronicon Placentinum*, RIS, XVI, 565.

65 P. Bonoli, *Istorie della città di Forlì*, Forlì, 1661, 44.

66 *Marcha di Marco Battagli*, ed. A. Massera, RIS, XVI, pt. III, 73 ; *Cronache malatestiane dei secoli XIV e XV*, ed. A. Massera, RIS, XV, pt. II, 141 ; Passerini in Litta, *Celebri famiglie italiane*, Milan, 1819–1923, IX, *sub nom.*

67 See for the Alidosi, C. Cortini, *Storia di Castel del Rio*, Imola, 1933, 9–19 ; for the Manfredi, BC. Faenza, Valgimigli Mss., *Storia di Faenza* ; for the Ordelaffi, P. Ravaglia, *Scarpetta degli Ordelaffi*, Forlì, 1955, 5–10 and E. Maltoni, ' La famiglia degli Ordelaffi dall' origine alla signoria ', *SR*, XI, 1960, 247–72 ; for the da Polenta, C. Ricci, ' Il castello e la chiesa di Polenta ', *AMR*, 3, IX, 1891, 15 ; for the Malatesti, Tonini, *Storia*, II, *passim*, and A. Massera, ' Note malatestiane ', *ASI*, 5, 49, 1911. In all that I write here and subsequently on the Malatesti, I have been guided by Dr. Philip J. Jones's Ph.D. thesis : ' The Malatesta of Rimini ', in the Bodleian Library, Oxford.

68 *Cronaca di Antonio Godi*, ed. G. Soranzo, RIS, VIII, II, 8–9 ; Gerardi Maurisii, *Cronica Dominorum Eccelini et Alberici*, ed. G. Soranzo, RIS, VIII, IV, 22 ; Nicolai Sirviregli, *Annales Vincentiae*, ed. G. Soranzo, RIS, VIII, V, 5. Probably he is the Alberghetto di Alberico, who with Manfredo di Alberghetto, witnessed an agreement between the great Romagnol houses of the Conti Guidi and the Traversari in 1216 ; F. Torraca, ' Su la " Treva " di G. de la Moro', *AMR*, XVIII, 1900. 113–14. He was *podestà* of Faenza in 1203 ; Tolosano, 118 n. 6. It has been denied by Valgimigli that there was any connection between the Manfredi and Alberghetti, but the evidence is too scanty for dogmatism.

69 Tolosano, 25–7.

70 Cortini, *Storia di Castel del Rio*, sees the count Alidosio de Malaperte who witnessed a mandate of the legate of Frederick I in 1159 as a member of the signorial family (see *Chartularium Imolense*, II, 196) ; and suggested that his descendants were rewarded with the Massa di Ambrogio as a fief, as a reward for services to the Empire. This seems doubtful (why for instance, should the later members of the family have abandoned the title of count?). But colour is lent to the speculation by the use of the imperial eagle on the Alidosi coat of arms, and their later claim to hold land in the Santerno valley ' by papal and imperial authority '. Certainly, Alidosio della Massa was witnessing a loan in the presence of the imperial count of Romagna in 1249 ; Ficker, *Forschungen*, IV, 426.

71 Tolosano, 57.

72 See Torraca, ' Su la " Treva " ', *passim*. Geremia da Polenta and a Pietro di Ordelaffo fought for the Traversari in 1170, Tolosano, 77. A Malatesta di Giovanni was married to Berta, daughter of Pietro Traversari in the second half of the twelfth century ; Tonini, *Storia*, II, 402.

73 Guido (di Lamberto?) da Polenta was *vicecomes* of the Archbishop in 1199 ; Fantuzzi, III, 302. Alberico da Polenta was the Archbishop's

vicecomes in Argenta in 1225 ; *Regesto della chiesa di Ravenna*, ed. V. Federici and G. Bizzi, Rome, 1911, I, 184. The Malatesti, too, are recorded later as holding similar positions in the archiepiscopal curia.

74 Tonini, *Storia*, II, 603–7 ; III, 408–11, 412–13.

75 Ricci, *Il castello*, cit. ; Ravaglia, 10.

76 AC. Imola, Liber Rubeus, 31.

77 Battagli, 29.

CHAPTER II

1 Benvenuto, III, 338.

2 Tolosano, 153 ; *Constitutiones et Acta Publica Imperatorum*, ed. L. Weiland, MGH, II, 311 ; Cantinelli, 3.

3 Cantinelli, 4 ; Fantuzzi, III, 81–2 ; L. Simeoni, ' Federico II all' assedio di Faenza ', *AME*, III, 1938 ; G. Rossini, ' Federico II e l' assedio di Faenza ', *AME*, VI, 1941.

4 *Epistolae Saeculi XIII*, MGH, ed. Pertz, II, 371 ; *Annales Placentini Gibellini*, ed. P. Jaffe, MGH. SS, XVIII, 497.

5 ' Pro despectu Bononiensium et aliorum qui partem ecclesiae sequebantur '; Battagli, 12–13. See F. Bernini, ' Federico II e la " Societas Lombardie, Marchie et Romanie " nel 1226 ', *Rivista Storica Italiana*, 1953, 496–513.

6 *Inferno*, XXVII, 49–50 ; see Benvenuto, II, 311. Similarly Matteo Visconti acted as Ghibelline in Lombardy and Guelf in Emilia ; V. Vitale, *Il dominio della Parte Guelfa in Bologna*, Bologna, 1901, 69.

7 Bartolus de Saxoferrato, ' Tractatus de Guelphis et Gebellinis ', in *Consilia, Quaestiones et Tractatus*, Venice, 1565, X, 151–2. There is an English translation of the ' De Guelphis ' and of ' De Tyrannia ' in E. Emerton, *Humanism and Tyranny*, Cambridge, Mass., 1925.

8 *Constitutiones et Acta Publica*, II, 311 ; *Ann. Caes.*, 1097, *Chronicon Este.*, ed. G. Bertoni and E. Vicini, RIS, XV, III, 17.

9 Cantinelli, 22–3 ; Salimbene, 183 ; E. Jordan, *Les Origines de la domination angevine en Italie*, Paris, 1909, 36. For the ambiguities on the question of Romagna in 1275, see L. Gatto, *Il pontificato di Gregorio X*, Rome, 1959, chapter vi.

10 Cantinelli, 3, describes Paolo Traversari's change of allegiance thus : ' dedit civitatem Ravenne communi Bononie '.

11 On the hegemony of Bologna ; A. Hessel, *Geschichte der Stadt Bologna, 1116–1280*, Berlin, 1910, 230–68, 479–95 ; Cantinelli, 6 ; *Corp. Chron. Bon.*, II, 136, 139.

12 See the effects of the Imolesi conflicts of 1263 ; Cantinelli, 8 ; and the discords ' occasione potestarie de Forolivio ' in 1269 ; *ibid.*, 10.

13 A. Massera, ' Il Serventese Romagnolo del 1277 ', *ASI*, 1914, Vol. I, 7.

14 Of the Bolognese family of the Alberti da Mangona. He is among the late repentant in *Purgatorio*, VI, 19. His father, Napoleone, and his uncle, Alessandro, are in the *Inferno*, XXXII, 41–60, as traitors to their kin.

15 Cantinelli, 12, 26–7, 16.

16 *Corp. Chron. Bon.*, II, 305.

17 Cantinelli, 47.

18 Cantinelli, 85. These are not untypical ; see for instance, *Corp. Chron. Bon.*, II, 298, 314–15 ; III, 381.

19 Salimbene, 190–1.

20 ACap. Imola, VI, 17, 14 December 1224.

21 Fantuzzi, III, 78.

22 *Ibid.*, II, 402.

23 *Ibid.*, IV, 398.

24 Cortini, *Castel del Rio*, 197. For the church of San Martino of Faenza, ' ob bella derelicta ' ; *Ad scriptores rerum italicarum cl. Muratori Accessiones Historicae Faventinae*, ed. J. Mittarelli, Venice, 1771 (henceforth cited as Mittarelli), 506.

25 *Ann. Caes.*, 1103.

26 S. Chiaramonte, *Caesenae Urbis Historiarum*, Cesena, 1641, reprinted in Graevius, VII, pt. II, 192.

27 Fantuzzi, III, LXIV.

28 Rubeus, 567

29 AS. Ravenna, S. Vitale, Vol. 616, *transunti*, 12 January 1362.

30 AN. Ravenna, M.13, To. II, 26r, 14 March 1363.

31 *Ibid.*, M.25, Pt. II, 19, 17 January 1376.

32 *Ibid.*, M.28, 7r, 8 February 1378.

33 AN. Imola, A. Monte, 3 July 1426.

34 Mittarelli, 575–6.

35 AC. Imola, VI, 32, 24 January 1369.

36 G. Franceschini, ' Un caduto del " Sanguinoso Mucchio ", il conte Taddeo di Montefeltro ', *SR*, VII, 1956, 48–9.

37 Cantinelli, 10 ; *Ann. Caes.* 1109.

38 *Epist. Saec. XIII*, III, 442.

39 Tarlazzi, I, 297–8.

40 Salimbene, 267.

41 Fantuzzi, III, 120. Fantuzzi dates these documents to the fourteenth century, but Guido ' Riccio ' died in January 1293 ; Cantinelli, 73.

42 Fantuzzi, III, 39.

43 Tonini, III, 566–7.

44 Fantuzzi, II, 238–9.

45 Tonini, III, 94–5.

46 Cantinelli, II, 15–16.

47 The Mendoli is purely a party name ; no family bearing it can be found. Salimbene, 370, says that Uguccione de' Binielli, beheaded by King Charles of Anjou, was succeeded in the leadership of the Mendoli by his brother Giovanni. Members of the Brizzi family are found in 1272 in the Society of Judges, Doctors, and Notaries ; AC. Imola, M. IV, 94.

48 Ficker, IV, 422–4 ; G. Salvioli, *Annali bolognesi*, Bassano, 1795, 111/1, 218 ; 111/2, 271–3 ; Cantinelli, 7, 18 ; *Corp. Chron. Bon.*, II, 160–1 ; Anon. (in fact by Alberghetti, though sometimes catalogued inaccurately under Benacci), *Storia di Imola*, Imola, 180, 172–3.

49 *Acta Imperii Inedita Seculi XIII et XIV*, ed. Winkelmann, Innsbruck, 1885, I, 524 ; Cantinelli, 3 ; *Ann. Caes.*, 1096.

50 L. Simeoni, ' Federico II all' assedio di Faenza ', 189–90 ; *Corp. Chron. Bon.*, II, 115 ; *Ann. Caes.*, 1097.

51 Mittarelli, 624–30 ; Salvioli, III/II, 326 ; Cantinelli, 7–8, 17–19, 22 ; *Corp. Chron. Bon.* II, 138–9.

52 Cantinelli, 10 and XXV.

53 His wife Monentessa was sister of Uberto, last count of Giaggiolo; Tonini, III, 563–5.

54 Dante Alighieri, *Il convivio*, ed. M. Barbi, Florence, 1954, IV, XXVIII.

55 *Inferno*, XXVII, 76–8. R. Honig, *Guido da Montefeltro*, Bologna, 1901, argues persuasively for his innocence of the crimes which Dante and others have attributed to him. See too, F. d' Ovidio, *Studii sulla Divina Comedia*, Milan, 1901, 27–75, 534–45, and G. Golubovich, ' Una pagina dantesca : notizie sul conte Frate Guido da Montefeltro ', *AFH*, III, 1910, 214–30.

56 Salimbene, 490.

57 Cantinelli, 18–22.

58 Battagli, 12. Against the date 1277, see, however, Waley, *The Popal State*, p.195, n.1.

59 Cantinelli, 24–6 ; *Ann. Caes.*, 1104, Cobelli, 49.

60 Salimbene, 369–70 ; Cantinelli, 38–9.

61 Salimbene, 605–6 ; *Corp. Chron. Bon.*, II, 114–15.

62 A. Tarlazzi, ' Riscontri critichi tra la Cronica di Fra Salimbene e gli storichi di Ravenna intorno alla decedenza della famiglia dei Traversari ', *AMR*, I, 1869, 37 ; G. Levi in *A.M. Modenesi e Parmensi*, 3, IV, 1886, 459–71.

63 Fantuzzi, III, 87, 89, Rubeus, 405–6, 431, 453, giving date 1275 ; A. Torre, ' La pace di Romagna del 1253 ', *AMR*, 1951–3, I, 165–80 ; Ricobaldus de Ferrara, *Pomerium Ravennatis Ecclesie*, RIS, IX, 141 ; *idem*, *Historia Imperatorum*, RIS, IX, 251 ; *idem*, *Compilatio Chronologica*, RIS, IX, 251 ; *Annales Ravennati*, RIS, 1, 2, 579 ; *Corp. Chron. Bon.* (Varignana), II, 192, giving date as 1275 ; *ibid.* (Rampona), II, 194, giving date as 1276. Guido di Lamberto, with Iacopo de' Corradini, is recorded as one of the two ' consules et rectores ' of Ravenna in 1275 ; Fantuzzi, III, 119.

64 L. Tonini, *Memorie storiche intorno a Francesca da Rimini*, Rimini, 1870.

65 Battagli, 31.

66 Giovanni Boccaccio, *Il commento alla Divina Comedia*, ed. D. Guerri, Bari, 1918, II, 137–8.

67 Battagli, 28 (but cf. Tonini, III, 71).

68 *Ann. Caes.*, 1101.

69 Battagli, 29.

70 Davidsohn, *Forschungen*, IV, 538. Salimbene, 368, speaks of 'Dominus Malatesta qui optime et fideliter partem ecclesie semper tenuit'.

71 Tonini, III, 538–40 ; *Corp. Chron. Bon.* II, 173.

72 *Annales Parmenses Maiores*, ed. P. Jaffe, MGH. SS, XVIII, 683.

CHAPTER III

1 Coluccio Salutati, *Tractatus de Tyranno*, ed. F. Ercole, Berlin and Leipzig, 1914, XXXX.

2 Theiner, I, 1–17, 198–9, 210–14 ; Ficker, II, 385–6. See Gatto, chapter vi ; Waley, *The Papal State*, 185.

3 G. Mollat, *Les Papes d'Avignon*, Paris, 1949, 213–16.

4 P. Sella, ' Costituzione per la Romagna pubblicate nel parliamento di Cesena dell' anno 1289 ', *ASI*, 1925, 243–50 ; L. Colini-Baldeschi, ' Le " Constitutiones Romandiolae " di Giovanni d' Appia ', *Nuovi Studi Mediaevali*, II, 221–52 ; P. Sella, ' Una costituzione inedita per la Romagna ', *RSDI*, II, 144–6.

5 Fantuzzi, III, 160.

6 Salimbene, 539 ; D. P. Waley, ' Papal armies in the Thirteenth century ', *EHR*, 1957, 2–6, 23–4.

7 Cantinelli, 64.

8 G. Ermini, ' I rettori provinciali dello Stato della Chiesa ', *RSDI*, IV, 1931, 34–6.

9 Benvenuto, II, 304.

10 *Poesie storiche relative all' Italia*, ed. V. Bartholomaeis, Rome, 1931, II, 288.

11 Cantinelli, 30, 38–9 ; Mittarelli, 513. G. Fasoli, ' La pace del 1279 tra i partiti bolognesi ', *ASI*, 1933, 49–75.

12 ' Il serventese dei Lambertazzi e dei Geremei ', ed. F. Pellegrini, *AMR*, 3, IX, 1891.

13 Cantinelli, 41.

14 *Ibid.*, 43.

15 G. Fasoli, ' Guelfi e Ghibellini di Romagna nel 1280–1 ', *ASI*, 1936, I, 157–80.

16 *Inferno*, XXXII, 122–3. Benvenuto, II, 514–15 ; *Annales Parmenses Maiores*, 689 (followed by *Chron. Este.*, 44), Salimbene, 370 ; G. Valgimigli, *Tebaldello Zambrasi*, Faenza, 1878. Cantinelli, 43–5.

17 Cantinelli, 41.

18 *Liber Pontificalis*, ed. L. Duchesne, Paris, 1955, II, 459–61 ; *Corp. Chron. Bon.*, II, 213–14 ; Waley, ' Papal armies ', 18.

19 *Inferno*, XXVI, 44 ; Cantinelli, 50–2.

20 *Histoire littéraire de France*, XXIII, Paris, 1856, 483.

21 *Inferno*, XII, 119–20.

22 *Les Régistres de Martin IV*, ed. F. Olivier-Martin, Paris, 1935, 214–15 ; F. M. Powicke, ' Guy de Montfort (1265–71) ', *Transactions of the Royal Historical Society*, 1935, 1–23.

23 F. Pipini, *Chronicon*, RIS, IX, 726 ; Cantinelli, 53 n.1.

24 *Codex Italiae Diplomaticus*, ed. J. Lunig, Frankfort, 1735, IV, 41–2.

25 For which, G. Zaccagnini, ' Maghinardo da Susinana ed il comune di Bologna ', *AMR*, 4, VIII, 1918, 52–146.

26 Cantinelli, 54 ; Azzurini, 124 ; *Inferno*, XXXIII, 109–57.

27 Cantinelli, 55–6, 62–3, 68, 71, 80–1, 85. Mittarelli, 517 ; Azzurini, 218–23.

28 Cantinelli, 55, 86 ; Fantuzzi, III, 186 ; *Ann. Caes.*, 1114.

29 *Ann. Caes.*, 1116. Maghinardo is described as Captain of Forlì in 1299, 1300, and 1301 ; Cantinelli, 92, 95, though only as Captain of Imola and Faenza in August 1302 ; *ibid.*, 95. ' Mainardo degli Ordelaffi ', found as *podestà* in 1300 in later works, is the confused creation of *Corp. Chron. Bon.*, born of the inaccurate recension of *Chron. Este.*, 52 : ' Mainardo e gli Ordelaffi '.

30 Cantinelli, 41, 43, 38.

31 Salimbene, 379.
32 Cantinelli, 55.
33 AC. Imola, M.IV, 4, 7 June 1287 — Lito della Massa, *defensor* with Paganino, *podestà* ; *ibid.*, M.IV, 9, 5 September 1287 — Lito, *defensor* found beside *podestà* and *anziani* ; *ibid.*, M.IV. 14, 29 June 1288, Alidosio degli Alidosi as *defensor* ; Schede Galli, 17 October 1289, Lito as ' Capitaneus populi Imole '.
34 Cantinelli, 62 ; *Ann. Caes.*, 1107.
35 Cantinelli, 65–7, 70. AC. Imola, M.IV, 114, 11 May 1292 — the Bolognese administration of Imola orders that none shall give aid to the Alidosi and their followers holding Linaro, Montecatone, Dozza, and Corvara. *Ibid.*, M.IV, 117, 31 May 1292 — the legate Ildebrandino da Romena places interdict on Imola for its attack on Montecatone and Linaro. Cf. *Corp. Chron. Bon.*, II, 236–7.
36 Rubeus, 478.
37 *Paradiso*, XV, 127 ; Benvenuto, V, 150–1.
38 Fantuzzi, III, 186 ; *Corp. Chron. Bon.*, II, 243–4 ; E. Goretta, *La lotta fra il comune bolognese e la signoria estense*, Bologna, 1906, 57–8.
39 Cantinelli, 92 ; see *Inferno*, XXVII, 37–9.
40 Cantinelli, 92 ; Benvenuto, III, 395 ; 9 ; Salimbene, 370 ; *Chron. Este.*, 52.
41 Cantinelli, 56.
42 Jacopo della Lana, *Commento*, Bologna, 1866, I, 433.
43 Rubeus, 440–1.
44 Cantinelli, 48–9 ; Rubeus, 445.
45 Tarlazzi, I, 370–1, 22 July 1285 ; Cantinelli, 61–2, 63, 75, 78 ; *Corp. Chron. Bon.*, II, 232–3 ; Ricobaldone, 143, ; *Compilatio Chron.*, 253.
46 Davidsohn, *Forschungen*, IV, 540–1.
47 S. Bernicoli, *Governi di Ravenna e di Romagna*, Ravenna, 1898, under dates ; E. Salzer, *Über die Anfänge der Signorie in Oberitalien*, Berlin, 1900, 56–60 ; Cantinelli, 79. Rubeus, 470–1 ; Fantuzzi, III, 168, 171.
48 Fantuzzi, V, 172 ; Cantinelli, 71. Cervia had been owned by the Archbishops of Ravenna, and the commune of Ravenna had exercised his power there from the beginning of the thirteenth century ; Rubeus, 359, 383.
49 Tonini, III, 631–2.
50 Fantuzzi, III, 143, 146.
51 Malatesta da Verucchio was described as Lord of Gradara in 1283. Giovanni di Malatesta was *podestà* of Pesaro in 1285, 1291, and from 1296 to 1304 ; Tonini, III, 143, 255–59. There was also a faction supporting the Malatesti in Urbino ; Cantinelli, 59.
52 Cantinelli, 57–8 ; 62–3.
53 Battagli, 30, Benvenuto, II, 309–10.
54 *Cronache malatestiane*, 5 ; *Ann. Caes.*, 1112.
55 Tonini, III, 170–1 ; 193–9.
56 Battagli, 30.
57 Chiaramonte, 162, 178. For Cesena, see : G. Franceschini, ' La signoria dei Conti di Montefeltro a Cesena', *SR*, V, 1954, 279–327.
58 *Ann. Caes.*, 1116.
59 Cantinelli, 63, 67 ; *Ann. Caes.*, 1111, 1120–2.

60 *Inferno*, XXVII, 25–54.

61 Dante called those who live in Italy south of the Po ‘ Latini ’. Those to the north he called ‘ Lombardi ’.

62 Benvenuto, II, 305, 308–9, 311.

63 No commentator has questioned the accuracy of Dante's line. Flavio Biondo of Forlì in the *Historia ab inclinatione Romanorum*, written in the middle of the fifteenth century, speaks of Dante's presence at Forlì on two occasions ; first before spring 1303 when the Whites were preparing to attack the Mugello ; second (though Barbi questions his accuracy here) in the second half of 1310. Biondo implied that his source was the letters of Pellegrino Calvi, the ‘ epistolarum magister ’ of Scarpetta Ordelaffi, which he believed had been also read by Benvenuto da Imola (though this again seems unlikely). See, M. Barbi, ‘ Sulla dimora di Dante a Forlì ’, *Problemi di critica dantesca*, Florence, 1934, I, 188–95 (also in *BSDI*, 1892, 21–8). Dante was not present at Forlì in 1308, nor was he secretary to Scarpetta as Troya asserted in *De Veltro Allegorico*.

CHAPTER IV

1 Theiner, II, 539.

2 P. Gaddi, ‘ Il testimonio di Maghinardo da Susinana ’, *Studi danteschi a cura della R. Dep. di Storia Patria per le provincie di Romagna*, ed. F. Costa, 1922, 61–88.

3 Salimbene, 370.

4 *Ibid.*, 605–6.

5 Tarlazzi, I, 455–6 ; *Ann. Caes.* 1110 ; Azzurini, 42 n.1 ; C. Ricci, *L' ultimo rifugio di Dante Alighieri*, Milan, 1891, 377–87,1 67–8 ; Passerini in Litta, *sub* Polenta.

6 A. Zaccaria, *Series Episcoporum Forocorneliensium*, Imola, 1820, II, 124 f., with which the undated document in Tarlazzi, I, 454–6, is connected.

7 Salimbene, 426–7 ; Cantinelli, 18 ; Azzurini, 41 n.1, 42 n.1.

8 Fantuzzi, III, 191–8.

9 *Inferno*, XXIII, 103. On this order, A. de Stefano, ‘ Le origini dei Frati Gaudenti ’, *Archivium Romanicum*, X, 1926, 305–50.

10 *Inferno*, XXXIII, 109–50.

11 Dates were more expensive than figs ; Alberico is saying that his cruel crime is being re-paid with doubled cruelty. The ‘ ill garden ’ is Faenza ; ‘ apellat Faventiam malum hortum quae produxit aliquando tam malos fructus in nobilibus suis ’ — Benvenuto, II, 504. The lines also refer to the signal Alberico gave for the attack : ‘ venga le frutte ’. These words became proverbial : ‘ perzò dise al vulgare : *Guardate da le fructe de fra Alberigho* ’ ; *Corp. Chron. Bon.*, II, 242.

12 G. Rossini, ‘ Il testamento di Frate Alberigo de Manfredi ’, *SR*, III, 1952, 524f ; G. Bertoni, ‘ Il testamento di Frate Alberico Manfredi e Ugolino Buzzola ’, *Archivium Romanicum*, V, 70–4.

13 *Inferno*, XXVIII, 70–90 ; Benvenuto, II, 363–6.

14 ‘ Tal è qui meco ’, is Curio, who according to Lucan advised Caesar to cross the Rubicon, flowing now through Malatesti territory. Focara is a headland between Fano and Cattolica.

15 *Il convivio*, ed. G. Busnelli and G. Vandelli, Florence, 1954, II, 3.
16 *Purgatorio*, XIV, 88–126.
17 Benvenuto, III, 388.
18 *Ann. Caes.*, 1177.
19 *Ibid.*, 1117.
20 *Corp. Chron. Bon.*, II, 380, 383, 396, 411–12 ; *Chron. Este.*, 98–9 ; *Ann. Caes.*, 1147 ; G. Villani, X, 138, 145.
21 Ricci, 420–44.
22 *Corp. Chron. Bon.*, II, 559 ; II, 561–2 ; *Chron. Este.*, 144–5.
23 *Ibid.*, 154.
24 Pedrino, II, 499.
25 *Corp. Chron. Bon.*, II, 357 ; *Chron. Malatest.*, 8–9.
26 *Ann. Caes.*, 1145.
27 *Corp. Chron. Bon.*, II, 429 ; *Ann. Caes.*, 1151 ; *Chron. Malatest.*, 10.
28 *Corp. Chron. Bon.*, II, 438 ; 455 ; *Chron. Malatest.*, 13 ; *Ann. Caes.* 1160.
29 Pedrino, II, 466–7.
30 Fantuzzi, V, 393.
31 M. Villani, X, 42 ; F. Guicciardini, *Opere inedite*, Florence, 1857–67, III, 393.
32 *E.g. Corp. Chron. Bon.*, II, 438 ; *ibid.*, II, 430, 436.
33 Quoted in I. Origo, *The Last Attachment*, London, 1949, 53.
34 Boccaccio, ' Trattatello ', 18.
35 That there was a university in Ravenna in the fourteenth century, and that Dante taught ' rettorica volgare ' in it has been propounded by Ricci, *L' ultimo rifugio*, 141–74 ; by P. Amaducci, ' Dante e lo studio di Ravenna ', *BSDI*, 1908, 132–42 ; by F. Filippini, ' L' insegnamento di Dante in Ravenna ', *Studi danteschi*, *AMR*, IV, 1922, 21–8 ; and by the same author in his, *Dante, scolaro e maestro*, Geneva, 1929. These opinions have been demolished by F. Novati, ' Se Dante abbia mai publicamente insegnato ', *Indagini e postille dantesche*, Bologna, 1899, 5–35, 113–25 ; by T. Casini, ' L' ultimo rifugio di Dante Alighieri ', *Studi danteschi*, Città di Castelli, 1913, 141–74 ; and by F. Torraca, ' Dante, maestro di scuola? ', in *Atti di R. Accedemia di Archeol. Lett. e Belle Arti*, Naples, 1926.
36 Boccaccio, ' Trattatello ', 34.
37 Gianozzo Manetti, ' Vita Dantis Poetae Florentini ' in *Vite di Dante*, 139.
38 ' Such as from bough to bough is gathered through the pine forest on the shore of Classe, when Aeolus lets forth Scirocco ' — *Purgatorio*, XXVIII, 19–21.
39 Guido's poetry has been published by C. Ricci, *L' ultimo rifugio*, 377–87. Giovanni Pascoli, suggested, however, that *Inferno*, V, 135, was taken by Dante from Guido Novello.
40 Boccaccio, ' Trattatello ', 28–9.
41 *Ibid.*, 62 ; Ricci, 187–93. His wife, Adaleta or Leta, was the daughter of ' messer Marchese ' (*Purgatorio*, XXIV, 31–4) of the Orgogliosi family of Forlì ; Rubeus, 571.
42 Boccaccio, ' Trattatello ', 36.

CHAPTER V

1 Bartolus, ' Tractatus de regimine civitatis ', *Consilia*, X.

2 Benvenuto, II, 514–15 gives this as the cause of Zambrasi's betrayal of Faenza. See also ' Serventese dei Lambertazzi ', cit.

3 Bartolus, ' De tyrannia ', *Consilia*, X, 117v.

4 C. Woolf, *Bartolus of Sassoferrato*, Cambridge, 1913, 164–9.

5 Davidsohn, *Forschungen*, III, 295.

6 G. Fasoli, ' Bologna e la Romagna durante la spedizione di Enrico VII ', *AME*, IV, 1939, 29 ; R. Caggese, *Roberto d' Angiò e suoi tempi*, Florence, 1922, I, 129, 346 n.1, II, 24–6 ; *Ann. Caes.*, 1132–6.

7 W. Preger, *Ueber die Anfänge des kirchenpolitischen Kampfes unter Ludwig dem Baier*, Munich, 1882, 169–70.

8 Fantuzzi, V, 391–7.

9 L. Ciaccio, ' Il cardinale legato Bertrando del Poggetto in Bologna ', *AMR*, 3, XXV, 85–196, 456–537 ; *Ann. Caes.*, 1153–6 ; *Chron. Este.*, 101–2 ; *Corp. Chron. Bon.*, II, 427.

10 *Corp. Chron. Bon.*, II, 518, 521–2, 530 ; E. Léonard, *Histoire de Jeanne Ier*, Monaco-Paris, 1932–7, I, 294 ; A. Mercati, ' Tentativo del duca d' Atene di ottenere l' investitura della Romagna ', *Rivista Storica degli Archivi Toscani*, IV, 1932, 153–63.

11 A Sorbelli, *La signoria di Giovanni Visconti a Bologna*, Bologna, 1901, ch. 1.

12 Mittarelli, 542–3.

13 L. Balduzzi, ' Il cardinale Bertrando del Poggetto e Bagnacavallo ', *AMR*, n.s., V, 1880 pt. I, 63 ff.

14 E. Orioli, ' Documenti bolognesi sulla fazione dei Bianchi ', *AMR*, 3, XIV, 1896, 7–10.

15 *Ann. Caes.*, 1123–1125 ; *Corp. Chron. Bon.*, II, 319, 332, 335–6 ; *Acta Aragonensia*, ed. H. Finke, Berlin and Leipzig, 1908, 271–2 ; G. Villani, IX, 18 ; Caggese, *Roberto*, I, 134, 147 ; Giovanni de Bazano, *Chronicon Mutinese*, ed. T. Casini, RIS, XV, pt. IV, 71 ; Bonoli, 133–4 (citing lost notarial deed) ; Fantuzzi, III, 326 ; *Chron. Este.*, 82 ; Ferreto de Ferreti, *Le opere*, ed. C. Cipolla, Rome, 1914, II, 215–16 ; Albertino Mussato, *De gestis Italicorum post Henricum VII*, in Graevius, VI, pt. 2, 282.

16 *Documenti tra Venezia e Ravenna*, 30 f.

17 Mittarelli, 535.

18 Azzurini, 165, 105. The particular importance which Faventine historians have given to Azzurini's words about Francesco for 2 January 1312 (pp. 125–6) : ' ascendit palatium pro defensione populi ', seems mistaken. Writing in the sixteenth century on the basis of documents now lost, Azzurini probably meant only that Francesco had received a temporary appointment as ' capitaneus et defensor populi '.

19 See form of letter of January 1313 ; Azzurini, 163.

20 Tonduzzi, 391–1 ; though Sinibaldo degli Ordelaffi was ' Defensor ' in 1316 ; *ibid.*, 26.

21 Azzurini, 176.

22 Azzurini, 199. See, too, Theiner, I, 512–13.

23 Azzurini, 86.

24 In 1324 he was called '*podestà* and captain', in 1327 and 1328, '*podestà*', and again in 1328, '*podestà* and captain'; Fantuzzi, V, 180, 181; III, 300; Tarlazzi, II, 194.

25 F. Grossaro, 'I poteri di Ostasio da Polenta', *FR*, 1951, f. 4, 67–75; f. 5, 65–80.

26 *Statuta Civitatis Cerviae*, Ravenna, 1558, in Jones, *Malatesta*, II, Appendix VI.

27 *Documenti tra Venezia e Ravenna*, 45–50.

28 Jones, *Malatesta*, I, 158, 181.

29 F. Battaglini, *Memorie istoriche di Rimino*, Bologna, 1798, 183–6; Jones, *Malatesta*, II, App. I, II, III; Tonini, *Rimini*, IV, 2, 134–8; Jones, 'The end of Malatesta rule', 222.

30 Tonini, *Rimini*, IV, 2, 137–8; Jones, *Malatesta*, I, 154–61.

31 BC. Imola, Ferri Mss., citing AC. Imola, M. VI, 34.

32 AC. Imola, M. VIII, 25; *ibid.*, 29 (22 April 1317), Ricciardo receives three-year appointment as captain; *ibid.*, M. VII, 52; M. VIII, II.

33 *Ibid.*, M. VIII, 29.

34 *Ibid.*, M. VII, 40.

35 *Corp. Chron. Bon.*, II, 384–5; G. Villani, X, 39; *Ann. Caes.*, 1147.

36 *Corp. Chron. Bon.*, II, 432, 436.

37 *Statuti di Imola*, 16–19.

38 In 1305; Davidsohn, *Forschungen*, IV, 555.

39 Theiner, II, 100.

40 G. de Vergottini, 'Ricerche sulle origini del vicariato apostolico' in *Studi di storia e dritto in onore di Enrico Besta*, Milan, 1939, II, 345, n.1. It was renewed by Clement VI to his son, Roberto, in December 1350; BC. Imola, Carte Galli, citing Archivio Vaticano, Arm. XXXXI, to. 26, 38.

41 Theiner, II, 531; 'farmentarium et sal recipiunt de campis Romane ecclesie'.

42 Léonard, *Jeanne I*, III, 112–14.

43 *Excerpta ex regestris Clementis VI et Innocentii VI*, ed. E. Werunsky, Innsbruck, 1885, 97–8; F. Filippini, 'La prima legazione del Cardinale Albornoz in Italia', *Studi Storichi*, V, 1896, 380–1, 405–7.

44 A. Gherardi, 'La guerra dei Fiorentini con Papa Gregorio XI detta la Guerra degli Otti Santi', *ASI*, 1867, and 1868 *passim*. *Corp. Chron. Bon.*, III, 307–19; Azzurini, 130; J. Temple-Leader and G. Marcotti, *Sir John Hawkwood*, London, 1889, chs. xiv–xxiv; J. Glénisson, 'Les Origines de la révolte de l'état pontifical en 1375', *Rivista di Storia della chiesa in Italia*, V, 1951, 145–68.

45 G. V. Marchesi, *Vitae Virorum Illustrium Foroliviensium*, Forlì, 1726, 457–70, for transcript of treaty with Ordelaffi. Probably the vicariate was given to the Manfredi at the same time; a notarial act of 23 February 1379 speaks of Astorgio as vicar; Azzurini, 87.

46 P. Jones, 'The vicariate of the Malatesta of Rimini', *EHR*, 1952, 321–51.

47 *La vita di Cola di Rienzo*, ed. Z. Re, Florence, 1854, chs. vii–xi *passim*. It is curious that the chronicler should suddenly interpose these chapters on Francesco in his life of Cola; possibly he saw a similarity in

the two men. His occasional inaccuracies (*e.g.* his assertion that Francesco held Imola) and his dialect show that he was not a native Romagnol.

48 Benedict XII writes to Francesco in 1335, warning him of the errors of the Fraticelli ; *Benoît XII : lettres closes et patentes*, ed. J. Vidal, Paris, 1913–42, I, 94.

49 *Ann. Caes.*, 1183, tells of the death of Ludovico in 1356, not as the Vita di Cola describes it, but in battle.

50 K. Schäfer, *Die Ausgaben der apostolischen Kammer unter Benedikt XII, Klemens VI and Innozenz VI*, Paderborn, 1914, 42.

51 Sacchetti, *Novelle*, XXV, tells the story with relish, adding that ' fu da davero '.

52 *Ann. Caes.*, 1164.

53 M. Villani, VII, 38.

54 E. Carrara, ' Cecco da Mileto e il Boccaccio ', *GSLI*, XLIII, 1904. Boccaccio's part in the expedition has been doubted ; F. Torraca, *Per la biografia di Giovanni Boccaccio*, Milan, 1912, 153–9.

55 M. Villani, VII, 69.

56 Boncompagni, *Liber de Obsidione Ancone*, ed. G. Zimolo, RIS, VI, pt. III, 42. On Aldruada, see Amaducci, ' Notizie storiche su gli antichi Conti di Bertinoro ', *AMR*, 3, XII, 1895, 188–249.

57 G. Villani, X, 224, giving date 19 September ; *Corp. Chron. Bon.*, II, 426–30, saying 28 September ; *Ann. Caes.*, 1153–6, saying 12 September.

58 *Ann. Caes.*, 1157.

59 *Ibid.*, 1157–65.

60 *Ibid.*, 1162 ; H. Otto, ' Benedikt XII als Reformator des Kirchenstaates ', *Römische Quartalschrift für christliche Altertumskunde und für Kirchengeschichte*, 1928, 88, 91.

61 Fantuzzi, III, 409. *Ann. Caes.*, 1165 gives a more sympathetic account, being indignant at the archbishop's ' usurpation '.

62 *Corp. Chron. Bon.*, II, 507 ; *Ann. Caes.*, 1178.

63 Léonard, *Jeanne I*, II, 18–19 ; *Corp. Chron. Bon.*, 579–80, 588–90 ; Pedrino, II, 413–14 ; *Ann. Caes.*, 1178–9 ; *Chron. Este.*, 156–7, 161.

64 *Ann. Caes.*, 1179–80 ; *Chron. Este.*, 108 ; M. Villani, I, 53.

65 M. Villani, I, 79.

66 M. Vecchiazzani, *Storia di Forlimpopoli*, Rimini, 1674.

67 M. Villani, VII, 38.

68 *Excerpta ex regestris*, 103 ; M. Villani, VII, 67.

69 *Vita di Cola*, IX, X ; M. Villani, VI, 14 ; VII, 58, 64, 68, 69, 77 ; *Ann. Caes.*, 1184 ; *Corp. Chron. Bon.*, III, 74–5.

70 M. Villani, VIII, 84.

71 M. Villani, IX, 36 believed wrongly that he had actually been invested with them.

72 P. Azarii, *Liber Gestorum in Lombardia*, ed. F. Cognasso, RIS, XVI, pt. I, 148–9 ; E. Martène and U. Durand, *Thesaurus Novus Anecdotorum*, Paris, 1717, II, 999 ; Pedrino, II, 418–19.

73 Theiner, II, 532.

74 Pedrino, II, 445. Bonoli, 175, writes of Giuliano being reinvested with the *castello* of Linaro in 1381 by the bishop of Sarsina. His ancestor had been invested with it in 1258.

75 Gherardi, VII, 224.

76 Bonoli, 170–2, cited the names of those families whose houses had been destroyed : ' i nomi di quali, conforme si ritrovano in certi manoscritti di Forlì, conservati in Casa de gli Albertini '.

77 Marchesi, 457–70.

78 Pedrino, II, 436.

CHAPTER VI

1 *Liber ruralium commodorum e Petro de Crescentiis compilatus*, Louvain, 1474, Preface.

2 *Ibid.*, I, 6 ; XIII, 8.

3 M. Placucci, ' Usi e pregiudizii de' contadini della Romagna ', Forlì, 1818, Titolo IV, reprinted in *Romagna tradizionale*, ed. P. Toschi, Bologna, 1952, 99 f. ; ' Documenti inediti relativi all' inchiesta napoleonica del 1811 nel dipartmento del Rubicone ', in *ibid.*, 33.

4 AS. Ravenna, Classe, CXVI, f. III, 21; f. IV, 24; Vol. 15 B, 54, 132.

5 BC. Faenza, *Statuta Vallis Hamonis*, Bk. III, R.7, f.70 ; labourers holding ' sive ad medietatem fructum, sive ad certam partem ' ought to ' rumpere, remanere [*i.e.* plough the second time], reterzare et requartere et quinto sulco seminare '. *Statuta Faventiae*, 228, for formula for vineland, ' eas diligenter putare, ligonizare et remanere '. See Tarlazzi, II, 97, for a contract of 1283. For other decrees, *Statuto di Ravenna*, 35–43 ; *Statuta Faventiae*, 225–31 ; *Statuti di Imola*, 83, 204, 232.

6 ' Gli statuti di Forlimpopoli ', ed. U. Santini, *AMR*, 3, XXII, 1904. In the statutes of the fourteenth-century printed by Santini, any labourer not working land as ordered in the statutes was supposed to give his lord four *sextarios* for each *tornature* he held ; p. 159. In the statutes of 1536, it was provided that he was to take no more than half a *staio* of corn from his patron for the sowing of each *tornatura* ; *ibid.*, 160.

7 A. Palmieri, ' I lavoratori del contado bolognese durante la signorie ', *AMR*, 3, 56 ; AN. Ravenna, M.15, 111r, 27 August 1360 — ' Indict. IV, Ravenne, in palacio Comunis penes banchum malleficiorum . . . Cum ad aures et noticiam Anthonii condam Ardoyni ser Montis pervenerit quoddam bannum factam per Donadinum publicum bannitorem Comunis Ravenne ex parte Magnifici D.D. Guidonis de Polenta vel eius vicarii quod omnes qui haberent vel tenerent aliqua bona immobilia ad affictum ab aliquibus personis deberent ipsa bona renunpciare [sic] et libere dimectere illis quorum sunt, quapropter dictus Anthonius nolens esse inobediens constitutis coram me notario et testibus infrascriptis coram Sapienti viro domino Johanne de Tirixiis de Parma vicario (Dni. Guidonis de Polenta vicarii generalis pro S.R.E.) renunciavit expresse Petro condam Dondidei de Mutina curatori Bernardini filii condam Fulchi de Polenta, cum non posset haberi presencia dicti Bernardini, 100 tornaturas terre positas in plebatu Forcoli S. Santerni '.

8 ' Statuti di Forlimpopoli,' 159.

9 *Statuta Faventiae*, 258–9. See ' Over-population and Underemployment in the Italian Countryside ' in R. Dumont, *Types of Rural Economy* (English translation), London, 1957, 237. On *mezzadria* see, too, F. Vochting, *Die Romagna : eine Studie uber Halbpacht und Landarbeiter Wesen in Italien*, Karlsruhe, 1927.

10 Theiner, II, 490–516. For succinct accounts of all the Romagnol feudality mentioned in Dante, see Casini, *Scritti danteschi* cit. and R. Torraca, *Scritti danteschi*, Naples, 1912 — especially ' Le rimembranze di Guido del Duca ', 131–7. See also G. Mini, *I nobili romagnoli della Divina Commedia*, Forlì, 1904, and P. Toynbee, *A dictionary of proper names and notable matters in the works of Dante*, Oxford, 1898.

11 Ezra Pound, *A Draft of Thirty Cantos*, London, 1954.

12 E. Gaddoni, ' Il testimonio di Maghinardo ' cit. The seals of Bernardino Orgogliosi, Alessandro de' Conti Romena, Malatesta da Verucchio, and Ugo dei Sassi are illustrated in G. Cencetti, ' Sigilli medievali del Museo Civico di Bologna ', *AMR*, 1951–3 (*Studi storici in memoria di Luigi Simeoni*, Vol. I). For the seals of Guido and Bernardino da Polenta, see plate 3 of G. Gerola, *A proposito dell' Aglugia da Polenta*, Florence, 1914.

13 *Ann. Caes.*, 1136 ; M. Villani, 1, 24.

14 M. Villani, IX, 97.

15 *I fioretti del glorioso messere Santo Francesco*, ed. G. Passerini, Florence, 1903.

16 *Ann. Caes.*, 1141–2 ; *Corp. Chron. Bon.*, II, 360–1.

17 Tarlazzi, II, 33 ; *Acta Imperii Inedita*, II, 161–5.

18 Tarlazzi, I, 209–11.

19 *E.g.* Theiner, I, 553–5.

20 Tarlazzi, II, 422–4 ; Theiner, II, 14.

21 Tarlazzi, I, 206.

22 F. Antonini, *Della antichità di Sarsina*, Faenza, 1769. 306–11. For a full discussion of the emphyteutic lease, see F. Grossara, ' La " concordia " ', *SR*, III, 1952.

23 AS. Ravenna, Porto, Vol. 1167, 21, segn. XXVI.

24 *Ibid.*, Classe, Vol. 14, 195r, 4 July 1432.

25 Fantuzzi, VI, 134.

26 P. Burchi, ' Regesto degli atti del notaio sarsinate Domenico da Firenzuola (1403–19),' *SR*, V, 1954, 52–167 *passim.*

27 Tarlazzi, II, 81, 2 May 1271.

28 Tonini, *Storia*, III, 24.

29 G. Ballardini, *Anno MCCXX: atto di liberazione dalla servitù della gleba e di concessione di un tenimento dell' agro faentino*, Faenza, 1907.

30 Tonini, *Storia*, III, 462–7, 26.

31 For the controversy on the abolition of serfdom in the Bolognese ; A. Palmieri, ' Sul riscatto dei servi della gleba nel contado bolognese ', *Archivio Giuridico*, 3, VI, 1906 ; Santini, *ASI*, 4, XVII, 1919, 142–5 ; Palmieri, ' Ancora sul riscatto dei servi alla gleba ', *AMR*, 4, IX, 1919, 142–5 ; *ibid.*, ' Lotte agrarie bolognesi nei secoli XIII e XIV ', *AMR*, 4, XXII, 1923, 7–63.

32 *Statuti di Forlì dell' anno 1359*, ed. E. Rinaldi, Rome, 1913, 106 ; *Statuta Faventiae*, 148, 157.

33 AN. Ravenna, M.I. a.c., XXIr, 16 July 1352 ; M.21, a.c. 49r, 23 March 1372 ; M.23 36r, 23 March 1374.

34 Burchi, 77, Antonini, 306–11 ; on later feudalism see G. Natali, ' La Repubblica Cispadana e l' abolizione dei feudi ', *AME*, III, 1938.

35 AC. Imola, M.V, 67, 28 April 1331, ' in nomine feudi, affictui seu servituti '.

36 *Ibid.*, ' unum quartum et dimidium frumenti boni, pulchri, necti et mundi '. A document of the same date in BC. Imola, Ferri Mss. VIII, 47, records thirteen men of Visignano and one of Castel Vielo with similar obligations, promising ' unum starium furmenti boni ' to Lippo Alidosi.

37 AC. Imola, M.V., 67 (cited), ' et custodias et castellanias ubicumque velluerit facere et exercitum et cavalcatum generalem et specialem predicto domino et eius filiis et heredibus atque successoribus totiens quotiens fuerit requisitus vel ei denumptatum fuerit per ipsum dominum seu ex parte ipsius Cecarelli '.

38 *Ibid.*, ' et laboreriis omnibus, angariis et perangariis honoribus et oneribus eidem domino respondere et stare et parere alte et base sub eius bannis preceptis et comdempnationibus et jurisdictione plenaria ipsius et ea adimplere in omnibus et per omnia que ad merum et mistum imperium et jurisdictionem plenariam pertinere nosscentur '.

39 BC. Imola, Mss. of Anchibene, 25 April 1399 ; Masio di Ca' Buraccia, for certain benefits received from Ludovico Alidosi, promised ' se esse servitorem et obedientem magnifice domine . . . pro decem annis proximis sequentibus et pro eodem facere chastelarium, exercitum et chavalchatos speciales et generales '.

40 *Capitoli del comune*, I, 576.

41 Tarlazzi, I, 169–70 ; 397 ; 308–10.

42 *Ibid.* I, 432–3.

43 *Capitoli del comune*, I, 95–7.

44 Mittarelli, 557.

45 BE. Modena, Campori, 44, 24 January 1369.

46 Fantuzzi, V, 423–6, — Gualdo is called ' Turrim et factoriam '.

47 The oath of the *gastald* of the canonry of San Cassiano in 1234 that he worked in return for a tenth part of all the revenues he received ; ACap. Imola, VI, 44. For the patrimonial properties of the da Polenta, see the *Codice Polentano* in Fantuzzi, III, 254–85. For the Malatesti, Dr. Jones's analysis of the *Codice Malatestiano* in *The Malatesta*, II, 695–8. For the Manfredi, there is much information in BC. Faenza, A. Zoli, ' Riassunto dei documenti in cui è ricordata la famiglia Manfredi esistenti nella Biblioteca Classense di Ravenna '.

48 BC. Faenza, *Statuta Vallis Hamonis*.

49 Fantuzzi, V, 337 ; Azzurini, 106–9 ; *Capitoli del comune*, I, 469–70.

50 There is a plan of Castiglioncho in D. Mini, *Marradi*, Castrocaro, 1892.

51 Cantinelli, 27 ; this Ranieri da Calboli is the hero of *Purgatorio*, XIV.

52 For adherents of Malatesti and Ordelaffi in 1389 ; *Documenti diplomatici tratti dagli archivi milanesi*, ed. L. Osio, Milan, 1864–72, I, 278–93.

53 Cobelli, XXII–XXIII.

54 G. Vitali, *Memorie storiche riguardanti la terra di M. Fiore*, Rimini, 1828, 33 f.

55 Sacchetti tells stories of three innkeepers in the province ; at Sant' Alberto (with seven daughters) ; at Tossignano (with a nagging wife) ; and at Cesenatico (with an unsavoury lavatory) ; *Novelle*, 216, 86, 196.

56 In these rural communes, often called the Casa Comunale; *e.g.* at Tossignano in March 1259 ' domus comunis ' — ACap. Imola, VII, 124. By the fifteenth century this had a *loggia* and a ' *sala maggiore* ' — AN. Imola, Rogiti di Nanne Zanelli di Tossignano (heceforth cited as Zanelli), 3 October 1433, 6 July 1433. Castel dell' Alpe met, ' in domo sive pallatio dicti Communis ', R. Caggese, *Classi e comuni rurali nel medio evo italiano*, Florence, 1907, I, 353. For a meeting of Castrocaro, ' in domo comunis in generali consilio comunis congregato ', under its *podestà* and vice-*podestà*, AN. Ravenna, Memoriale I, 1 May 1304.

57 *Statuta Montis Florum*, Olivo Cesari, Urbino, 1579, summarised in Vitali; these are the statutes of 1471.

58 In other *castelli*, and probably too, at Montefiore, when it was under the Malatesti, justice was largely in the hands of the Captain or Vicar appointed by the authorities of the town to which they were subject. In 1458, Marco di Roberto di Broccardi, Captain of Tossignano, was writing to Taddeo Manfredi for authorisation to act in a case of tutelage; AN. Imola, Zanelli, 15 May 1458.

59 As for the submission of the ' commune of San Stefano and S. Francesco of Tossignano ' to the Duke of Milan (at that time holding Imola) in 1424; *ibid.*, 29 February 1424. Six years earlier, the ' Consiglio Generale and Arrengo ' convoked by Sandro da Codronco, Vicar of the Castello for Ludovico Alidosi, had appointed the celebrated Imolese jurist, Antonio Tartagni, as its procurator to seek the reappointment of Ludovico as papal vicar of the *castello*; *ibid.*, 30 December 1418.

60 As in Tossignano's dispute with Casale in 1461; ' super collectis gravaminibus impositionibus et oneribus realibus personalibus et mixtis hominum et personarum habentium terras et alia immobilia bona in villa Garatorii et Riverie et Seragli '; *ibid.*, 26 July 1461.

61 In 1351, the men of Castel Meleto, for example, in the house of the commune appointed procurators to renew the forty-nine year lease of their *castello* from the Abbey of San Giuliano. The re-entry fine was eightpence, and the annual rent twopence. There are records of the renewals of the lease in 1399; Tonini, *Storia*, IV/2, 175–6, 429–32. The *massarius* of the *castello* of Lugo leased, ' locum vocatum Castrum Campioni cum tota curte sua et suis pertinentibus et cum omnibus et singulis terris; et vineis, pratis, buschis et paludibus seu aquastrinis in dicta curia Campioni positis et sitis, et omnes et singulos reditus, pensiones, prestationes, fidelitates etc.' for sixty-nine years, *ad renovandum*, for a rent of two Bolognesi pennies each March; AN. Imola, Rogiti di Antonio Monte (henceforth cited as A. Monte), 18 April 1418. In 1383, the Commune of Castel Gatteo, in the vicariate of Sant' Arcangelo, bought land with a house on it within the court of the *castello*, for £50; AN Faenza, Bartolo di Bonaccorsi da Trentola, 26 November 1383. In 1417, the representative of the same commune paid four brace of ducks to the Monastery of Classe in return for lands in the parish of Sant' Angelo in Salute; AS. Ravenna, Classe, Volume 21, 101r, 20 April 1417.

62 In 1363, Tossignano promised to guard 1,000 florins gold from all fortuitous chances, and to return it within ten days to Azzo and Roberto Alidosi. The commune acknowledged that if it were unable to make the repayment then, it would, at a later date, pay a sum of 2,000 florins gold. This appears to be a disguised usurious contract; but the circumstances

behind it are obscure. It was drawn up in the episcopal palace of Bishop Lito Alidosi, the brother of Azzo and Roberto ; AC. Imola, M.IX, 17, 26 April 1363. In 1405, the *massarius* of Bagnacavallo repaid a loan of £R.20 1 9, and on the same day contracted a loan of 200 ducats for two months at an interest of eightpence in the pound per month with a Jew called Lucio ; AN. Ravenna, Porto, Vol. 1192, 127r.

63 In Tossignano, there was a half-product contract (see page 137) for working ' in lana bisella ' in 1433 ; AN. Imola, Zanelli, 7 June 1433. A weaver was admitted to citizenship of Montefiore in 1376, Vitali, 239. See also Sorbelli, *Comune rurale*, 313, for Antonio Mazzani, ' mercator panni coloris ' at Dovadola in 1401, and for the domestic loom.

64 Vitali, 76–7. At Tossignano, Perla, daughter of Vitale of Fano and wife of Manuel di Issiah of Viterbo, residing in Tossignano, acted as *tutrix* of her sons David and Bonaventura and Abraham in 1445 ; AN. Imola, Zanelli, 4 November 1445.

65 Markets within the *contadi* are noted by Sorbelli, *Comune rurale*, 331, at Tossignano, Bertinoro, Meldola, Sant' Arcangelo, Mercato Saraceno, and Mercatale. In 1391, Zolo, rector of the church of Sant' Ambrogio della Massa, *gastald* of the Alidosi family, sold ' omnes et singulas gabellas ' of the Mercatale of the Massa Alidosia to Cecco da Modena for £B.230, with the provisio that the contract was to be void, ' si propter guerram generalem, homines non possent venire ad mercatum ' ; AC. Imola, XI, 15, 13 December 1391.

66 Sanudo, V, 278, 300, 347, 510–11, 602–3. But the evidence of population is confusing ; *apud* 278 for the *castello* itself — ' 1,000 anime ' ; *ibid.*, 602, ' fa con el territorio anime 6,000 ' ; *ibid.*, 603, ' 3,000 anime soto el qual territorio '.

67 For the duties of the *massarius*, *Statuti di Imola*, 35–7 ; *Statuta Faventiae*, 61–2, 85, 182. In Ravenna, he was known as ' capitularius ' ; *Statuto del sec. XV*, 33–5. On the rural communes, see further, below, pages 175–7.

68 See below, Chapter VIII, note 81. Linaro was still meeting there in 1454 ; AN. Imola, Rogiti di Luca di Antonio del Monte (henceforth cited as L. Monte), 12 February 1454.

69 BC. Imola, Galli Mss., citing Archivio della Mensa, 22 June 1311 ; AN. Imola, L. Monte, 14 May 1439. This commune met ' on the highway near the cemetery of Santa Maddalena ' ; *ibid.*, Rogiti di Giacomo di Battista di Fontanalice di Ricci (henceforth cited as Ricci), 27 October 1459.

70 Ibid, A. Monte, 18 March 1418, 4 March 1442. The lease described as ancient in 1418, was for sixty-nine years, with a re-entry fine of £B.20.

71 In 1418, Linaro in Sarsina bought ploughland to the value of £B.25 from Bishop Zanfilippo ; Burchi, 95–6. In 1443, the commune of Montecatone bought ' unam domum cum solo, tecto, curte et omnibus iuris ' in the *cappella* of S. Cristina in Imola. In 1462, the men of Linaro in the Imolese, bought a house in the *cappella* of San Donato ; AN. Imola, L. Monte, 16 January 1443, 22 February 1462. In 1427, the *massarius* and the men of Dozza (fifty-seven in all over the age of fourteen) give a lease of land for twenty-nine years *ad renovandum* ; AC. Imola, XI, 87, 9 June 1427.

72 BC. Ravenna, *Statuti polentani*, f.23r. Whoever was elected to the office was exempt thenceforth until all other members of the *scola* had held it in their turn. *Statuta Faventiae*, 215–17, 222–3, 264.

73 U. Toschi, *Un comune del Subappenino Romagnolo*, Imola, 1928, 30.

74 ' Documenti relativi all' inchiesta napoleonica del 1811 nel dipartimento del Rubicone ' in *Romagna tradizionale*, 21.

75 *Ibid.*, 35, 41, 108 ; G. Bagli, ' Bandi malatestiani ', *AMR*, 3, II, 1885.

76 M. Spallicci, *La poesia dialettale romagnola*, Forlì, 1953, 17–26.

77 F. Cocco, ' Analisi storica e semantica della parola " Trébbo " ', in *Il mondo agrario tradizionale nella Valle Padana*, Modena, 1963, 105–112, and U. Foschi, ' Antichi giochi dei contadini romagnoli ', *ibid.*, 127–140. Sorbelli, *Comune rurale*, 249–55.

78 *Ibid.*, 255–8 ; Sorbelli, 239, cites a farm in the *montagna* of Rimini with a pair of oxen, an ass, five sheep, and four goats — but this would be exceptional. The *Statuta Faventiae*, 281, mention hoes, spades, ploughshares, knives, hatchets, sickles, and saws ; — smiths were to charge no more than twopence for sharpening these.

79 ' Capo d' ogni grosseza d' ingegno ' ; *The Literary Works of Leonardo da Vinci*, ed. Richter, Oxford, 1939, II, 192.

80 Crescentius, XI, 8 ; I, 12 ; *Statuta Faventiae*, 225 ; ' Dazii di Forlì ', 109.

81 Benvenuto, II, 89–91.

82 *Ann. Caes.*, 1160.

83 BC. Imola, Anchibene Mss. citing Archiv. Vat. Arm. XXXVI, tom. 26, n.22.

84 AS. Florence, Missive, Registro, XXXIV, 36, 7 December 1431 ; Reg. XL, 93, 29 November 1454 ; Reg. XL, 71v, 11 September 1454.

85 Ibid, Missive, Reg. XLIV, 137, 8 February 1463 ; Reg. XLIV, 78, 23 April, 1463 ; Reg. XLIV, 115, 11 October 1463.

86 Sorbelli, *Comune rurale*, 248, 274–5, generalising for the whole of the Apennine *montagna*, believed that *mezzadria* was much less frequent than lease. Most rents, he thought, were equivalent to 10–12 per cent of the value of the land.

87 A. Zoli, ' La caccia nel territorio di Ravenna nel secolo XIII ', *La Romagna*, 1910, 235. In 1304, the Abbot of San Vitale leased to one Domenico ' fisherman ' the ' vallem de Bartina ad piscandum, venandum et aucupandum, illuminandum pro tertia parte piscium et venationis ' — AS. Ravenna, A.C.R.S., Vitale, Volume 623, f.23, 19 January 1304. These rights were also leased for money. Two years later, the Abbot leased hunting and fishing rights for the ' vallem Bartinae ' for £R.27 a year, *ibid.*, ACR, S. Vitale, Vol. 623, f.24, 1306.

88 P. Jones, ' A Tuscan monastic lordship in the later Middle Ages ', *Journal of Ecclesiastical History*, V, 1954, 181 ; Mittarelli, 526.

89 Theiner, II, 513.

90 The men of the rural commune of Massa Lombarda promise to Beltrando Alidosi, Signore of Imola, sixty-six *corbe* of spelt for each ox and cow that went in the following year to the woods of the commune of Imola ; BC. Imola, Ferri Mss., X.40, 3 December 1380. Ludovico Alidosi gives to Antonio Tartagni all rights for the exploitation of the pasture of

the commune from the river Sillaro to Castel Guelfo, AN. Imola, Marconi, 10 December 1426. Syndic of Taddeo Manfredi concedes to Andrea Bolognetti the right of pasturage for thirty beasts in the *valle* of the commune for the month of September for 1/- Bon. ; *ibid.*, L. Monte, 22 June 1465.

91 Thus in 1460, the *podestà* of Imola condemned some men of Conselice to a fine of £B.50 each for taking wood and digging a ' *cavamentus* in form of a canal ' in the wood of the commune ; BC. Imola, Ferri Mss., XII, 15 September 1460. The same year, the four *conductores* of the *dazii* of pasturage allow the men of the commune of Castel Bolognese to seek wood from Via Selice to Via Dozza ; *ibid.*, Ferri Mss., XII, 14, 5 September 1460. See also Statuti di Imola, 242 ; Bagli, ' Bandi malatestiani ', 36–7.

92 Fantuzzi, VI, 171–4, for regulations of Venice for pasturing in Ravenna in 1491 ; *ibid.*, IV, 469–72, for regulations for woods in same year.

93 AN. Ravenna, M.5, To.1, 109r, 29 October 1357.

94 AN. Imola, Rogiti di Baioli, 20 October 1365 ; one Palmiero leaves in a will 5 *corbe* of corn for ' colatico medietatis duorum boborum pretii XXIIII libras b '. owed to Margerita, wife of Azzo di Roberto di Alidosi. This notary records many contracts *ad colaticum.*

95 *Ibid.*, Rogiti do Rosegati, 13 November 1340 ; in return for 40 sol. bon. Sino di Baldo of Viduino promises to consign to Guido Bandoli of Imola, in the field of the said Guido, thirty-five ' cunnis Letaminis boni scilicet bovium, pecundum et equorum '.

96 *E.g.* to drive mills, in 1194, Tolosano, 14 ; in 1220, Mittarelli, 472 ; in 1225, Tolosano, 150–1 ; in 1254, Tonduzzi, 287–8 ; for drainage and repair of canals in 1235, 1264, Tonduzzi, 269, 298 ; and in 1278, Cantinelli, 27. See also *Statuti di Imola*, 288–9, — to prevent ' plenitudines aquarum ' a diversion should be made at the expense of the commune.

97 Tolosano, 130–2 ; Cantinelli, 19–20.

98 *E.g.*, in the middle of the fifteenth century — since the possessors of fields in Le Tombe at Linaro are not able to rid their lands of water, they agree in common to make ' unam clavigiam suttilis canale comunis Imole per quam dicte aque decurrere habent ' — AN. Imola, L. Monte, 10 May 1439. Note also the public and private work of Lamberto da Polenta in constructing the Tossa Lama and the Canale Dimizio near the Pineta ; Rubeus, 514.

99 L. Quadri, *Vita massaese attraverso i secoli*, Massa Lombarda, 1910.

100 AC. Imola, A. del Monte, 7 September 1448.

101 *Ibid.*, Guasconi —

22 Feb. 1459 — 400t.	24 Feb. 1459 — 200t.	4 Oct. 1459 — 200t.
4 Oct. 1459 — 400t.	4 Oct. 1459 — 200t.	4 Oct. 1459 — 50t.
26 Apr. 1460 — 114t.	26 Apr. 1460 — 100t.	26 Apr. 1460 — 100t.
23 May 1460 — 200t.	15 June 1460 — 1000t.	16 June 1460 — 110t.
23 June 1460 — 500t.	25 June 1460 — 700t.	23 July 1460 — 80t.
2 Aug. 1460 — 150t.	7 Aug. 1460 — 150t.	18 Sept. 1460 — 50t.
9 Oct. 1460 — 150t.	13 Dec. 1460 — 100t.	18 Dec. 1460 — 100t.
15 Jan. 1460 — 50t.		

102 AC. Imola, Guasconi, 4 October, 1459.

103 *Ibid.*, 15 June 1460.

104 Sorbelli's evidence for *dissodamento* and the enclosure of common property comes almost entirely from the sixteenth century, Sorbelli, 235–8. Palmieri sees a rise in the value of land in the second half of the fifteenth century ; A. Palmieri, *La montagna bolognese*, Bologna, 1929, 370.

CHAPTER VII

1 For the bell of Ravenna, F. Beltrami, *Il forestiero istruito nelle cose notabili di Ravenna*, Ravenna, 1783, 42. It is uncertain when clocks were first brought to the towns ; mention is made of one in 1371 at Cesena. At Imola in 1462, ' the circumspect man, Battista di Baldassare di Baffadi, procurator of the commune, in execution of the deliberation taken by the *anziani* and council of Imola concerning the clock to be made by Cristoforo da Merlo ' gave to him the tax upon foreigners until it yielded £B.100. In return he was to construct a clock within a year, ' in the place of the old clock of Imola ' ; AN. Imola, Guasconi, 24 January 1462.

2 For fire in Cesena, destroying Palazzo Popolo, Palazzo Maggiore, and surrounding houses in April 1303 ; *Ann. Caes.* 1124 ; another fire, August, 1314 *ibid.*, 1134. At Forlì, a fire in 1382, which burnt twenty-four houses ; Pedrino, II, 444. At Bagnacavallo, fire in 1363, in which a third of the village burnt down ; *Corp. Chron. Bon.*, III, 174. For regulations on firefighting, *Statuti di Imola*, 210, 307.

3 The *Statuti di Imola*, 294, specifically allows anyone to build a balcony or portico on to their house. In the fifteenth century at Faenza, Astorgio Manfredi ordered that all porticos in the town should be demolished, possibly because they were unsafe ; Azzurini, 241. For sleeping under the porticos, see Salimbene, 191.

4 AN. Faenza, Rogiti di G. Casali, 14 November 1369, 10 March 1371, 10 May 1371, 1 July 1373, 5 April 1374.

5 BC. Ravenna, *Statuti polentani*, 53, each citizen obliged to remove mud every Friday ; *Statuti di Imola*, 294, 208–9 ; Clementini, *Raccolto istorico della fondazione di Rimino*, Rimini, 1617, II, 362.

6 G. Majoli, Palazzi, *Case e casate di Ravenna del passato*, Ravenna, 1956, 24.

7 BC. Imola, Ferri Mss. Estratti I, 259 ; 30 April 1334 ; ' Nobilis vir Odorichus de Nordiglis vendidit Michaeli olim Porcelli de Primartinis de Imola unum necessarium et clausum parietibus lapideis sive muris et cum medietate muri unius inter ipsam Michaelem emptorem et ipsum odorichum venditorem . . . pro pretio 15 librarum bon. parvorum in summa.'

8 *Statuta Faventiae*, 170.

9 *Statuti di Imola*, 217.

10 *Statuti di Forlì*, 100 ; BC. Faenza, *Statuta Vallis Hamonis*, Bk. I, R.15, f.15–16.

11 Rubeus, 514.

12 Ricci, 3 ; *Statuti di Imola*, 213, 245–6.

13 Cantinelli, 56. This practice seems the cause of the attack of the people of Faenza on the bishop in 1184 ; ' granaria et cellaria frangens ' ; Tolosano, 92.

14 Tonini, *Le imposte*, 33.

15 See the report of the Florentine Commissary at Faenza to Piero de' Medici in 1494 ; ' ricordandovi che quasi tucte le alterationi di questa cipta sono processe da Carestia ; et quando il Signor M. Carlo et il Vescovo furono cacciati di questa cipta, ne fu grandissima cagione la carestia ' ; AS. Florence, Medici av. P. XVIII, 317, 7, October 1494.

16 ' Reprisals ' were ordered by Ravenna against Argenta in 1298, for goods to the value of £R.40, taken from a Ravenna citizen ; Tarlazzi, I, 422–4. In 1308, the Venetian guards of Marcabò recorded : ' Mag. dom. Calegario de Favencia, qui per aquas vallium prope Postam Fenarole portabat pelles subtilares concholos, moltoncevelles, peccias pignolati de Ravenna ad terram Lugi ' ; *Acta et Diplomatica e R. Tabulario Veneto*, III, sct. I, 142. Sacchetti, *Novelle*, 86, speaks of Michele Porcello of Imola, ' faccendo sua mercanzia di merce per Romagna e per Toscana ', but the importance of his trade can be inferred from the fact that he married an innkeeper's widow. Probably such a man was typical of ' the merchants of Romagna ' found in Pisa in the thirteenth century ; D. Herlihy, *Pisa in the Early Renaissance*, New Haven, 1958, 28.

17 Giraldus Cambrensis, 240 ; he wished to cash a bill of exchange for Modenese currency that he had obtained at Troyes.

18 G. Mazzini, ' Una vertenze fra i medici e il comune d' Imola nel secolo XIII ' extracted from *Bollettino dell' Istituto Storico italiano dell' Arte Sanitaria*, Rome, May-June 1930.

19 Transcript in AS. Ravenna from Memoriale dell' Anno 1314 c.23v in AS. Bologna 23 February 1314.

20 A. Palmieri, ' L' esercizio dell' arte medica nell' antico Apennino bolognese ', *AMR*, 4, I, 1911, 1–224.

21 G. Manacorda, *Storia della scuola in Italia*, I, 1913, pt. II, 297 : S. Bernicoli, ' Maestri e scuole letterarie in Ravenna ', *FR*, 1925, 61–9, 90–99 ; Carlo Tonini, *La coltura letteraria e scientifica in Rimini*, Rimini, 1884, 4.

22 Davidsohn, *Forschungen*, I, 314 ; *Statuta Faventiae*, 284.

23 AN. Imola, Rosegati 5 October 1341 ; the Lady Antonia di Bonmartino sells to Niccolo Ugodonici, three quarters of sixty-six parts of the new *beccharia*. The protocols of the same notary have many deeds drawn up, ' in foro bovium civitatis'. For regulations on working in the *beccaria*, *Statuti di Imola*, 198–9, 295.

The Societas Becchariorum veterum of Cesena took a sixty year lease of 100t. of meadow land in the parish of Russi in Cesena from the Monastery of Classe in 1364. The entry-fine (*pro mercede*) was fixed at forty shillings, the re-entry fine (*pro rennovatione*) at twenty shillings, and the rent (*pro pensione*), ' one good kid ' ; AS. Ravenna, Classe, Volume 18 p. 167.

24 AN. Imola, 11 January 1464, a tenth of the *pescheria* auctioned for £B.230.

25 AN. Ravenna, Memoriale 3, 67r, 13 May 1354, sale of ' unam barcham de rupore cum omnibus suis careriis pro precio VII ducatorum auri'. *Ibid.*, M.5, Tom. I, 31v, 24 March 1357, sale of ' unam barcham marsiliariam, que barcha vocatur Santo Antonio et Santo Leonardo nunc positam in aquis Ravenna capacitatis XX mazorum, cum omnibus suis careriis et paratibus pro precibus LXXX ducatorum auti '. *Ibid.*, M.29,

120v, 15 August 1380, sale of ' unum navilium copertum capacitatis trigintasex anforanum vel idcirca longum 40 pedibus et larghum in bocha 12 pedibus cum duobus arboribus, duabus velis duabus temonis, et cum omnibus suis sartiis, cannis aoredis, ferris etc.' for 280 ducats gold. *Ibid.*, M.7 Tom. II, 70r, 14 August 1359. ' Iacopinus filius condam Ollitavanni de Burgo S. Domini Comitatus Parme de contrata Bastelli promisit prestare operas et servicium persone sue hinc ad tres annos Zanino condam Marmorie navilia, in barcha dicti Zanini.'

26 AS. Ravenna, S. Vitale, Vol. 642, 52, 8 January 1335, Bagnacavallo, ' sub porticu ecclesie S. Michaelis. . . . Sandrus de Castaldis de Borfaglaga comitatus Ravenne promittit Johanni muratori aportare cum curru et bobus ad fornacem dicti Johannis que est extra terram in latere Porte Bulgarellorum per totum mense madii p. v. ligna et fraschas pro coquendo lapides et supos ad unam bucham tantum de alveo dicte fornaciis pro precio 6 librar. et 10 sold. bon.' ; Archivio Notarile di Imola, Volpe 1 April 1387, Michele di Giacomo and two companions promise Bonaventura di Cola di Mezzamice, to work at the kiln outside Imola until the middle of the following September. They were to make ' quadraginta milaria supporum, quinquaginta milaria lapidum et decem millaria tavellarum de terreno ' and to place these ' super arca in greza '. Bartoloneo was to provide the clay. Their salary was to be 19/- bon. a month.

27 AN. Ravenna, 23 October 1359 ; Francesco di Ser Ridolfo de Marchisini and other ' magistri lignaminis ', citzens of Forlì, promise to Leo da Polenta, on behalf of the new church of S. Niccolo, ' fideliter laborare totum lignamen quod debet inponi super muris ipsius ecclesie et affides et tectium et complere totum ipsum laborerium cum lanbrettis supra exceptis cuppis et non teneantur dicti magistri depingere affides vel catinellas sive sechare cum secha grossa vel magna, pro salario 75 librarum Rav. et 10 soldorum '.

AN. Imola, Della Volpe, July 1391 ; Toniolo di Bonmercato della Massa, Paolo di Bettolo di Chiasura, Giovanni di Nerio di Tossignano, workers in wood promise to Fra Tebaldi, Guardians of the Friars Minor of Imola, to construct a roof for the dormitory of the friars.

AN. Ravenna, 5 Tom. II, 66r, 8 May 1357, for a lease by the Archbishop of land to the ' maioribus et officialibus Societatis et Universitatis Scole Carpentorum civitatis Ravenna '.

28 C. Malagola, *Memorie storiche sulle maioliche di Faenza*, Bologna, 1880 ; G. Liverani, ' La ceramica in Imola ' in *SR*, VI, 1955 ; L. Tonini, *Figuline riminese*, Rimini, 1870 ; Bernicoli and Grigioni, ' La ceramica in Ravenna,' *FR*, 1911 and 1912.

29 *Nuovi testi fiorentini del dugento*, ed. A. Castellani, Florence, 1952, II, 911 ; A. Sapori, ' Un bilancio domestico a Firenze alla fine del dugento ' in *Studi di storia economica*, I, 354, 367, 368 ; Sacchetti, *Novelle*, L.

30 BC. Faenza, *Matricola de larti del la lana de magnifica citade de Faenza* (1470).

31 AN. Ravenna, M.15, 119r–120r, 10 July 1366 ; in the shop of the Jewish goldsmith Michino di fu Jacob di Ser Melchisides, Michino makes a contract to work with Francesco Niccolo of Florence in the church of San Giovanni in Florence. *Ibid.*, M.1, 2r. for the lease of a goldsmith's shop, with description of his tools in June 1352.

32 AN. Ravenna, M.29, 47r–48r for an inventory of a chemist's shop, 29 January 1379. AN. Imola, Della Volpe, 29 July 1392, for lease of 'stationem sive apothecam aptam ad artem speciarie' for £B.100 for two years.

33 *Ibid.*, Broccardi, 18 April 1387, for Floriano di Ugolino of Bologna and his wife Daria, living in Imola, 'in arte et mercatione cartolarie esercenda'.

34 *Statuta Faventiae*, 277–8, 281, 284.

35 AC. Imola, M.VI, 94 ; in 1312, there was also an Art of Tailors.

36 BC. Faenza, *Matricula de larti de la lana*, cit. f. 27r ; similar provisions in *Statuti dell' arte della gentile* (*1417*), 28v.

37 *Ibid.*, *Matricola dell' arte dei fabbri in Faenza* (18 June 1466), Cap.1 ; the *massarius* and consuls of the Orders to attend mass in S. Pietro (the cathedral) on the first Sunday of each month, where a mass was to be said for the dead of the Art ; two shillings bon. was to be given to the priest.

38 G. Ballardini, *Inventario critico e bibliografico dei codici e pergamene dell' archivio del comune di Faenza*, Faenza, 1905, XXXIX, for decree of Arts prohibiting work on feast days, 8 March 1332.

39 *Ibid.*, for deliberation of March 1326, fixing minimum price of shoes at fourpence.

40 BC. Faenza, *Matricola dei fabbri*, Cap. IV ; C. Spreti, *Statuti e rubriche dell' ordine della Casa Matha*, Ravenna, 1820, 8–9 (statutes of 1304).

41 F. Sacchetti, *I sermoni evangelici*, Florence, 1857, 52.

42 *Statuti di Imola*, 141–3, 147–8, *Statuta Faventiae*, 98–9, 277, 358. See too, the terms of Carlo Malatesti's ban against usury in 1398 ; Bagli, 'Bandi malatestiani,' 84–5.

43 *Statuti di Imola*, 106–11, 123 ; *Statuta Faventiae*, 97–100, 107–8. Tarlazzi II, 119, for sequestration of goods, and see II, 149.

44 Thus Girolamo Riario wrote to Ercole d' Este asking him to capture two men, debtors of Melchior Torresano for £B.800, 'como ne appare scriptura de mano de dicto Melchior secundo lordine mercantile'; Archivio di Stato di Modena, Carteggio di Principi e Signorie, Imola, Busta I, 30 October 1478.

45 C. Roth, *The History of the Jews in Italy*, Philadelphia, 1946, 70, 121–2, 130–3, 147–9 ; Fantuzzi, III, 75–6 ; G. Balli, 'Gli Ebrei a Lugo', *SR*, III, 1953, 145 *et seq.*

46 BC. Imola, Mss. 943, 1 November 1458.

47 AS. Florence, *Statuti di communità e luoghi autonomi*, *Statuto di Castrocaro*, 165.

48 A. Bernardi, *Cronache forlivesi*, Bolgona, 1895, I, 304–5.

49 In Florence interest rates remained at an average 20–30 per cent through the fourteenth century ; A. Sapori, 'L' interesse del denaro a Firenze nel trecento', in *Studi di storia economica*, I, 223–43. Interest on loans against pledge in Siena was 20 per cent in 1457 ; in Lucca, 40 per cent in 1372, 33½ per cent in 1431, 30 per cent in 1482 ; N. Piccolomini, *Il Monte dei Paschi di Siena*, Siena, 1891, I, 144. In the Marche with an economy similar to that of Romagna, interest varied with the size of the loan. At Gemmana in 1395, loans of less than half a mark under full security took 37 per cent interest, those of above, 22–23 per cent. In

Fano in 1425, interest varied from 20–25 per cent against pledges and rose to 28 per cent and above against public instrument; G. Luzzato, *I banchieri ebrei in Urbino nell' età ducale*, Padova, 1903, 16, 32–3. Sacchetti distinguished the *foenator* from the usurer, the first lending at simple, the second at compound interest, but it is doubtful if bankers in normal transactions in Romagna capitalised interest; A Sapori, ' L' usura nel dugento a Pistoia ', I, 187. In all Romagnol documents of this era the two terms are used interchangeably.

50 AN. Imola, A. Monte, 20 August 1428.

51 AN. Ravenna, M.5, T.1, 13 March 1357.

52 Fantuzzi, III, 429–30.

53 In that year, the Jews of the province asked that papal taxation should not exceed 200 ducats gold; E. Rinaldi ' Gli Ebrei in Forlì ', *AMR*, 4, X, 1920, 313–15.

54 A bank in Forlì in 1485 had a capital of £B.8000; Rinaldi, 315–23. In 1335, Eli son of Solomon made a contract with Solomon son of Manuel, by which the latter should manage his bank in Ravenna for the following year with a salary of 18 ducats gold; AN. Ravenna, M.3, 2a, 31v.

55 AS. Ravenna, S. Vitale caps. IX, f. III, n. 12, 8 November 1416.

56 In 1453, for instance, the heirs of Gaio, Jew of Cento, brought a case against Emmanuel before the judges of Faenza. Emmanuel was accused of fraud and breach of contract while acting as partner in Gaio's bank at Faenza; Mittarelli, 581.

57 AN. Imola, A. Monte, 1 September 1456.

58 Sacchetti, *Novelle*, CXC; Pedrino, II, 432.

59 G. Bertoni, ' Banchieri ad Imola nel secolo XIII ', in *Studi Mediaevali*, III, 1911, 683; A. Lettes, ' Il libro giornale d' un mercante toscano ad Imola nel secolo XIII ', in *Rivista di Diritto Commerciale*, IX, 1911. The Council of Faenza allowed two Florentine merchants to establish a bank in the town in June, 1379; Mittarelli, 563. A Florentine is found lending money in Ravenna in 1289; Tarlazzi, II, 103–4. See, too, E. Fiumi, *Storia economica e sociale de San Gimignano*, Florence, 1961, 92–3.

60 Under this formula, for instance, Anna, *meretrix* of Ravenna, acknowledged a loan of £B.30 to be repaid within two months from Masio de Rigoletti; AN. Ravenna, M.21. 4 November 1372. For two other similar loans to prostitutes, *ibid.*, M.22, 115, 119, 11 August 1373.

61 AN. Imola, Della Volpe, 23 July 1378. In some cases the creditor took only a third of the profits. So, with a loan of £R.51 for working in *arte pannorum bisellorum* at Ravenna in 1356; M.4, 9 August 1356. For other examples: *ibid.*, M. 19, 2 August 1356; AN. Faenza, A. Piccini, 18 May 1476; AN. Imola, R. Broccardi, 14 September 1338.

62 AN. Imola, Rosegati, 11 April 1389.

63 BC. Imola, Anchibene, 10 May 1383.

64 AN. Imola, L. Monte, 5 May 1442; 2 November 1461. A. Monte, 15 March 1423; 30 March 1423.

65 *Ibid.*, A. Monte, 4 March 1423, 7 April 1428; L. Monte, 17 September 1454.

66 *Ibid.*, A. Monte, 28 September 1423; P. Marconi 18 December 1439; A. Monte 20 August 1418; 30 June 1436; AN. Ravenna, M.17, 120r.

67 AN. Imola —

Broccardi	21 Sept.	1422	£B. 30 to a flaxworker
A. Monte	9 Feb.	1423	£B.100 to the same man
A. Monte	7 March	1423	£B. 15 to a clothworker
L. Monte	26 Feb.	1426	£B. 25 to a haberdasher
L. Monte	24 March	1426	£B. 25 to a butcher
L. Monte	27 May	1426	£B. 33 to a chemist
L. Monte	31 March	1427	£B. 25 to a clothworker
L. Monte	15 March	1429	£B.150 to a flaxworker

In 1454, his heirs invested £B.100 with a goldsmith ; *ibid.*, L. Monte, 1 January 1454.

In the same period the Rogiti of A. Monte contain the following contracts of Bartolomeo :

8 Feb.	1422	lease of ox at colatico
12 Dec.	1422	lease of 15t at mezzadria
9 Jan.	1423	purchase of ploughland of 3t for £B.6
20 May	1423	purchase of house for £B.24
7 Jan.	1425	lease of 4t of vineland at mezzadria
14 March	1428	lease of 7t in San Prospero
21 March	1428	purchase of 2t in Fontanella for £B.16
8 Aug.	1428	purchase of orchard in cappella of S. Cassiano
5 Oct.	1429	makes will

68 *Ibid.*, A. Monte, 9 April 1423.

69 Rolandino Passagieri, *Summa Artis Notarie*, Venice, 1565, preface to Part III. For the disguise of usurious contracts, see A. Pertile, *Storia del diritto italiano*, Turin, 1893, IV, 595 *et seq.*, and Sapori, ' Saggio sulle fonti della storia economica mediaevale ' in *Studi di storia economica*, I, 7–9.

70 Jewish bankers lent money under this formula ; AN. Imola, M.21, 19 March 1372. A *lapsus calami* of a notary in another document ; ' instrumentum depositi seu mutui ' reveals the real meaning of leaving money in deposit ; *ibid.*, M.21, 14 January 1396.

71 For an example of this contract see Tarlazzi, II, 233–5, 27 January 1340.

72 Fantuzzi, VI, 70–4.

73 AN. Imola, A. Monte, 30 December 1458.

74 *Ibid.*, L. Guasconi, 24 March 1465.

75 See Sapori, ' I mutui dei mercanti fiorentini del trecento e l' incremento della proprieta fondaria ', in *Studi di storia economica*, I, 191–221.

76 BC. Imola, Anchibene, 28 February 1404.
AN. Imola, A. Monte, 12 July 1419.

77 AN. Faenza, G. Casali, 26 February 1386.

78 AS. Ravenna, San Vitale, Volume 624, *campione* 54, 29 March 1355.

79 AN. Ravenna, M.5, T.1, 27 October 1357.

80 AN. Ravenna, M.5, T.11, 27 June 1357.

81 *Ibid.*, M.32, 9 April, 1397.

82 *Epistolario di Coluccio Salutati*, ed. F. Novati, Rome, 1896, III, 449–50.

83 Bernardi, I, 304.

84 Cited by Sacchetti, *Novelle*, 86 (set in Romagna, and a good illustration of prevailing thought on the subject) and Boccaccio, *Decamerone*, IX, 9.

85 AN. Imola, Zanelli, 5 April 1453. The *Statuti polentani* (Biblioteca Classense), 46v, permitted the beating of wives, ' dum tamen verbatio non sit enormis '.

86 AN. Imola, Rogiti di Sigismondo Marconi, 10 October 1498.

87 AN. Ravenna, M.12, T.11, 23r.

88 As in the annulment of marriage between Ser Giovanni di Ser Bentivegna de Pusterla, and Marina di Rigo de' Mainardi, in 1360; *ibid.*, M.8, 20v, 5 February 1360.

89 *Ibid.*, P.11, 205v–206r; Obizzo di Guido da Polenta creates Giovanni Pietro di San Lorenzo in Campo his procurator at the baptisms of the male child of Francesco da Ferrara, dwelling in Forlì, ' et ipsi infanti nomen in Batismate predicto prout per ipsum Franciscum statutum fuerit imponendi '. *Ibid.*, P.14, 39v, Ginevra di Gian Galeazzo Manfredi, wife of Ostasio da Polenta, appoints procurator, ' ad ellevandum in sacro fonte Batismatis ' a girl of Pietro de' Conti da Bagno.

90 Tonini, *Storia*, IV/I, 247–8.

91 G. Cerchiari, *Ristretto storico della città d' Imola*, Bologna, 1847, 46.

92 BC. Imola, Galli Mss. citing M.VI, 32, 9 March 1372.

93 AN. Ravenna, M.28, 24r, 23 February 1377; Iacopo di Chele of Castel San Pietro, cook of Guido da Polenta, receives dowry of £50 for Cortesa, daughter of Pietro of Florence. The dowry of one marrying a doctor of medicine in 1353 was £R.400; *ibid.*, M.2, 68, 2 March 1353.

94 *Ibid.*, M.5, II, 76v, 9 June 1357; ' reservato beneficio statuti Comunis Ravenne quo loquitur si uxor premoriatur sine filiis comunibus eorum vir lucrari debeat medietatem constituti '.

95 Tarlazzi, II, 77–9, 82–4.

96 Salimbene, 428–9.

97 *Statuti di Imola*, 236, 247. The regulations of Faenza of January 1497 show that syphilis was already rife; Mittarelli, 792–5.

98 AS. Ravenna, Estranee, Caps. XXV, 5, 44, 16 April 1310; *ibid.*, XXV, 5, 4, 23 January 1313.

99 *Statuti di Imola*, 223; see also sumptuary law of Beltrando Alidosi in 1372; Cerchiari, 46.

100 Rubeus, 558.

101 AN. Ravenna, MXXXI, 101v–103r, 18 November, 1384.

102 *Ibid.*, M.XXXV. (Testamenti I), 54r, 24 November 1357.

103 S. Muratori, ' Vesti, ornamenti e oggetti d' uso in alcuni inventarii ravennati dei secoli XIV–XV ', *La Romagna*, 1913, 283–99.

104 Cerchiari, 165.

105 AN. Ravenna, M.26, 22r, 19 May 1376; on slavery in Italy see I. Origo ' The Domestic Enemy: The Eastern Slaves in Tuscany in the Fourteenth and Fifteenth Centuries ', *Speculum*, 1955, 321–66.

106 AN. Ravenna, M.32, 76r, 11 March 1397.

107 AN. Imola, A. Monte, 28 April 1440.

108 F. Filippini ' Inventario dei libri e dei beni posseduti dall' archiv. di Ravenna Petrocino nel 1369 ', *Studi storici*, VI, 1897, 3–32, 473–93 ; S. Bernicoli ' La Biblioteca dell' Archivescato di Ravenna (1321) ' *FR*. 1930, 25–6.

109 R. Weiss, ' Il Petrarca e i Malatesti ' in *Il primo secolo dell' umanesimo*, Rome, 1949, 73. A. Massera, ' Iacopo Allegreti da Forlì ', *AMR*, 4, XVI, 1926, 137–203.

110 See above, pages 75, 93 ; N. Sapegno, *Il trecento*, Milan, 3rd ed., 1948, 282, 456 ; R. Sabbadini, *Giovanni da Ravenna*, Como, 1934.

111 Dante, *De Vulgari Eloquentia*, ed. A. Merigo, Florence, 1957, I, XV ; G. Zaccagnini, ' Due rimatori faentini del secolo XIII ', *Archivium Romanicum*, XIX, 1953, 79–106.

112 N. Matteini, *Il più antico opositore politico di Dante : Guido Vernani da Rimini*, Padua, 1958 ; C. Tonini, *La coltura letteraria e scientifica in Rimini*, Rimini, 1884, Chapter II ; G. Leff, *Gregory of Rimini*, Manchester, 1961.

113 C. Tonini, *La coltura*, Chapter ii ; B. Brandi, *Vita e dottrina di Raniero da Forlì*, Turin, 1885.

114 F. Güterbock, ' Forliveser Annalen des Pietro Ravennate ', *Neues Archiv der Gesellschaft für ältere Deutsche Geschichtskunde*, XXIV, 1899, 736–42. The *Annali forlivesi* are not to be confused with the *Annales Forolivienses* (or *Cronaca Moratina*), compiled in the fifteenth century.

115 Hieronymus Foroliviensis, 29 ; G. Ballardini, ' Alcuni lettere dei Manfredi al Gonzaga ', *AME*, I, 1936, 18. On the popularity of the Romagnol spas, see R. Davidsohn, *Firenze ai tempi di Dante*, Florence, 1929, 602.

116 *Statuti di Imola*, 201–2.

117 *Statuta Faventiae*, 294–5.

118 *Rimatori comico-realistici del duecento e trecento*, ed. M. Vitale, Turin, 1956, II, 279–80, 184.

119 BC. Imola, Ferri Mss. citing AC. Imola, VIII, 174, 20 October 1334.

120 ' Statuti di Forlimpopoli ', 52 ; *Statuti di Forlì*, 107.

121 Full list of charges in *Statuti di Forlì*, 75–82.

122 BC. Ravenna, *Statuti polentani*, 42v De Protocollis Tabellionum Defunctorum ; AN. Ravenna, M.14, T.11a, 6v, 2 January 1365 — General Council concedes to Francesco de Bellolis the protocols of Ugolino di fu Severino. *Ibid.*, M.26, 77v–78r, 24 August 1376, grant by council of protocols of Ser Menghino Mezzani (the friend of Dante) to Vitali di Giovanni.

123 L. Baldisseri, *Benvenuto da Imola*, Imola, 1921.

124 For these creations see Ficker, IV, 509–10 (by Carlo di Guido di Battifolle) ; AN Ravenna, M.3, 1r, 29 December 1354, by Count Bartelotto ; *ibid.*, M.21, 85r, 1 July 1372, ' in domo habitacionis sive scola magistri Johannis ser Guaspar de Bonzanis de Parma rectoris scolarum quam conducit a Blaxio de Scarabigolis ' and 2 July 1372 (*ibid.*, 85v) ' in scola magistri Phylipini condam ser Phylipini ', Count Staffanode Henzera creates six notaries. *Ibid.*, M.30, 157v, Count Iacholo di Cerno of

Zara, 18 March 1381, and *ibid.*, 12 July 1381, M.30, 128r, and, *ibid.*, 20 September 1381, M.XXX. 163v–164r. This archive contains many other examples, see also Burchi, 92, 94, 95 etc. for creations by the Bishop of Sarsina, Count Palatine of Bobbio. Burchi's register of the acts for 1403–19 of Domenico da Firenzuola, notary of Sarsina, gives a representative sample of the character of the notary's work in the *contado*. There are 657 *rogiti* in all.

125 AC. Imola, L. Monte, 21 February 1465 ; the college of procurators and notaries of Imola gathered in the house of Marco di Mamelli of Bagnara and twenty-one men present forming over two-thirds of the society, after dining, enrolled one of Marco's sons in the *Marticula*. In Ravenna, the society had its own house ; AN. Ravenna, M.6, 85r, 1 October 1358.

126 AN. Imola, A. Monte, 13 May 1438.

127 Vitali, 298.

128 AC. Imola, II, 79.

129 *Ibid.*, M.VIII, 91 ; Fantuzzi, III, 71.

130 See D. Baldisseri, *Il castello di Mordano*, Imola, 1925, 28.

CHAPTER VIII

1 Bartolo da Sassaferrato, ' De regimine civitatis ', *Consilia*, X, 152v.

1 See F. Ercole, *Dal comune al principato*, Florence, 1929, 99–118.

2 Sacchetti, *Novelle*, CCII.

3 Dino Compagni, *La cronica*, ed. I. Lungo, RIS, IX, part 2, 151–2. but one wonders how much Compagni knew about Scarpetta. In 1302 he describes him as ' vicario per la chiesa ' in Forlì, which seems extremely improbable. Scarpetta might perhaps have been the recipient of some local vicariate in the *contado*. Extremely dubious is Compagni's assertion, *op. cit.* 202–3, that the Florentines caused Forlì to prohibit the entry of Cardinal Orsini in 1306.

4 Cobelli, XXV.

5 Theiner, II, 253.

6 Spreti, 20.

7 *Ann. Caes.*, 1143.

8 M. Villani, IX, 12.

9 *Ibid.*, I, 58.

10 *Corp. Chron. Bon.*, III, 155–6, 158–9, 160–1.

11 Giovanni da Bazzano, 142, shows him as *podestà* for the d' Este in 1352.

12 *Corp. Chron. Bon.*, III, 197–8 ; *Chron. Este.*, 487.

13 AC. Imola, IX, 14, reproduced in L. Rossi-Case, *Ancora di Maestro Benvenuto da Imola*, Imola, 1893.

14 BC. Imola, Galli Mss. citing Arch. Sgr. Vat. Urban V de cura, Anno I–II–III, Vat. 261, 198–9.

15 *Corp. Chron. Bon.*, III, 207–8.

16 Theiner, II, 531.

17 AC. Imola, VIII, 91.

18 *Ibid.*, IV, 10 ; VIII, 22.

19 G. Cerchiari, *Ristretto storico della città d' Imola*, Bologna, 1847, 39 ; G. Mazzini, ' Una vertenze fra i medici ed il comune di Imola nel secolo XIII ', *Bollettino dell' Istituto Storico Italiano dell' Arte Sanitaria*, Rome, May, 1930.

20 BC. Imola, Ferri Mss. citing M.VI, 51, 56.

21 *Ibid.*, citing M.VI, 84, 16 October 1312.

22 Ricci, 13 ; Rubeus, 444, 449, 458, 488 ; Cantinelli, 72, 97 ; *Chronicon parmese*, ed. G. Bonazzi, RIS, IX, pt. IX, 76–7 ; *Corp. Chron. Bon.*, II, 274 ; Mussato, *De gestis*, 125 ; Davidsohn, *Forschungen*, IV, 51.

23 Pedrino, II, 434–5.

24 Tonini, III, 193–5. Similar household for the *podestà* of Faenza ; *Codex Italiae Diplomaticus*, IV, 66 ; *Statuta Faventiae*, 1, 3.

25 *Statuta Faventiae*, 32–3.

26 F. Sacchetti, *I sermoni evangelici, le lettere ed altri scritti inediti e rari*, ed. O. Gigli, Florence, 1857, 230. For appointment of *podestà* at Rimini and Fano ; Jones, *Malatesta*, II, 727–8, 765.

27 F. Sacchetti, *Lettere volgari*, Imola, 1880, 35–36. Piero Crescenzii, the Bolognese writer upon agriculture, might be taken as a representative of the professional judge-advocate to the *podestà* — an office which he filled for thirty years in various towns (including Imola in 1283) ; L. Frati, ' Pier de Crescenzi e l' opera sua ', *AMR*, 4, IX, 1919. 146–64.

28 Sacchetti, *Sermoni evangelici*, 233–4.

29 Sacchetti, *Lettere volgari*, 42.

30 Pedrino, I, 20 — they were pardoned the crime.

31 *Ibid.*, II, 1654.

32 AN. Ravenna, M.18, 70r, 7 July 1369.

33 So Azzurini, 74 n.1, but the system was flexible. In 1386, for instance, the ' Judex ordinarius ad discum leonis ' was creating *tutores* for minors ; AN. Faenza, Giovanni Casali, 26 February 1386. In Ravenna there was the judge ' ad discum aquile juris civilis ' ; AN. Ravenna, M.5, T.1, 79r.

34 *Statuta Faventiae*, 57.

35 AN. Ravenna, M.5, T.1, 57r, 17 May 1357 ; Agnesia, daughter of Giovanni, hanged for theft of £R.18 18. *Ibid.*, M.16, 127, 12 July 1367, registration of condemnation of man for theft, ' quod per gulam suspendatur ita taliter quod penitus moriatur '.

36 AN. Imola, Della Volpe, 27 February 1388.

37 Pedrino, II, 1478.

38 *Statuta Faventiae*, 47.

39 *Statuti di Imola*, 51.

40 E.g. Matteo di Pietro gives kiss of peace to Marco de Mari, ' de quodam vulnere illato per dictum Marchum in cossa sinistra dicti Methei cum una daga ' ; AN. Ravenna, M.28, 99r, 22 September 1378. Michele from Casanigo and Como Pietro make ' pactum perpetuum finis, remissionis atque concordiae ' under pain of £B.25 for non-observance, AN. Faenza, G. Casali, 16 August 1386.

41 AN. Imola, 31 July 1389. Yet according to *Statuti di Imola*, 69–72, boundary disputes and the division of property, were supposed to be settled by two *ingrossatores*, one a judge, one a notary, working two days a week in the Palazzo Nuovo.

42 AN. Imola, Della Volpe, 28 April 1387.

43 *Statuti di Imola*, 59–67.

44 *Statuta Faventiae*, 96. During the rule of Galeotto Manfredi this was enlarged to all cases concerned with sums below £B.10 ; *Accessiones Faventiae*, 792.

45 As in the trial of Pietro Giovanni Zervaxi by Obizzo and Aldrovandino da Polenta in 1396 ; AN. Ravenna, M.32, 82, 23 December 1396.

46 Sacchetti, *Novelle*, CCII.

47 Jones, *Malatesta*, II, 731.

48 Pedrino, II, 454, 466.

49 *Statuti di Imola*, 43–4 ; AN. Imola, Della Volpe, 28 April 1378.

50 *Statuti di Forlì*, 74. Deposit with the friars was customary in all Italy ; H. E. Bell, 'Italian Archives', *Studies presented to Hilary Jenkinson*, London, 1957.

51 In Ravenna one finds Nanne Guelfo, ' Orator dignus ac secretarius Magnifici Oppizonis de Polenta ', AS. Ravenna, S. Giovanni Evangelists, 15 June 1427.

52 *Statuti di Imola*, 21 ; *Statuta Faventiae*, 67 ; *Statuto di Forlì*, 10–16.

53 Sacchetti, *Novelle*, CCXXII.

54 Imola, Archivio Sassatelli, III, 23 October 1334 ; ' Congregatis, Maxio de Ghismadis, Vicario Nobilis viri Domini Lippis de Allidoxis honorabilis Capitaneus civitatis Imole et antianis dicte civitatis super logia palatii novi dicti communis ad sonum campane more solito, providerunt, deliberaverunt et firmaverunt et Alberico dela Bordella, Massario Communis Imole licentiam concesserunt ut det, consolvat infrascriptis nuntiis communis quod iverunt pro factis Communis infrascriptas quantitates pecuniae . . .' follows the names of three men to be paid four shillings each. The document is sealed twice. The statutes provided that all extraordinary payments of the town should be proposed by the captain and approved by a two-thirds majority of the *anziani*, and subsequently ratified either in the Great Council, or should the captain prefer it, in the Council of the twenty-four *savii* (cit. I, XX). This, however, did not apply to the payments of *nuncios* and spies up to a pound.

55 G. Santini, 'I dazii egidiani in Forlì nel 1364', *AMR*, 4, IV, 1914.

56 BC. Faenza, B.18a, 1421, for certificate for quittance of *gabelle* of dowry.

57 Cristoforo di Antonio of Imola, ' conductor dacci bestiarum et becherie, who possessed the licence to give strangers permission to take wood in the woods of the commune of Imola ', gives a licence to some men of Solarolo and their families, to *silvizare* in the said woods. He also allows them to give licences to do the same to any men of Solarolo. This in return for £B.20 ; AN. Imola, L. Monte, 19 January 1460. Isabella da Polenta leased for two years the ' passus Primarii ' with its *hospitio* or refuge, and boats, to Lorenzo di Antonio and his associates. In addition to his work at the ferry, he was allowed to pasture thirty head of cattle in the neighbourhood. This in return for a payment of £R.355 ; AS. Ravenna, M.40, 67, 105, 6 August 1432.

58 *Gabelles* of *macinatura* and *Vino al minuto* sold to two men for £B.6,300 ; AN. Imola, Della Volpe, 3 March 1388.

59 As in Forlì, where two groups of citizens offer £B.19,500 and £B.20,000 respectively ; Pedrino, I, III.

60 Tonini, *Le imposte*, 8–19, and see Bagli, ' Bandi malatestiani ', 87–9, for Roberto Malatesti's new ' esteem ' of 1432. A new ' esteem ' was drawn up in Imola in 1311, AC. Imola, VI, 35, February 1311. The rules for the construction of the ' esteem ' in Faenza follow the same pattern ; *Statuta Faventiae*, Book VIII. Forlì in 1417, had ' una colta de suoldi VI per lira et suoldi X per cavo d' estimo ' ; Pedrino, I, 32.

61 AC. Imola (through Ferri Mss), VIII, 2, 27 May 1301.

62 *Statuto di Forlì*, 45, provided that nothing was to be proposed in the councils unless it had first been examined by the captain or *podestà*. In Rimini in 1398, the ' Consilium et consiliarii ' were ' electi per Mag. et potentem dm. Carolum . . . et per consiliaros ad hoc deputatos ' ; Tonini, *Storia*, IV, 2, 422. The very change of name — from General Council, to Council of the 400, suggests that the same process had taken place in Forlì by 1321 ; *Documenti . . . Venezia e Ravenna*, 30. In Imola by 1424, the General Council had similarly been limited ; there were only 192 present in March of that year ; BC. Imola, Galli Mss. citing Arch. Vat. Arm. 34, N8, f. 1, 16 March 1424. See too, Jones, *Malatesta*, II, 744–8.

63 BC. Ravenna, *Statuti polentani*, 7–8.

64 *Statuti di Imola*, 30–1.

65 Mittarelli, 535.

66 *Statuti di Ravenna*, 1–3.

67 *Ibid.*, 34, 234. AN. Ravenna, M.15, 132r, 1 September 1366 ; ' in guaita S. Agate maioris. Congregatis hominibus de guaita S. Agate maioris ex parte d. Johannis de Tenisiis de Parma vicarii in civitate Ravenna pro D. Guidone de Polenta, in ecclesia S. Agate maioris ex causa eligendi duos maiores in dicta guaita ', they elect two men for six months. The *Statuti polentani*, 23 (BC. Ravenna) ' De maioribus Gaiaytarii elegendis ' declared that two were to be elected from each *guaita* in March.

68 AN. Imola, L. Monte, 26 June 1447.

69 *Statuto di Forlì*, 59–60.

70 *Statuta Faventiae*, 69.

71 ' uno omo per casa per tutti la sua forza ' ; *Chron. mal.*, 39. Dr. Jones has observed that this was merely a temporary expedient ; *Malatesta*, II, 736.

72 Azzurini, 238.

73 Waley, ' Papal armies ', 20 ; G. Villani, VIII, 76.

74 There are large numbers of contracts of *condotte*, between the Venetian government and Romagnols in June and July 1356, and in June 1378 in the AN. Ravenna.

75 AN. Ravenna, M.12, T.11, 74r, 25 April 1362 ; *ibid.*, M.16, 128r, 15 June 1367.

76 Giovanni Fiorentino, *Il pecorone*, Milan, 1804, I, 140–54.

77 AN. Imola, A. Monte, 11 July 1407 ; ' lo Francesco de Borniolo da Balcone da Dozza spontaneamente prometto al magnifico signor mio messer Ludovico degli aliduxi di Imola e suo contado et di star et habitar personalmente e marcho mio figliolo con tutta la mia famiglia in la roccha di sotto del Castello di Dozza de di e di notte e quella bene e diligentemente guardare e salvare . . . e none uscire se marcho mio figliuolo predetto non remane dentro della fortezza '. He promised not to give or sell

the castle without licence of the *signore*, and to keep it well furnished with six months provision of wine, wood, bread, flesh, salt, oil, and vegetables.

78 BC. Imola, XI, 11 September 1408.

79 *Ibid.*, X, 49, 21 December 1382.

80 *I.e.*, ' mero et misto imperio in fare, et fare fare raxone in loro tireno et fonza '. In return they promised ' se farne raccomandadi del Majestico et Possente Signore Misser Ludovico deli Alidoxii, et promettere essere soi leali servidori, tenere i soi amixi per amixi, e i inimixi per inimixi, e fare paxe e guerra segondo che sera de piaxere e commendamento al ditto signore et di obedire suo commendamento ' ; BC. Imola, Ferri Mss. II, 25 May 1411.

81 AC. Imola, IV, 113–40, 6–12 June 1292.

82 BC. Faenza, Valgimigli Mss, VIII, 168–9, 8 September 1376.

83 Tonini, III, 33, 511–15. For later extent of the *contado* (and for the *contadi* of all the communes) ; Theiner, II, 490–516. For its fate in the fifteenth century ; Sanudo, V, 604–9.

84 G. Gasperoni, ' Il comune di Savignano ', *AMR*, 3, XXVI, 1908, 245–84. See the dispute between the men of Penna and Maciano on the payment of their vicar in 1413 ; Tonini, IV/2, 94–5.

85 Jones, *Malatesta*, II, 742–3, analyses the systems of *contado* rule in the dependent territories of the Malatesti in Romagna and elsewhere. See also ibid, 784 n.4 for list of *castra* that were communes.

86 Pedrino, II, 427 ; *Chron. Mal.*, 48.

87 AN. Ravenna, M.1, 1 May 1304.

88 BC. Faenza, Busta 16, 7 March 1389.

89 AS. Ravenna, Classe, Volume 30, 41, 4 August 1416, shows Ser Iacopo Paganini, the *locumtenens* of Baldassare degli Ubaldini, ' capitaneus terre seu civitatis Forumpopoli pro Magnifico et potente domino Zeorgio de Ordelaffi vicario Forolivii '.

90 See C. Mor, ' Predappio e la genesi dei suoi statuti ', *Bolletino Storico Italiano*, 58.

91 M. Fuzzi, *L' ultimo periodo degli Ordelaffi in Forlì*, Forlì, 1937, 59 citing Cronaca Albertina, 476.

92 AN. Ravenna, M.2, 113r, 30 March 1353.

93 *Ibid.*, M.28, 87–8, ' in broilo domini Guidonis de Polenta ', 25 July 1378 ; an *instrumentum treuge* between the Todeschi and the Tomasini, both from the *villa* of Vigo. *Ibid.*, M.VI, 131v–132r, 30 May 1358 ; the Lord Bernardino makes peace in his orchard between two families of Melsa. *Ibid.*, M.33, 117 f., ' in camera viridi situ apud salam novam palacii Dominorum de Polenta ', 5 March 1405, peace made between, on the one hand, the Accari and Santi, and on the other the Pasolino of Granarola (presumably some forebear of the historian), by the Lady Alidosia, wife of Obizzo da Polenta.

94 AS. Ravenna, S. Vitale, Vol. 622, 12, 9 January 1429 ; in the piazza of Russi, Obizzo da Polenta makes peace between two families.

95 Fantuzzi, III, 103.

96 As did Casaselvatica, Villa Lombardia, Sabloneria, Filio, Longastrino, Fossapudolo, Umana, and Sant' Adalberto ; AN. Ravenna, M.II, I, 141 f., 5–9 July 1362.

97 *Statuta Faventiae*, 72–3 ; A. Metelli, *Storia di Brisighella e della valle di Amone*, Faenza, 1869, I, 305.

98 G. Ballardini, ' La costituzione della contea di Brisighella e di Val d' Amone', *Valdilamone*, VII, 1927, prints the Bull.

99 BC. Faenza, *Statuta Vallis Homonis*, Bk. 1, I-VII, 3–10.

100 BC. Faenza, ' *Memorie e documenti della famiglia Paganelli* ', 19, transcribes a record of a General Council of 1477, in which were present, ' necnon dd. Gubernatoribus vallis Hamonis in sufficienti numero videlicet decem ex duodecim '. In 1488, the Florentine ambassador described them as ' i dodici della valle che sono i primi huomini ' ; A. Missiroli, *Astorgio III Manfredi*, Bologna, 1912, 61.

101 The ' quattuor dd. castri Russi, Solaroli, Granaroli, et Orioli, representantibus eorum comunis et regiminis ' appear in the general council of 1477, mentioned in the preceding note. They are referred to in the sixteenth century statutes ; BC. Faenza, *Magnificae civitatis Faventiae Ordinamenta*, Bk. 1, XVI. ' unus praetor castri Russi, unus vicarius castri Aureoli, unus vicarius castri Solaroli, unus vicarius Granaroli '. In fact, the office of ' commisarius Solaroli ' already existed in 1412 ; Azzurini, 90–1.

102 L. Baldisseri, ' L' episcopato imolese nel secolo XII ', *Rivista storica di Scienze Teologiche*, 1912 ; A. Rustici, ' Il castello di San Cassiano di Imola ', *La Romagna*, 1915 ; G. Fasoli, ' I conti e il comitato di Imola ', *AMR*, 1943–5, 120 f. ; G. de Vergottini, ' Il papato e la comitatinanza nello stato della Chiesa (sec. XIII–XV)', *AMR*, n.s.3, 1952–3, 150f. S. Alvisi, *Il comune di Imola nel secolo XII*, Bologna 1909, is highly imaginative.

103 The commune is first recorded, 6 September 1298, Tarlazzi, II, 134.

104 AC. Imola, VI, 25, 29 (through Ferri Mss).

105 *Ibid.*, VI, 22 June 1310.

106 *Ibid.*, VII, 19, 20.

107 ACap. Imola, VII, 28, 3 September 1317, ' in domo comunis comitatus Imole ' ; AC. Imola (through Ferri Mss), M.VIII, 28, 1375, ' in domibus et palatio dicti Comitatus Imole '.

108 Theiner, II, 527.

109 Theiner, I, 558, ' Introitus Comitatus Imole '.

110 Biblioteca del Senato del Regno, *Statuta Comitatus Imole*, Bk. IV, ' De legationibus comitatus ' — from which it appears that there had previously been five legations. The legation of Serra was now incorporated with Monte Mauro.

111 BC. Imola, Mss. 960, ' Atto di sottomissione del contado di Imola al comune di Bologna ', 7 April 1376. The communes asked the following conditions : (i) that their statutes should still continue in force ; (ii) that no *gabelles* should be imposed ; (iii) that they should pay taxes according to the ' esteems ' of the *contado*. This mss. is a transcript of AS. Bologna, Diritti del Comune di Bologna dal 1300 al 1400, rog. di Morandino da Croara.

112 A. Palmieri, ' Gli antichi vicariati dell' Apennino bolognese e la costituzione amministrative moderna ', *AMR*, 3, XX, 1902, 348, 376.

113 G. Cortini, *Brevi notizie storiche sul comune di Casalfiumanese*, Imola, 1926, II.

114 AC. Imola, XI, 59–61 ; Azzurini, 93.

115 BC. Imola, Mss. 1015, 14 December 1407.

116 For Fontanalice, AN. Imola, Ricci, 22 March 1457. The vicariate of Castel del Rio was presumably created after the fall of the Alidosi from *signoria*. It was a means by which the new *signorie* held down the still surviving branch of the family. There was a Michele da Battaglini, ' Capitaneus Masse Alidosiorum, Castri Rivi, Piancaldoli, Tirli, Castiglionelli et Montis pro illustri et excelso domino, domino Comite Hieronymo vicecomite de Riario ' in 1481 ; AN. Imola, R. di Piero Massucci, 27 January 1481.

117 In 1415, Mongiardino is correcting its ' esteem,' ' pro collectis dicto comitatu impositis per parliamentum generalem dicti comitatus ' ; AN. Imola, R. di Paolo Marco, 27 April 1415. The BC. Imola preserves the statutes of the *contado* of 1347, translated into Italian in 1461.

118 AN. Imola, Zanelli, 30 December 1418, 11 April 1428, 21 March 1429, 6 July 1432, 20 February 1424 : 27 August 1442 ; *Ibid.*, Ricci, 16 December 1451, 26 July 1461, — all record meetings of the vicariates. For *gabelles* see *ibid.*, Zanelli, 15 January 1465 ; and BC. Imola, Galli Mss. citing ' Lettere di Castelli Soggetti,' 26 February 1432.

119 See E. Fiumi, ' Sui rapporti economici tra città e contado nell' età comunale ', *ASI*, 1956, 18–68.

120 See, for instance, S. Gaddoni, ' L' estimo di bubano del Sec. XIV ', *AMR*, 4, II, 1911, 321f.

121 Tonini, *Storia*, IV/2, 347–50, 372–5.

122 AC. Imola, XI, 145, 1 October 1432.

123 AN. Imola, Zanelli, 17 June 1453, 20 April 1459.

CHAPTER IX

1 G. Giulini, *Memorie spettanti alla storia di Milano*, Milan, 1854–7, VII, 278.

2 I. Döllinger, *Beiträge zur Sektengeschichte des Mittelalters*, Munich, 1890, I, 53. For what follows, see, in general, G. Volpe, *Movimenti religiosi e sette ereticali nella società medievale italiana*, Florence, 2nd ed., 1961, especially 91–2, and E. Dupré-Theseider, *Introduzione alle eresie medievali*, Bologna, 1953.

3 *Un Traité néo-manichéen du XIII*[e] *siècle : le Liber de Duobus Principiis*, ed. A. Dondaine, Rome, 1939, 70.

4 *Acta Pontificum Romanorum Inedita*, ed. J. von Pflugk-Harttung, Graz, 1958, III, 317–18 ; Tonini, *Storia*, II, 589.

5 Innocent III, *Opera Omnia* (Volumes 214–17 of Patrologia Latina), II, 319–20.

6 Tonini, *Storia*, III, 442 ; *Epist. Saec. XIII*, I, 259.

7 L. A. Muratori, *Antiquitates Italicae Medii Aevii*, Milan, 1741, V, 131 ; G. Mussoni, ' I patarini in Rimini ', *La Romagna*, II, 1905, 400–11.

8 Döllinger, II, 273–9. For recent studies of Catharist belief see A. Borst, *Die Katharer*, Stuttgart, 1953, and F. Niel, *Albigeois et Cathares*, Paris, 1959.

9 Innocent III, *Opera Omnia*, II, 819–20, 1042–3, 1057.

10 Salimbene, 255–94.

11 H. Lea, *A History of the Inquisition of the Middle Ages*, London, 1888, III, 107–9.

12 Muratori, *Antiquitates*, VI, 471–2 ; Griffoni, 15 ; Pipino, 704 ; *Corp. Chron. Bon.*, II, 151–2 ; see N. Cohn, *The Pursuit of the Millennium*, London, 1957, Chapter vi.

13 *Acta Sanctorum*, ed. J. Bollandus, Paris and Rome, 1863–84, *Aprilis*, III (29 April), 692–703 ; J. Guiraud, *Histoire de l'Inquisition au Moyen Age*, Paris, 1938, II, 503–4.

14 *Acta Sanctorum*, *Iunii*, III (13 June), 199–229. I accept the assurance of the *Catholic Encyclopaedia* that the miracle of the horse took place, not in Bruges, as Wadding has it, nor in Forlì, as the *Acta* claim, but in Rimini.

15 G. Fussenberger, ' De manipulo documentorum ad usum inquisitoris haereticae pravitatis in Romandiola : Saec. XIII ', *AFH*, XLIV, 1951, 71–86 ; P. Mariano d' Alatri, *L' inquisizione francescana nell' Italia centrale nel secolo XIII*, Rome, 1954, 55–7 ; ' Tractatus de Hereticis Zanchini Ugolini ' in *Tractatus Illustrium Iurisconsultorum de Iudiciis Criminalibus S. Inquisitionis*, XI, pt. II. Venice, 1584, 234–71 ; Lea, II, 234, 242 ; III, 307 ; A. Dondaine, ' Le Manuel de l' inquisiteur ', *Archivium Fratrum Predicatorum*, XVII, 1947, 124.

16 S. Gaddoni, ' Documenta ad historiam trium ordinum S. Francisci in Urbe Imolensi ', *AFH*, V, 1912, 63.

17 See L. Fiumi, *Eretici e ribelli nell' Umbria : studio storico di un decennio, 1320–1330* (reprinted from *Bolletino della R. Deputazione per Umbria*), 1916 ; E. Dupré-Theseider, ' L' eresia a Bologna nei tempi di Dante ', *Studi storichi in onore di G. Volpe*, Florence, 1958, 381–441 (based largely on documents registered in L. Aldrovandini, ' Acta Sancti Officii Bononiae ab anno 1291 asque ad annum 1309 ', *AMR*, 3, XIV, 1896, 225–300.)

18 See Volpe, 151–2.

19 A.C. Imola, X, 22, 3 March 1371.

20 *Rationes Decimarum Italiae nei secoli XIII e XIV : Aemilia*, ed. A. Mercati, E. Nasalli-Rocca, and P. Sella, Vatican, 1933, 197–221.

21 Cantinelli, 56.

22 Tolosano, 108.

23 *Rationes Decimarum*, 210, 64, 91, 105, 83, 104, 171, 178, 184, 191 ; C. Rivalta, ' La chiesa della commenda di Faenza e la sede di Cavalieri Gerosolimitani ', *AME* III, 1937–8, 218 ff. Presumably Templar property passed to the Hospital after 1310. By the sixteenth century the Great Priory of the Hospitallers at Venice included ' legations ' at Ravenna, Faenza, and Forlì, with *commanderie* at Rimini, Cesena, and Imola : *Cartulaire général de l'ordre des Hospitaliers de S. Jean de Jérusalem*, ed. J. Delaville de la Roux, Paris, 1894–1906, I, CXX-CXXXIV ; II, 473, IV, 13.

24 Rossi, 520–3 ; *Chron. Parm.*, 113.

25 See above, page 61.

26 Fantuzzi, III, 387.

27 *Chron. Mal.*, 14 ; Battagli, 50–1 refers to the enterprise (on which see A. Attiya, *The Crusade in the Later Middle Ages*, London, 1938, 290–5) without mentioning any Romagnol participation.

28 BC. Imola, Galli Mss. citing M.V, 32, 9 March 1372.

29 L. Frati, ' Tradizioni storiche del Purgatorio di S. Patrizio ', *GSLI*, LXIII, 1914, 174–5.

30 *Statuta Faventiae*, 294 n.3.

31 AS. Ravenna, Classe V, 16, 7–8, 1 February 1345 ; AN. Ravenna, M.34, 29, 18 August 1408.

32 *Ibid.*, P.3, 49, 4 January 1327 ; AS. Ravenna, Classe, Busta 326, n.8, 43, 12 February 1388.

33 *Acta Sanctorum, Augustii*, V, 845–7.

34 G. Garampi, *Memorie ecclesiastiche appartenenti all' istoria della B. Chiara di Rimini*, Rome, 1755. Despite the enthusiasm of Garampi and C. Tonini, *La coltura*, 48, I cannot throw off the suspicion that the manuscript life of Chiara is a forgery.

35 Giovanni Fiorentino, *Il pecorone*, Milan, 1804.

36 Azzurini, 196 ; F. Lanzoni, ' La cronaca del convento di Sant' Andrea in Faenza ', *Archivio Muratoriano*, I (RIS), 1904, 511–48 ; *ibid.*, ' I conventi domenicani in Romagna ' in *Il VII centenario di S. Domenico*, Rome, 1921, 350.

37 F. Lanzoni, *I primordi dell' ordine francescano in Faenza*, Faenza, 1910 ; *ibid.*, ' Le antiche carte del convento di S. Chiara in Faenza ', *AFH*, V, 1912, 216–76, 482–93 ; S. Gaddoni, *I frati minori in Imola*, Florence, 1911, and ' Documenta ad historiam trium ordinum S. Francisci in Urbe Imolensi ', *AFH*, V, 1912, 52–73, 544–72, 710–26 ; VI, 1913, 291–321 ; VII, 1914, 683–705 ; VIII, 1915, 23–55, 482–527 ; L. Wadding, *Annales Minorum*, Rome, 1731–1886, III, 219 ; IV, 45, 178.

38 *Statuta Faventiae*, 345, n.1.

39 AN. Imola, A. Monte, 6 February 1400.

40 As at Sant' Ambrogio della Massa (in Castel del Rio) ; *ibid.*, A. Monte, 11 March 1456. The right in this passage was exercised as early as the 12th century : *Chart. Imol.*, I, 533. For episcopal confirmation of the right of the parishioners at Castel Pagano : AN. Imola, A. Monte, 2 December 1439.

41 As with the churches in the upper Senio valley : Burchi, 52–67 *passim*, and in the Imolese at, *e.g.*, Montebattaglia ; AN. Imola, Ricci, 1 October 1458 ; at Santa Maria di Osta, *ibid.*, 29 June 1453 ; at San Pietro di Valsalva, *ibid.*, 3 December 1460 ; at S. Martino in Viduino, *ibid.*, Rogiti di Ludovico Guasconi, 1 June 1444 ; at S. Martino in Gallisterna, *ibid.*, 27 May 1446. Two notarial deeds were formally made out ; the first for the election itself ; the second when the priest was presented to the bishop or his vicar. Thus in 1444, Cristoforo da Riolo appeared before the Vicar of the Bishop, declaring that he had been entrusted by the other men of the village with the presentation of Oderic of Frankfort ' de partibus Alemanie ' whom they had elected as parish priest of S. Andrea di Ossano in Laderchio. His election was confirmed : *ibid.*, Guasconi, 1 June 1444.

42 *Ibid.*, Zanelli, 27 August 1442. There are similar financial gifts to the church at Tossignano, *ibid.*, Zanelli, 4 September 1431, and at Ortodonico, *ibid.*, A. Monte, 7 October 1453. At Linaro in Sarsina the commune lent its rector £B.215 to help in the repair of the church, Burchi, 104.

43 AN. Imola, L. Monte, 3 January 1474.

44 *Ibid.*, Zanelli, 13 April 1449.

45 See above, pages 30–1.

46 AS. Ravenna, S. Vitale, Vol. 619, 93–4, 26 November 1358.

47 AN. Imola, Zanelli, 3 November 1456; 29 May 1461; on Don Valeriano, see A. Campana, 'Antico epitafio di Benvenuto da Imola', *SR*, VI, 1955, 344–8.

48 AN. Imola, Ricci, 12 September 1461.

49 *Ibid.*, Della Volpe, 7 December 1373.

50 *Ibid.*, Della Volpe, 24 September 1387; Broccardi, 24 September 1422; Capucci, 10 October 1446.

51 See on this controversy, *AFH*, III, 1910, 306.

52 Cantinelli, 42, who was a contemporary. See, too, F. Lanzoni, 'Una vita del Beato Novellone Faentino', *AFH*, VI, 1913, 623–53.

53 F. Lanzoni, 'L' antico archivio di S. Francesco di Faenza', *AFH*, XX, 1927, 589–95.

54 F. Lanzoni, 'Cose francescane faentine', *AFH*, XIV, 1921, 435–41; 'Una laude in onore di S. Emiliano' (for *battuti* of S. Maria della Grazie), Azzurini, 392–5.

55 AN. Imola, A. Monte, 11 August 1449.

56 *Ibid.*, 1 December 1426, 3 February 1423. The hospital of the Devout stood in fact by the bridge of the Santerno, and in the middle of the fourteenth century was endowed with lands and with an inn in the *cappella* S. Paolo, which were granted out on lease by the society; *ibid.*, A. Bolgarelli, 20 August 1352, 8 September 1353, 20 September 1353.

57 See Tonini, *Storia*, IV/1, 451–63, for the eighteen hospitals noted in the Riminese.

58 Among the hospitals noted in the Imolese are that of San Carlo e San Domenico, outside the Porta Spavuglia; Zaccaria, 143; the Ospedale dei Devoti by the Santerno, and the Hospital of Penitence. In 1413, the rectors of the Hospital of San Bernardo sold its mobile goods because its walls were falling down; AN. Imola, A. del Monte, 1 February 1413. In the Ravennate, stood the Hospital of Mercy of Ravenna 'for the succour of the poor'; AS. Ravenna, *Ospedale della Misericordia*, CXIX, i, n.4, 12 September 1313. At Piratello was the Hospital of San Lazzaro; AN. Imola, Della Volpe, 10 March 1390. The hospital of Santa Maria of Russi was supervised by the village of Russi; AN. Ravenna, M.8, 40, 31 March 1360.

59 See, for instance, *Registri dei cardinali Ugolino d' Ostia e Ottaviano degli Ubaldini*, ed. G. Levi, Rome, 1890, 77–81; Guiraud, II, 387–8; A. Torre, 'Le controversie fra l' arcivescovo di Ravenna e Rimini nel sec. XIII', *SR*, III, 1951, 333–55; G. Rossini, 'Un antica controversia per il possesso di Lugo e di S. Potito', *SR*, IV, 1953, 103–17.

60 *Statuta Faventiae*, 34, 175.

61 *Ibid.*, 155, 276.

62 *Ibid.*, 285–6.

63 Cantinelli, 56.

64 *Liber Censuum*, II, 105.

65 Tonini, *Storia*, IV, 404, yet local election seems to have continued in Ravenna. At Faenza in 1465, Federigo Manfredi, the son of Astorgio II, was unanimously elected Bishop by the chapter but the election was quashed at Rome, perhaps because this was an infringement of papal rights, perhaps because he was only twenty-two years old at the time. He was in fact elected again in 1472; Azzurini, 55–6. Normally however, election seems to have gone by petition; see Azzurini, 55.

66 A. Manzoni, *Episcoporum Corneliensium sive Imolensium Historia*, Faenza, 1719, 250–1, 234; A. Zaccaria, *Series Episcoporum Forocorneliensium*, Imola, 1820, 124–6. Leale, illegitimate son of Malatesta Guastafamiglia, after serving as Bishop of Pesaro (1370–4), was translated to Rimini (1374–1400). Rinaldo da Polenta was elected, though not consecrated, as archbishop of Ravenna in September 1321. Scarpetta, the natural son of Francesco II Ordelaffi, was bishop of Forlì in 1391. That Bishop Riccardo of Faenza (f. 1339) was the son of Alberghetto Manfredi is a myth; cf. Ughelli, *Favent. Epsicopus*, with Valgimigli, VII, 272. A natural son of Francesco Manfredi, however, was bishop of Trivento in the Regno; Azzurini, 129, n.5.

67 See, for instance, above, page 60.

68 BC. Imola, *Primo estratto delle scritture delle monache di San Domenico d' Imola* (in Ferri Mss.), 563. The Religious ladies of the Sisters of the Virgin of Imola, eleven in all in 30 July 1357, were far less aristocratic in composition; Ferri, *Estratti*, 272. In Ravenna, the Chapter of the Sisters of Santa Chiara of Ravenna had a pronounced noble element; in 1359 its members included Iacopa da Rasponi, Beatrice de' Mainardi, Lucia da Bertinoro, Chiara da Polenta, Rengarda and Polentesa da Polenta, Chiara da Balbi and Traversaria da Bertinoro. The same element dominated in 1389; AN. Ravenna, M.7, II, 74r; 20 August 1350; P.7, 8, 30 November 1358.

69 Zaccaria, 141–3; Manzoni, 225–6.

70 Zaccaria, 143; AC. Imola, IX, 8, for concessions of lands in Bagnara and Zagonara to Roberto.

71 Manzoni, 247; see Chapter VI, n. 62.

CONCLUSION

1 F. Petrarch, *Epistolae Seniles*, XIV, 1, printed as a separate treatise: 'De Rep. Opt. Administranda Liber', in *Opera Omnia*, Basle, 1581, 372–86.

2 Giulini, VII, 278–81.

APPENDIX I

1 C. Diehl, *Études sur l'administration byzantine dans l'Exarchat de Ravenne*, Paris, 1888, 52.

2 G. Comelli, 'Dei confini naturali e politici della Romagna', *AMR*, 3, XXVI, 1908, 30–44.

3 Biondo da Forlì, *Roma ristaurata*, 132.

4 Pius II, *Commentaries, Books II and III*, translated F. Cragg, Smith College Studies in History, XXV, 1939–40, 175.

5 Alberti, 266.

6 P. Pasolini, *I tyranni di Romagna e i papi nel medioevo*, Imola, 1888, 2–3.

7 G. Merlini, 'Unità regionale dell' Emilia e Romagna', *RGI*, 1946, 60–9.

8 *E.g.*, A. Vesi, *Ragionamenti intorno ai veri confini della Romagna*,

Faenza, 1841 ; T. Casini, ' Toscana e Romagna ', *Scritti danteschi*, Città di Castello, 1913, 65.

9 *Statuto del secolo XIII*, 15.

10 Salimbene, 509.

11 Tarlazzi, I, 419. See, too, G. Ermini, ' I rettori provinciali dello stato della chiesa ', *RSDI*, IV, 1931, 38–9.

12 Against it one could point out that in his commentary on *Purgatorio*, XIV, Benvenuto (III, 387) clearly assumed that Dante was describing Romagna. Yet, Jacopo della Lana, *Commento*, Bologna, 1866, II, 161, seems to be surprised at this : ' e nota ch' elli include infra questi termini Bologna '.

13 F. Torraca ' Il dialetto romagnolo e il bolognese nel " De Vulgari Eloquentia " ', *AMR*, 4, XVII, 1927, 346–57.

14 To my ear. F. Schurr, ' La posizione storica del Romagnolo fra i dialetti contermini ', *Revue de Linguistique Romaine*, IX, 1933, 203–28, claims a basic unity of dialects between the Panaro and Foglia.

15 See article ' Romagna ' in *Enciclopedia Italiana*.

16 Liber Censuum, I, 441, 443 ; P. Amaducci, ' Notizie storiche ', 248–9 ; Waley, *The Papal State*, 18.

17 L. Tonini, *Storia*, III, 238.

18 See L. Bertarelli, *Marche*, Milan, 1937, 91, for boundaries of Montefeltro.

19 P. Franciosi, ' Il Montefeltro, sotto l' aspetto geografico, etnico, storico, devesi considerare come facente parte del territorio di Romagna ', *AMR*, 4, XVI, 1926, 1–19.

20 P. Fabre, ' Massa d' Arno, Massa di Bagno, Massa Trabaria ', *ASR*, XVIII, 1894, 5–17 ; T. Codignola, ' Ricerche storico-giuridiche sulla Massa Trabaria nel XIII secolo ', *ASI*, 1939–40.

APPENDIX II

1 Theiner, II, 527–39.

2 *Ibid.*, 516–27.

3 *Ibid.*, 490–516.

4 K. Beloch, *Bevölkerungsgeschichte Italiens*, Berlin, 1939–40, II, 84–90.

5 L. Gambi, ' Il censimento del cardinale Anglic in Romagna nell' anno 1371 ', *RGI*, 1947, 221–49.

6 ' Ce coefficient-standard, beaucoup ont cru le trouver ' ; R. Mols, *Introduction à la démographie historique des villes d'Europe*, Louvain, 1955, II, 100–130. Mols, while underlining the difficulties it presents, approves its use. How to decide between Beloch (who follows, knowingly or unknowingly, Fantuzzi, V, VIII) and Gambi on this point? Palmieri, working from statistics in the Bolognese *montagna*, confined himself to asserting that there were few families with more than nine mouths and many with only three or four : A. Palmieri, *La montagna bolognese*, chapter called Demografia, 236–42. G. Salvioni, ' La popolazione di Bologna nel secolo XVII ', *AMR*, 3, VII, 1890, in a brief analysis of Anglic's description of Bologna assigned four souls to each family.

7 Giving a mean density of thirty souls per km². In this century

with a population of *circa* 1,438,860, the density is 163 per km².

8 This rate is found in Tuscany in 1240; P. Santini, *Documenti dell' antica costituzione del comune di Firenze*, Florence, 1895, 473; Waley, *Papal State*, 254.

9 AC. Imola, M.VI, 32, Racio Talearum comitatus Imole Sex Annorum:

'tangit pro quolibet fumante sol. XVIII den II et sexta parte alterius.

Et sic in anno pro quolibet fumante lib. II sol. XVII den. VI et med.'

The same document states that there were three 'terms' each year. Thus terminal payments of 19/2 and sixth of penny on each *fumante* yielded £2 17 6½. The author of the document enumerated a total of 667¾ *fumantes* for the *contado*. This should have yielded approximately £1,921 3 5¼. (£2 17 6½ cannot be multiplied by ¾ to yield an exact monetary equivalent) — that is to say, six to six and half times more than in 1371.

10 Gambi, 228. There is no question of these being different villages with the same names.

11 Theiner, II, 354. There are also some mistakes in arithmetic. Thus Castrocaro and its *contado* were allotted 204 *fumantes* in all. For this at a rate of twenty-six pennies they were assessed justly enough at a *fumanteria* of £22 2 –. Yet the *Descriptio* enumerates previously 214 *focularia* thus:

Castrum Castrocarii	120
Villa Ceule	24
Averni et Golforis	20
Converselli et Moroni	17
Carpeneti, Bagnoli and Risalsi	16
Montecli et Cayboris	10
Valliselle	7
	214

I have not checked all the arithmetic in the *Descriptio* but have noticed in passing three other errors: in a similar way, Civitella was assessed at 78 instead of 79, Meldola at 199 instead of 200, and the Archbishop of Ravenna's properties at 222 instead of 212 *fumantes*. *Ibid.*, 501–2, 511, 500.

12 G. Villani, IX, 80. On which see H. Lucas, 'The great European famine of 1315, 1316 and 1317', *Speculum*, 1930, 343–77.

13 *Ann. Caes.*, 'accidit stupenda mortalitas, tam immensa per totum fere mundum, sed in provincia Romandiole acerbior . . .'. It began in 1318; by May 1319, it was so severe that many in Romagna were buried without the rites of the Church.

14 *Chron. Este.*, 110; and see for Florence, G. Villani, XI, 114.

15 *Chron. Mal.*, 17.

16 G. Villani, XIII, 84; Battagli, 54, compares it to the flood ('et pro dei gratia ego evasi'); *Corp. Chron. Bon.*, II, 854–6, 589–90; *Chron. Este.*, 159–60; Griffoni, 56.

17 *Corp. Chron. Bon.*, III, 143.

18 *Ibid.*, 201.

19 *Annal. Foroliv.*, 66. There are also records of plague in Bologna

in 1312 (*Corp. Chron. Bon.*, II, 324) and 1362 (*ibid.*, III, 151–2 ; Griffoni, 66), although no specific mention of plague in Romagna is made.

20 On which compare Rodolico, ' Note statistiche su la popolazione fiorentina nel XIV secolo ', *ASI* 1902, with the more hopeful findings of G. Pardi, ' Disegno della storia demografica di Firenze ', *ASI*, 1916.

21 Beloch II, 84, citing *Storia d' Imola*, 189–90. Beloch mistakenly believed that the number of *fumantes* has doubled by 1371. He was misled by Anglic's assertion : ' summa omnium focular. dicti districtus 1624 '. Closer examination shows that this figure includes 1,338 *focularia* for the town and 286 for the district. Failing to realise this, Beloch added the 1,338 of the town to the 1,624 of the town and districtus, to reach the illusory total of 2,962. Yet even without this error the number of *focularia* is greater than in 1288.

22 Cerchiari, 171.

23 AS. Bologna, Diritti del Comune, ' Quaternus fumantium comitatus Imole', 1265.

24 AC. Imola, M.VI, 32.

25 BE. Modena, Campori 44, 22 January 1369.

26 AC. Imola, M.VI, 29, 8 June 1305, ' fodrum regale sive fumantarium '.

27 *Annales Camuldalenses*, ed. J. Mittarelli and A. Costadeni, Venice, 1794, IV, 299–300.

28 G. Tomasetti, ' Sale e focatico del comune di Roma nel medio evo ', *ASR*, 1897, 333.

29 L. Fiumi, *I registri del Ducato di Spoleto della serie, ' Introitus et Exitus ' della Camera Apostolica presso l' Archivio segr. Vaticano*, Perugia, 1913, 205, cited in Beloch, 59.

30 C. Calisse, ' Costituzione del Patrimonio di San Pietro in Tuscia nel secolo XIV ', *ASR*, XV, 1892, 30–1.

31 C. Bauer, ' Studi per la storia delle finanze papali durante il pontificato di Sisto IV ', *ASR*, 1927, 334.

32 Beloch, II, 37.

33 *Capitoli del comune*, I, 496–7.

34 Sorbelli, *Comune rurale*, 294. Curiously enough neither Sorbelli nor Palmieri utilised the *Descriptio* in their studies.

35 Theiner, II, 352.

36 Palmieri, *Montagna bolognese*, 381–3 ; see, too, the curious notice in *Corp. Chron. Bon.*, III, 387, — but perhaps *fumanteria* is here a misprint for *formentaria*?

37 Theiner, I, 147.

38 G. Santini, ' Dazii egidiani ', 51–2.

39 *Ibid.*

40 C. Tonini, *Storia*, VI, pt. I, 85. In 1524, the population of Rimini over five years of age was calculated at 5,500 in the town, and 6,500 in the *contado* ; Jones, ' The end of Malatesta Rule ', 235.

APPENDIX III

1 Imola in 1305 paid only £B.200 for two years' *fumanteria*. A receipt of 1307 shows the same payment of £B.100 for that year ; BC.

Imola, Ferri Mss. citing AC. Imola, M.VI, 29, 8 June 1305, M.VI, 28, 23 February 1307.

2 Theiner, I, 588, from which it appears that the tax was sold. For 1371, *ibid.*, II, 490–516.

3 See above, page 211. However, in the fifties it may have been less. In 1354, Bernardino da Polenta paid only £R.154 for *fumanteria* for Ravenna, Cervia, and Polenta; AN. Ravenna, M.3, 84, 6 July 1354. Probably the 1330 level was maintained to at least 1336, when Rimini paid £R.600; Tonini, *Storia*, IV/I, 101.

4 Theiner, II, 532.

5 L. Balduzzi, 'Bagnacavallo e i Manfredi', 189 f.; Tonini, *Storia*, IV/I, 100–1; Theiner, II, 490–516.

6 There are other records of payment of *tallia*. In 1283, Jean d' Eppe imposed £B.2,250 *tallia* upon Imola, for which the commune had to take a loan of £B.2,217 from a Bolognese banker; BC. Imola, Ferri Mss. citing M.III, 158, 30 April 1283. In 1282 it paid 805 gold florins for the support of the papal army at Meldola; Alberghetti, 187. In 1305 it paid the *tallia stipendiorum* of £B.140 for the year; AC. Imola, M.VI, 29. In 1311 it paid £B.425 *pro parte*, and later, £B.53 *pro complementu* of the year's *tallia*; *ibid.*, M.VI, 47, 7 November 1311, M.VII, 48, 29 November 1311. Rimini paid 780 florins in 1310, and conceded £4,294 in the parliament of Bertinoro in 1321; Tonini, *Storia*, IV, pt. I.

7 Theiner, II, 358. This change is found in all the papal states; Peter Partner, *The Papal State under Martin V*, London, 1958, 112–13.

8 This was after the da Polenta had taken their profit. As part owners, the family ratified all treasury leases of salt; *e.g.* AN. Ravenna, 29, 42.

9 'Ex antiqua consuetudine cuius primordii non extitit memoria barateria civitatis Ravenne et districtus vendita est et proventus sive dacium dicte Baraterie fuit preceptum per emptores eiusdem tam sub actuali dominio Ecclesie olim quam ecciam ante et post usque nunc'; AN. Ravenna, M.10, Tom. II, 6, 6 January 1361, and see *ibid.*, M.3, 84, 6 July 1354, for payment. In Imola the 'datia barateria seu bordellarum' had been abolished by the Bolognese administration in 1277; AC. Imola, M.11, 22. It was restored with the government of the church, and deeds of sale by the Marshall of the province for 1323, 1324, 1335, and 1357 still survive. In 1323 it yielded 60 gold florins, in the other years 50; *ibid.*, M.VIII, 14, 25, 87, M.XIII, 37 (through Ferri Mss.). It was more profitable in Faenza where under the Angevin rectorate it yielded 14 gold florins a month; Mittarelli, 546; and in 1326, £B.327 a year; Azzurini, 310. The pious scruples of Tonini persuaded him that the examples of papal sales of *barateria*, which he found in the archives of Rimini, involved only gaming, and not brothels. The horror expressed by Anglic for the tax shows that this is not so; Theiner, II, 529.

10 Alberghetti, 187; AC. Imola (through Ferri Mss.), M.III, 158, 30 April 1283.

11 Fantuzzi, III, 138.

12 *Ibid.*, III, 165.

13 AC. Imola (through Ferri Mss.) VI, 36.

14 *Ibid.*, 21 May 1315, M.VII, 19, 20. For other fines, Theiner, I, 347–76; 587–9.

15 Theiner, II, 516. Pierre, Archbishop of Bourges, estimated the same yield from Romagna in 1371 ; M. Antonelli, ' La dominazione pontificia nel patrimonio negli ultimi venti anni del periodo avignonese ', *ASR*, 31, 1908, Appendix IIIa.

16 See above, page 81.

17 Fantuzzi, V, 391–7.

18 *Ibid.*, 398–408.

19 Theiner, I, 593 ; and see *Annal. Caes.*, 1138, ' male sibi obediverunt provinciales, nisi in Italia ac Fumontana solvendo ' ; sic for ' nec in tallia nec Fumanteria solvendo ' (of Aimeric de Chalus).

20 Jones, ' The Vicariate ', 345–7, considers that this exemption from *tallia* refers only to ordinary payments, and that *tallia* might still be raised as an extraordinary payment through a grant by the provincial parliament. But whatever the position in the Marche whence Dr. Jones draws his evidence, there is no reference to either parliament or *tallage* in Romagna after this date. It is significant that to raise money for the building of the Castle of Faenza, Anglic resorted to a levy of *fumantes* rather than to a *tallage* for which a parliament might be called. Again, in granting vicariates to the Alidosi the church expressly reserved its rights to *fumanteria*, though *tallia* was unmentioned ; Theiner, III, 92–3, 224–9, 229–31.

21 Marchesi, *Vitae*, 457–70.

22 Fantuzzi, III, 352.

23 Theiner, III, 229–31 ; Hieronimo da Forlì, 30.

24 Partner, 198.

25 Partner, 189.

26 Jones, ' The Vicariate ', 347–9.

27 Partner, 117 n.6.

28 AN. Imola, Broccardi, 27 November 1451 ; L. Monte, 15 December 1461.

29 Pedrino, II, 1645.

30 Theiner, II, 490–516.

31 G. Orlandelli, ' Le finanze della comunità di Forlì sotto il vicariato di Baldassare Cossa ', *SR*, VIII, 1956, 183–92.

32 See above, pages 210–12.

33 Tonini, *Storia*, IV/I, 102.

34 Pandolfo Malatesti paid Martino da Faenza, one of his captains in Lombardy, over £50,000 in the years 1411–14 ; Jones, *Malatesta*, II, 689.

35 Fantuzzi, III, 131.

36 P. Broccoli, ' Su le piu antiche monete della zecca faentina ', *La Romagna*, XIV, 1923 ; *idem*, ' Di uno quattrino dei Manfredi da Faenza ', *La Romagna*, IV, 1907 ; *idem*, *Di due altri quattrini di Astorgio Manfredi, signore di Faenza*, Iesi, 1908 ; F. Argani, *Cenni storichi sulla zecca, sulle monete e medaglie de' Manfredi*, Faenza, 1886 ; G. Zanetti, *Delle monete di Faenza*, Bologna, 1777.

37 Battaglini, 220 ; Jones, *Malatesta*, II, 769.

LIST OF WORKS REFERRED TO

I PRINTED SOURCES

(i) *Statutes, and collections of Documents*

Acta Aragonensia. Ed. H. Finke. Berlin and Leipzig, 1908.
Acta et Diplomatica e R. Tabulario Veneto. Ed. A.-S. Minotto. Venice, 1873.
Acta Imperii Inedita Seculi XIII et XIV. Ed. E. Winkelmann. Innsbruck, 1885.
Acta Pontificum Romanorum Inedita. Ed. J. von Pflugk-Harrtung. Graz, 1958.
Ad scriptores rerum italicarum cl. Muratori Accessiones Historicae Faventinae. Ed. J. Mittarelli. Venice, 1771.
Annales Camuldalenses. Ed. J. Mittarelli and A. Costadeni. Venice, 1794.
Appendice ai monumenti ravennati. Ed. A. Tarlazzi. Ravenna, 1869–76.
Benoît XIII; Lettres closes et patentes. Ed. J. Vidal. Paris, 1913–42.
Capitoli del comune di Firenze. Ed. C. Guasti. Florence, 1864–93.
Cartulaire général de l'ordre des Hospitaliers de S. Jean de Jérusalem (1100–1310). Ed. J. Delaville de la Roux. Paris, 1894–1906.
Chartularium Imolense. Ed. S. Gaddoni and G. Zaccherini. Imola, 1910–1913.
Codex Italiae Diplomaticus. Ed. J. Lünig. Frankfort, 1735.
Commissioni di Rinaldo degli Albizzi. Ed. C. Guasti. Florence, 1867.
Constitutiones et Acta Publica Imperatorum. Ed. L. Weiland. MGH.
Documenti diplomatici tratti dagli archivi milanesi. Ed. L. Osio. Milan, 1864–72.
Documenti riguardanti antiche relazioni tra Venezia e Ravenna. Ed. P. Pasolini. Imola, 1881.
Epistolae Saeculi XIII. Ed. Pertz. MGH.
Excerpta ex regestris Clementis VI et Innocentii VI. Ed. E. Werunsky. Innsbruck, 1885.
Liber Pontificalis. Ed. L. Duchesne. Paris, 1955.
Magnificae Civitatis Faventiae Ordinamenta. Faenza, 1527.
Monumenti ravennati de' secoli di mezzo. Ed. M. Fantuzzi. Venice, 1801–4.
Négotiations diplomatiques de la France avec la Toscane. Ed. G. Canestrini. Paris, 1859.
Rationes Decimarum Italiae nei secoli XIII e XIV: Aemilia. Ed. A. Mercati, E. Nasalli-Rocca, and P. Sella. Vatican, 1933.
Regesto della chiesa di Ravenna. Ed. V. Federici and G. Bizzi. Rome, 1911.
Registres de Martin IV. Ed. F. Oliver-Martin. Paris, 1935.
Registri dei Cardinali Ugolino d' Ostia e Ottaviano degli Ubaldini. Ed. G. Levi. Rome, 1890.
Statuta Faventiae. Ed. G. Rossini. RIS, XXVIII, pt. V, 1.
Statuta Montis Florum. Urbino, 1579.

Statuti di Forlì dell' anno 1359. Ed. E. Rinaldi. Rome, 1913.
'Statuti di Forlimpopli.' Ed. U. Santini. *AMR*. 3, XXII, 1904.
Statuti di Imola del secolo XIV. Ed. S. Gaddoni. Milan, 1931.
Statuto del secolo XIII del comune di Ravenna. Ed. A. Zoli and S. Bernicoli. Ravenna, 1904.
Theiner, A. *Codex Diplomaticus Dominii Temporalis S. Sedis*. Rome, 1861–2.
Thesaurus Novus Anecdotorum. Ed. E. Martène and U. Durand. Paris, 1717.

(ii) *Chronicles and other Literary Sources*

Acta Sanctorum. Ed. J. Bollandus. Paris and Rome, 1863–84.
Alberti, F. *Descrittione di tutta Italia*. Venice, 1557.
Annales Caesenates. RIS, XV.
Annales Forlivienses. Ed. G. Mazzatinti. RIS, XXII, pt. II.
Annales Parmenses Maiores. Ed. P. Jaffe. MGH, SS. XVIII.
Annales Placentini Gibellini. Ed. P. Jaffe. MGH, SS. XVIII.
Annales Ravenati. RIS, I.
Azarii, P. *Liber Gestorum in Lombardia*, ed. F. Cognasso. RIS, XVI, Pt. I.
Azzurini, B. *Chronica Breviora*, ed. A. Messeri. RIS, XXVIII, pt. III.
Bambaglioli, Graziolo de'. *Il commento più antico*, ed. A. Fiamazzo, Udine, 1892.
Bartolus de Saxoferrato. 'Tractatus de Guelphis et Gebellinis. Tractatus de regimine civitatis.' In *Consilia, Quaestiones et Tractatus*. Venice, 1565.
Battagli, Marco. *Marcha*, ed. A. Massera. RIS, XVI, pt. III.
Bazano, Giovanni de. *Chronicon mutinese*, ed. T. Casini. RIS, XV, pt. IV.
Benvenuto de' Rambaldi di Imola. *Commentum super Dantis Aldigherii Comoediam*. Florence, 1887.
Bernardi, A. *Cronache forlivesi*. Bologna, 1895.
Biondo da Forlì, Flavio. *Roma ristaurata et Italia illustrata*. Venice, 1543.
Biondo da Forlì, Flavio. *Historiarum ab inclinatione Romanorum*. Basel, 1569.
Boccaccio, Giovanni. *Il commento alla Divina Commedia*, ed. D. Guerri. Bari, 1918.
Boccaccio, Giovanni. *Il Decameron*, ed. U. Bosco. Rome, 1946.
Boccaccio, Giovanni. *Trattatello in laude di Dante*. See *Vite di Dante*, etc.
Boncompagni. *Liber de Obsidione Ancone*, ed. G. Zimolo. RIS, VI, pt. III.
Cantinelli, P. *Chronicon*, ed. F. Torraca. RIS, XXVIII, Pt. II.
Chiaramonte, S. *Caesenae Urbis Historiarum*. Cesena, 1641. In Graevius, VII, pt. II.
Chronicon Estense. Ed. G. Bertoni and E. Vicini. RIS, XV, III.
Chronicon Marchiae Tarisinae et Lombarduae. Ed. L. Boltegli, RIS, VIII, pt. III.
Chronicon Parmense. Ed. G. Bonazzi. RIS, IX, pt. IX.
Cobelli, L. *Cronache forlivesi*, ed. G. Carducci and E. Frati. Bologna, 1874.

Compagni, Dino. *La Cronica*, ed. I. Lungo. RIS, IX, pt. 2.
Corpus Chronicorum Bononiensium. Ed. A. Sorbelli. RIS, XVIII, pt. I, II.
Crescenzii, Pietro di. *Liber ruralium commodorum*. Louvain, 1474.
Cronache malatestiane dei secoli XIV e XV. Ed. A. Massera. RIS, XV, pt. II.
Dante Alighieri. *De Monarchia*, ed. E. Moore. Oxford, 1916.
Dante Alighieri. *Epistolae*, ed. P. Toynbee. Oxford, 1920.
Dante Alighieri. *Le opera di Dante*. Florence, 1921.
Dante Alighieri. *Il convivio*, ed. M. Barbi. Florence, 1954.
Dante Alighieri. *De Vulgari Eloquentia*, ed. A. Merigo, Florence, 1957.
Ferreti, Ferreto de. *Le opere*, ed. C. Cipolla. Rome, 1914.
Ghirardacci, C. *Della historia di Bologna*. Bologna, 1605.
Giovanni Fiorentino. *Il pecorone*. Milan, 1804.
Giraldus Cambrensis. *Opere*, ed. J. Brewer. Rolls Series, London, 1863.
Godi, Antonio. *Cronaca*, ed. G. Soranzo. RIS, VIII, pt. II.
Graevius, J. G. *Thesaurus Antiquitatum et Historiarum Italiae*. Leyden, 1704–25.
Griffoni, Matteo. *Memoriale Historicanum*. Ed. A. Frati and L. Sorbelli. RIS, XVIII, pt. II.
Guicciardini, F. *Opere inedite*. Florence, 1857–67.
Guicciardini, F. *Le cose fiorentine*. Florence, 1945.
Hieronomo da Forlì. *Chronicon*, ed. A. Pasini. RIS, IX, pt. V.
I fioretti del glorioso messere Santo Francesco. Ed. G. Passerini. Florence, 1903.
Innocent III. *Opera Omnia*. *Patrologia Latina*, 214–17.
Lana, Jacopo della. *Commento*. Bologna, 1866.
Machiavelli, N. *Opere*, ed. M. Bonfantini. Milan, n.d.
Manetti, Gianozzo. *Vita Dantis Poetae Fiorentini*. In *Vite di Dante*, cit.
Maurisius, Gerardus. *Cronica Dominorum Eccelini et Alberici*, ed. G. Soranzo. RIS, VIII, pt. IV.
Mussato, Albertino. *De gestis Italicorum post Henricum VII*. In Graevius, VI, pt. 2.
Mussi, Giovanni de. *Chronicon Placentinum*. RIS, XVI.
Nuovi testi fiorentini del dugento. Ed. A. Castellani. Florence, 1952.
Pedrino, Giovanni di M. *Cronica del suo tempo*, ed. G. Borghezio and M. Vattasio. Vatican City, 1929–34.
Pegoletti, F. Balducci. *La pratica della mercatura*, ed. A. Evans. Cambridge, Mass., 1936.
Petrarch, F. *Opera Omnia*. Basle, 1581.
Pipini, F. *Chronicon*. RIS, IX.
Pius II. *Commentaries*, Books II and III. Translated F. Cragg. Smith College Studies in History, XXV, 1939–40.
Poesie storiche relative all' Italia. Ed. V. Bartholomaeis. Rome, 1931.
Ricobaldus de Ferrara. *Compilatio Chronologica*. RIS, IX.
Ricobaldus de Ferrara. *Historia Imperatorum*. RIS, IX.
Ricobaldus de Ferrara. *Pomerium Ravennatis Ecclesie*. RIS, IX.
Rimatori comico-realistici del due e trecento. Ed. M. Vitale. Turin, 1956.
Rubeus, H. *Italicarum et Ravennatum Historiarum Libri XI*. Graevius, VII, pt. I.

Sacchetti, Franco. *I sermoni evangelici, le lettere ed altri scritti inediti e rari*, ed. O. Gigli. Florence, 1857.
Sacchetti, Franco. *Le novelle*. Milan, 1874.
Sacchetti, Franco. *Lettere volgari*. Imola, 1880.
Salimbene de Adam. *Cronica*. Ed. O. Holder-Egger. MGH., SS. XXXII.
Salutati, Coluccio. *Epistolario*, ed. F. Novati. Rome, 1896.
Salutati, Coluccio. *Tractatus de Tyranno*, ed. F. Ercole. Berlin and Leipzig, 1914.
Sanudo, M. *I diarii*. Venice, 1879–1902.
Sidonius. Letters, tr. W. B. Anderson. Harvard, 1936.
Sirviregli, Nicolai. *Annales Vincentiae*, ed. G. Soranzo. RIS, VIII, pt. V.
Spreti, Desiderio. *De urbis amplitudine, vastatione, et instauratione, Libri tres*. In Graevius, VII, I.
Thomas Tuscius. *Gesta Imperatorum et Pontificum*, ed. E. Ehrenfeuchter. MGH., SS. XXII.
Tolosanus. *Chronicon Faventinum*, ed. G. Rossini. RIS, XXVIII, pt. 1.
Tractatus Illustrium Iurisconsultorum de Iudiciis Criminalibus. Volume XI, pt. II. Venice, 1584.
Uberti, Fazio degli. *Il dittamondo*, ed. G. Cersi. Bari, 1952.
Un Traité néo-manichéen du XIIIe siècle : le Liber de Duobus Principiis. Ed. A. Dondaine. Rome, 1939.
Villani. *Croniche di Giovanni, Matteo e Filippo Villani*. Trieste, 1857.
Vinci, Leonardo da. *The Literary Works*, ed. Richter. Oxford, 1939.
Vita di Cola di Rienzo. Ed. Z. Re. Florence, 1854.
Vita di Dante, Petrarca e Boccaccio. Ed. A. Solerti. Milan, 1904.

II OTHER WORKS

Affò, I. *Dizionario della poesia volgare*. Parma, 1777.
(Alberghetti). *Compendio della storia di Imola*. Imola, 1810.
Aldrovandini, L. ' Acta Sancti Officii Bononiae ab anno 1291 usque ad annum 1309.' *AMR*, 3, XIV, 1896.
Amaducci, P. ' Notizie storiche su gli antichi conti di Bertinoro.' *AMR*, 3, XII, 1895.
Amaducci, P. ' Guido del Duca e la famiglia Mainardi.' *AMR*, 3, XX, 1902.
Amaducci, P. ' Guido del Duca di Romagna.' *AMR*, 3, XXIII, 1905.
Amaducci, P. ' Cenni topografici su Ravenna antica.' *AMR*, 3, XXV, 1907.
Amaducci, P. ' Dante e lo studio di Ravenna.' *BSDI*, 1908.
Antonelli, M. ' La dominazione pontificia nel patrimonio negli ultimi venti anni del periodo avignonese.' *ASR*, XXXI, 1908.
Antonini, F. *Della antichità di Sarsina*. Faenza, 1769.
Argnani, F. *Cenni storichi sulla zecca, sulle monete e medaglie de' Manfredi*. Faenza, 1886.
Attiya, A. *The Crusade in the Later Middle Ages*. London, 1938.
Bagli, G. ' Bandi malatestiani.' *AMR*, 3, II, 1885.
Bagli, G. ' L' archivio Sassatelli in Imola.' *AMR*, 3, VI, 1888.

Bagli, G. 'Contributo agli studi di bibliografica storica romagnola.' *AMR*, 3, XIII, 1895, and, 3, XIV, 1896.
Baldisseri, L. *I castelli di Cunio e Barbiano*. Imola, 1911.
Baldisseri, L. 'L' episcopato imolese nel secolo XII.' *Rivista storica di Scienze Teologiche*, 1912.
Baldisseri, L. *Benvenuto da Imola*. Imola, 1921.
Baldisseri, L. *Il castello di Mordano*. Imola, 1925.
Balduzzi, L. 'Bagnacavallo e i Manfredi.' *AMR*, II, pt. I, 1881.
Balduzzi, L. 'Bagnacavallo e i conti di Cunio.' *AMR*, 2, II, 1875.
Balduzzi, L. 'Il cardinale Bertrando del Poggetto e Bagnacavallo.' *AMP*, n.s., V, 1880, pt. I.
Ballardini, G. *Inventario critico e bibliografico dei codici e pergamene dell' archivio del comune di Faenza*. Faenza, 1905.
Ballardini, G. *Anno MCCXX : atto di liberazione dalla servitù della gleba*. Faenza, 1907.
Ballardini, G. 'Di una impresa dei Manfredi.' *FR*, 1912.
Ballardini, G. *La costituzione della contea di Brisighella, e della Val d' Amone*. Valdilamone, VII, 1927.
Ballardini, G. 'Alcuni lettere dei Manfredi al Gonzaga.' *AME*, I, 1936.
Balli, G. 'Gli Ebrei a Lugo.' *SR*, III, 1953.
Barbi, M. *Problemi di critica dantesca*. Florence, 1934.
Barbieri, G. 'Lo sviluppo storico delle vie di communicazione tra Firenze e Bologna.' *RGI*, 1947.
Battaglini, F. *Memorie istoriche di Rimino*. Bologna, 1798.
Bauer, C. 'Studi per la storia delle finanze papali durante il pontificato di Sisto IV.' *ASR*, 1927.
Bell, H. E. 'Italian Archives.' In *Studies presented to Hilary Jenkinson*. London, 1957.
Beloch, K. *Bevölkerungsgeschichte Italiens*. Berlin, 1939–40.
Beltrami, F. *Il forestiero istruito nella cose notabili di Ravenna*. Ravenna, 1783.
Beltrami, P. *Maghinardo Pagani da Susinana*. Faenza, 1908.
Bernicoli, S. *Governi di Ravenna e di Romagna*. Ravenna, 1898.
Bernicoli, S. 'Maestri e scuole letterarie in Ravenna.' *FR*, 1925.
Bernicoli, S. 'La biblioteca dell' Archevescovato di Ravenna (1321).' *FR*, 1930.
Bernicoli and Grigioni. 'La ceramica in Ravenna.' *FR*, 1911 and 1912.
Bernini, F. 'Federico II e la "Societas Lombardie Marchie et Romanie" nel 1226.' *Rivista Storica Italiana*, 1953.
Bertarelli, L. *Marche*. Milan, 1937.
Bertoni, G. 'Banchieri ad Imola nel secolo XIII.' *Studi Medievali*, III, 1911.
Bertoni, G. 'Il testamento di Frate Alberico Manfredi e Ugolino Buzzola.' *Archivium Romanicum, V*.
Bonaini, F. *Gli archivi delle provincie d' Emilia*. Florence, 1861.
Bonoli, P. *Istorie della città di Forlì*. Forlì, 1661.
Borst, A. *Die Katharer*. Stuttgart, 1953.
Brandi, B. *Vita e dottrina di Raniero da Forlì*. Turin, 1885.
Brandi, B. *L' archivio storico del comune di Forlì*, Rome, 1892.
Broccoli, P. 'Sul le più antiche monete della zecca faentina.' *La Romagna*, XIV, 1923.

Broccoli, P. ' Di uno quattrino dei Manfredi da Faenza.' *La Romagna*, IV, 1907.

Broccoli, P. *Di due altri quattrini di Astorgio Manfredi*. Iesi, 1908.

Burchi, P. ' Regesto degli atti del notaio sarsinate, Domenico da Firenzuola (1403–19).' *SR*, V, 1954.

Caggese, R. *Classi e comuni rurali nel medio evo italiano*. Florence, 1907.

Caggese, R. *Roberto d' Angiò e suoi tempi*. Florence, 1922.

Calisse, C. ' Costituzione del patrimonio di San Pietro in Tuscia nel secolo XIV.' *ASR*, XV, 1892.

Calvi, E. *Tavole storiche dei comuni italiani*. Rome, 1907.

Campana, A. ' Antico epitafio di Benvenuto da Imola.' *SR*, VI, 1955.

Carrara, E. ' Cecco da Mileto e il Boccaccio.' *GSLI*, XLIII, 1904.

Casini, T. *Scritti danteschi*. Citta di Castello, 1913.

Castiglione, A. ' Il salasso nell' arma gentilizia dei Manfredi.' In ed. C. Singer and H. Sigerist, *Essays in the History of Medicine presented to Professor K. Suidhoff*. London, 1925.

Cencetti, G. ' Sigilli medievali del Museo Civico di Bologna.' *AMR*, 1951–3.

Cencetti, G., and Fasoli, G. ' Gli studi storici sulle signorie romagnole.' *AME*, IV, 1939.

Cerchiari, G. *Ristretto storico della città d' Imola*. Bologna, 1847.

Chelazzi, C. *Catalogo della raccolta di statuti del medioevo alla fine del secolo XVIII*. Biblioteca del Senato della Repubblica, 1943f.

Ciaccio, L. ' Il cardinale legato Bertrando del Poggeto in Bologna.' *AMR*, 3, XXV, 1906.

Ciasca, R. *L' arte dei Medici e Speziali*. Florence, 1927.

Clementini. *Raccolto istorico della fondazione di Rimino*. Rimini, 1617.

Codignola, T. ' Ricerche storico-giuridiche sulla Massa Trabaria nel XIII secolo.' *ASI*, 1939.

Cohn, N. *The Pursuit of the Millennium*. London, 1957.

Colini-Baldeschi, L. ' Le " Constitutiones Romandiolae " di Giovanni d' Appia.' *Nuovi Studi Medievali*, II.

Comelli, G. ' Dei confini naturali e politici della Romagna.' *AMR*, 3, XXVI, 1908.

Cortini, G. *Brevi notizie storiche sul comune di Casalfiumanese*. Imola, 1926.

Cortini, C. *Storia di Castel del Rio*. Imola, 1933.

Cortini, G. *Storia di Imola e della valle di Santerno*. Mss. in Biblioteca dell' Archiginnasio, Bologna.

Davidsohn, R. *Forschungen zur älteren Geschichte von Florenz*. Berlin, 1896–1908.

Davidsohn, R. *Firenze ai tempi di Dante*. Florence, 1929.

De Montalbo, Astrudo, di Riella. *Dizionario della Repubblica di San Marino*. Paris, 1898.

Diehl, C. *Études sur l'administration byzantine dans l'Exarchat de Ravenna*. Paris, 1888.

Döllinger, I. *Beiträge zur Sektengeschichte des Mittelalters*. Munich, 1890.

Dondaine, A. ' Le Manuel de l'Inquisiteur.' *Archivium Fratrum Predicatorum*, XVII, 1947.

Dumont, R. *Types of Rural Economy*. London, 1957.

Dupré-Theseider, E. *Introduzione alle eresie medievali*. Bologna, 1953.

Dupré-Theseider, E. ' L' eresia a Bologna nei tempi di Dante.' *Studi storici in onore di G. Volpe*, Florence, 1958.

Eckstein, L. ' The Guidi and their relations with Florence.' *EHR*, XIV, 1899.

Emerton, E. *Humanism and Tyranny*. Cambridge, Mass. 1925.

Ercole, F. *Dal comune al principato*. Florence, 1929.

Ermini, G. ' I rettori provinciali dello stato della chiesa.' *RSDI*, IV, 1931.

' Esame di alcuni diplomi e carte stampate gia nell' Ughelli.' *Nuova Raccolta d' Opusculi*, Venice, 1771.

Fabre, P. ' Massa d' Arno, Massa di Bagno, Massa Trabaria.' *ASR*, XVII, 1894.

Fasoli, G. ' La pace del 1279 tra i partiti bolognesi.' *ASI*, 1933.

Fasoli, G. ' Guelfi e Ghibellini di Romagna nel 1280–1.' *ASI*, 1936.

Fasoli, G. ' Bologna e la Romagna durante la spedizione de Enrico VII.' *AME*, IV, 1939.

Fasoli, G. ' I conti e il comitato di Imola.' *AMR*, 1943–5.

Ficker, J. *Forschungen zur Reichs- und Rechtgeschichte Italiens*. Innsbruck, 1868–74.

Filippini, F. ' La prima legazione del Cardinale Albornoz in Italia.' In *Studi storichi*, V, 1896.

Filippini, F. ' Inventario dei libri e dei beni posseduti dell' Archiv. di Ravenna Petrocino nel 1369.' *Studi storichi*, VI, 1897.

Filippini, F. *Dante, scolaro e maestro*. Geneva, 1929.

Filippini, F. *Il cardinale Egidio Albornoz*. Bologna, 1933.

Filippini, F. ' L' insegnamento di Dante in Ravenna.' In *Studi danteschi*, ed. Costa.

Fiumi, E. ' Sui rapporti economici tra città e contado nell' età comunale.' *ASI*, 1956.

Fiumi, E. *Storia economica e sociale di San Gimignano*. Florence, 1961.

Fontana, L. *Bibliografica degli statuti dei comuni dell' Italia superiore*. Turin, 1907.

Foschi, U. ' Bibliografia cervese.' *SR*, XI, 1960.

Franceschini, G. ' La signoria dei Conti de Montefeltro a Cesena.' *SR*, V, 1954.

Franceschini, G. ' Un caduto del " Sanguinoso Mucchio ", il conte Taddeo di Montefeltro.' *SR*, VII, 1956.

Franceschini, G. *Saggi di storia montefeltresca e urbinate*. Selci Umbro, 1957.

Franchini, V. ' Appunti di diritto marittimo riminese nel secolo XIV. ' *La Romagna*, 1913.

Franciosi, P. ' Il Montefeltro.' *AMR*, 4, XVI, 1926.

Frati, L. ' Tradizioni storiche del Purgatorio di S. Patrizio.' *GSLI*, LXIII, 1914.

Frati, L. ' Pier de' Crescenzi e l' opera sua.' *AMR*, 4, IX, 1919.

Fumi, L. *I registri del Ducato di Spoleto della serie ' Introitus et Exitus ' della Camera Apostolica*. Perugia, 1913.

Fumi, L. ' Eretici e ribelli nell' Umbria : studio storico di un decennio, 1320–1330.' (Reprinted from *Bollettino della R. Deputaz. di St. P. per Umbria*.) 1916.

Fussenegger, P. ' De manipulo documentorum ad usum Inquisitoris Haereticae Pravitatis in Romandiola.' *AFH*, XLIV, 1951.
Fuzzi, M. *L' ultimo periodo degli Ordelaff. in Forlì*. Forlì, 1937.
Gaddi, P. ' Il testimonio di Maghinardo da Susinana.' In *Studi danteschi*, ed. Costa, 1921.
Gaddoni, P. *I Frati Minori in Imola*. Imola, 1911.
Gaddoni, S. ' Documenta ad historiam trium ordinum S. Francisci in Urbe Imolensi.' *AFH*, V, 1912 ; VI, 1913 ; VII, 1914 ; VIII, 1915.
Galli, R. *I manoscritti e gli incunabuli della biblioteca comunale di Imola*. Imola, 1894.
Gambi, L. ' Il censimento del Cardinale Anglic in Romagna nell' anno 1371.' *RGI*, 1947.
Garampi, G. *Memorie ecclesiastiche appartenenti all' istoria della B. Chiara di Rimini*. Rome, 1755.
Gasperoni, G. *Saggio di studi storichi sulla Romagna*. Imola, 1902.
Gasperoni, G. ' Il comune di Savignano.' *AMR*, 3, XXVI, 1908.
Gatto, L. *Il pontificato di Gregorio X*. Rome, 1959.
Gerola, G. *A proposito dell' Aguglia da Polenta*. Florence, 1914.
Gherardi, A. ' La guerra dei Fiorentini con Papa Gregorio XI.' *ASI*, 1867, 1868.
Gill, J. *The Council of Florence*. Cambridge, 1959.
Ginanni, P. *Memorie dell' antica ed illustre famiglia Alidosia*. Rome, 1735.
Giulini, G. *Memorie spettanti alla storia di Milano*. Milan, 1854–7.
Glénisson, J. ' Une Administration médiévale aux prises avec la disette.' *Le Moyen Age*, 1951.
Glénisson, J. ' Les Origines de la révolte de l'état pontifical en 1375.' *Rivista di Storia della Chiesa in Italia*, V, 1951.
Golubovich, G. ' Una pagina dantesca : notizie inedite sul Conte Frate Guido da Montefeltro.' *AFH*, III, 1910.
Goretta, E. *La lotta fra il comune bolognese e la signoria estense*. Bologna, 1906.
Grierson, P. ' The Coin List of Pegoletti.' In *Studi in onore di A. Sapori*. Milan, 1957.
Grossara, F. 'I poteri di Ostasio da Polenta.' *FR*, 1951.
Grossara, F. ' La " Concordia inter clericos et laycos de Ravenna ".' *SR*, III, 1952.
Guiraud, J. *Histoire de l'Inquisition au Moyen Age*. Paris, 1938.
Güterbock, F. ' Forliveser Annalen des Pietro Ravennate.' *Neues Archiv der Gesellschaft für ältere Deutsche Geschichtskunde*, XXIV, 1899.
Herlihy, D. *Pisa in the Early Renaissance*. New Haven, 1958.
Hessel, A. *Geschichte der Stadt Bologna, 1116–1280*. Berlin, 1910.
Honig, R. *Guido da Montefeltro*. Bologna, 1901.
Huillard-Bréholles, J. *Vie et correspondance de Pierre de la Vigne*. Paris, 1865.
Il mondo agrario tradizionale nella Valle Padana. Modena, 1963.
Jacob, E. (ed.) *Italian Renaissance Studies*. London, 1960.
Jones, P. ' The Vicariate of the Malatesta of Rimini.' *EHR*, 1952.
Jones, P. ' A Tuscan monastic lordship in the Later Middle Ages.' *Journal of Ecclesiastical History*, V, 1954.
Jones, P. *The Malatesta of Rimini*. Ph.D. thesis in Bodleian Library, Oxford.

Jordan, E. *Les Origines de la domination angevine en Italie.* Paris, 1909.
Lanzoni, F. ' La cronaca del convento di Sant' Andrea in Faenza.' *Archivio Muratoriano* (RIS), *I*, 1904.
Lanzoni, F. *I primordi dell' Ordine Francescano in Faenza.* Faenza, 1910.
Lanzoni, F. ' Le antiche carte del convento di S. Chiaro in Faenza.' *AFH*, V, 1912.
Lanzoni, F. ' Una vita del Beato Novellone Faentino.' *AFH*, V, 1912.
Lanzoni, F. ' Cose francescane faentine.' *AFH*, XIV, 1921.
Lanzoni, F. ' I conventi domenicani in Romagna.' In *Il VII centenario di S. Domenico*, Rome, 1921.
Lanzoni, F. ' L' antico archivio di S. Francesco di Faenza.' *AFH*, XX, 1927.
Lattes, A. ' Il libro giornale d' un mercante toscano ad Imola nel secolo XIII.' *Rivista di Diritto Commerciale*, IX, 1911.
Lea, H. *A History of the Inquisition in the Middle Ages.* London, 1888.
Leff, G. *Gregory of Rimini.* Manchester, 1961.
Lenel, W. *Die Entstehung der Vorherrschaft Venedigs an die Adria.* Strassburg, 1897.
Lenel, W. ' Ein Handelsvertrag Venedigs mit Imola.' *Vierteljahrschrift für Social- und Wirtschaftsgeschichte*, VI, 1908.
Léonard, E. *Histoire de Jeane I*[re]. Monaco-Paris, 1932–7.
Litta. *Celebri famiglie italiane.* Milan, 1819–1923.
Liverani, G. ' La ceramica in Imola.' *SR*, VI, 1955.
Lucas, H. ' The great European famine of 1315, 1316, and 1317.' *Speculum*, 1930.
Luzzatto, G. *I banchieri ebrei in Urbino nell' età ducale.* Padua, 1903.
Luzzatto, G. *Storia economica di Venzia.* Venice, 1961.
Luzzatto, G. *An economic history of Italy.* Translated P. Jones. London, 1961.
Majoli, G. *Palazzi, case e casate di Ravenna del passato.* Ravenna, 1956.
Malagola, C. *Memorie storiche sulle maioliche di Faenza.* Bologna, 1880.
Maltoni, E. ' La famiglia degli Ordelaffi dall' origine alla Signoria.' *SR*, XI, 1960.
Manacorda, G. *Storia della scuola in Italia.* 1913.
Mancini, F. ' I fondi speciali manoscritti della biblioteca comunale d' Imola.' *SR*, IV, 1955.
Manzoni, A. *Episcoporum Corneliensium sive Foroliviensium Historia.* Faenza, 1719.
Marchesi, G. V. *Vitae Virorum Illustrium Foroliviensium.* Forlì, 1726.
Mariano d' Alatri. *L' inquisizione francescana nell' Italia centrale nel secolo XIII.* Rome, 1954.
Massèra, A. ' Note malatestiane.' *ASI*, 1911.
Massèra, A. ' Il serventese romagnola del 1277.' *ASI*, 1914.
Massèra, A. ' Iacopo Allegretti da Forlì. *AMR*, 4, XVI, 1926.
Matteini, N. *Il più antico oppositore politico di Dante : Guido Vernani da Rimini.* Padua, 1958.
Mazzatinti, G. *Gli archivi della storia d' Italia.* Rocca San Casciano, 1899–1915.
Mazzini, G. ' Una vertenze fra i medici e il comune d' Imola nel secolo XIII.' In *Bollettino dell' Istituto Storico Italiano dell' Arte Sanitaria*, 1930.

Mercati, A. ' Tentativo del Duca d' Atene di ottonere l' investitura della Romagna.' *Rivista storica degli Archivi Toscani*, IV, 1932.
Merlini, G. ' Unità regionale dell' Emilia e Romagna.' *RGI*, 1946.
Messeri, A. *Galeotto Manfredi*. Faenza, 1904.
Messeri and Calzi. *Faenza nella storia e nell' arte*. Faenza, 1909.
Metelli, A. *Storia di Brisighella e della valle di Amone*. Faenza, 1869.
Mini, G. *I nobili romagnoli della Divina Commedia*. Forlì, 1904.
Mirot, L. ' La Question des blés dans la rupture entre Florence et le saint-siège.' *Mélanges d'Archéologie et d'Histoire*, 1896.
Missiroli, A. *Astorgio III Manfredi*. Bologna, 1912.
Mollat, G. *Les Papes d'Avignon*. Paris, 1949.
Mols, R. *Introduction à la démographie historique des villes d'Europe*. Louvain, 1955.
Mor, C. ' Predappio e la genesi dei suoi statuti.' *Bollettino Storico Italiano*, 58.
Muratori, L. A. *Antiquitates Italicae Medii Aevii*. Milan, 1741.
Muratori, S. ' Vesti, ornamenti e oggetti d' uso in alcuni inventarii ravennati dei secoli XIV–XV.' *La Romagna*, 1913.
Mussoni, G. ' I patarini in Rimini.' *La Romagna*, II, 1905.
Nadiani, P. *Guido Selvatico da Dovadola*. Forlì, 1936.
Nadiani, P. *Il Guido Guerra Dantesco*. Forlì, 1938.
Natali, G. ' La repubblica cispadana e l' abolizione dei feudi.' *AME*, III, 1938.
Niel, F. *Albigeois et Cathares*. Paris, 1959.
Novati, F. ' Se Dante abbia mai publicamente insegnato.' In *Indagini e postille dantesche*, Bologna, 1899.
Origo, I. *The Last Attachment*. London, 1949.
Origo, I. ' The Domestic Enemy : The Eastern Slaves in Tuscany.' *Speculum*, 1955.
Orioli, E. ' Documenti bolognesi sulla fazione dei Bianchi.' *AMR*, 3, XIV, 1896.
Orlandelli, G. ' Le finanze della comunità di Forlì sotto il vicariato di Baldassare Cossa.' *SR*, VIII, 1956.
Orlandelli, G. ' Gli archivi della valle del Bidente.' *SR*, X, 1959.
Otto, H. ' Benedikt XII als Reformatur de Kirchenstaates.' In *Römische Quartalschrift für christliche Alterumskunde und für Kirchengeschichte*, 1928.
Ovidio, F. d'. *Studii sulla Divina Commedia*. Milan, 1901.
Palmieri, A. ' Gli antiche vicariati dell' Appennino bolognese e la costituzione amministrativa moderna.' *AMR*, 3, XX, 1902.
Palmieri, A. ' Sul riscatto dei servi della gleba nel contado bolognese.' *Archivio Giuridico*, 3, VI, 1906.
Palmieri, A. ' L' esercizio dell' arte medica nell' antico Appennino Bolognese.' *AMR*, 4, I, 1911.
Palmieri, A. ' Le strade medievali fra Bologna e la Toscana.' *AMR*, 4, VIII, 1918.
Palmieri, A. ' Ancora sul riscatto dei servi alla gleba.' *AMR*, 4, IX, 1919.
Palmieri, A. ' Lotte agrarie bolognesi nei secoli XIII e XIV.' *AMR*, 4, XXII, 1923.
Palmieri, A. *La Montagna bolognese nel medioevo*. Bologna, 1929.

Palmieri, A. ' I lavatori del contado bolognese durante le signorie.' *AMR*, 3, 56.
Pardi, G. ' Disegno della storia demografica di Firenze.' *ASI*, 1916.
Parks, G. *The English Traveler to Italy*. Rome, 1954.
Partner, Peter. *The Papal State under Martin V*. London, 1958.
Pasolini, P. *I tyranni de Romagna e i papi nel medioevo*. Imola, 1888.
Pecci, G. *La casa da Caboli*. Rome, 1934.
Pellegrini, F. ' Il serventese dei Lambertazzi e dei Geremei.' *AMR*, 3, IX, 1891.
Perez, J. *El Cardenal Albornoz*. Madrid, 1950.
Pertile, A. *Storia del diritto italiano*. Turin, 1893.
Piccolomini, N. *Il Monte dei Paschi di Siena*. Siena, 1891.
Placucci, M. *Usi e pregiudizii de' contadini della Romugna*. Forlì, 1818.
Plessi, G. ' Gli archivi di Cervia.' *SR*, XI, 1960.
Powicke, F. ' Guy de Montfort (1265–1271).' *Transactions of the Royal Historical Society*, 1935.
Preger, W. *Über die Anfänge des Kirchenpolitischen Kampfes unter Ludwig dem Baier*. Munich, 1882.
Quadri, L. *Vita massese attraverso i secoli*. Mass Lombarda, 1910.
Ranke, L. *The History of the Popes*. London, 1896.
R.A.S. Firenze. *Statuti di comunità e luoghi autonomi*. Florence, 1903.
Ravaglia, P. *Scarpetta degli Ordelaffi*. Forlì, 1955.
Ravaglia, P. ' I signori di Ravaldino.' *SR*, X, 1959.
Ricci, C. *L' ultimo rifugio di Dante Alighieri*. Milan, 1891.
Rinaldi, E. ' Gli Ebrei in Forlì.' *AMR*, 4, X, 1920.
Rodolico. ' Note statistiche su la popolazione fiorentina nel XIV secolo.' *ASI*, 1902.
Romagna tradizionale. Ed. P. Toschi. Bologna, 1952.
Roover, R. de. *The Rise and Decline of the Medici Bank*. Cambridge, Mass., 1963.
Rossi-Case, L. *Ancora di Maestro Benvenuto da Imola*. Imola, 1893.
Rossini, G. ' Federico II e l' assedio di Faenza.' *AMR*, VI, 1941.
Rossini, G. ' La sistemazione delle fonti archivistici locali.' *SR*, I, 1950.
Rossini, G. ' Il testamento di Frate Alberigo de' Manfredi.' *SR*, III, 1952.
Rossini, G. ' Un antica controversia per il possesso di Lugo e di S. Potito.' *SR*, IV, 1953.
Roth, C. *The History of the Jews of Italy*. Philadelphia, 1946.
Rustici, A. ' Il castello di San Cassiano di Imola.' *La Romagna*, 1915.
Sabbadini, R. *Giovanni da Ravenna*. Como, 1934.
Salvioli, G. *Annali bolognesi*. Bassano, 1795.
Salvioni, G. ' La popolazione di Bologna nel secolo XVII.' *AMR*, 3, VII, 1890.
Salzer, E. *Über die Anfänge der Signorie in Oberitalien*. Berlin, 1900.
Santini, P. *Documenti dall' antica costituzione del comune di Firenze*. Florence, 1895.
Santini, G. ' I dazii egidiani in Forlì nel 1364.' *AMR*, 4, 1914.
Sapegno, N. *Il Trecento*. Milan, 1948.
Sapori, A. *Studi di storia economica*. Florence, 1955.
Schäfer, K. *Die Ausgaben der Apostolischen Kammer unter Johann XXII*. Paderborn, 1911.

Schäfer, K. *Deutsche Ritter und Edelknechte in Italien während des 14. Jahrhunderts*. Paderborn, 1911.
Schäfer, K. *Die Ausgaben der Apostolischen Kammer unter Benedikt XII, Klemens VI und Innocenz VI*. Paderborn, 1914.
Schurr, F. ' La posizione storica del Romagnolo fra i dialetti contermini.' *Revue de Linguistique Romaine*, IX, 1933.
Sella, P. ' Costituzione per la Romagna, pubblicate nel parliamento di Cesena dell' anno 1289.' *ASI*, 1925.
Sella, P. *Glossario latino-emiliano*. Rome, 1937.
Sella, P. ' Una costituzione inedita per la Romagna.' *RSDI*, II.
Simeoni, L. ' Federico II all' assedio di Faenza.' *AME*, III, 1938.
Sorbelli, A. *La signoria di Giovanni Visconti a Bologna*. Bologna, 1901.
Sorbelli, A. *Il comune rurale dell' Appennino emiliano nei secoli XIV e XV*. Bologna, 1910.
Spallicci, M. *La poesia dialettale romagnola*. Forlì, 1953.
Spreti, C. *Notizie spettanti all' antichissima scuola de' Pescatori in oggi denominata Casa Matha*. Ravenna, 1820.
Stefano, A. de. ' Le origini dei Frati Gaudenti.' *Archivium Romanicum*, X, 1926.
Studi danteschi a cura della R. Dep. di Storia Patria per le provincie di Romagna. Ed. F. Costa, 1922.
Tarlazzi, A. ' Riscontri critichi tra la Cronica di Fra Salimbene e gli storichi di Ravenna intorno alla decedenza della famiglia dei Traversari.' *AMR*, I, 1869.
Temple-Leader, J., and Marcotti, G. *Sir John Hawkwood*. London, 1889.
Tomassetti, G. ' Sale e focatico del Comune di Roma nel medioevo.' *ASR*, 1897.
Tonduzzi, G. *Historie di Faenza*. Faenza, 1675.
Tonini, L. *Storia civile e sacra riminese*. Rimini, 1848–88.
Tonini, L. *Il porto di Rimini*. Bologna, 1864.
Tonini, L. *Figuline riminese*. Rimini, 1870.
Tonini, L. *Memorie storiche intorno a Francesca da Rimini*. Rimini, 1870.
Tonini, L. *Le imposte pagate a Rimini nel secolo XIV*. Bologna, 1872.
Tonini, C. *La coltura letteraria e scientifica in Rimini*. Rimini, 1884.
Torraca, F. ' Su la " Treva " di G. de la Moro.' *AMR*, XVIII, 1900.
Torraca, F. *Per la biografia di Giovanni Boccaccio*. Milan, 1912.
Torraca, F. *Scritti danteschi*. Naples, 1912.
Torraca, F. ' Dante, maestro di scuola?' *Atti di R. Accademia di Archeol. Lett. e Belle Arti*, Naples, 1926.
Torraca, F. ' Il dialetto romagnolo e il bolognese nel " De Vulgari Eloquentia ".' *AMR*, 4, XVII, 1927.
Torre, A. ' Le controversie fra l' archievescovo di Ravenna e Rimini nel sec. XIII.' *SR*, III, 1951.
Torre, A. ' I patti fra Venezia e Cervia.' *SR*, XI, 1960.
Torre, A. ' La pace di Romagna del 1235.' *AMR*, 1951–3.
Toschi, U. *Un comune subappennino romagnolo*. Imola, 1920.
Toynbee, P. *A Dante Dictionary*. Oxford, 1898.
Ubaldini, G. L. *Istorie della casa de Gli Ubaldini*. Florence, 1588.
Valgimigli, G. *Tebaldello Zambrasi*. Faenza, 1878.
Valgimigli, G. *Storia di Faenza*. Mss. in BC. Faenza.

Vechiazzani, M. *Storia di Forlimpopoli*. Rimini, 1674.
Veggioni, A. 'La fusione dello zolfo dal XV al XVIII secolo nelle miniere di Romagna.' *SR*, VI, 1955.
Vergottini, G. de. 'Ricerche sulle origini del vicariato apostolico', in *Studi di storia e dritto in onore di Enrico Besta*. Milan, 1939.
Vergottini, G. de. 'Il papato e la comitatinanza nello stato della chiesa.' *AMR*, n.s., 3, 1952–3.
Vesi, A. *Ragionamenti intorno ai veri confini della Romagna*. Faenza, 1841.
Villari, L. *The Republic of Ragusa*. London, 1904.
Vitale, V. *Il dominio della Parte Guelfa in Bologna*. Bologna, 1901.
Vitali, G. *Memorie storiche riguardanti la terra di M. Fiore*. Rimini, 1828.
Vochting, F. *Die Romagna : eine Studie über Halbpacht*. Karlsruhe, 1927.
Volpe, G. *Movimenti religiosi e sette ereticali nella società medievale italiana*. Florence, 2nd ed., 1961.
Wadding, L. *Annales Minorum*. Rome, 1731–1886.
Waley, D. P. 'Papal Armies in the Thirteenth Century.' *EHR*, 1957.
Waley, D. P. *The Papal State in the Thirteenth Century*. London, 1961.
Weiss, R. *Il primo secolo dell' umanesimo*. Rome, 1949.
Wicksteed, P., and Gardner, E. *Dante and Giovanni Virgilio*. Westminster, 1902.
Woolf, C. *Bartolus of Sassoferrato*. Cambridge, 1913.
Wurm, H. *Cardinal Albornoz*. Paderborn, 1892.
Zaccagnini, G. 'Maghinardo da Susinana ed il comune di Bologna.' *AMR*, 4, VIII, 1918.
Zaccagnini, G. 'Due rimatori faentini del secolo XIII.' *Archivium Romanicum*, XIX, 1935.
Zaccaria, A. *Series Epsicoporum Forocorneliensium*. Imola, 1820.
Zama, P. *Indice e cronologia dei notai del vecchio archivio faentino*. Faenza, 1925.
Zanetti, G. *Delle monete di Faenza*. Bologna, 1777.
Zoli, A. 'Ravenna e il suo territorio nel 1309.' *AMR*, 3, XVIII, 1900.
Zoli, A. 'La caccia nel territorio di Ravenna nel secolo XIII–XIV.' *La Romagna*, 1910.

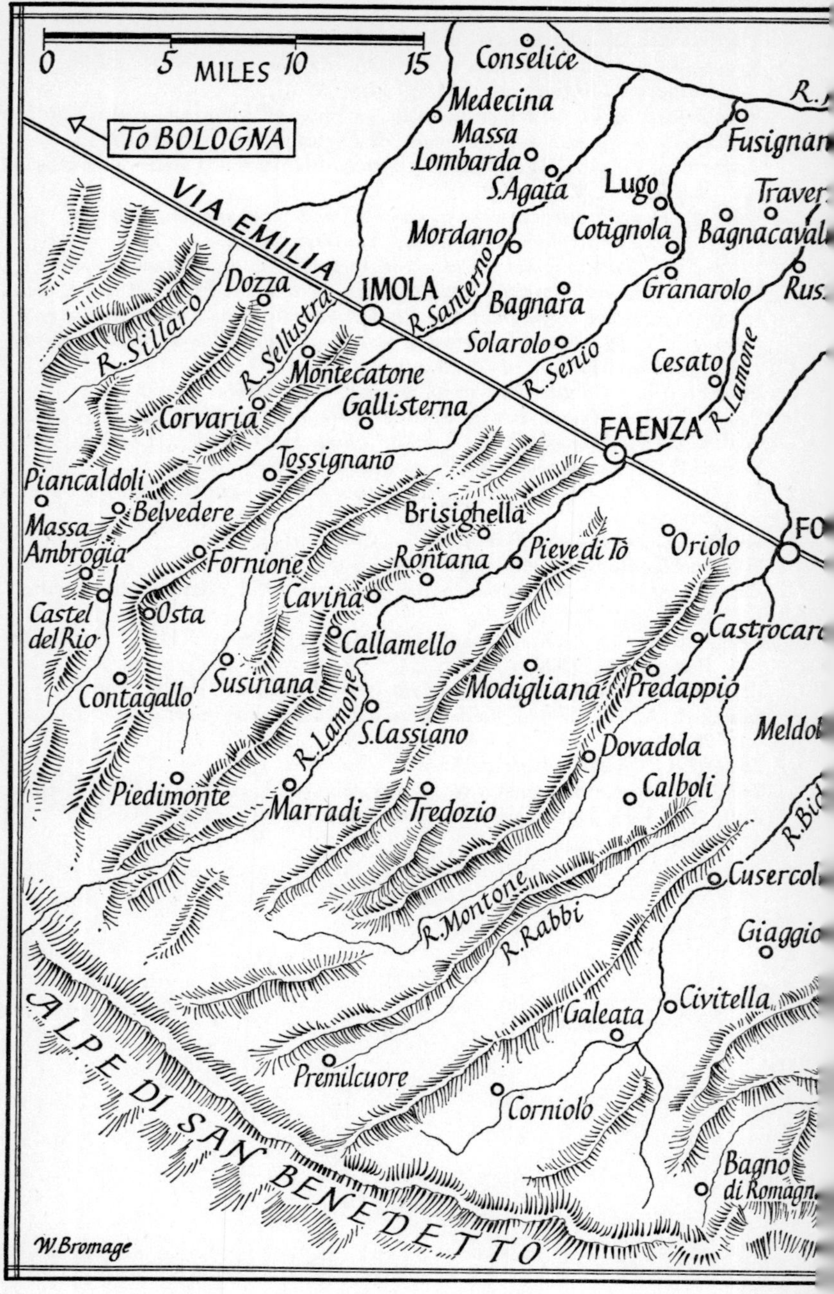
0 5 MILES 10 15
To BOLOGNA
VIA EMILIA
Conselice
Medecina
Massa Lombarda
S.Agata
Lugo
Mordano
Cotignola
Granarolo
Bagnara
IMOLA
R.Santerno
Dozza
R.Sillaro
R.Sellustra
Solarolo
R.Senio
Cesato
R.Lamone
Montecatone
Gallisterna
Corvaria
FAENZA
Tossignano
Piancaldoli
Belvedere
Brisighella
Massa Ambrogia
Fornione
Rontana
Pieve di Tò
Oriolo
Castel del Rio
Osta
Cavina
Callamello
Susinana
Contagallo
Modigliana
Predappio
R.Lamone
S.Cassiano
Dovadola
Piedimonte
Marradi
Tredozio
Calboli
R.Montone
R.Rabbi
Civitella
Galeata
Premilcuore
Corniolo
ALPE DI SAN BENEDETTO
W.Bromage

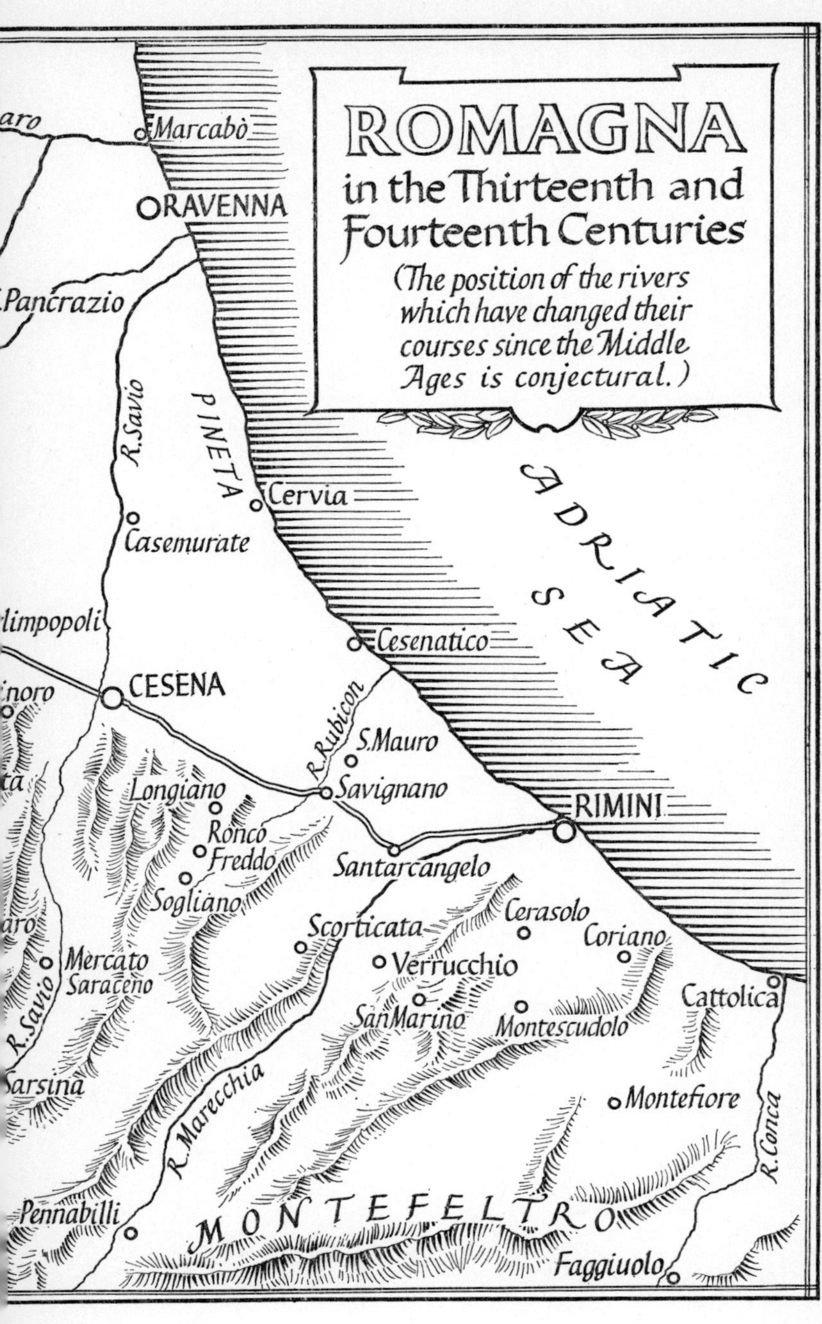
ROMAGNA
in the Thirteenth and Fourteenth Centuries
(The position of the rivers which have changed their courses since the Middle Ages is conjectural.)
Marcabò
RAVENNA
Pancrazio
R. Savio
PINETA
Cervia
Casemurate
limpopoli
ADRIATIC SEA
Cesenatico
CESENA
R. Rubicon
S. Mauro
Savignano
RIMINI
Longiano
Ronco Freddo
Santarcangelo
Sogliano
Scorticata
Cerasolo
Coriano
Mercato Saraceno
Verrucchio
Cattolica
San Marino
Montescudolo
R. Savio
Sarsina
R. Marecchia
Montefiore
R. Conca
Pennabilli
MONTEFELTRO
Faggiuolo

INDEX

PRINTED BY R. & R. CLARK, LTD., EDINBURGH